Writing Poems

Writing Poems

Robert Wallace
Case Western Reserve University

Little, Brown and Company

BOSTON · TORONTO

for Sharon

Library of Congress Catalog Card No. 81–84227

ISBN 0-316-91996-9

9 8 7 6 5 4 3

MV

Published simultaneously in Canada
by Little, Brown & Company (Canada) Limited

Printed in the United States of America

ACKNOWLEDGMENTS

W. M. Aberg. "The Lark and the Emperor." Copyright © 1980 by W. M. Aberg. Reprinted by permission.
A. R. Ammons. "First Carolina Said-Song" is reprinted from *Collected Poems 1951–1971* by A. R. Ammons, with the permission of W. W. Norton & Company, Inc. Copyright © 1972 by A. R. Ammons.
Richard Armour. "Going to Extremes" from *Light Armour* by Richard Armour. Reprinted by permission of the author and McGraw-Hill Book Company.
John Ashbery. "These Lacustrine Cities" from *Rivers and Mountains* by John Ashbery. Reprinted by permission of John Ashbery and Georges Borchardt, Inc. Copyright © 1962 by John Ashbery.
W. H. Auden. "Musée des Beaux Arts." Copyright 1940 and renewed 1968 by W. H. Auden. Reprinted from *W. H. Auden: Collected Poems*, by W. H. Auden, edited by Edward Mendelson, by permission of Random House, Inc., and Faber and Faber Limited.
Pamela Azusenis. "Salvation." Copyright © 1978 by Pamela Azusenis. Reprinted by permission.
Basho. "Breaking the silence . . ." reprinted from *Basho: The Narrow Road to the Deep North & Other Travel Sketches*, trans. Nobuyuki Yuasa (Penguin Classics, 1966), p. 9. Copyright © Nobuyuki Yuasa, 1966. By permission of Penguin Books Ltd.
Michael Benedikt. "Rose," copyright © 1969 by Michael Benedikt. Reprinted from *Sky* by permission of Wesleyan University Press. "The Atmosphere of Amphitheatre," copyright © 1976 by Michael Benedikt. Reprinted from *Night Cries* by permission of Wesleyan University Press.
Bruce Bennett. "Smart." Copyright © 1978 by Bruce Bennett. Reprinted by permission.
E. C. Bentley. "Sir Christopher Wren" from *Clerihews Complete* by E. C. Bentley. Reprinted by permission of Curtis Brown Ltd. on behalf of The Estate of E. C. Bentley.
Elizabeth Bishop. "First Death in Nova Scotia." Reprinted by permission of Farrar, Straus and Giroux, Inc. from *The Complete Poems* by Elizabeth Bishop. Copyright 1940, © 1962, 1969 by Elizabeth Bishop.
Deborah Bliss. "Van Busbeke Discovers the Tulip, 1550," © 1967 by Deborah Bliss. Reprinted by permission.
Robert Bly. "Looking at a Dead Wren in My Hand" from *The Morning Glory* by Robert Bly. Copyright © 1969, 1970 by Robert Bly. "Come with Me" from *The Light Around the Body* by Robert Bly. Copyright © 1964 by Robert Bly. Both reprinted by permission of Harper & Row, Publishers, Inc. Translations of two haiku by Issa, © 1969 by Robert Bly. Reprinted with permission of Robert Bly. "Waking from Sleep" and "Taking the Hands" from *Silence in the Snowy Fields* (Wesleyan University Press, 1962). Reprinted with permission of Robert Bly.
Joseph Bruchac. "The Release," © 1979 by Joseph Bruchac. Reprinted by permission.
Timothy Calhoun. "A Band of Poets Desert from the Red Army, Forever," © 1977 by Timothy Calhoun. Reprinted by permission of the author and Willow Springs Magazine. "The Lament of an Old Eskimo Woman," © 1982 by Timothy Calhoun. Used by permission.
Jared Carter. "Second Sheet." Copyright © 1979 by Jared Carter and reproduced by permission.

(continued on page 412)

FOREWORD

Do Poets Need
to Know Something?

One of the advantages to being a poet, says an elder statesman among poets, Robert Francis, is that you aren't required to know anything in particular.

Not that Francis believes that for a minute. Slyly, he is just stating a prevalent misconception: the view of the poet as an empty-headed blatherer of beautiful words. When you reflect about it, though, most poets have to soak up a great deal that needs knowing. First, they must learn to strum that colossal and resonant harp, the English language, a temperamental instrument that calls for practiced fingering. Perhaps a good half of the poet's art consists in knowing exactly how to proceed and exactly when. At times, the poet barges ahead with confidence, setting down words as surely and rapidly as a Japanese master brush artist draws a leaping carp upon paper so porous that a second's hesitation may run the ink to the tip of his brush, producing a botch. At other times, the poet slows down and takes pains, casting and recasting a line of a poem till it hooks fast. All this is only basic working knowledge, to which poets add anything they can learn. Just for fun, W. H. Auden drew up the curriculum for an imaginary college for poets that encompassed such matters as archaeology, mathematics, cooking, gardening, and the care of chickens and goats. Auden's point, I take it, was that poetry may thrive on any old soil of learning. Quality of observation, not mere breadth of experience, seems to be what makes poetry out of what a poet knows. To find the raw material for poems, you don't need to backpack to Katmandu. No doubt some have done so and returned knowing less than Emily Dickinson knew from watching hummingbirds and garter snakes in the meadow across the road past her home.

That in order to be a poet you have to know something, college students have long taken for granted. At least, they keep signing up for courses in writing poetry as if they expect such studies to impart something valuable. Nowadays, with the tendency of basic composition courses to include a unit or two of creative writing, it is a rare student who escapes being asked to write a poem at some moment in the college experience. Things were not always so. When, in 1931, Paul Engle founded his celebrated Writers' Workshop at the University of Iowa, academic traditionalists (as Engle later recalled) thought the term "creative writing" an obscenity. (To me, the term seems closer to blasphemy. In a sense, only the Unmoved Mover creates; all a writer does is assemble things from words.)

In colleges today, the titular poet in residence doesn't ever simply reside, but has to teach, like the rest of the faculty. But in most departments of English, the teacher of poetry writing is generally envied. Peers look upon this teacher in much the way that musicians in a band, struggling to pack their amplifiers and timpani after a concert is over, cast jealous eyes upon the piano player, who casually picks up the sheet music and goes home. To the instructor of composition—*prose* composition—struggling to reread "On Civil Disobedience" before the next bell for class and groaning under four sets of essays on Thoreau's nonconformity, it would appear that the poetry writing teacher has a racket. The latter, having asked students to run off copies of a poem or two they have written, apparently strolls into class without a preparation in mind, has the students read aloud their poems, and chats about them.

But this is another misconception. Like the piano player, a teacher of poetry writing has to possess innate ability, devotion to craft, and the strength to endure a professional training that never ends. I doubt that even a brain surgeon, who (these are Richard Brautigan's delectable words) removes "with a sudden but delicate motion . . . a disordered portion of the imagination," puts longer hours or finer skill into the art than does the instructor who detaches a rickety line from a student poem and suggests how to tighten it. To ferret out the weakness in a poem—or the strength—may take far more time and thought than to fathom a student essay. A deep satisfaction of the job, and yet a continuing responsibility, is that the student-teacher relationship often lasts. Although students of freshman composition, after their onerous course is through, don't usually want anything further to do with their instructors, students of poetry writing may persist for years in looking to their instructors for support and encouragement. A decade after the poetry workshop has disbanded, the instructor may still be asked to criticize a book manuscript, or to testify on a former student's behalf to some grant-giving institution.

However hard they toil, instructors of poetry writing continually feel expected to justify their existence. Most often, they defend their profession in one of two ways. Either they claim that, by trying to write poems, students come to understand poetry from the inside, and so become more astute readers; or else they argue that the attempt to write poetry benefits the students' more mundane writing, enabling them to wield words with greater skill and keener sensitivity when they write term papers and job applications. Both these reasons make pretty good sense to me, but I would add still another. Although it happens rarely, sometimes a workshop in poetry brings together an inspired teaching poet and an inspired student poet—mind to mind, face to face. And when any such situation brings John Crowe Ransom together with Robert Lowell, or Robert Lowell together with Sylvia Plath and Anne Sexton, it achieves something unique and remarkable. Perhaps, in a relatively small way, it even strengthens the flickering light of civilization.

I would say, then, that courses in the writing of poetry are, by and large, wholesome and morally sweet activities. They wouldn't be were they to make huge and misleading claims, but they never do. They don't offer, directly, practical and remunerative job training. They don't even promise to usher the student's writings into print. No self-respecting instructor of poetry writing pretends to ready the young for a money-making future in literature—a profession that, Wallace Stegner said, barely exists. Robert Wallace makes all this clear in his chapter "Oddments" in *Writing Poems*. He offers the young poet this frank and succinct advice: "Get a job."

Designed to help a student write poetry—financially unprofitable poetry— Wallace's textbook isn't a usual one at all. Until I met it, I had seen one or two other textbooks purporting to aid the novice poet in writing poems, but none that I thought would greatly help anybody. That we have not previously had a really useful textbook in the subject isn't hard to explain. It is demonstrably impossible to tell another human being how to write a poem, and even to suggest how to get ready to write poetry is a task fraught with boobytraps and complexities. Moreover, instructors of poetry writing usually know their own minds. As often as not, they have favorite teaching techniques, and it is a brave and foolhardy textbook author who would push techniques on them.

Like most who have taught courses in poetry writing, I had thought I knew how to do it decently, and so, when the publisher first asked me to look at Wallace's book in manuscript, I began to read with skepticism. I was won over. Wallace doesn't tell the student how to write a poem; he doesn't lay down arbitrary laws. Instead, he carefully arrays all the possibilities. Starting with the assumption that the student, in order to write a poem, would do well to read poetry and see what goes on in it, he sets forth poems, elements of poetry, suggestions for writing, and a generous bag of wisdom and advice. Soon I was turning his pages in astonishment, nodding in doglike assent, struck many times by insights that had never occurred to me. Whatever the instructor's persuasions, this book is a flexible instrument. Some matters will seem basic (the line, the metaphor, how to revise), and the instructor may care to take them up with the entire class. Other matters may seem of more limited interest (say, how to write in syllabics), and the instructor may wish simply to point them out to the student who asks about them. Wallace gives us, in one book, a highly teachable classroom text; a compact and lively anthology including greats such as Shakespeare, Donne, Walt Whitman, and Anonymous; a work of reference; a practical, worldly wise companion (see the chapter "Business"); and a poetical *Guide to the Perplexed*. Instructors can fruitfully employ it however they will.

To his task, Wallace brings outstanding credentials. In the first place, he is himself a fine and original poet, as readers can tell from his collections (*This Various World*, 1957; *Views from a Ferris Wheel*, 1965; *Ungainly Things*, 1968; and *Swimmer in the Rain*, 1979) and his poems in many anthologies. No doubt being a poet helps a teacher of poetry writing, although I can't agree with Ezra Pound's counsel to pay no heed to the criticism of anyone who hasn't written a notable work. The teaching of poets is in this respect like the training of boxers: there are distinguished instructors whose own poems haven't stood up for three rounds, yet who have been instrumental in the care and nurturing of champions. As a writer of prose, Wallace knows how to put subtle matters clearly, and he radiates forthrightness, modesty, and good cheer. That he has taught the writing of poetry for a long time and thought hard about it, his every page reveals. Besides, as an editor for Bits Press at Case Western Reserve University, he is steeped in the swim of literary publishing. All these knowledges lend an air of conviction to his words, and a freshness seldom achieved in textbooks on writing.

At this moment, the whole idea of teaching poetry writing is—as usual—under bombardment. Lately, a few observers have blamed creative writing programs for the sort of poetry that now clutters our little magazines: a poetry that seems composed by some electronic word processor smothered in mothballs, a poetry lacking in music and grace, passion and intelligence. Such observers assume that there once was a golden age when every poem in the little magazines shone like a Krugerrand, and that in these dull days we have sadly fallen from it. But a critical browse through an old file of *Poetry* from the 1930s or *Evergreen Review* from the 1960s will puncture this illusion in a hurry. David Bromwich, writing in the *Times Literary Supplement* for June 6, 1980, foresees no hope for the quality of American poetry until programs in creative writing are drastically scaled down and students taught how to read better. Robert Wallace, however, would go for the latter goal *within* a creative writing class. My own suspicion is that our current poetry glut (as Karl Shapiro calls it) or superabundance (as I'd rather call it) may be the result of a larger cultural situation and pernicious forces at large in the body politic. Today, more and more Americans seem driven by a need to switch off their television sets and stand and proclaim that they're persons. Evidently, one way to do so is to publish poetry. This frenzy to charge headfirst into print with a signed lyric, no matter how poor, has been intensified by the cheapness and convenience of offset printing. Anybody with a hundred dollars in hand can bring out a chapbook of poems or a new little magazine tomorrow. Some teachers of creative writing, perhaps, have egged their students on to premature and reckless publication. But the best teachers, aware that it takes time for good poets to arrive, don't try to accelerate them. If anything, such teachers gently apply the brakes by insisting on excellence.

Whatever the facts of our situation, and whatever you make of them, it seems unlikely that creative writing programs are going to dwindle in a hurry. Clearly, their workshops serve fledgling poets as sounding boards and training camps, and if colleges were to start closing them down, their students would probably revive the traditional *Hair*-era custom of torching administration buildings. Rather than do away with creative writing, we might try to make it better than it is: more demanding, more widely humane, more generously informative.

Robert Wallace's *Writing Poems* offers a way to begin. From it, with the instructor's help, students will surely learn much about poetry from the inside, acquire more sensitivity to words, and almost certainly learn a good deal that will be useful in writing poems, should they write any. And if Wallace's book should stick around, and instructors come to swear by it, eventually the magazines should be printing new poems we will want to remember. To help a single memorable poem come into the world—what instructor wouldn't call that ample reward for a lifetime of reading manuscripts? That would be justification enough for a thousand poetry writing courses.

X. J. Kennedy

PREFACE

I am not sure writing poems can be taught, but I know it can be learned. This book is intended to help provide the circumstances for that learning.

I have tried to write it simply, but without simplifying. Because poetry happens all at once in writing a poem—as it does in reading a poem—the division into sections on form, content, and process; and of these sections into chapters, is primarily a convenience of exposition, not an implicit theory. Readers, or teachers, are invited to skip around freely, following their own direction or interest. Properly, a book orders the material and a teacher orders the course. Partly to spread out the clumps of very technical information in Chapters 2 (on free verse), 3 (on meter), and 4 (on diction, syntax, alliteration, assonance, rhyme, and texture), I might assign Chapters 1, 2, 6, and 11 first; then 3, 7, and 12; and so on—more or less raising simultaneous matters simultaneously. Establishing a personal emphasis, another teacher might choose to begin with Chapter 8 (on metaphor) or Chapter 9 (on the non-rational).

Flexibility is important in creative writing courses. Far more than in subject matter courses, one is teaching not material, but *students*. An individual response matters, and an awareness of backgrounds, needs, and goals. Because so much class time is devoted to discussing students' writing, a significant value of this book should be to let the teacher put the exposition of principles on automatic pilot. It is discouraging, after an especially exciting semester, to recall that a class never really got to metaphor, or to the basics of meter.

This book is also designed to serve as a mini-anthology. The selection favors the modern and contemporary, though I wish still more poems and poets could have been represented. A few of my own poems are here because I can bear witness about them. I have also included a number of poems written by students (whose names are marked by asterisks) both because they are good poems and because they may serve as friendly models of what beginning poets can accomplish. "Poems to Consider" after each chapter provide the reader with plenty to do independently, as do "Questions and Suggestions." These are intended to supplement, not replace, the instigations a thoughtful teacher can supply.

A rule I have rarely broken is not to use "bad" examples. All poets write (and learn from) their own bad poems, and the beginning poet will be able to do so without unhappy illustrations. Early versions of poems, particularly in Chapters 12 and 13 (on revising), offer instances of clumsiness or wrongheadedness—as well as the assurance that problems can be solved.

Writing poems—trying to handle one's deepest feelings and to present one's most serious view of the world—is always an intimate, vulnerable activity. In a sense, all good poems are lucky hits. Beginning poets, then, especially those faced with deadlines, should always consider the poems they present as *experiments*, valuing those which succeed, letting go of those which do not. One doesn't grade all the poems, only the best.

Everything I know about writing poetry I have learned from somebody. I am grateful to all the teachers, poets, editors, students, and colleagues whose touch is on this book.

Robert Wallace

CONTENTS

II   Content: The Essential Something

I

Form:
The Necessary Nothing

Verse Is:
Catsup and Diamonds

Shakespeare was seventeen. None of his great poems was written, nor even imagined. That year—perhaps a year or two earlier or later—admiring a poem, he wrote one similar to it. Possibly his wasn't a very good poem, but it pleased him. He enjoyed having written it, enjoyed saying it over to himself aloud as he walked along. When the occasion arose, he wrote another poem, then another. Like him, all poets begin. Like them, Shakespeare had chosen to write in a form called verse.

He might as easily have chosen to write in prose since it is more akin to both the ordinary and the elevated speech of everyday affairs. Prose, too, may be impassioned, complex, and finely wrought, as is that of Shakespeare's contemporary, John Lyly. Some writers are drawn to prose and to the essays, stories, and novels for which prose is suitable. Others, electing the odd and ancient conventions of verse, write the poems that verse makes possible. What is verse, then? What are the substantial differences between verse and prose?

We may begin to answer that question by identifying the obvious difference. When you open a book, how do you know whether you are looking at prose or verse? Prose always continues across the printed page from left margin to an even right margin because the right margin is set arbitrarily, *externally*, by the printer. The printer determines when a new line begins, and the wider the page, the longer the line. In the extreme, and on a page wide enough, an entire book of prose theoretically could be printed on one line.

Verse, however, is a system of writing in which the right margin, the line-turn, is determined *internally* by a mechanism contained within the line itself. Thus, no matter how wide the page, a poem is always printed in the same way. It is the poet, not the printer, who determines line length, or measure.

The Greek word for measure is *meter* (as in *thermometer*, "heat measure"). In poetry the word *meter* traditionally refers to the conventions of English verse by which poets measure their lines (for instance, iambic pentameter). *All* verse, though, even free verse, has some kind of measure—some rationale or system by which the poet breaks or ends his lines. The choice of the measure may be intuitive or trained, but the nature of verse demands that the poet have a clear perception of the identity of each line, even if he or she cannot articulate the reasons.

This crucial aspect of verse is hidden in the etymology of the word itself. *Verse* comes from the Latin *versus*, which derives from the Latin verb *verso*, *versare*, meaning "to turn." (This root appears in such familiar words as *reverse*, "to turn back.") Originally the past participle of the verb, *versus* literally meant *"having turned."* As a noun it came to mean *the turning of the plough*, hence *furrow*, and ultimately *row* or *line*. Thus, the English word *verse* refers to the *deliberate turning from line to line* that distinguishes verse from prose.

This deliberate turning of lines adds an element to verse that prose does not possess. The rhythm of prose is narrowly restricted by the cadence of the voice; in verse, however, this cadence constantly plays over the relatively fixed unit of **line.** The element of line gives verse an extraordinary, complex rhythmic potential of infinite variation.

Line-breaks may coincide with grammatical or syntactical units. This reinforces their regularity and emphasizes the normal speech pauses.

How many times,
I thought,
must winter come
and with its chill whiteness
slip-cover
field and town.

Line-breaks also may occur between grammatical or syntactical units, creating pauses and introducing unexpected emphases.

How
many times, I thought, must
winter
come and with its chill

whiteness
slip-cover field and
town.

When the end of a line coincides with a normal speech pause (usually at punctuation), the line is called **end-stopped,** as in these lines by John Milton
(1608–1674) from *Paradise Lost*:

> As killing as the canker to the Rose,
> Or taint-worm to the weanling Herds that graze,
> Or Frost to Flowers, that their gay wardrobe wear

Lines that end without any parallel to normal speech pause are called **run-on** or
enjambed (noun: **enjambment**), as in these lines of Milton:

> Of man's first disobedience,‖and the Fruit
> Of that forbidden Tree,‖whose mortal taste
> Brought Death into the World,‖and all our woe.

A **caesura** (‖), a normal speech pause that occurs within a line, may produce
further variations of rhythm and counterpoint that are not possible in prose.

By varying the use of end-stop, run-on, and caesura and by playing sense,
grammar, and syntax against them, the poet may produce an infinite range of
effects. In the following passage note how Milton creates an effect of free-falling
with these devices:

> Men called him Mulciber: and how he fell
> From Heaven they fabled, thrown by angry Jove
> Sheer o'er the crystal battlements: from morn
> To noon he fell, from noon to dewy eve,
> A summer's day, and with the setting sun   5
> Dropt from the zenith, like a falling star,
> On Lemnos, th' Aegean isle.

The emphatic pauses, or divisions of the action, occur within the lines; and the
line-ends are primarily run-on.

Line

Line is the core of verse. The poet's sensitivity to line, an awareness of its
effect on the other elements of a poem, is central to craftsmanship. Consider

this poem by an anonymous poet (ca. 1300), born more than two centuries before Shakespeare. Probably young and in love, he composed a quatrain we have entitled "Western Wind":

> Western wind, when wilt thou blow,
>   The small rain down can rain?
> Christ, if my love were in my arms
>   And I in my bed again!

Perhaps a sailor away from home and missing his girl, the poet longs impatiently for spring when he will return to her. In prose he might have written something like this:

> I long for spring to come, with its westerly wind and its fine, nurturing rain; for then at last I will again hold my love in my arms and we will be in bed together!

Compare the poem and its prose imitation. What makes the poem especially effective?

Speaking *to* the wind, for instance, suggests isolation as well as loneliness, whereas in prose we address inanimate objects only rarely (as a man who has just struck his thumb with a hammer may address the hammer). In the poem both wind and the "small rain" are personified—**personification** is treating something inanimate as if it had the qualities of a person, such as sex or (here) volition—and "can rain" suggests that the rain shares the speaker's impatience for spring. By parallel, the direct address to the wind suggests that the exclamatory "Christ" in line 3 is also, in part, a prayer. The sailor's world (if a sailor he was) is a world of forces—wind, rain, and Christ—as the merely human world of my prose statement is not. The poem expresses the natural procreativity of the speaker's desire more passionately than the prose version does, so that the human in the poem seems, too, a force among forces. The incomplete conditional of lines 3–4 conveys more by ellipsis than the prose's explicit but flat "we will be in bed together." What is longed for is simply beyond words to characterize. The poem's singular "I in my bed again!" seems at once more vigorous and, because it is in some measure joking, less intimidated by circumstance than does the rather passive prose.

All of this—the dramatization, personification, implication—might be presented in prose, but it occurs more naturally, more succinctly in verse. The compression of verse calls for an alertness of attention, word by word, line by line, that we rarely give to prose. More happens in less space (and fewer words) in verse than in prose, which is habitually discursive and given to adding yet something further, drawing us onward to what is next and then next, and next again. We half expect the prose to continue, whereas the poem seems finished, complete, inviting us again and again to explore it. Prose, like a straight line, extends to the horizon. Verse, like a spiral, draws us into itself.

This reflexiveness of verse causes us to attend to, hear, *feel*, the poem's rhythm as we do not the prose's rhythm. Only two syllables in lines 1–2 (the second syllable of "Western" and "The") are not heavy. The lines are slow, dense, clogged, expressing the speaker's anguish and the ponderousness of waiting. By contrast, filled with light syllables (only "Christ," "love," "arms," "I," and "bed" have real weight), lines 3–4 seem to leap forward, expressing the speaker's eagerness for the eventual release of longing into forthright action. The poem's measuring of lines is also a measuring of feeling. Rhythm is meaning. The "equal" lines of verse differ more tellingly from one another than the elements of the freer, looser prose can do. The young sailor's desire, carrying its own music with it, is less a speech than a song.

Inviting attention line by line, verse holds a spatial dimension that prose cannot imitate. Consider "Me up at does" by E. E. Cummings (1894–1962).

Me up at does

out of the floor
quietly Stare

a poisoned mouse

still who alive   5

is asking What
have i done that

You wouldn't have

Here is the prose translation:

From the floor, a poisoned mouse, which is still alive, stares up at me quietly, asking, "What have I done that you wouldn't have?"

Note that the lines of the poem break the flow of the statement, isolating its elements for emphasis. Despite the poem's odd syntax, the scene seems easier to visualize in verse than in prose. The poem's verticality aids us in perceiving the ironic verticality of the exchange between the two protagonists: the "Me" appropriately stands above the "poisoned mouse." Like the speaker's gaze, the lines of the poem travel downward to the mouse. But the mouse's stare, and more-than-human indignation, travel up. It is as if the force of this counterface not only disconcerts the speaker but causes the poem's dislocations of syntax as well. In a sense the poem happens all at once on the page, while the coherently linear prose does not.

The disordered language registers the speaker's discomposure and simultaneously allows the poet to present the pieces of the scene in a dramatically effective sequence. He begins with the self-conscious, tense "Me up at does" and concludes with the mouse's silent question (which interestingly does not exhibit the rattled incoherence of the speaker's observation). The disorder permits the poet to echo multiple meanings with the use of a single word: "still," for example, means *however, motionless,* and *yet.* The poem's four capitalized words ("Me," "You," "Stare," "What") sum up the little drama: the human arrogance of the poison, the bewildered dignity of the question. The lower-case "i" of the mouse's question underlines the simplicity of the animal in the face of the human. The speaker's "who" in line 5, instead of "which," suggestively registers his guilt.

The poem seems spontaneous, a fragmentary and unpremeditated evocation of the dramatic moment. But it is, in fact, carefully and very precisely structured. Every line has exactly four syllables. In effect, there are two stanzas, half-rhymed: *a b b a* ("does-floor-Stare-mouse" and "alive-What-that-have"); the trenchant sound of the poem is hardly accidental. Each stanza, with its open lines, seems an eye. There are two eyes—an eye above, an eye below. There are two I's, too—two creatures regarding one another across an irredeemably tragic distance.

Ultimately, the inimitable effect of the poem derives from the *lines* of its verse. Cutting across the scene and feeling at mechanical intervals, the line-breaks bring the poem to life. As must be obvious from both "Western Wind" and "Me up at does," having something to say is only half the problem in writing a poem, and may be the easier half. In everyday situations we value what is being said, not the way it is said. We require only that language be reasonably clear and informative. Even in newspapers and best sellers, we pay attention to **content** (the what-is-being-said), not to **form** (the way-it-is-said).

Literature, however—whether prose or verse—is language in which form is equal in importance to content. Poetry joins perfectly these two invariable halves: form and content, mode and meaning. We value a poem as we value a diamond for the form that the carbon content takes under pressure. "What oft was thought, but ne'er so well expressed," said Alexander Pope. Shakespeare's *King Lear,* for example, is not only a great statement about the *human condition,* it is also a *great statement* about the human condition. The difference between a pretty girl and one not so pretty is a matter of the arrangement of features, the form of content.

Form

Why do we value form? Perhaps the answer lies in the secrets of our musculature, in our dark roots. Why do we live in square rooms? Why do we draw mechanical doodles when we are bored? Why do we tap our feet to music? Perhaps there is a profound link between the meter of verse and the human pulse, the rhythm of life itself—*te TUM te TUM te TUM.* The rhythmical impulse runs deep in us, and it is the basis of all the arts. Our pleasure in symmetry is undeniable, whether it is the child's delight in colored blocks of wood or the poet's need to make words rhyme. Hanging around language, seeing what tricks it can perform, is often a crucial fascination for the poet. W. H. Auden says:

> As a rule, the sign that a beginner has a genuine original talent is that he is more interested in playing with words than in saying something original; his attitude is that of the old lady, quoted by E. M. Forster—"How can I know what I think till I see what I say?"

Form is valuable because it preserves content, like our use of verse to remember which months have thirty days. We write a poem to keep fresh an experience or a person we care about; thus, the motive for writing a poem or story is not unlike that for taking photographs. We want to retain, however dimly or crudely, the light and the look of the moment. In a poem the thing is fixed, tied down, in the tightness of lines and rhymes. "Form alone," Henry James said, "*takes,* and holds and preserves substance—saves it from the welter of helpless verbiage that we swim in as in a sea of tasteless, tepid pudding."

When we try to express the thought, feeling, or event so well that it lasts as long as language itself, we escape (a little) the unremitting passage of all things into time, and we escape (a little) the endless bombardment of our senses. Works of art are machines for saving and clarifying experience. Robert Frost thought of a poem as "a momentary stay against confusion."

As simply as possible, form is the nothing, the magic or pressure, that is necessary to transform the ordinary carbon of experience into the forever-diamonds of art. Here is a simple example of so lofty a concept, "Going to Extremes" by Richard Armour (b. 1906):

> Shake and shake
>   The catsup bottle.
> None'll come—
>   And then a lot'll.

That catsup bottles are so poorly designed that they blurt out gobs of the red goo is all too ordinary, familiar information. What makes us laugh is Armour's clever rhyme ("bottle-lot'll") with its surprising imitation of catsup's last-second blurting out. Form more than the content here is meaning.

Of course, form and content are inseparable in practice. Any utterance has both, and it is virtually impossible to distinguish precisely between them. As consciousness is always embodied, every idea or feeling, when stated, has only the shape of the words used. Even the telephone book has form and rhythm ("Anderson, D. D., Anderson, D. R., Anderson, D. S., Anderson, E. B., Anderson, George"); but in a poem that pleases us, what works is the concord of the two qualities, form and content. Often, when a poem "doesn't work," there may be a discord of the two; an elegy written in galloping rhythm is ludicrous:

My old Harry is dead and is gone to his rest,
Who was always in all ways the bravest and best.

Fluid and Solid Forms

Poetic form may be thought of as being of two general kinds. In "A Retrospect," Ezra Pound distinguishes between what he calls "**fluid**" and "**solid**" **forms.** Some poems, he says, "may have form as a tree has form, some as water poured into a vase." Mighty literary quarrels have been fought over the preference, movements have been formed, manifestoes hurled. But both sorts of poetic form make good poems. Fluid (or **open**) form is organic, like a tree's growth. Solid (or **closed**) form is symmetrical, like water poured into a vase. Both are natural, and so long as the poet is willing not to be theory-bound, he may use whichever a given poem wants.

Fluid, organic form, in which the form "only" expresses the content, is an ideal no one could disagree with. Emerson suggested succinctly, "Ask the fact for the form." Charles Olson, elder statesman of the "Beats" and proponent of fluid form, presents the ideal this way in his famous essay "Projective Verse":

FORM IS NEVER MORE THAN AN EXTENSION OF CONTENT. (Or so it got phrased by one R. Creeley, and it makes absolute sense to me, with this possible corollary, that right form, in any given poem, is the only and exclusively possible extension of content under hand.)

In practice, however, it must remain a dangerous matter of faith or pride for a poet to conclude that he or she has found the "only and exclusively possible" form for what he or she is saying. A poet's freedom to invent or discover a poem's form while writing experimentally is too valuable to restrict, but fluid form is a hard discipline. It has made possible poems as finely wrought as Walt

Whitman's "A Noiseless Patient Spider" (page 13), Ezra Pound's exquisitely conversational "The Garden" (page 19), and Charles Simic's magical "Stone" (page 21). But it has also, unhappily, justified a deluge of sloppy, raggedy, cavalier poems, more fluid than form—as many, surely, as there have been sloppy, overstuffed, padded sonnets or villanelles.

The problem with wanting form to be nothing more than expression of content is that it is impossible. The beginning poet might pin to the lampshade on his desk "Glass" by Robert Francis (b. 1901):

> Words of a poem should be glass
> But glass so simple-subtle its shape
> Is nothing but the shape of what it holds.
>
> A glass spun for itself is empty,
> Brittle, at best Venetian trinket.   5
> Embossed glass hides the poem or its absence.
>
> Words should be looked through, should be windows.
> The best word were invisible.
> The poem is the thing the poet thinks.
>
> If the impossible were not   10
> And if the glass, only the glass,
> Could be removed, the poem would remain.

Ideally, form is the necessary nothing.

A proponent of solid or fixed form—such as the sonnet or sestina, meters and rhymes—might make a case for the pleasure, usefulness, or psychological accuracy of such forms. Regular rhythms (as in music) or the chiming of well-managed rhymes are pleasurable. Having at hand such highly adaptable forms as conventional meters, couplets, or quatrains may be simply useful—every new cook needn't reinvent the frying pan. In any case, even the staunchest proponent of fixed or solid form affirms the importance of form and content's fitting each other.

Whether fluid or solid, form must express content. Because each poem is a new creation, one ideally gives it the form it needs, without regard to theory. Invented forms are neither better nor worse, in general, than adapted forms, only better or worse for the job at hand.

The sonnet, for instance, is one of the most difficult fixed forms, but its structure may well *help* the poet write a poem, just as a good interviewer's questions draw a coherent account from a witness. Consider how the material of Sonnet 73 by William Shakespeare (1564–1616) fills and fits the three quatrains and single couplet of the Elizabethan sonnet:

That time of year thou mayst in me behold
When yellow leaves, or none, or few, do hang
Upon those boughs which shake against the cold,
Bare ruined choirs° where late the sweet birds sang.   *choirlofts*
In me thou see'st the twilight of such day   5
As after sunset fadeth in the west,
Which by-and-by black night doth take away,
Death's second self that seals up all in rest.
In me thou see'st the glowing of such fire
That on the ashes of his youth doth lie,   10
As the deathbed whereon it must expire,
Consumed with that which it was nourished by.
    This thou perceiv'st, which makes thy love more strong,
    To love that well which thou must leave ere long.

The theme is the poet's aging. In the three quatrains he compares his age to
three things: autumn, the dying of the year; twilight, the dying of the day; and
glowing ashes, the dying of the fire. Because the fixed quatrains emphasize the
threefold comparison, Shakespeare has accurately used an Elizabethan sonnet
(three quatrains and a couplet) rather than a Petrarchan sonnet (octave and
sestet). The couplet at the end, with its difference in tone, presents a resolving
statement of the problem offered in the quatrains. Form and content are in
harmony.

Note that the order of the quatrains corresponds to a mounting anguish of
feeling. The movement is, in the first place, from a bare winter-daylight scene
to a twilight scene, and then to a night scene, the time when a fire is usually
allowed to die. The progression from day to dusk to night emphasizes and supports the image of night as "Death's second self" and possibly suggests night as
the time one most fears dying.

Another progression is at work in the three images: each of the "dyings" is
shorter and more constricted than the last, as though the speaker were aware of
the quickening of death's approach. The first comparison is to a season's dying,
the second to a day's dying, and the third to a fire's dying. In its preoccupation
with time, the first quatrain looks backward to summer, when "late the sweet
birds sang." The second looks forward to "Death" explicitly and inevitably ("by-
and-by"). The third imagines the coming night/death, when death is no longer
a prospect but a reality: "deathbed." The increasingly narrow, bleak images of
the three quatrains enhance the speaker's sense of loss and depletion in aging.
There echoes throughout the poem's images a story of an old man's death during
the night after a cold winter day.

The constraint of the sonnet form dramatically matches that of the
speaker. The poet addresses the trouble of aging only indirectly, through inanimate images, as though he held its personal implications at a distance. The
apparent composure is, however, deceptive. Each of the three images begins

with a more positive tone than it ends with. The increasingly self-diminishing revisions in line 2 offer a clear example: "yellow leaves, or none, or few." The yellow leaves, like the "twilight" and the "glowing" of the fire, are attempts at an optimism that the speaker cannot maintain. In each of the images he is compelled to say what he originally seems to have wanted to withhold, even from his own consciousness.

Intended as a compliment to the lover on the strength of her love, the couplet begins on a positive note: "This thou perceiv'st, which makes thy love more strong." But the next line betrays the speaker's fears because he does not say, as we might expect, "To love that well which thou must *lose* ere long"; rather, "To love that well which thou must *leave* ere long." He sees his death as *her* leaving him, not the other way around. Throughout the poem, the speaker has expressed, not his self-image, but what he imagines to be his lover's image of him: "thou mayst in me behold," "In me thou see'st," and "This thou perceiv'st." By "leave" in line 14 he need not mean more than "leave behind," but the bitter taste of jealousy is on the word. He does not say, "To love *me* well whom,*" nor even "To love *him* well *whom,*" but "To love *that* well *which.*" The poet refers to himself as a thing, as though time had robbed him, in his lover's eyes, of manhood. Thus, the full weight of his fear of being rejected, replaced, falls on his odd choice of the word "leave." The complimentary statement of the poem stands, of course, but we feel the swirl of dramatic currents beneath its surface.

Such delicate precision of content in form is equally possible in fluid forms, as in "A Noiseless Patient Spider" by Walt Whitman (1819–1892):

A noiseless patient spider,
I marked where on a little promontory it stood isolated,
Marked how to explore the vacant vast surrounding,
It launched forth filament, filament, filament, out of itself,
Ever unreeling them, ever tirelessly speeding them.   5

And you O my soul where you stand,
Surrounded, detached, in measureless oceans of space,
Ceaselessly musing, venturing, throwing, seeking the spheres to con-
    nect them,
Till the bridge you will need be formed, till the ductile anchor hold,
Till the gossamer thread you fling catch somewhere, O my soul.   10

The spacious lines, unreeling loosely out across the page, correspond to the long filaments the spider strings out into the wind when it is preparing to construct a web. The two equal stanzas, one for the description of the spider, one for the soul's "musing, venturing, throwing, seeking," perfectly shape the poem's central comparison.

The comparison of the spider's "unreeling" and the soul's "throwing" is not presented mechanically. The spider's activities, described in stanza 1, are neither explained nor resolved until the last line of stanza 2. The success of the soul's "gossamer thread," catching and anchoring, implies a similar success for the spider. Notice the verbal echoes between various words in the two stanzas: "stood"/"stand," "surrounding"/"Surrounded," "tirelessly"/"Ceaselessly." Similar links bridge the images, as in the contrast of small to grand scale with "on a little promontory," followed in stanza 2 by "measureless oceans of space." After "promontory" (a headland or cliff jutting out into the ocean), the images of "oceans of space," "bridge," and "anchor" lend unity to the comparison. Like the spider's action, the poem's apparent randomness is in fact careful and purposeful.

Whitman's alliteration and assonance give some of the lines a unity of sound and emphasize the linear, filamentlike structure: *m*'s in line 2, *v*'s in line 3, *f*'s in line 4, and long *e*'s in "unreeling" and "speeding" in line 5. The half-hidden rhyme in lines 9—10 ("hold"/"soul") suggests the success of both the spider's and the soul's ventures. The caesural pause after "somewhere," so near the end of the last line, also suggests that the long line makes contact with something akin, not alien.

Although Shakespeare's Sonnet 73 is an example of solid form and Whitman's "A Noiseless Patient Spider" of fluid form, these poems are more alike, as verse, than different. Both demand and reward careful attention. There need be no war to the death between fluid and solid form, between sonnets and free verse. Practically, there is a richness of choice for the poet concerned with writing his or her next poem. Classic forms such as sonnets are as new or contemporary as they are useful for fresh purposes. So in "next to of course god america i" (page 120) E. E. Cummings and in "Acquainted With the Night" (page 119) Robert Frost employ the sonnet freshly. The poet, writing as one must in the language and styles of a particular time, but keeping an eye on what one's predecessors have done, must neither accept the moment's fashions too easily nor fear them.

Space and Object

Because nothing in a poem is waste, even the space between the lines or stanzas may be significant. As in Cummings's "Me up at does" or Whitman's "A Noiseless Patient Spider," the relationship between space and object is no less the concern of the poet than it is of the sculptor. Consider the sometimes misunderstood "Dust of Snow" by Robert Frost (1874—1963):

The way a crow
Shook down on me

The dust of snow
From a hemlock tree

Has given my heart   5
A change of mood
And saved some part
Of a day I had rued.

The division of the poem into two stanzas reveals the balance of the two elements in its statement: subject and predicate; the scene and the feeling it produced; cause, effect. The symmetry draws attention to the fact that the poem's
statement is a paradox.

A crow is generally regarded as negative, a bad omen. The image "dust of
snow" is mainly unpleasant, suggesting disuse, neglect, or even a kind of
baptism in the cold of death or ruin; and the hemlock, a cemetery tree, as well
as one from which a poison is made, suggests death. Thus, the event described
in stanza 1 is unpleasant, and ought to make the speaker miserable. Surprisingly,
the feeling produced is cheering: "saved some part / Of a day" he would
otherwise have regretted.

Frost doesn't say anything so banal as that something good happened to
him and made him feel good. Rather, something uncomfortable made him,
strangely enough, feel better. The most significant detail in the poem may well
be that space between the quatrains, the two parts of the speaker's thought, that
makes us balance and compare. "Dust of Snow" leaves unanswered the question
of why the speaker was cheered by a disagreeable experience. But the mystery
makes us puzzle over the poem and pushes us back to the first line: "The *way* a
crow." How might a crow shake snow from a tree so that someone would feel
his day had been "saved"? By alighting, by resettling, or by departing? The
poem seems to hint that any reader should be able to imagine which of these it
was.

A good poem nearly always lets the reader complete it by suggesting,
implying more than it states.

QUESTIONS AND SUGGESTIONS

1. Here are two poems printed as prose. Experiment with turning them into
verse by dividing the lines in different ways for different effects. The originals,
as well as all further notes to the Questions and Suggestions, will be found in
Appendix I.

a) *For a Lady I Know*

> She even thinks that up in heaven her class lies late and snores, while poor
> black cherubs rise at seven to do celestial chores.

b) *Potatoes*

> Grandpa said potatoes reminded him of school. Potatoes and school. He said
> he'd wake nearly freezing, kindle a fire and throw two potatoes on. Going to
> school he carried them to warm his hands. To warm his feet he ran. He said by
> noontime those potatoes almost froze, said he ate a lot of cold potatoes for
> lunch.

2. Compare the next poem with Whitman's "A Noiseless Patient Spider" (page
13). How has what the poet is saying influenced her formal decisions? Perhaps
write a poem of your own about a spider, choosing the form carefully.

Spider

JAN M. W. ROSE*

Afraid for both of them,
her movements, uncertain,
she lightfoots it between

twelve intersections of thread
and an odd collector's item: 5
a strange dark bug she keeps

knotted in a silk pouch
tight as a cherry pit.
Gnats hover in the moist air

languorous with conversation.   10
"She's strange" they murmur,
riding tiny currents of air.

About her are slung
a dozen males,
bulging in their white hammocks,   15

shimmering in porch light.
Even as she wanders,
legs tapping the wires

like piano strings,
they bob up and down,   20
suspended hard in sleep.

*Throughout *Writing Poems,* an asterisk following the poet's name indicates that the poem was
written when the poet was a student.

But her long worn Utility
chooses none; the captive males
curl tighter in their nets;

and dropping her blue-white line,   25
for a moment—she fidgets—
then turns into shadow.

3. Consider how much "In the Morning, In the Morning," written in 1895 by
A. E. Housman (1859—1936), depends on implication. How do we know that
the characters are lovers? How are we led to understand what has happened?
What lets us know that they are regretful?

In the morning, in the morning,
    In the happy field of hay,
Oh they looked at one another
    By the light of day.

In the blue and silver morning
    On the haycock as they lay,
Oh they looked at one another
    And they looked away.

4. Study the line-breaks of this poem. Is any principle of division deducible
from the length or handling of line or from the poem's appearance? Why has
the poet not used stanzas?

Move into the Wheat

SUZANNE RASCHKE*

Blond heads of grain gods
Loll on the hills.
Farmers understand.
The rest of us keep
Small towns between these hills,   5
Watch the sway of hair,
And try to brush off
Our ripening desire
To move into the wheat
And sleep among gods.   10
Like golden bodies from the black
Earth, sun-bleached tassels stretch
Into August. It is September,
Still they sleep until
Farmers go to wake them,   15
Turn the golden bodies,
Toss back their heads and comb

Hair from their faces.
We see their eyes,
Black as the empty beds   20
Where they slept until harvest.
Later, when I watch
Grains of gold in your eyes
Hide, at dark, I see
Their eyes. Tonight   25
While you sleep my desire
Ripens. I tell myself, "Tomorrow
I will move into the wheat."

5. In the spring of 1854 Henry David Thoreau (1817—1862) jotted down a
couplet in his journal. He gave it *two* last lines, and himself never chose
between them. If it were your poem, which version of the second line would
you choose? Why?

a) When the toads begin to ring,
   Then thinner clothing bring.

b) When the toads begin to ring,
   Off your greatcoat fling.

POEMS TO CONSIDER

The Girl in the Red Convertible   1971

GARY GILDNER   (b. 1938)

The girl in the red convertible
with the heater going full blast
and her throat knocking
turns off the lights
on the road to Winterset   5
and rolls toward the moon
resting expressionless
on the next hill.

When the car stops coasting
it is still June, and   10
she is at the edge
of a field, waiting . . .
She has a
"fifty-fifty chance." It—
that expression—is quietly   15
eating her eyeballs . . .

At dawn a cow appears; then
another. Taking all the time
they need. If only something
would break—break open   20
so she could scream—
Finally there are nine lined up
along the fence—
like visitors to the zoo.

The Garden   1916

En robe de parade.

SAMAIN

EZRA POUND (1885–1972)

Like a skein of loose silk blown against a wall
She walks by the railing of a path in Kensington Gardens°,   *park in London*
And she is dying piece-meal
        of a sort of emotional anæmia.

And round about there is a rabble   5
Of the filthy, sturdy, unkillable infants of the very poor.
They shall inherit the earth.

In her is the end of breeding.
Her boredom is exquisite and excessive.
She would like some one to speak to her,   10
And is almost afraid that I
        will commit that indiscretion.

Player Piano

1958

JOHN UPDIKE (b. 1932)

My stick fingers click with a snicker
And, chuckling, they knuckle the keys;
Light-footed, my steel feelers flicker
And pluck from these keys melodies.

My paper can caper; abandon   5
Is broadcast by dint of my din,
And no man or band has a hand in
The tones I turn on from within.

At times I'm a jumble of rumbles,
At others I'm light like the moon,   10
But never my numb plunker fumbles,
Misstrums me, or tries a new tune.

Loving in Truth, and Fain in Verse My Love to Show

1591

SIR PHILIP SIDNEY (1554–1586)

Loving in truth, and fain in verse my love to show,
That she, dear she, might take some pleasure of my pain,
Pleasure might cause her read, reading might make her know,
Knowledge might pity win, and pity grace obtain,
I sought fit words to paint the blackest face of woe,   5
Studying inventions fine, her wits to entertain,
Oft turning others' leaves, to see if thence would flow
Some fresh and fruitful showers upon my sunburnt brain.
But words came halting forth, wanting Invention's stay;
Invention, Nature's child, fled step-dame Study's blows;   10
And others' feet still seemed but strangers in my way.
Thus great with child to speak, and helpless in my throes,
Biting my truant pen, beating myself for spite:
"Fool," said my Muse to me, "look in thy heart and write."

Stone

CHARLES SIMIC   (b. 1938)

Go inside a stone
That would be my way.
Let somebody else become a dove
Or gnash with a tiger's tooth.
I am happy to be a stone.   5

From the outside the stone is a riddle:
No one knows how to answer it.
Yet within, it must be cool and quiet
Even though a cow steps on it full weight,
Even though a child throws it in a river;   10
The stone sinks, slow, unperturbed
To the river bottom
Where the fishes come to knock on it
And listen.

I have seen sparks fly out   15
When two stones are rubbed,
So perhaps it is not dark inside after all;
Perhaps there is a moon shining
From somewhere, as though behind a hill—   20
Just enough light to make out
The strange writings, the star-charts
On the inner walls.

The Idea of Order at Key West

WALLACE STEVENS   (1879–1955)

She sang beyond the genius of the sea.
The water never formed to mind or voice,
Like a body wholly body, fluttering
Its empty sleeves; and yet its mimic motion

Made constant cry, caused constantly a cry,   5
That was not ours although we understood,
Inhuman, of the veritable ocean.

The sea was not a mask. No more was she.
The song and water were not medleyed sound
Even if what she sang was what she heard,   10
Since what she sang was uttered word by word.
It may be that in all her phrases stirred
The grinding water and the gasping wind;
But it was she and not the sea we heard.

For she was the maker of the song she sang.   15
The ever-hooded, tragic-gestured sea
Was merely a place by which she walked to sing.
Whose spirit is this? we said, because we knew
It was the spirit that we sought and knew
That we should ask this often as she sang.   20

If it was only the dark voice of the sea
That rose, or even colored by many waves;
If it was only the outer voice of sky
And cloud, of the sunken coral water-walled,
However clear, it would have been deep air,   25
The heaving speech of air, a summer sound
Repeated in a summer without end
And sound alone. But it was more than that,
More even than her voice, and ours, among
The meaningless plungings of water and the wind,   30
Theatrical distances, bronze shadows heaped
On high horizons, mountainous atmospheres
Of sky and sea.
                    It was her voice that made
The sky acutest at its vanishing.
She measured to the hour its solitude.   35
She was the single artificer of the world
In which she sang. And when she sang, the sea,
Whatever self it had, became the self
That was her song, for she was the maker. Then we,
As we beheld her striding there alone,   40
Knew that there never was a world for her
Except the one she sang and, singing, made.

Ramon Fernandez°, tell me, if you know,   *a French critic*
Why, when the singing ended and we turned
Toward the town, tell why the glassy lights,   45
The lights in the fishing boats at anchor there,
As the night descended, tilting in the air,
Mastered the night and portioned out the sea,
Fixing emblazoned zones and fiery poles,
Arranging, deepening, enchanting night.   50

Oh! Blessed rage for order, pale Ramon,
The maker's rage to order words of the sea,
Words of the fragrant portals, dimly-starred,
And of ourselves and of our origins,
In ghostlier demarcations, keener sounds.   55

2

Free Verse:
Invisible Nets and Trellises

Fluid form has several names, including organic or open form. The most familiar name, of course, is **free verse.** Borrowed from the French *vers libre,* the term means verse written without a particular or recognizable meter. Since verse requires some system of measure, some internal signal when a new line should begin, the term *free verse* may seem self-contradictory. Indeed, verse that really is free of any measure often ends up as arbitrary, random, "chopped-up prose." Robert Frost compares such verse to playing tennis without a net—too easy, without challenge, no fun. W. H. Auden describes the problem:

> The poet who writes "free" verse is like Robinson Crusoe on his desert island: he must do all his cooking, laundry and darning for himself. In a few exceptional cases, this manly independence produces something original and impressive, but more often the result is squalor—dirty sheets on the unmade bed and empty bottles on the unswept floor.

Even Ezra Pound, who championed free verse in 1912, was very soon complaining about the sloppy free verse being written:

> Indeed *vers libre* has become as prolix and as verbose as any of the flaccid varieties that preceded it. It has brought faults of its own. The actual language

and phrasing is often as bad as that of our elders without even the excuse that the words are shovelled in to fill a metric pattern or to complete the noise of a rhyme-sound.

He concluded:

Eliot has said the thing very well when he said, No *vers* is *libre* for the man who wants to do a good job.

Despite the dangers of slackness, free verse is a popular, well-established form. *The Princeton Encyclopedia of Poetry and Poetics* notes that free verse "has become so common as to have some claim to being the characterisic form of the age." Many finely wrought, even formal poems have been written in free verse; and finally that must be the test—the form is good that works.

For the beginning poet, however, there is little practical theory of free verse. Poets who have written successfully have done so largely through intuition. A well-tuned ear—a delicate sensitivity to language—finds the right form, right rhythm, which, in Pound's words, "corresponds exactly to the emotion or shade of emotion to be expressed." Poets often do this without being able to explain how, just as readers may respond to such rhythms without knowing, technically, why. Olson's view, passed along by Allen Ginsberg, that length of line is somehow determined by the poet's breath, seems purely impressionistic and of little use in practice. (Do poets who write very short lines, for instance, suffer from emphysema?) William Carlos Williams's notion of the "variable foot," suggestive though it is, is also vague. His rhythms and forms may be imitated, but there is no satisfactory account of the principles underlying them.

To discover what will be useful to you as a beginning poet, you must find tempting models and work intuitively or experimentally from them in developing your own free verse. And, until there is an adequate theory (and historical account), you may find a few rough distinctions valuable. Three basic types of free verse, I think, can be distinguished. They may be called end-stopped, run-on, and spatial, though, of course, any given poem may be a mixture of these and there are a number of subtypes of each.

End-Stopped Free Verse

The father of modern end-stopped free verse is Walt Whitman (1819–1892), although there are historical antecedents in the "verse" of the King James Bible of 1611 (especially in Psalms, Ecclesiastes, and chapter 38 of Job), in Christopher Smart's *Rejoice in the Lamb,* and in William Blake's prophetic poems in the eighteenth century. Walt Whitman's "A Noiseless Patient

Spider" (page 13) exemplifies end-stopped free verse, as does the first section of "Song of Myself" (1855):

> I celebrate myself, and sing myself,
> And what I assume you shall assume,
> for every atom belonging to me as good belongs to you.
>
> I loaf and invite my soul,
> I lean and loaf at my ease observing a spear of summer grass.   5
>
> My tongue, every atom of my blood, formed from this soil, this air,
> Born here of parents born here from parents the same, and their
>   parents the same,
> I, now thirty-seven years old in perfect health begin,
> Hoping to cease not till death.
>
> Creeds and schools in abeyance,   10
> Retiring back a while sufficed at what they are, but never forgotten,
> I harbor for good or bad, I permit to speak at every hazard,
> Nature without check with original energy.

In this passage the line-breaks occur at syntactical or grammatical pauses or intervals; that, simply, identifies end-stopped free verse. Although the lines of the Whitman poem vary considerably in length, they are generally long and loose, allowing for great variety in rhythm with or without internal pauses (caesuras). They are essentially in prose rhythm, that is, rangy and irregular, but are heightened by recurring phrases, as in lines 7−8, or by recurring parallel structures, as in lines 4−5. Whitman's rhythms and patterns of rhythms are often oratorical and prophetic, as are the rhythms in the later end-stopped free verse of Carl Sandburg or Allen Ginsberg ("A Supermarket in California," page 251, or "America," page 367). Typically, the Whitman manner and gesture are grand. It is interesting that the first line is written in traditional iambic pentameter:

> Ĭ célĕbráte mўsélf, ănd síng mўsélf.

Whitman's use of that meter seems to imply that his free verse was essentially an opening up of the traditional line of English metrical verse.

End-stopped free verse tends toward long lines because they permit internal pauses and greater internal rhythmic variation. When there are pauses and syntactical intervals that do not fall at line-ends, those that do are doubly emphatic, whereas the internal pauses are minimized and lightly passed over. The muscular cadence of end-stopped free verse (a particularly appropriate form for the oratorical statement) derives in large part from the tension between these two kinds of pauses.

Short lines of end-stopped free verse diminish the possibility of internal pause and variation. In the logical extreme—where every syntactical unit is given an individual line—the tension disappears and all that remains is chopped prose. Suppose the sixth line of the passage were rearranged:

My tongue,
every atom of my blood,
formed from this soil,
this air . . .

The result is stacked prose (lines piled on top of one another in a way that merely parallels the syntactical units of a prose statement). Beginners often mistakenly divide the lines this way, and the impact is about as arresting, in its lack of variety, as a stack of lumber or dishes. Line in verse, however one measures or defines it, must somehow *cut across* the natural flow of sentences, at least often enough to allow one to distinguish its rhythm from prose.

End-stopped free verse may, of course, be written in lines shorter than Whitman's. "The Garden" by Ezra Pound (page 19) is an instance, as is his very droll "The Three Poets":

Candidia has taken a new lover
And three poets are gone into mourning.
The first has written a long elegy to 'Chloris,'
To 'Chloris chaste and cold,' his 'only Chloris.'
The second has written a sonnet   5
                upon the mutability of woman,
And the third writes an epigram to Candidia.

The syntactical units are long enough to allow for rhythmical variation, and Pound has treated the end of the very long line 5 as a "dropped" line ("upon the mutability of woman") to provide further variation and indicate subordination. While this phrase is long enough to justify a line of its own, note how wooden the movement is when the line begins at the left margin:

The second has written a sonnet
Upon the mutability of woman,
And the third writes an epigram to Candidia.

The dropped-line not only adds flexibility but also prepares, like a whip whirling backwards, for the rhythmic decisiveness and snap of the last line. After the first three lines, each of which contains a simple sentence structure (subject, verb, object), the fourth line ("To 'Chloris chaste . . .' ") is a subordinate appositional clause on a line by itself—and with a caesural pause as well. Throughout, not one of the poem's three sentences lies across the verse lines in the same way. As a consequence, the pace is lithe and sinewy, albeit with the slim sinews of good prose. Such line-to-line syntactical variations make the poem's rhythm flexible and lively.

"The Three Poets" superbly illustrates how syntax may be used to enhance tone and meaning. Overall, the light, swift rhythm supports the satiric nature of this poem. For example, treating line 6 as a dropped line transforms what might otherwise be a rather weighty statement into a sardonic aside. The comma at the end of the line, where we might expect a period, hurries the voice on to the last line where the trenchant wit then seems appropriately offhand. Finally, the shift to the present tense in the last line indicates that Pound's speaker *is* the third poet referred to, and that this poem is his "epigram to Candidia."

Other poems in end-stopped free verse to which an interested reader may want to look ahead are J. D. Reed's "The Weather Is Brought to You" (page 188) and Kenneth Koch's "You Were Wearing" (page 230).

Run-On Free Verse

Along with others, most notably William Carlos Williams and Marianne Moore, Ezra Pound explored and enhanced the possibilities of run-on free verse. The first stanza of his "The Return" exemplifies the form:

See, they return; ah, see the tentative
    Movements, and the slow feet,
    The trouble in the pace and the uncertain
    Wavering!

The rhythmic character of the passage primarily derives from the very strong run-on lines broken between the adjectives and the nouns: "the tentative / Movements" and "the uncertain / Wavering!" Both force a slightly abnormal pause, and this extra hesitation evokes rhythmically the tentative, uncertain feeling. Given a line by itself, "Wavering!" unexpectedly ends the stanza's flow, leaving it on an appropriately awkward diminuendo.

Since no formal meter determines where the lines must end, the choice of breaking them is arbitrary in run-on free verse. Line-breaks tend to occur where there is no major grammatical or syntactical pause. Of course, the last line of a poem is inevitably end-stopped, as other lines may be. The texture of run-on free verse may vary, not only with the mixing in of end-stopped lines but also with the alterations in "pull" of the various run-ons. Just as end-stopped free verse tends to longer lines, run-on free verse characteristically tends to shorter lines.

Long lines allow for caesural pauses and for any number of rational places to break lines in end-stopped free verse. The speed or "pull" of run-ons in similarly long lines of run-on free verse, however, would be obtrusive and seem abnormal, competing with the slower, deliberate pace of the main part of the line. Indeed, when free verse mixes very short and very long lines, it is often unsuccessful—bumpy and unpaced. Pace is important in free verse, especially since line-breaks are relatively arbitrary. Thus, some roughly equal line-length seems necessary to unify a poem or passage.

William Carlos Williams (1883–1963) is the major innovator in run-on free verse, and his "To Waken an Old Lady" is a primary example of the form:

> Old age is
> a flight of small
> cheeping birds
> skimming
> bare trees 5
> above a snow glaze.
> Gaining and failing
> they are buffeted
> by a dark wind—
> But what? 10
> On harsh weedstalks
> the flock has rested,
> the snow
> is' covered with broken
> seedhusks 15
> and the wind tempered
> by a shrill
> piping of plenty.

The short, oddly broken lines convey the speed and skittery movement of the small birds. (As always, the criterion is whether the form, free or strict, expresses its content.) We may scan the poem in two ways. One is to mark the accented (´) and unaccented (˘) syllables. The other is to mark the force, or "pull," of the run-on line-ends: three slashes (///) for strong pull; two (//) for moderate pull; one (/) for weak pull; and zero (0) for end-stopped lines.

> Óld áge ĭs   //   ⟵───────
>
> ă flíght ŏf smáll   //   ───────⟶

chéepĭng bírds   /   ←——————→

skímmĭng   //   ←——————

báre trées   /   ←——————→

ăbóve ă snów gláze. 0   ——————→

Gáinĭng ănd fáilĭng /   ←——————

théy ăre búffetĕd   /   ←——————

bў ă dárk wínd—   0   ——————→

Bút whát?   0   ←——————→

Ŏn hársh wéedstálks /   ——————→

thĕ flóck hăs réstĕd, 0   ←——————→

thĕ snów   /   ——————→

ĭs cóvĕred wĭth brókĕn /// ←——————→

séedhúsks   /   ←——————→

ănd thĕ wínd témpĕred //   ——————→

bў ă shríll   ///   ——————→

pípĭng ŏf pléntў.   0   ←——————

Of the poem's eighteen lines, thirteen are run-on and only five end-stopped. Seven lines have weak run-ons; four, moderate run-ons; and two, strong run-ons. Relative to run-ons, the poem has three movements. Lines 1–5 are moderately active (//-//-/-//-/). Lines 6–13 are weakly active (0-/-/-0-0-/-0-/). Lines 14–18 are strongly active (///-/-//-///-0). These relative movements correspond to the three phases of the poem. In lines 1–6 the birds are active and mobile, in flight, "skimming." In lines 7–13, they are defeated by the dark wind—the weak run-ons of lines 7–8 suggest their efforts ("Gaining") and their unsuccess ("and failing")—and come to rest on the "harsh weedstalks." The defeat, however, is temporary, for in lines 14–18 the activity is resumed, even increased, as they feed. The strong run-on of line 14—"is covered with broken /// seedhusks"—suggests or imitates the breaking open of the husks; and the strong run-on of line 17, again separating adjective and noun, emphasizes the activity of "shrill /// piping of plenty."

No doubt Williams felt the rightness of the rhythms not by calculation but intuitively, which is what having a good ear means. Scanning the syllables per line confirms just how good Williams's ear is. Lines range in length from two to six syllables. Lines in the middle of the poem, where action is diminished, are generally longer than those at the beginning or end. Around the stark interrogative at the poem's center ("But what?") are six lines of four or five syllables, while shorter lines are characterisic of the more active parts of the poem.

Local effects of the rhythm are also telling. The only two syllable lines that come together—"skimming // bare trees"—give an impression of the swiftness of the birds' flight. In:

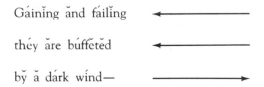

Gáinĭng ănd fáilĭng

théy ăre búffĕtĕd

bў ă dárk wĭnd—

the "drag" or backward leaning of the first two lines (accented followed by unaccented syllables) suggests their difficulty in making headway, whereas the advance or forward leaning of the third line (unaccented syllables running to accented) suggests the irresistible force of the wind. I have marked this drag or advance with arrows alongside the scansion.

The similarly short, oddly broken lines of Williams's "Poem" offer an interesting contrast, conveying rather than speed and skittery movement a feeling of catlike hesitancy and care:

As the cat
climbed over
the top of

the jamcloset   5
first the right
forefoot

carefully
then the hind
stepped down

into the pit of   10
the empty
flowerpot

Short lines do not necessarily produce rhythmic speed, any more than long lines necessarily produce slowness or ponderousness (Whitman's spider works rapidly), but in most cases they do. How, then, does Williams achieve the virtual slow-motion of "Poem"?

Ăs thĕ cát	/	⟶
clímbed óvĕr	///	⟵—
thĕ tóp ŏf	///	⟷
thĕ jámclósĕt	0	⟷
fírst thĕ right	///	⟷
fórefóot	//	⟷
cárefŭllў	/	⟵
thén thĕ hínd	/	⟷
stépped dówn	/	⟷
íntŏ thĕ pít ŏf	///	⟶
thĕ émptў	//	⟷
flówĕrpót	0	⟷

The use of stanzas, none of which is end-stopped, clearly accentuates the very deliberate rhythm, as does the fact that the poem is all one fairly long sentence. Neither of these explanations is sufficient, however, to account for the rhythm. The marking of run-ons shows that the poem is strongly run-on; only two lines are end-stopped. (I have counted the end of the subordinate clause after "jamcloset" as end-stopped, though Williams omits the expected comma.) Generally, the run-ons are strongest where the action of the cat is least decisive, most slow-motion; and are weakest in lines 5–8 where the actual steps of the cat are described. The strongest run-ons—between preposition and object, or between adjective and noun—occur in lines 2, 3, 5 and 10. Strangely, these seem to produce the effect of the least movement, the reverse of what we might expect.

The explanation becomes clear from the scansion of syllables. Only three of the poem's twelve lines show either drag or advance (lines 1–2 and 7). Nine of the lines are balanced, or static (shown by the double-headed arrows). In "To Waken an Old Lady" there were only six lines in balance, with five showing drag and seven showing advance. In "Poem" the preponderance of lines in balance causes a feeling of stasis, which even the sentence's momentum can scarcely overcome. For the rest, the range of line-length is from two to five syllables. Eight of the twelve lines, however, have three syllables; only two have two syllables, and only one each has four or five. The stronger syllabic norm in "Poem" may also contribute to the slow-motion of the rhythm.

Run-on free verse continually plays its line structure against the speech flow of the poem. Other poems in run-on free verse include Gerald Costanzo's "Potatoes" (page 392) and John Ciardi's "Counting on Flowers" (page 49). "The Racer's Widow" by Louise Glück (b. 1943) shows the effect of longer lines in run-on free verse:

> The elements have merged into solicitude.
> Spasms of violets rise above the mud
> And weed and soon the birds and ancients
> Will be starting to arrive, bereaving points
> South. But never mind. It is not painful to discuss   5
> His death. I have been primed for this,
> For separation, for so long. But still his face assaults
> Me, I can hear that car careen again, the crowd coagulate on asphalt
> In my sleep. And watching him, I feel my legs like snow
> That let him finally let him go   10
> As he lies draining there. And see
> How even he did not get to keep that lovely body.

Line length ranges from eight to nineteen syllables, and the pattern of run-ons is strong: 0-//-/-///-//-0-///-//-/-/-//-0. The widow's assertion that "It is not painful to discuss // His death" is contradicted by the run-ons that flow to or from internal pauses very near the line-ends, as well as by the imagery that suggests how distraught she is ("Spasms of violets"; "I can hear . . . the crowd coagulate on asphalt"). Run-ons into lines 3 ("above the mud // And weed"), 5 ("bereaving points /// South"), 6 ("to discuss // His death"), 8 ("his face assaults /// Me"), and 9 ("on asphalt // In my sleep"), and from line 11 ("And see // How even he") conform to this pattern. The effect is an odd starting and stopping, a smooth assertiveness and an odd careening around corners. The repetition in line 10—"That let him finally let him go"—sounds natural but of course is not. The sentence fragment at poem's end has the same effect: "And see . . ." which is by ellipsis parallel to "I feel my legs. . . ." The poem's rhythm, jerking forward in very forced run-ons and smoothing in the relatively long lines, appropriately conveys the widow's repressed but unconcealed emotional turmoil.

Many poems are a mixture of end-stopped and run-on free verse. Each free verse poem establishes its own norms, one of which is the range of line-length. Once a pattern of lines of relatively consistent length has been established, it should be maintained. Lines very much shorter, or longer, than the norm pattern stand out too much and may seem awkward or contrived. A one-word line in "The Racer's Widow," for example, would seem out of place, as would a very long line in Williams's "To Waken an Old Lady."

Visible Stanzas

Historically, before the invention of printing in the fifteenth century, poetry was primarily an oral and aural art, rather than a written one. It was heard, rather than seen. Songs were sung; epics and narratives were declaimed by traveling bards. Formal meters, clearly accented and countable, allowed a poem's form to be followed by its hearers—just as rhyme, aside from its musical qualities, served to mark the turn from line to line like a typewriter bell. Since the sixteenth century, and especially after the rise of general literacy in the nineteenth century, poetry has become ever more a visual art through almost imperceptible evolution. Today we are more accustomed to seeing a poem than to hearing it, and students must be reminded to read poems aloud, particularly older poems, lest they miss an essential element.

The rise of free verse in the twentieth century corresponds, I suspect, to the acceleration of the evolution of poetry toward the visual. Free verse permits us to *see* the difference from prose. More in run-on than in end-stopped free verse, this visual quality represents the development of new formal possibilities, of visual forms. The visual will not replace the oral (poetry always relies on speech for its vigor) but will complement it, enriching and widening the poet's resources. William Carlos Williams is unquestionably the American master of run-on free verse, his poems a virtual library of effects. One of his significant innovations is free verse in stanzas of the same number of lines, and frequently of the same shape, as in "Poem." Such stanzas provide a regularity in visual form on the page, within which the language and the content can ebb and flow. The stanzaic regularity, reassuringly suggesting order and decisiveness to the eye, complements or counterpoints the freedom of speech inside the form. In the case of one poem, "The Nightingales," as Williams reports in *I Wanted To Write a Poem,* he changed a stanza of five lines to four to match the poem's other stanza. The original version:

My shoes as I lean
unlacing them
stand out upon
flat worsted flowers
under my feet.

Nimbly the shadows
of my fingers play
unlacing
over shoes and flowers.

The revision:

My shoes as I lean
unlacing them
stand out upon
flat worsted flowers.

Nimbly the shadows
of my fingers play
unlacing
over shoes and flowers.

"See," he says, "how much better it conforms to the page, how much better it looks?" One reason we prefer the final version, aside from the symmetry of stanzas of an identical number of lines, is that the poem is tighter without losing anything. Line 5 in the original was weak and redundant.

Traditionally, stanzas are structural units of thought and are end-stopped, as in "The Nightingales." They may be run-on as well, however, as in Williams's poem about the cat or Frost's "Dust of Snow." As with lines, stanzas provide an additional element of modulation and flow. Late in his career, Williams often used an indented pattern of three lines, as in this excerpt from "Asphodel, That Greeny Flower":

The sea! The sea!
          Always
                    when I think of the sea
there comes to mind
          the *Iliad*
                    and Helen's public fault
that bred it.
          Were it not for that
                    there would have been

5

```
no poem but the world                                      10
        if we had remembered,
                those crimson petals
    spilled among the stones,
            would have called it simply
                        murder.                             15
```

These triads gave Williams a fixed but flexible medium for longer poems—for
starting and stopping, speeding and slowing the voice. Notice the quickness
with which, in line 10, the second part of the compound sentence begins,
prompting a momentarily mistaken but relevant reading of "no poem but the
world" as a syntactical unit (with "but" as preposition, in the sense of "except,"
rather than as conjunction). Notice also the weight with which the sentence
comes to its end on the one-word line, "murder." (See page 266 for another
excerpt from this poem.) Similarly, lines of regularly *differing* lengths, repeated
from stanza to stanza, as in "The Double Play" (page 49) or "The Girl Writing
Her English Paper" (page 348) offer, on Williams's model, any number of fresh
possibilities for the control and organization of free verse.

Free verse stanza patterns such as Williams's are trellises; they are the
framework of visual regularity on which the morning-glory of the new poem
fluidly and freely twines. An alliance with form does not necessarily imply the
loss of freedom. Even when the choice of stanza length or shape seems arbitrary,
its uses may be organic and expressive of the content. Stanza structure may
produce run-on free verse as precise and formally made as a metrical poem.

Robert Creeley (b. 1926) deftly develops free-flowing content on the arbitrary trellis of stanzas in his dramatic "I Know a Man":

```
As I sd to my
friend, because I am
always talking,—John, I

sd, which was not his
name, the darkness sur-                                     5
rounds us, what

can we do against
it, or else, shall we &
why not, buy a goddamn big car,

drive, he sd, for                                           10
christ's sake, look
out where yr going.
```

Both lines and stanzas are strongly run-on, with line-breaks occurring at awkward places: "my / friend" or "I / sd" or "against / it." Even the word "sur- / rounds" is broken. The effect is a feeling of disorder, confusion, haste. Abbreviations ("sd" for "said," "yr" for "you're," "&" for "and") support this impression of flurry. The speaker is highly agitated, rattled. Realizing that the "darkness" in line 5 is not merely physical (one can't *do* anything against merely physical darkness), we also know that the speaker's agitation is a kind of frantic, desperate outburst about the negative circumstances of life. In the last stanza, his friend recalls him from this general complaint to an immediate danger: "drive, he sd." This makes the poem's point that it is better to deal practically with real problems than to worry about abstract, symbolical issues of good and evil. In this context, "for / christ's sake" takes on a deeper meaning, suggesting perhaps that goodness consists not in generalizations but in specific acts, not in vague, ineffective opposition to evil but in particular resistance. Here the specific resistance is to the temptation of despair ("& / why not, buy a goddamn big car") or of being careless of others.

A major part of the poem's effect comes from the choice of a form in which the run-on lines imitate the confusion, haste, and irrationality of the speaker. Breaking "sur- / rounds," for instance, emphasizes the sense of being surrounded by appearing to point both right and left; the "turn" of the line seems a gesture in all directions. Further, note that the poem is one long sentence. The mere comma after "car" in line 9 does not prepare us for the change of speaker, as would the normal period or dash. Our sudden realization in line 10—"drive, he sd"—that the voice has changed imitates the suddenness of danger, the unexpectedness with which an "accident" can occur when one is morally off guard. The terse urgency of the warning reinforces this abruptness. That comma after line 9 is a master stroke.

The title, "I Know a Man," which at first seems emptily descriptive, comes finally to mean something like "I know a *real* man, one who isn't flustered by moral complaint or danger." The overtone of both "goddamn" and "for / christ's sake," which at first seem mere vulgarity, suggests that manliness may be very much a moral or spiritual matter. The regular three-line stanzas contain, box in, and so *measure* the frustrations and confusion of the speaker. Like the "friend," they are a reminder of restraint and, thus, stand as a formal expression of the poem's theme. (**Theme** is what a poem *as a whole* says, or more often implies, about its subject matter. We might think of it as the poem's central thought, its drift, its consensus of meaning.)

The use of a visual, stanzaic form explains the popularity of William Carlos Williams's strangely effective little poem, "The Red Wheelbarrow":

so much depends
upon

a red wheel
barrow

glazed with rain   5
water

beside the white
chickens

The stanzas focus on each detail separately, giving the poem its intense, painterly concentration—and emphasizing the important first statement which, so isolated, can't just be passed over. Then, convinced by the color and clarity of the images, we wonder how such details are significant. The poem's theme resonates with possibilities: the natural fecundity of land and rain and labor on which we depend for food; the ancient human inventiveness ("wheel," perhaps "glaze") of which the simple farmyard scene reminds us and on which our sophisticated civilization thoughtlessly depends; the enduring values of a plain and honest daily life, which the unmentioned farmer, whose tools and concerns they are, represents; and not least (because it is Williams's poem) the spiritually nutritious perception of the beauty of the ordinary.

Each stanza is, indeed, shaped roughly like a wheelbarrow, with the longer first line suggesting the handle. Less obviously, the second line of each couplet is reached by a very strong run-on. In the first couplet the forced run-on causes the voice to come down on the preposition "upon" more heavily than the word normally deserves and so emphasizes it. In the last three couplets the line-break divides an adjective from its noun: "a red wheel /// barrow," "glazed with rain /// water," "beside the white /// chickens." In stanza 2 the run-on in fact divides, though without hyphen, the single word "wheelbarrow." That both "wheel" and "rain" are nouns used as adjectives reinforces the pull of the run-ons. Rhythmically, we might illustrate these strong run-on lines this way:

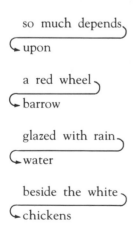

If the stanzas are shaped like tiny wheelbarrows, these turning run-ons rhythmically suggest the wheels. Probably the fascination of this apparently quiet little poem comes from the way its combined visual and aural form mirrors its subject. This tiny still-life catches energy in stasis, a complex vitality only momentarily at rest.

Like a vine that goes up and spreads on its trellis instead of blooming in a heap on the ground, the free verse in all these poems uses visual form—stanza shapes and relative line-lengths—to express the inner shape or movement of their subjects and feelings. What is important is not the stanza forms (they are empty shapes) but the way they are used, the way the vine of the language has been trained upon them. Any form, any measure, whether free or conventionally metrical—or something else—is only as valuable as the use that is made of it.

Syllabics

That something else might be **syllabics**: a formal measure in which only the number of syllables in each line is counted. Strictly speaking, syllabics is not free verse. (Compare Dylan Thomas's "Fern Hill," p. 173.) But neither, strictly, are the fixed shape stanzas we have been discussing. Both are, more than anything else, forms of free verse; and recognizing them as such is a further step toward an adequate theory of the major verse form of the twentieth century. Since the counting of syllables in English syllabic verse cannot be done by ear (that is, syllabics is not a measure or rhythm we can hear), syllabics is merely mechanical form. It is a development of free verse, as is the measure of counting the number of *words* per line (pioneered by Robert Francis) or, indeed, the counting of any other nonrhythmical element or feature of the language. Like shape-stanzas, such forms provide a trellis for the rhythmically free cadence. Like William Carlos Williams, Marianne Moore (1887–1972) must be regarded as one of the masters of free verse. Here is her syllabic "To a Steam Roller":

The illustration
is nothing to you without the application.
    You lack half wit. You crush all the particles down
        into close conformity, and then walk back and forth on them.

Sparkling chips of rock   5
are crushed down to the level of the parent block.
    Were not "impersonal judgment in aesthetic
        matters, a metaphysical impossibility," you

might fairly achieve
it. As for butterflies, I can hardly conceive   10
    of one's attending upon you, but to question
        the congruence of the complement is vain, if it exists.

Each first line has five syllables; each second line, twelve; each third line, twelve; and each fourth line, fifteen. Especially in stanzas 1 and 3, the longer last lines mimic, both visually and rhythmically, the effect of something rolled over and flattened by a steam roller. And the rhyme in each stanza's lines 1–2 (on top, where the too mechanical steam roller would be) is followed by the *lack* of rhymes in lines 3–4, as if the last two lines had been squashed. Even the mechanical chopping off of the run-on "achieve / it" in lines 9–10 seems something the steam roller would do. "To a Steam Roller" is a graceful and sardonic little poem in syllabic run-on free verse.

Spatial Free Verse

A spatial or visual element has been important in a number of the poems already discussed, such as "Me up at does" or "The Red Wheelbarrow." In these poems the visual quality remains subordinate to the aural. In other poems, however, the visual predominates; and even the elementary structure of line becomes secondary or may disappear. A simple case:

The

    ball

        bumps

            down

                the

                    steps . . .

Here the lines themselves are clearly secondary to the visual image they create. A poem like "The Murder of Two Men by a Young Kid Wearing Lemon-colored Gloves" by Kenneth Patchen (1911–1972) can't in any normal sense be *read*, but is perceived:

                    Wait.

                                                    Wait.

                                        Wait.

                            Wait. Wait.

                Wait.

                                                    Wait.

                                W a i t.

                    Wait.

                                            Wait.

                                                    Wait.

                        Wait.

                                            Wait.

                Wait.

                    NOW.

E. E. Cummings, who brilliantly wrote "mOOn," has been the most influential experimenter with visual effects in poetry and with spatial free verse. In poems like "O sweet spontaneous" (page 50) or "chanson innocente" (page 133), Cummings uses spacing as a sort of musical notation for emphasis, for speeding or slowing the voice. Consider, for instance, the differences in the three repetitions of the phrase "far and wee" in "chanson innocente." But he also writes poems in which the oral is effectively replaced by the visual or spatial as the primary medium. This fine little poem, whose first line is "l(a," defies reading aloud. Study it carefully so as not to let me ruin the surprise.

l(a

le
af
fa

ll

s)
one
l

iness

The poem is the word "loneliness" and, inside it, parentheses containing the image of a single leaf falling as an example of loneliness. The poem is symmetrical, alternating stanzas of one line and three lines; and the broken way the image of the leaf twists down from line to line perhaps suggests the turning descent of the leaf, rocking as it drops. Compare this commonplace rearrangement:

loneliness
(a leaf falls)

Cummings's version of the identical statement is visually textured and, because it requires us to puzzle it out, fresh. The vital detail of the poem is not found in the rearrangement: in the formal splintering of the word "loneliness," we are shown an almost heartbreaking accident of the language. The lower case "l" and the arabic numeral "1" are designed the same way (one key serves for both on the standard typewriter). What the poem's form unmistakably tells us is that loneliness is "l-one-l-iness." That is what loneliness is, one-one-one-iness.

Another rearrangement of the poem—omitting the stanza breaks—suggests how much its form is its necessary nothing. The poem seems to lose its precision, feels cluttered:

l(a
le
af
fa
ll
s)
one
l
iness

Spatial poetry may be as simple as the visually punning "In the Fields" by Barry Spacks (b. 1931):

Rainingrainingraining.

Or it may be as complex as **picture poems,** which use the shape of an object as their form. Picture poems are an old tradition. "Easter Wings" by George Herbert (1593–1633), written in meter, is an early example:

Lord, who createdst man in wealth and store,
Though foolishly he lost the same,
Decaying more and more
Till he became
Most poore;
With thee
O let me rise
As larks, harmoniously,
And sing this day thy victories;
Then shall the fall further the flight in me.

My tender age in sorrow did beginne;
And still with sicknesses and shame
Thou didst so punish sinne,
That I became
Most thinne.
With thee
Let me combine,
And feel this day thy victorie;
For if I imp my wing on thine,
Affliction shall advance the flight in me.

19 *imp:* to engraft feathers on a damaged wing (term from falconry).

Decreasing and then increasing the lines of each stanza by one foot, Herbert not only makes the poem look like two pairs of angels' wings but also embodies the poem's theme of personal diminution and regrowth.

Twentieth-century picture poems have been written in the shape of Coca-Cola bottles, traffic cloverleafs with Model T's and Model A's circling them, and umbrellas. In 1969 John Hollander (b. 1929) published *Types of Shape,* in which there are poems shaped like a key, a light bulb, a bell, a heart, New York State, and even a swan and its shadow. Here is "Eskimo Pie":

```
        I shall
     never pretend
    to have forgotten
    such loves as those
    that turned the dying
   brightness at an end of
   a childs afternoon into
   preludes To an evening of
   lamplight To a night dark
   with blanketing To mornings
   of more and more There deep
   in the old ruralities of play
   the frosted block with papery
  whisps still stuck to it kissed
  me burningly as it arose out of
  dry icy stillnesses And there now
  again I taste first its hard then
  its soft Now I am into the creamy
 treasure which to have tasted is to
 have begun to lose to the heat of a
 famished sun But O if I break faith
 with you poor dreadful popsicle may
 my mouth forget warm rains a tongue
 musty Pauillac cool skin all tastes
              I see
              sweet
              drops
              slide
              along
              a hot
              stick
              It is
              a sad
              sorry
              taste
              which
              never
              comes
              to an
              end
```

Pauillac: a very fine French wine.

So-called "concrete poems" lie halfway between poetry and graphics. Here is one of the most famous, by Reinhard Döhl (b. 1934). "Apfel" is the German word for apple.

```
        .ipfelApfelApfelApter..
       ,telApfelApfelApfelApfelA,
      ,felApfelApfelApfelApfelApfe
    ApfelApfelApfelApfelApfelApf,
   pfelApfelApfelApfelApfelApfel/
  [ApfelApfelApfelApfelApfelApfe
  pfelApfelApfelApfelApfelApfelA
  ApfelApfelApfelApfelApfelApfe
  )felApfelApfelApfelApfelApfel/
  \pfelApfelApfelApfelApfelApf
   elApfelApfelApfelWurmAp'
   'elApfelApfelApfelApfel/
    `ofelApfelApfelApfel^
     ^felApfelApfelA-
      ' ^felAnfel^
```

Whatever its form, free verse—because it may be invented to suit its occasion or subject—is always changing and fresh. It is not merely poetry written any-old-which-a-way.

QUESTIONS AND SUGGESTIONS

1. Using a recent free verse poem of your own with which you aren't really satisfied, experiment with arranging it in stanzas. Don't spare the paper.

2. Write a poem in syllabics. Or write a picture poem about a carrot, a hat, an alarm clock, or some other common object. Or write an **acrostic** poem, using your own name or the name of someone you know. An acrostic is a poem in which the first letters of each line have a meaning when read downward, like:

Here lies an
English teacher who was
Never
Really
Young at heart.

Let him rest in peace,
Every word spelled right,
Every period in its place.

3. How have these student-poets reinvented and used free verse for their purposes?

a) FRANCES SLACK*

> I think the needle is stuck
>   ink the needle is stu
>   ink the needle is stu
>   ink the needle is stu
>   ink the needle is stu
>   ink the needle is stu
>   ink the needle is stu

b) *disappearances*

SHEILA HEINRICH*

> was a man of many disguises
> was a man of few words and
> one day when they looked where he had been
> they found
>
> and no one said
> so no one ever

c) *The Butterfly Collective*

CURT MANLEY*

> Fluttering in in their silks,
> Your high-heeled, radiant ladies
> Invite themselves, unannounced,
>   And as we finish our supper,
>   They frolic about the furniture,   5
>   Pulsing like children at play.
>
> As you step
> Into their circle of secret laughter,
> Their smiles pull off your old clothes,
> Stretch you into your raw ebon silk,   10
> Your tie, carefully masking your curves,
> Your sex.
> And when they've hidden your braids
> Beneath a wide, dark brim,
> They own and obey you,   15
> Clutching your arms
> As you lead them again into the night,
>   Drawn down to the
>   Neon flickerings of a faster life
>   Where you are every bit a man.   20

Gold-pinned marriage became your chrysalis.
Changed, to something less fragile,
You've not yet thought to
Cut me loose
Or remove the meaningless ring: 25
    Alone in the Venetian-slit darkness
    I spin my own cocoon around me,
    But when the light returns
    I am unchanged.

After a year,   30
This
Is all it comes to.
    How much worse can it finally be
    When your claws rake me aloft
    To shake me off the last time?   35

4. In "Smart" by Bruce Bennett (b. 1940) what *gestures* do you find the poet making in his choice of line-breaks and stanzas? Does Bennett's omission of capitalization and punctuation help his fable?

Smart

like the fox
who grabs a stick
and wades
into the water

deep   5
and deeper
till only his muzzle's
above it
his fleas

leap   10
up and up
onto his head
out onto the stick

which he lets go

off it floats   15
as he swims back
and shakes himself dry

5. How has James Wright (1927–1980) used line-length, run-on and end-stopped lines, and caesura, to represent his meaning in his rhythm? (This is one of two poems given the joint title "Two Hangovers.")

I Try to Waken
and Greet the World Once Again

In a pine tree,
A few yards away from my window sill,
A brilliant blue jay is springing up and down, up and down,
On a branch.
I laugh, as I see him abandon himself   5
To entire delight, for he knows as well as I do
That the branch will not break.

POEMS TO CONSIDER

On the Lawn at the Villa   1963

LOUIS SIMPSON   (b. 1923)

On the lawn at the villa—
That's the way to start, eh, reader?
We know where we stand—somewhere expensive—
You and I *imperturbes,* as Walt would say,
Before the diversions of wealth, you and I *engagés.*   5

On the lawn at the villa
Sat a manufacturer of explosives,
His wife from Paris,
And a young man named Bruno,

And myself, being American,   10
Willing to talk to these malefactors,
The manufacturer of explosives, and so on,
But somehow superior. By that I mean democratic.
It's complicated, being an American,
Having the money and the bad conscience, both at the same time.   15
Perhaps, after all, this is not the right subject for a poem.

We were all sitting there paralyzed
In the hot Tuscan° afternoon,   Tuscany (Italy)
And the bodies of the machine-gun crew were draped over the balcony.
So we sat there all afternoon.   20

To the Stone-Cutters   1924

ROBINSON JEFFERS   (1887–1962)

Stone-cutters fighting time with marble, you fore-defeated
Challengers of oblivion,
Eat cynical earnings, knowing rock splits, records fall down,
The square-limbed Roman letters
Scale in the thaws, wear in the rain. The poet as well   5
Builds his monument mockingly;
For man will be blotted out, the blithe earth die, the brave sun
Die blind and blacken to the heart:
Yet stones have stood for a thousand years, and pained thoughts found
The honey of peace in old poems.   10

Counting on Flowers   1962

JOHN CIARDI   (b. 1916)

Once around a daisy counting
she loves me / she loves me not
and you're left with a golden
button without a petal left to
it. Don't count too much on   5
what you count on remaining
entirely a flower at the end.

The Double Play   1961

ROBERT WALLACE   (b. 1932)

In his sea-lit
distance, the pitcher winding
like a clock about to chime comes down with

the ball, hit
sharply, under the artificial   5
banks of arc lights, bounds like a vanishing string

over the green
to the shortstop magically
scoops to his right whirling above his invisible

shadows   10
in the dust redirects
its flight to the running poised second baseman

pirouettes
leaping, above the slide, to throw
from mid-air, across the colored tightened interval,   15

to the leaning-
out first baseman ends the dance
drawing it disappearing into his long brown glove

stretches. What
is too swift for deception   20
is final, lost, among the loosened figures

jogging off the field
(the pitcher walks), casual
in the space where the poem has happened.

E. E. CUMMINGS   (1894–1962)   *1923*

O sweet spontaneous
earth how often have
the
doting

          fingers of   5
prurient philosophers pinched
and
poked

thee
, has the naughty thumb
of science prodded
thy

    beauty   . how
often have religions taken
thee upon their scraggy knees
squeezing and

buffeting thee that thou mightest conceive
gods
    (but
true

to the incomparable
couch of death thy
rhythmic
lover

    thou answerest

them only with

        spring)

3

Meter:
Genie-Bottles
and Spiderwebs

Solid form includes poem forms (like sonnets), stanza forms (like couplets or quatrains), and conventional meter, the basic underlying rhythmic pattern of the *line* of verse in English for about five hundred years. This chapter describes the mechanics of meter. While free verse is more formal than its name indicates, meter is happily less formal than it may seem—and less complicated than its thicket of terminology suggests.

Meter means "measure." Some recurring element of the language is used as the unit of measurement. As the music of speech varies with each language, each uses distinctive elements as the basis for poetic meter. Latin verse, for example, used the duration of vowels, long or short, as the measuring element. Chinese and Japanese, in which all words are monosyllabic, use syllables as the measuring element. More strongly accented in the manner of the Germanic languages, English has always used **accent** as the measuring element. Accent is the emphasis—in loudness, pitch, or duration—with which a syllable is spoken, relative to adjacent syllables. For metrical purposes only two levels of accent (or **stress**) are counted: relatively *heavily* accented syllables (called accented) and relatively *lightly* accented syllables (called unaccented).

Anglo-Saxon (Old English) meter used two simple elements, accent and alliteration. A line of verse had four main accents, two on each side of a heavy caesura; and at least three of the four accented syllables were alliterated (usually with a consonant). Unaccented syllables were not counted. In the twentieth century Richard Wilbur (b. 1921) has employed this meter in a poem called "Junk." Notice the splitting of each line into distinct halves and the alliterated accent-syllables "*axe, angles, ashcan*" in line 1, "*Hell's, handiwork, hickory*" in line 2, and so on.

> *Huru Welandes*
> > *worc ne geswiceð*
> *monna ænigum*
> > *ðara ðe Mimming can*
> *heardne gehealdan.*
> > WALDERE

An axe angles
           from my neighbor's ashcan;
It is hell's handiwork,
           the wood not hickory,
The flow of the grain
           not faithfully followed.
The shivered shaft
           rises from a shellheap
Of plastic playthings,
           paper plates,   5
And the sheer shards
           of shattered tumblers
That were not annealed
           for the time needful.
At the same curbside,
           a cast-off cabinet
Of wavily-warped
           unseasoned wood
Waits to be trundled
           in the trash-man's truck.   10
Haul them off! Hide them!
           The heart winces
For junk and gimcrack,
           for jerrybuilt things
And the men who make them
           for a little money,

Bartering pride
                    like the bought boxer
Who pulls his punches,
                              or the paid-off jockey   15
Who in the home stretch
                              holds in his horse.
Yet the things themselves
                              in thoughtless honor
Have kept composure,
                              like captives who would not
Talk under torture.
                    Tossed from a tailgate
Where the dump displays
                              its random dolmens,   20
Its black barrows
                    and blazing valleys,
They shall waste in the weather
                              toward what they were.
The sun shall glory
                    in the glitter of glass-chips,
Foreseeing the salvage
                    of the prisoned sand,
And the blistering paint
                    peel off in patches,   25
That the good grain
                    be discovered again.
Then burnt, bulldozed,
                    they shall all be buried
To the depth of diamonds,
                    in the making dark
Where halt Hephaestus°
                    keeps his hammer
And Wayland's work
                    is worn away.   30

29 *Hephaestus:* lame Greek god, patron of artists who worked in iron or metal.

The epigraph, from an Anglo-Saxon poem about the legendary smith Wayland,
reads as Wilbur translates it: "Truly, Wayland's handiwork—the sword Mim-

ming which he made—will never fail any man who knows how to use it bravely." The choice of the archaic Anglo-Saxon alliterative form for this poem is a good one, because it emphasizes the theme: contrasting the well-made old with modern plastic, mismade "junk."

Accentual-Syllabic Meter

Later, more or less during Chaucer's time, when modern English influenced by French (brought by the Normans to England) was emerging, the old alliterative meter disappeared. It gave way to what is called **accentual-syllabic meter,** which has been standard in English since the sixteenth century. Accentual syllabic has been a rich metrical tradition, as varied as the poets who have used it: Shakespeare, Donne, Milton, Pope, Wordsworth, Keats, Yeats, Frost, Stevens, and in recent decades Richard Wilbur, Robert Lowell, Howard Nemerov.

In theory both the number of accents and the number of syllables are counted, and it is the *pattern* of accented and unaccented syllables that forms the meters. The elementary unit is called a **foot** (note the analogy to dance). The basic metrical unit is the *iambic foot,* or **iamb,** which is an unaccented followed by an accented syllable: tĕ TÚM, as in "ăvóid" or "tŏ bréak" or "thĕ tíme‖lĕss trées." Note, as in the third example, that a word may be part of two separate feet.

Lines may be composed of any given number of feet, though lines of four or five feet (eight or ten syllables) have been the norm. **Monometer** is a line consisting of one foot: ˘ ´. It is rarely used; but "Upon His Departure Hence" by Robert Herrick (1591−1674) is an example:

Thŭs Í
Passe by,
And die:
As One,
Unknown,   5
And gon:
I'm made
A shade,
And laid
I'th grave,   10
There have
My Cave.
Where tell
I dwell,
Farewell.   15

Dimeter, also rare, is a line consisting of two feet: ˘ ´ | ˘ ´. Although it deviates a little from strict iambic dimeter, "For My Contemporaries" by J. V. Cunningham (b. 1911) is a twentieth-century example. (A final unaccented syllable at the end of the line—a "feminine" ending—is not counted and does not change the meter.)

Hŏw tíme | rĕvér|sĕs

Thĕ próud | ĭn héart!

Ĭ nów | măke vér|sĕs

Whŏ áimed | ăt árt.

But I sleep well.   5
Ambitious boys
Whose big lines swell
With spiritual noise,

Despise me not!
And be not queasy   10
To praise somewhat:
Verse is not easy.

But rage who will.
Time that procured me
Good sense and skill   15
Of madness cured me.

Trimeter is a line consisting of three feet: ˘ ´ | ˘ ´ | ˘ ´, as in the wonderfully waltzing "My Papa's Waltz" by Theodore Roethke (1908–1963):

Thĕ whís|kĕy (´)ŏn | yŏur bréath

Cŏuld máke | ă smáll | b(˘)ŏy díz|zў;

Bŭt Í | h(˘)ŭng ón | lĭke déath:

Sŭch wáltz|ĭng wás | nŏt éas|ў.

We romped until the pans   5
Slid from the kitchen shelf;
My mother's countenance
Could not unfrown itself.

The hand that held my wrist
Was battered on one knuckle;   10
At every step you missed
My right ear scraped a buckle.

You beat time on my head
With a palm caked hard by dirt,
Then waltzed me off to bed   15
Still clinging to your shirt.

Tetrameter, very common and serviceable, is a line consisting of four feet: ˘ ´ |
˘ ´ | ˘ ´ | ˘ ´ , as in A. E. Housman's "Loveliest of Trees":

Lóvelı̆est | ŏf trées, | thĕ chér|rў nów

Ĭs húng | wı̆th blóom | ălóng | thĕ bóugh,

Ănd stánds | ăbóut | thĕ wóod|lănd rı́de

Wéar|ı̆ng whíte | fŏr Éas|tĕrtíde.

Now, of my threescore years and ten,   5
Twenty will not come again,
And take from seventy springs a score,
It only leaves me fifty more.

And since to look at things in bloom
Fifty springs are little room,   10
About the woodlands I will go
To see the cherry hung with snow.

Pentameter is a line consisting of five feet: ˘ ´ | ˘ ´ | ˘ ´ | ˘ ´ | ˘ ´ . Iambic
pentameter has been the standard line of verse in English from Shakespeare to
Frost. When it is unrhymed, it is also called **blank verse,** as in Robert Frost's
"An Old Man's Winter Night":

Ăll óut|-ŏf-dóors | lŏ̆oked dárk|lў (´) ı̆n | ăt hím

Thrŏugh thĕ | thín fróst | ălmóst | ı̆n sép|ărăte stárs,

Thăt gáth|ĕrs (´) ŏn | thĕ páne | ı̆n émp|tў róoms.

Whát képt | hı̆s éyes | frŏm gív|ı̆ng báck | thĕ gáze
Was the lamp tilted near them in his hand.   5

What kept him from remembering what it was
That brought him to that creaking room was age.
He stood with barrels round him—at a loss.
And having scared the cellar under him
In clomping here, he scared it once again   10
In clomping off;—and scared the outer night,
Which has its sounds, familiar, like the roar
Of trees and crack of branches, common things,
But nothing so like beating on a box.
A light he was to no one but himself   15
Where now he sat, concerned with he knew what,
A quiet light, and then not even that.
He consigned to the moon, such as she was,
So late-arising, to the broken moon
As better than the sun in any case   20
For such a charge, his snow upon the roof,
His icicles along the wall to keep;
And slept. The log that shifted with a jolt
Once in the stove, disturbed him and he shifted,
And eased his heavy breathing, but still slept.   25
One aged man—one man—can't keep a house,
A farm, a countryside, or if he can,
It's thus he does it of a winter night.

Hexameter (or **Alexandrine**) is a line consisting of six feet: ˘ ´ | ˘ ´ | ˘ ´ | ˘ ´
| ˘ ´ | ˘ ´ . Because it tends to be long and sluggish in practice, it is rare.
Howard Nemerov (b. 1920) uses it deftly, however, in his epigram, "Power to
the People":

Whý ăre | thĕ stámps | ădórned | wĭth kíngs | ănd prés|ĭdénts?

Thăt wé | măy líck | thĕir hínd|ĕr párts | ănd thúmp | thĕir héads.

Heptameter, a line consisting of seven feet, is awkward and very rare. The
example is from "The Book of Thel" by William Blake (1757–1827):

Thĕ Lí|lĭy ŏf | thĕ vál|lĕy, bréath|ĭng ĭn | thĕ húm|blĕ gráss,

Ánswĕred | thĕ lóve|lĭy máid | ănd sáid: | "Ĭ ám | ă wát|'rĭy wéed,

Ănd Í | ăm vér|ĭy smáll | ănd lóve | tŏ dwéll | ĭn lów|lĭy váles;

Sŏ wéak, | thĕ gíld|ĕd bút|tĕrflý | scărce pérch|ĕs ŏn | mĭy héad.
Yet I am visited from heaven, and he that smiles on all   5

Walks in the valley, and each morn over me spreads his hand,
Saying, 'Rejoice, thou humble grass, thou new-born lily flower,
Thou gentle maid of silent valleys and of modest brooks;
For thou shalt be clothed in light, and fed with morning manna,
Till summer's heat melts thee beside the fountains and the springs,   10
To flourish in eternal vales.'

Over the centuries, tetrameter and pentameter lines have become the norm; they are neither too short and clipped nor too long and clumsy. Monometer or dimeter lines tend to occur only in stanzaic poems of varying line lengths, such as George Herbert's "The Collar" (page 106) or John Donne's "Song" (page 107).

The iamb (tĕ TÚM) is the basic foot. But, as suggested by anomalies in the scansions already marked, five other feet may be substituted for iambs without changing the metrical pattern. They are:

Trochee (trochaic): accented followed by unaccented syllable: TÚM tĕ.

> ónlў   tótăl   ców ănd   the | fárm bĕ|low

Anapest (anapestic): two unaccented followed by an accented: tĕ tĕ TÚM.

> ĭntĕrvéne   fŏr ă whíle   lov|ĕr ŏf míne

Dactyl (dactylic): accented followed by two unaccented: TÚM tĕ tĕ

> mérrĭlў   tíme fŏr ă   lóvĕr ŏf | mine

Spondee (spondaic): two accented syllables together: TÚM TÚM.

> bréad bóx   in the | swéet lánd   stróng fóot

Double-iamb: two unaccented followed by two accented: tĕ tĕ TÚM TÚM.

> ŏf thĕ swéet lánd   ĭn ă gréen sháde

Instead of the double-iamb, most accounts include the **pyrrhic** foot, two unaccented syllables: tĕ tĕ. But since it contains no accent, the pyrrhic is awkward to hear as a unit, and it is almost invariably followed by a spondee. This pattern is so frequent that it seems simpler and more natural to think of it as a double-iamb. A double-iamb, of course, counts as two feet.

Substitution and Variations

Any of these other feet—trochees, anapests, dactyls, spondees, or double-iambs—may be *substituted* for iambs in the norm line. (The noun is **substitution**.) "Slid from" is a trochee substituted as the first foot in the second line of "My Papa's Waltz" (page 56):

We rómped ŭntíl thĕ páns

Slíd fròm | thĕ kítch|ĕn shélf

The slightly unexpected tipping in the rhythm imitates (perhaps) the described action of pans sliding from a shelf. A trochee, an anapest, and a spondee are substituted in lines 13–14:

Yŏu béat | tíme ŏn | mў héad

Wĭth ă pálm | cáked hárd | bў dírt

"Whý ăre" is a trochaic substitution in Nemerov's "Whý ăre | thĕ stámps | ădórned | wĭth kíngs | ănd prés|ĭdénts?" Note the double-iamb and the anapest substituted in the second line of Frost's "An Old Man's Winter Night" (page 57):

Thrŏugh thĕ thín fróst, | ălmóst | ĭn sép|ărătĕ stárs

Substitution allows an almost infinite rhythmical variety, and it is frequently the means of imitative, expressive effects. Used heavily or awkwardly, of course, it can break the flow of the meter. But used deftly, it is the freedom of the formal poem. Meter might best be thought of, not as something that must be rigidly followed, but as something the poet is free to vary whenever it suits his or her purpose.

Substitution of anapests or dactyls (feet of three syllables) tends to simplify accentual-*syllabic* meter toward what may be called **accentual meter,** in which the syllables of a line are less strictly counted. When unaccented syllables are not counted at all, accentual meter in effect escapes the conventions and approaches a loosely patterned free verse, as in the seventeen-line opening passage of T. S. Eliot's *The Waste Land* (1922). Although a number of Eliot's lines may be scanned with conventional substitution, lines like "Dúll róots with spring rain" and "I réad, much of the níght, and go sóuth in the wínter" make any system unintelligible. Similarly idiosyncratic are lines of what Gerard Manley Hopkins called "sprung rhythm," such as "As a skate's héel sweeps smóoth on a bow-bénd: the húrl and glíding" in "The Windhover."

Three further aspects of the metrical system are important. First, meter is a simplification of what we actually hear. In speech it is possible to distinguish a wide and subtle range of accents. In metered verse, however, the distinction is narrow and clear-cut: syllables are counted as either **accented** or **unaccented.** That meter is two-valued, for counting, does not of course reduce the variety of accents of natural speech that play over it. Thus, regular meter need never be goose-step or wooden. Further, the distinction between accented and unaccented syllables is relative; that is, we count a syllable as accented or unaccented *in relation to* the syllables next to it, not by an absolute measurement. The first line of "An Old Man's Winter Night" is scanned this way:

Ăll óut|-ŏf-dóors | lŏŏked dárk|lў ĭn | ăt hím

We can hear the meter ticking along regularly under the speech rhythm. Although "looked" counts as an unaccented syllable (being next to the more heavily accented "dark-") and although "in" counts as an accented syllable (being next to the still slightly less accented "-ly" and "at"), purely objectively "looked" is more accented than "in."

A second important aspect is that a line may be scanned—that is, interpreted or heard—somewhat differently by different readers. A single reader may often be aware of more than one obvious possibility. In the Frost line, for instance, I can also hear "lŏŏked dárk-" as a spondee; it is the ominous center of the statement and both words might be read as equally heavily accented. Another reader might hear, and mark, the first foot in the line as a spondee, too: "Ăll óut-." In scanning, parentheses arc often useful to call attention to such other obvious possibilities, so that the rhythmical flexibility of a line won't be lost in the description of it. Similarly, parentheses mark what may be called **"courtesy" accents:** syllables that should be treated as accented even though they barely deserve it, like "in" in "dárk|lў ĭn | ăt hím." The parentheses indicate that, although the scanner primarily hears a line in a certain way, he is also aware of other ways of hearing it. As the accents of meter are essentially relative, **scansion** should be wisely tentative and undogmatic. In scanning, we do not seek the "correct" answer, but a notation of accents that allows us to perceive and discuss accurately the subtleties of the line.

A third aspect of the metrical system is the **feminine ending,** a final unaccented syllable at the end of the line, as in Roethke's

Cŏuld máke | ă smáll | bŏy díz|kў

or in Frost's

Thĕ lóg | thăt shíft|ĕd wíth | ă jólt

Ónce ĭn | thĕ stóve, | dĭstúrbed | hím ănd | hĕ shíft|ĕd.

Because they are unaccented, feminine endings are regarded metrically as extras and are uncounted; thus, these lines remain iambic trimeter (Roethke) and iambic pentameter (Frost). Feminine endings may, however, be rhythmically useful for expressive or imitative effects. In Frost's lines the nearly unaccented syllable "with" lets the voice speed toward the abrupt "jolt," and the trochaic substitution "Ónce ĭn" helps to mimic the loose and jolting motion of the log in the fire. The trochaic substitution that puts two unaccented syllables together— "hím ănd | hĕ shíft-"—helps to suggest the old man's restiveness resulting from the fire's disturbing noise. The feminine ending "ănd | hĕ shíft|ĕd" completes the effect by also suggesting the old man's restlessness and the unfinished, unsatisfying, indecisive quality of his movement as contrasted with the abrupt, finished movement of the log's "jolt" at the (so-called) **masculine ending**—on an accented syllable—of the preceding line. The feminine ending lets the line end with four syllables, only one of which ("shift-") is accented, giving an effect of slight but unresolved movement. Contrast the effect of the same line with a masculine ending: "Once in the stove, disturbed | hím ănd | hĕ stírred."

Metrical verse may be more or less strict, depending on: 1) how closely the rhythm approximates the meter's beat; 2) the occurrence of substitutions and feminine endings; and 3) the frequency of caesural pauses and run-on lines. Strict meter would avoid anapestic or dactylic substitutions, which add syllables to a line. More leisurely meter might use these substitutions for loosening or variation. The poet's problem of how to choose and use a conventional meter is similar to the problem of how to choose and use a free verse measure. Meter is (simply) a more complex trellis. In his deceptively offhand way, Frost summed up the matter when he remarked that there are really only two meters in English, strict iambic and loose iambic.

Rhythm

Meter is a purely mechanical pattern of unaccented and accented syllables: te TUM te TUM te TUM, always *exactly* regular and arbitrary. An iamb is an iamb, just as an inch is an inch. But something happens when the words of a poem are laid over meter. The result is never precisely regular, is no longer mechanical. The usual stresses of words, their varying importance or placement in the statement, their sounds, as well as the pauses and syntactical connections between them, all work to give the line an individual movement, flavor, weight. This we call **rhythm:** the play of the words across the rigid metrical pattern.

Meter measures speech, the varied flow of a voice. Rhythm is the result of blending the fixed (meter) with the flexible (speech). The result isn't exactly the te TUM te TUM of meter nor a reproduction of actual speech. A poem is read neither as inflexible meter nor as wholly flexible speech, but always as something between the two.

Although all iambic pentameter lines have exactly the same meter, no two lines have exactly the same rhythm. Variations in rhythm can never be exhausted. The poet, thus, need not fear being trapped by the regularities of meter, but may delight in the freedom of searching out the qualities of rhythm that will make each line unique.

Consider a simple example, the sentence which is part of the first line of Richard Wilbur's "Juggler" (page 75): "A ball will bounce, but less and less." It is as inaccurate to read the line mechanically by the meter ("a BALL will BOUNCE, but LESS and LESS") as it is to read it as one might speak it ("a ball will BOUNCE, but less and less"). In speech, we usually dash off everything but the most emphatic part. In fact, depending on the intention, we might place the primary accent on *any* of the eight words in the sentence. If we are distinguishing a ball from a glass bottle, for instance, we might well say, "a BALL will bounce, but less and less." If we are distinguishing a single ball from a box of balls, we might well say, "A ball will bounce, but less and less." Similarly, in speech, we might find a perfectly good reason for saying "a ball WILL bounce, but less and less" or "a ball will bounce, BUT less and less," and so on, depending on what we are trying to say in a particular context.

We read this sentence in "Juggler" neither according to the rigid meter nor according to any of those possible speech emphases. In the poem the meter changes the speech-run a little, giving the sentence a more measured movement; and the speech-run of the sentence loosens the march-step of the meter. The result is distinctive—rhythm. Speech flowing over meter produces rhythm.

Normally, the unique qualities of rhythm, especially in its imitative potential, occur where the strength of the speech-run dislodges the meter, that is, where substitution occurs. When the poet is doing his job, substitutions and the consequent variations in rhythm will be significant, as in the Frost and Roethke lines discussed. Almost every substitution in the poems cited has some useful expressive effect. Consider the second stanza of Cunningham's "For My Contemporaries" (page 56):

But I sleep well.

Ambitious boys

Whose big lines swell

With spiritual noise

Line 3, with its four heavy syllables (two spondees), suggests the pompous, proud rhetoric of the poets Cunningham is describing; and the alliterated b's of "Ambitious boys" climax emphatically in "big," reenforcing the rhythmical effect. Line 4 is particularly interesting. The anapestic second foot—"-itual noise"—is made rather gummy due to the already elided "-ual" of normal pronunciation, though it might be enunciated as "-ŭăl." This possibility of four syllables in the foot—"-ĭtŭăl nóise"—makes us somewhat mouth the line to keep on track. The little muddle is deliberate: it is Cunningham's rhythmic imitation of, and comment on, the muddled intellect he finds in such pompous poetry. The contempt is conveyed by more than the choice of the word "noise."

In Roethke's "My Papa's Waltz" (page 56) note the probable spondee in line 2—"Cŏuld máke | ă smáll | bŏy díz|zў̆"—three accents together, which, along with the feminine ending syllable of "díz|zў̆," might suggest force and the twisting movement that is described. Notice in line 3—"Bŭt Ī | húng ón | lĭke déath"—the imitative "hanging on" of the spondaic "húng ón." All three feet in that line might almost be read as spondees: the voice maintains a nearly even pitch throughout the line.

Another common variation is the omission of the initial unaccented sylla-ble at the beginning of a line. In Housman's "Loveliest of Trees" (page 57) this occurs three times: in lines 4 ("Wéar|ĭng whíte | fŏr Éas|tĕrtíde"), 6 ("Twén|tў̆ wĭll | nŏt cóme | ăgáin"), and 10 ("Fíf|tў̆ spríngs | ăre lít|tlĕ róom"). If such monosyllabic feet occurred elsewhere in the line, they would mark a major hiatus in the rhythm; but, occurring innocuously at the beginning of lines, they scarcely disturb the flow. In two of these three instances in "Loveliest of Trees," in lines 6 and 10, this almost unnoticeable metrical shortening emphasizes the brevity of the "Twenty" years that "will not come again" and of the "Fifty springs" which are "little room."

Typically, the unique qualities in rhythm occur where substitutions occur. (One purpose of scansion is to locate such qualities so that they can be dis-cussed accurately.) Even a perfectly regular line, however, may have its own deliciously characteristic, even imitative rhythm. Consider again Wilbur's "A ball will bounce, but less and less," containing four perfectly regular iambs, te TUM te TUM te TUM te TUM. Within that regularity or, rather, precisely because of it, small differences in stress give the effect of less and less force and so seem to imitate the way a ball dribbles to a stop in smaller and smaller hops. The first two accents are made fairly forceful by the alliterated b's—"A ball will bounce"—while the liquid l's of "less and less" are softer and the s's seem to stretch. The second "less" naturally gets less force than the first, but it is the difference in the accents that is crucial in establishing the line's rhythm. The first iamb is strongest because the contrast between the negligible "A" and the sharp "ball" is very large: "a BALL." Comparatively, the second iamb seems less forceful because the unaccented syllable—"will"—gets some emphasis from its near-rhyme with "ball" and is much less sharply contrasted, in force, with "bounce." The second iamb, "will bounce," is more evenly spread, softer. The same is true of the third iamb, "but less": "but" picks up a little extra emphasis from the already alliterated b's of "ball" and "bounce"; thus the contrast of the unaccented syllable with the accented syllable seems more muted still than in "will bounce." The fourth iamb, "and less," is weaker in both parts. In short, the *difference* between each unaccented syllable and its accented syllable diminishes with each foot. We might show it pictorially, imagining each foot as a piece of string proportionally arranged according to accent:

A ball will bounce, but less and less.

Or we could simply draw the relative rise in each foot:

A ball will bounce, but less and less.

This is rhythmical mastery of a high order, like performing a magic trick without props. Such effects are possible with meter, which tunes the ear to careful measurements. "The strength of the genie," Wilbur has said, "comes of being confined in the bottle."

Just as a taut web allows the spider to feel the slightest disturbance, tight metrical structures let us perceive the slightest variation as significant. Tuned to that expectation—te TUM te TUM—we can respond sensitively to the smallest subtleties or counterpoint. Alexander Pope's justly famous "sound of sense" passage from *An Essay on Criticism* (page 74) is a treasury of metrical effects. Here, for instance, is the couplet about the Greek hero in the Trojan War, Ajax:

When Ájăx stríves sŏme róck's vást wéight tŏ thrów,

Thĕ líne tóo lăbŏrs, ănd thĕ wórds móve slów

Pope uses several spondaic substitutions to produce the feeling of weight and then of effort. In the second line, in addition to the two spondees—"tóo láb-" and "móve slów"—the third foot is broken by the caesura—"-ŏrs,‖ănd"—so that the somewhat forced accent on "and" seems itself slow and effortful. In the first line the two spondees (or near spondees) put five heavy syllables together and so weight the center of the line, as Ajax lifts the boulder he means to hurl. The secret of the line, however, isn't merely a matter of dumping a heavier foot or two into it. The craft lies in the perfectly regular iamb in the fifth foot, "tŏ thrów." It is in that small te TUM gesture that we *feel* Ajax's effort. After five nearly even strong syllables, the contrast in weight between "to" and "throw" rhythmically mimics Ajax's gesture:

When Ajax strives some rock's vast weight to throw

Pope's skill is evident in his having varied slightly the normal word order of the sentence. If we move "to throw" back to its normal place, the effect disappears, and Ajax is left standing there with the rock sagging in his hands:

When Ájǎx stríves tǒ thrów sǒme róck's vǎst wéight

Read the two versions of the line aloud. The little fillip of a perfectly regular foot makes us feel the actual attempt to heave the rock. The embodiment of content in form could hardly be more remarkable.

Scansion

"Excellence" by Robert Francis is a subtle example of rhythmic sleight-of-hand:

Excellence is millimeters and not miles.

From poor to good is great. From good to best is small.

From almost best to best sometimes not measurable.

The man who leaps the highest leaps perhaps an inch

Above the runner-up. How glorious that inch   5

And that split-second longer in the air before the fall.

Try your hand at scanning this poem to see what its meter is and how it works. Mark the meter with a pencil or on a separate sheet before you look at the scansion that follows. (*Note:* Omitting the unaccented syllable from the *first* foot of a line is a very normal variation. Here, the first foot is "Éx-." The effect is to push the poem off to a sharp, confident start. When such a defective foot occurs *within* a line, however, it is called a **"lame" foot** and usually suggests disorder or a dramatic break. The last foot of this line from Francis's "The Base

Stealer" (page 71) is a lame foot: "Póised bĕ|twĕen gó|ing ón | ănd báck, | ˣpúlled." The missing syllable is indicated by an x.)

In scanning, listen to the poem without imposing a metrical pattern on it. Read each line aloud slowly and more than once. It may also be a good idea to scan several lines tentatively before marking them, to determine what the *norm* of the poem is. Having that norm in mind may help you resolve difficult or ambiguous spots in the rhythm. Since unique qualities most readily appear in variations from the norm, don't te *TUM* so hard that you miss something interesting. Mark ambiguous syllables (those you can imagine two ways) with your preferred interpretation in parentheses. Like substitutions, such feet will very likely lead to a secret of the rhythm.

Éx|cĕl|lénce | ĭs míl|lĭmét|ĕrs ⁽ʼ⁾and | ⁽ʼ⁾nŏt míles.

Frŏm póor | tŏ góod | ĭs gréat. | Frŏm góod | tŏ bést | ĭs smáll.

Frŏm ál|mŏst bést | tŏ bést | ⁽ʼ⁾sŏmetímes | ⁽ʼ⁾nŏt méa|sŭráb⁽ʼ⁾|lĕ.

Thĕ mán | whŏ léaps | thĕ hígh|ĕst léaps | pĕrháps | ăn ínch

Ăbóve | thĕ rún|nĕr-úp. | Hów glór⁽ʼ⁾|ĭóus | thăt ínch

Ănd thát | splít-séc|ŏnd lóng|ĕr ⁽ʼ⁾in | thĕ áir | bĕfóre | thĕ fáll.

The norm meter in "Excellence" is iambic hexameter, which may appear an odd choice for a poem about athletic legerity, the lightness of the high-jumper. Perhaps the poet's first line—"Excellence is millimeters and not miles"—gave him the meter. Having said that to himself, or written it down, he had at least to consider writing the poem in hexameters, "sluggish" as they may seem (Pope's characterization). He might have changed the line to "Excellence is inches and not miles" and had a lighter, pentameter line. Since he uses "inch" later in the poem, it wouldn't have been out of place to make that change. But probably he liked the *feel* of "is millimeters and not miles," as the alliterated m's contrast the tiny and vast units of measure.

However accidental, hexameters were an excellent choice. The poem is less interested in the jumper's lightness or ease than in his difficulty, the extra push or effort that earns excellence, that buys the additional "inch / And that split-second longer in the air." Possibly because hexameter feels as though it goes on a little beyond the pentameter norm of English—seems to have to somehow push its way to its end—it was a perfect choice. Having made that choice, the poet exploits it beautifully, especially in the poem's last line where, after we have become accustomed to lines of six feet, he pushes it just a little farther and ends with a heptameter. We don't see that extra length because the words are shorter, but we hear it, even if we don't count the feet. The line itself lasts in the ear just a second longer than the others.

Something subtle, and perhaps not very noticeable to a casual reader, is going on rhythmically in every line of "Excellence." In the first line, the almost spondaic "not miles" provides a rhythmical emphasis on the line's contrast between millimeters and miles, tiny and large, as do the short "i" of "mil-" and the long "i" of "miles." In line 2, the unrelenting monosyllables and the caesural pause may suggest the distance between "poor" and "best," a distance that can be crossed only by such a dogged pace as the line itself has. In line 3 the main effect is in the last foot, where the almost completely unaccented secondary accent of the word "méas|ŭráb|lĕ," followed by the unaccented feminine syllable, blurs the beat so much that we almost have to force the voice to record it. (We can't bring ourselves to say "MÉAS-ŭr-ÁB-lĕ.") And so the line's end perfectly mimes the meaning of "not measurable." This effect is heightened, too, by the temptation to hear an off-rhyme between the last syllable of "measurable" and "miles" and "small," and so to displace the accent falsely onto that last syllable.

Like line 2, line 4 is metrically regular; but the movement is not broken by a caesura. It continues without pause to its end, where, after three end-stopped lines, the run-on to line 4 suggests the leap itself. In line 5 a light secondary accent on the last syllable of "glór|ĭoŭs" hurries us along to the poem's second run-on. This run-on and the spondee of "split-séc-" in line 6 appropriately hold the voice a bit longer than we expect. The very light accent on "ĭn" perhaps suggests the momentary suspension of the jumper "before the fall."

Metrical Potential

Of all the qualities meter may be said to provide, including our pleasure in symmetry, the focusing of attention, or the lull of the trance it may induce, none is more important than its stretching the web tight so that every effect may be felt. But there is one function the poet will be aware of, and a reader perhaps not. Once chosen, meter, like stanza shape in free verse, provides a trellis for the tendrils of the unfolding poem to wind around. Though a good poet takes advantage of rhythmical possibilities and imitative effects, every phrase, every line cannot be jeweled. There will be flat portions—necessary exposition, transition, or preparation for effects to come—and for these the poet will be grateful that the meter, the form, is simply *there*. Its presence allows her or him, without being particularly brilliant, to keep the poem going, the voice talking, the ball in the air. Often enough, the real magic is the unnoticed craft with which the poet gets the rabbit *into* the hat.

As a beginning poet you may find meter hard to manage at first; it may seem wooden, mechanical. As Pope says, though,

> True ease in writing comes from art, not chance,
> As those move easiest who have learned to dance.

With practice, meter becomes second nature. It is really a rule-of-thumb, simple, binary system; and it usually bends (substitution) to fit any purpose. Like the skillful tennis player who no longer has to think about form and so can concentrate on the ball and the game, as a skillful poet you will have your eye on the subject, your mind on the poem.

Once the form, whether metrical or stanzaic, is launched in a poem, it will suggest possibilities for dealing with the subject that might never have occurred to the poet otherwise. This must have happened in the writing of Francis's "Excellence" and perhaps happens in the writing of nearly every good poem. You cannot know the potential until you get there. Rhythmical discoveries result from intuition or trial-and-error. The poet says something and tests it across the meter; it doesn't feel right so she or he restates it and tries again until the right rhythm just "happens." Persistence can make one lucky.

QUESTIONS AND SUGGESTIONS

1. Scan the following poems, considering the significance of rhythmical variations. (For comparison, my scansions are in Appendix I.) *Clue:* Larkin's "First Sight" is iambic tetrameter with the first unaccented syllable of each line "omitted." *Clue:* Francis's "The Base Stealer" is difficult because there are so many variations (substitutions, lame feet) that the line norm is hard to detect. Mostly it is tetrameter, but lines 1, 5, 6, 8, and 10 may be more precisely scanned as pentameter. There isn't even one iamb in the last line! It is most simply scanned as four dactyls and a lame foot, with the long pause at the dash replacing the omitted syllable. Is there a thematic purpose in all this metrical jumpiness?

a) *Epigram: Of Treason*

SIR JOHN HARINGTON (1561–1612)

Treason doth never prosper, what's the reason?

For if it prosper, none dare call it treason.

b) *Death of the Day*

WALTER SAVAGE LANDOR   (1775–1864)

My pictures blacken in their frames

    As night comes on,

And youthful maids and wrinkled dames

    Are now all one.

Death of the day! a sterner Death

    Did worse before;

The fairest form, the sweetest breath,

    Away he bore.

c) *Tribute*

JOHN FANDEL   (b. 1925)

What the bee knows

Tastes in the honey

Sweet and sunny.

O wise bee. O rose.

d) *First Sight*

PHILIP LARKIN   (b. 1922)

Lambs that learn to walk in snow

When their bleating clouds the air

Meet a vast unwelcome, know

Nothing but a sunless glare.

Newly stumbling to and fro   5

All they find, outside the fold,

Is a wretched width of cold.

As they wait beside the ewe,

Her fleeces wetly caked, there lies

Hidden round them, waiting too,   10

Earth's immeasurable surprise.

They could not grasp it if they knew,

What so soon will wake and grow

Utterly unlike the snow.

e) *The Base Stealer*

ROBERT FRANCIS (b. 1901)

Poised between going on and back, pulled

Both ways taut like a tightrope-walker,

Fingertips pointing the opposites,

Now bouncing tiptoe like a dropped ball

Or a kid skipping rope, come on, come on,   5

Running a scattering of steps sidewise,

How he teeters, skitters, tingles, teases,

Taunts them, hovers like an ecstatic bird,

He's only flirting, crowd him, crowd him,

Delicate, delicate, delicate, delicate—now!   10

2. Translate the following passage from Lewis Thomas's *The Lives of a Cell*
(Viking Penguin, 1974, pp. 12—13) into blank verse (unrhymed iambic pentameter). As much as possible, use the language of the prose. But stretch or
compress and, where necessary, add your own touch. For comparison, a version
in rhymed couplets is in Appendix I.

A solitary ant, afield, cannot be considered to have much of anything on his mind: indeed, with only a few neurons strung together by fibers, he can't be imagined to have a mind at all, much less a thought. He is more like a ganglion on legs. Four ants together, or ten, encircling a dead moth on a path, begin to look more like an idea. They fumble and shove, gradually moving the food toward the Hill, but as though by blind chance. It is only when you watch the dense mass of thousands of ants, crowded together around the Hill, blackening the ground, that you begin to see the whole beast, and now you observe it thinking, planning, calculating. It is an intelligence, a kind of live computer, with crawling bits for its wits.

3. Consider, in these poems by students, how appropriate is the choice of a very loose meter, bouncy with anapests? Do the rhythms enhance and convey the poems' tones?

a) *Cherries Jubilee*

   —meditations while pie-eating

   JOSEPH URBAN*

   The cherries in pies are all gooey and soft
   unlike the firmness of little red buttocks
   that float in fruit cocktail and bob upside down
   or the round maraschino my father will munch
   having drained a Manhattan on our kitchen barstool.   5
   There are cherries in ice cream and cherry preserves
   to spread on hot muffins on cold winter mornings.
   The proverbial cherry has always been found
   at the top of the heap of whipped cream on a sundae.
   Cough syrup is cherry and Smith Brothers' drops.   10
   Pink popsicles. Pastries with cherry insides.
   Down on the corner the barber who slicks
   the cowlicks on little boys' heads with hair tonic
   gives the ones who don't cry a surprise lollipop
   and cherry is always the flavor as well   15
   as those little red boxes of Christmas hard candies
   handed out as a prize by department store Santas
   to cherry-eyed three-year-olds slobbering kisses
   on his big cherry nose with their small cherry lips
   like holiday cherubs with little round faces   20
   and cheeks cherry red from the chill of December.
   In fifth grade Fat Freddy whom everyone hated
   was caught lighting cherry bombs in the boys' room
   and sent to Miss Wakeley who wore cherry rouge,
   the cherry bun tied on her head with red ribbon.   25
   There are cherries on trees (which is where they all started)
   that blossom on Washington's streets during April

like the one that our country's father chopped down
and couldn't lie to *his* father about.
But now boys his age have no trouble lying   30
about all the cherries they've popped in their time.
The name of the Cherry's been taken in vain.
I can't even drink a bottle of pop
without conjuring visions of sexual conquest.
Ma Chérie, my dear one, I'm still on your side.   35
I still eat my pie with a fork and yet this
even this that was once just an act pure and simple
has somehow turned phallic. I stab through the crust
piercing five at a time and savor the flavor—
the only known fruit so exquisite and tiny   40
to serve as the one word summation of all
our most infinite innocence, intimate drives.

b) *Belfast Ballad*

TIM LUCAS*

I was born on the rug of a two-story snug
And fueled up with heroic desires.
For old Ireland's cause I'd have broken all laws
And perished in Protestant fires.

Mum weaned me on stories of the Catholic glories   5
Of Charlie Parnell and his men.
I wanted the same for it seemed a grand game
For a lad and his mates to be in.

So I dreamed of the day when I'd join in the fray
And the English limbs I'd dismember;   10
That when Ireland was free, I'd sit—lads on knee—
Spinning legends in which I'm a member.

While wearing the green I caressed my machine
Gun and kept it ready and loaded;
And to my Priest's horror, I screamed "Faith Begorra!"   15
On learning Mountbatten° exploded.

But last Sunday I made my first Belfast raid
And didn't get on with the gore.
'Twas Sean Riley's arm that caused my alarm
As it fell, in three parts, to the floor.   20

16 *Mountbatten*: Lord Louis Mountbatten (1900–1979) killed by IRA terrorists.

4. Try making the rhythm and syntax, flow and pauses, of a long *prose* sentence imitate the movement of a skier (mountain climber, bowler, or quarterback fading back to pass). Try the same in a few lines of free verse, then in a few lines of iambic tetrameter.

from *An Essay on Criticism*   1711

ALEXANDER POPE   (1688–1744)

But most by numbers judge a poet's song;
And smooth or rough, with them, is right or wrong:
In the bright muse though thousand charms conspire,
Her voice is all these tuneful fools admire;
Who haunt Parnassus° but to please their ear,   5
Not mend their minds; as some to church repair,
Not for the doctrine, but the music there.
These equal syllables alone require,
Though oft the ear the open vowels tire;
While expletives their feeble aid do join;   10
And ten low words oft creep in one dull line:
While they ring round the same unvaried chimes,
With sure returns of still expected rhymes;
Where'er you find "the cooling western breeze,"
In the next line, it "whispers through the trees":   15
If crystal streams "with pleasing murmurs creep,"
The reader's threatened (not in vain) with "sleep":
Then, at the last and only couplet fraught
With some unmeaning thing they call a thought,
A needless Alexandrine ends the song,   20
That, like a wounded snake, drags its slow length along.
Leave such to tune their own dull rhymes, and know
What's roundly smooth, or languishingly slow;
And praise the easy vigor of a line,
Where Denham's° strength, and Waller's° sweetness join.   25
True ease in writing comes from art, not chance,
As those move easiest who have learned to dance.
'Tis not enough no harshness gives offense,
The sound must seem an echo to the sense:
Soft is the strain when Zephyr° gently blows,   *the west wind*   30
And the smooth stream in smoother numbers flows;
But when loud surges lash the sounding shore,
The hoarse, rough verse should like the torrent roar:
When Ajax° strives some rock's vast weight to throw,
The line too labors, and the words move slow;   35

Not so, when swift Camilla° scours the plain,
Flies o'er th' unbending corn, and skims along the main.

5 *Parnassus*: Greek mountain, sacred to the Muses.　　25 *Denham*: poet Sir John
Denham (1615–1669); *Waller*: poet Edmund Waller (1606–1687).　　34 *Ajax*: Greek
warrior in *The Iliad*.　　36 *Camilla*: ancient Roman queen, reputed to run so swiftly
that she could skim over a field of grain without bending the stalks, over the sea
without wetting her feet.

Juggler　　　　　　　　　　　　　　　　　　　　　　1950

RICHARD WILBUR　(b. 1921)

A ball will bounce, but less and less. It's not
A light-hearted thing, resents its own resilience.
Falling is what it loves, and the earth falls
So in our hearts from brilliance,
Settles and is forgot.　　　　　　　　　　　　　　　　　　　5
It takes a sky-blue juggler with five red balls

To shake our gravity up. Whee, in the air
The balls roll round, wheel on his wheeling hands,
Learning the ways of lightness, alter to spheres
Grazing his finger ends,　　　　　　　　　　　　　　　　　10
Cling to their courses there,
Swinging a small heaven about his ears.

But a heaven is easier made of nothing at all
Than the earth regained, and still and sole within
The spin of worlds, with a gesture sure and noble　　　　15
He reels that heaven in,
Landing it ball by ball,
And trades it all for a broom, a plate, a table.

Oh, on his toe the table is turning, the broom's
Balancing up on his nose, and the plate whirls　　　　　20
On the tip of the broom! Damn, what a show, we cry:
The boys stamp, and the girls
Shriek, and the drum booms
And all comes down, and he bows and says good-bye.

If the juggler is tired now, if the broom stands   25
In the dust again, if the table starts to drop
Through the daily dark again, and though the plate
Lies flat on the table top,
For him we batter our hands
Who has won for once over the world's weight.   30

Learning by Doing   1967

HOWARD NEMEROV   (b. 1920)

They're taking down a tree at the front door,
The power saw is snarling at some nerves,
Whining at others. Now and then it grunts,
And sawdust falls like snow or a drift of seeds.

Rotten, they tell us, at the fork, and one   5
Big wind would bring it down. So what they do
They do, as usual, to do us good.
Whatever cannot carry its own weight
Has got to go, and so on; you expect
To hear them talking next about survival   10
And the values of a free society.
For in the explanations people give
On these occasions there is generally some
Mean-spirited moral point, and everyone
Privately wonders if his neighbors plan   15
To saw him up before he falls on them.

Maybe a hundred years in sun and shower
Dismantled in a morning and let down
Out of itself a finger at a time
And then an arm, and so down to the trunk,   20
Until there's nothing left to hold on to
Or snub the splintery holding rope around,
And where those big green divagations were
So loftily with shadows interleaved
The absent-minded blue rains in on us.   25

Now that they've got it sectioned on the ground
It looks as though somebody made a plain
Error in diagnosis, for the wood
Looks sweet and sound throughout. You couldn't know,
Of course, until you took it down. That's what   30
Experts are for, and these experts stand round
The giant pieces of tree as though expecting
An instruction booklet from the factory
Before they try to put it back together.

Anyhow, there it isn't, on the ground.   35
Next come the tractor and the crowbar crew
To extirpate what's left and fill the grave.
Maybe tomorrow grass seed will be sown.
There's some mean-spirited moral point in that
As well: you learn to bury your mistakes,   40
Though for a while at dusk the darkening air
Will be with many shadows interleaved,
And pierced with a bewilderment of birds.

Adam's Curse   *1904*

WILLIAM BUTLER YEATS   (1865–1939)

We sat together at one summer's end,
That beautiful mild woman, your close friend,
And you and I, and talked of poetry.
I said: 'A line will take us hours maybe;
Yet if it does not seem a moment's thought,   5
Our stitching and unstitching has been naught.
Better go down upon your marrow-bones
And scrub a kitchen pavement, or break stones
Like an old pauper, in all kinds of weather;
For to articulate sweet sounds together   10
Is to work harder than all these, and yet
Be thought an idler by the noisy set
Of bankers, schoolmasters, and clergymen
The martyrs call the world.'

                    And thereupon
That beautiful mild woman for whose sake   15
There's many a one shall find out all heartache
On finding that her voice is sweet and low
Replied: 'To be born woman is to know—
Although they do not talk of it at school—
That we must labour to be beautiful.'   20

I said: 'It's certain there is no fine thing
Since Adam's fall but needs much labouring.
There have been lovers who thought love should be
So much compounded of high courtesy
That they would sigh and quote with learned looks   25
Precedents out of beautiful old books;
Yet now it seems an idle trade enough.'

We sat grown quiet at the name of love;
We saw the last embers of daylight die,
And in the trembling blue-green of the sky   30
A moon, worn as if it had been a shell
Washed by time's waters as they rose and fell
About the stars and broke in days and years.

I had a thought for no one's but your ears:
That you were beautiful, and that I strove   35
To love you in the old high way of love;
That it had all seemed happy, and yet we'd grown
As weary-hearted as that hollow moon.

The Sound of Sense:
Of Pitchers and Petticoats

In the "sound of sense" passage (page 74) Pope is having fun with the possibilities of language, showing the tricks it can be made to perform. But the fun has a serious side, for smooth "numbers," regularity of meter, is not enough. Nor is avoiding the common faults he mocks—though what were laughable blunders in 1711 aren't likely to seem nimble graces two and a half centuries later. The crux is that "The sound must seem an echo to the sense." The rest of the passage is a library of effects.

When he mentions the gluey effect of open vowels, he provides a line of them: "Though oft the ear the open vowels tire." He illustrates how filler words like "do" make awkward lines: "While expletives their feeble aid do join." Or how monotonously monosyllables can move: "And ten low words oft creep in one dull line." He makes an illustrative hexameter sinuously sluggish:

A needless Alexandrine ends the song,
That, like a wounded snake, drags its slow length along.

He contrasts the "roundly smooth" with the "languishingly slow," and shows how quick and easy a line can be: "And praise the easy vigor of a line." He makes sound imitate the difference between a "smooth stream" and "loud surges," or between weight or effort and speed or agility:

> Soft is the strain when Zephyr gently blows,
> And the smooth stream in smoother numbers flows;
> But when loud surges lash the sounding shore,
> The hoarse, rough verse should like the torrent roar.
> When Ajax strives some rock's vast weight to throw,
> The line too labors, and the words move slow;
> Not so, when swift Camilla scours the plain,
> Flies o'er th' unbending corn, and skims along the main.

Interestingly, like the line showing the hexameter's snakelike slowness, the line showing Camilla's speed is a hexameter! Plainly, it isn't so much the metrical *what* as the rhythmical *how*.

A number of other things are at work in the sound effects of the passage, and this chapter will have a look at these cogs in the rhythmical machinery: *diction, syntax, alliteration and assonance,* and *rhyme.*

Diction

The precise choice of words for what you want to say is more important than sound. Meaning itself must be overriding—the exact word, not merely something near it. Poetry has no room for the *I mean's* and *you know's* by which, in everyday conversation, we stumble toward being understood. The poet, like his or her best reader, will have keen antennae for the overtones and nuances, the connotations and suggestions that most words carry with them. Connotations are the feelings, the approval or disapproval, that go along with essentially the same denotative information in different words. Consider S. I. Hayakawa's amusing example: the difference between *Finest quality filet mignon* and *first-class piece of dead cow.* Or the difference between *slim* or *slender* (approving), *thin* (approximately neutral), and *skinny* (disapproving). The language is happily full of words that are near but slightly differing in meaning, and a good thesaurus (like *Roget's New Pocket Thesaurus in Dictionary Form,* edited by Norman Lewis) is one of the handiest books a poet can own. When you are stuck for a word, a look in the thesaurus can set you off in a fresh direction. Often the overtones or nuances of a word come from its etymological derivation, as the word *thesaurus* itself comes from a Greek word meaning "treasury" or as our word *verse* has hidden in it the Latin root "to turn."

Under *old,* Roget cites some eighty-seven adjectives, including *aged, elderly, ancient, hoary, antiquated, archaic, antique, timeless, geriatric, senile, timeworn, worm-eaten, old-fashioned, out-of-date, outmoded, passé, stale, veteran, experienced, seasoned.* Several basic meanings of *old* appear among these, applying, for instance, to people (*elderly, senile*) or to things and manners (*archaic, antique, old-fashioned, stale*). Depending on how we felt about him, the same old man might be described as *old-fashioned* or *seasoned* or as *timeless* or *timeworn.*

As we choose words, we should consider more than meaning and nuance. A word, in general, ought to be of the same level as the other words in the context. A fancy polysyllable, for example, might not fit among more everyday words. We wouldn't say, "Mr. Jones was senectuous"; we would say simply, "old." Sometimes, however, an odd word, from another level or range of meaning, provides exactly the sense and the surprise the poet wants, as with Larkin's "vast unwelcome" in "First Sight" or Cunningham's "spiritual noise." In "My Papa's Waltz," Roethke chooses the less predictable word "countenance" rather than "face":

> My mother's countenance
> Could not unfrown itself

The greater formality and strangeness of "countenance" emphasize the stiffness and the oddness, to the boy, of her expression, as the word "face" could not. Countenance is also a shade more precise, since it primarily connotes the look or appearance of a face. (Lurking behind it, perhaps, is "countenance" as a verb.) The surprise of an unexpected word when it turns out to be especially appropriate to the poet's intention is exemplified by Robert Herrick's choice of "liquefaction" in "Upon Julia's Clothes" (page 115) or by X. J. Kennedy's use of "instruments" in "First Confession" (page 115) where he describes, from the point of view of a small boy, a little girl's genitals.

> I'd bribed my girl to pee
> That I might spy her instruments.

The witty "instruments" suggests both the sexual neutrality of the boy's interest and, along with "spy," implies the almost scientific quality of his curiosity.

Clichés—stale, timeworn, too familiar words and phrases—are best avoided in favor of freshness. The language of poetry pays attention, and it is the nature of a cliché not to pay attention. Recently a newspaper carried this sentence: "'I think we are enjoying the backlash of the moral decline that peaked in Watergate,' Dr. Weber said." Enjoying a lash of any kind seems unlikely; and the *peak* of a *decline* is language that isn't listening to itself at all.

Poetry often generates a kind of cliché all its own, **"poetic diction,"** which is fancy, pompous, or ornate language that gets used and reused until it becomes simply dull. Contractions like *o'er* for *over* or *ere* for *before* and elegant pronouns like *thou* are examples. So are such eighteenth-century elegant variations as *finny tribe* for *fish*, or such twentieth-century buzz words as *ceremony*, *stardust*, or *parameters*. The best rule is never to use in a poem a word that you wouldn't use in speech.

So, roundabout, we come to the sound of words, which is a secondary but important property of diction. In general, the sounds of the words in a passage should be cleanly enunciated, smooth, and easy to say; or, when they are awkward, clogging, and hard to say, it should be for a reason related to the sense, as with Pope's deliberately clumsy "Though oft the ear the open vowels tire" or deliberately harsh "The hoarse, rough verse should like the torrent roar." The effect of a word on the other words near it, both in rhythm and in music (euphony or cacaphony), is basic. In the line about Ajax, for example, Pope might have chosen other words: "When Ajax *tries*," instead of "*strives*." But not only is "strives" more intense in meaning (suggesting "strife"), it is also a little harder to enunciate; "tries" would lose the slight difficulty of the two *s*-sounds, "A-jacks *s*trives," a clear enunciation of which requires a small but effortful pause. Or he might have written, instead of "some rock's vast weight," "a boulder's weight." But the line would lose the massing of accents for the merely regular. And it would lose the further *s*-sound difficulty of "strives some," as well as the heavy clotting of consonants in "some rock's vast weight." Try saying the two versions of the line:

When Ajax tries a boulder's weight to throw

When Ajax strives some rock's vast weight to throw

Some words have their own sound effects built in: words like *hiss*, *buzz*, *snap*, *pop*, *smash*, *whisper*, *murmur*, *shout*. Such words are called *onomatopoetic* (noun: **onomatopoeia**). Never mind the Greek name, but keep your ear tuned for such inherent sound effects. More words than one might think have something of this quality. Notice the light vowels in *thin*, *skinny*, *slim*, *slender*, *spindly*. Or the long vowels or clotting consonants in *fat*, *hefty*, *gross*, *huge*, *stout*, *pudgy*, *thick*. Notice how lightly "*delicate*" hits its syllables, how heavily "*ponderous*" does. Feel how your mouth says *pinched*, *tight*, *open*, *round*, *hard*, *soft*, *smooth*.

It isn't that particular sounds, particular vowels or consonants, have meanings as such; *slight* and *threadlike* don't sound much like their meanings. Often, though, there seems to be some at least latent correlation between the meaning and the noise of words that the poet can use. The most familiar example of onomatopoeia is Tennyson's

The moan of doves in immemorial elms
And murmuring of innumerable bees

"Moan" and "murmur" are onomatopoetic, and the rather slurred, hard-to-count syllables of "innumerable" might also qualify. The hum of the lines, the alliterated *m*'s, *n*'s, and *r*'s that pick up the sounds of "moan" and "murmuring," seems imitative throughout.

Such effects should be used sparingly. In the extreme they quickly become silly or obtrusive and overwhelm meaning, as in "The Bells" by Edgar Allan Poe (1809—1849):

> Hear the sledge with the bells—
> Silver bells!
> What a world of merriment their melody foretells!
> How they tinkle, tinkle, tinkle,
> In the icy air of night!   5
> While the stars that oversprinkle
> All the heavens, seem to twinkle
> With a crystalline delight;
> Keeping time, time, time,
> In a sort of Runic rhyme,   10
> To the tintinnabulation that so musically wells
> From the bells, bells, bells, bells,
> Bells, bells, bells—
> From the jingling and the tinkling of the bells.

And so it goes for a further ninety-nine lines, which we can do Poe the favor of ignoring.

Syntax

Syntax is the way that words are put together to form phrases, clauses, or sentences. The poet can take advantage of a language's many alternative patterns for formulating or constructing sentences. Placement of modifiers, apposition, series, restrictive or nonrestrictive clauses, active or passive voice, and inversion are obvious formulas. The word *syntax* comes from the Greek *syn* ("together") and *tassein* ("to arrange"): "to arrange together." Also from *tassein* we get the word *tactics,* a military image that may suggest the value of syntax to the poet in deploying his or her forces.

The syntactical qualities of good writing in general, with main ideas in main clauses and subordinate ideas in subordinate clauses, apply in poetry.

Pope's "some rock's vast weight to throw," instead of "to throw some rock's vast weight," is a simple example of the reenforcement of meaning by syntax—by **inversion** of normal word order. So is the fussiness implied by the overcarefully inserted "with them" in:

> But most by numbers judge a poet's song,
> And smooth or rough, with them, is right or wrong

The syntax, not the statement itself, communicates the slight contempt, as if Pope were holding the words "with them" away from his nose. In "Excellence" (page 66) Robert Francis achieves a syntactical effect simply by choosing to make two sentences of the line "From poor to good is great. From good to best is small." The syntactical ambiguity of Francis's "The Base Stealer" (page 71) is part and parcel of the subject's dancing, tentative, uncertain quality. Just try to find the main clause, much less diagram the poem's one sentence! As with every aspect of form, the very arrangement of words into clauses and sentences can be useful.

In these lines from John Donne's "Satire III," the complex and entwined syntax, played skillfully over the line-breaks, rhythmically suggests the difficulty through which "Truth" is approachable.

> On a huge hill,
> Cragged, and steep, Truth stands, and he that will
> Reach her, about must, and about must go;
> And what the hill's suddenness resists, win so

Syntactical displacement and inversions constantly impede the lines' movement. Compare a more normal prose version:

> On a huge, cragged, and steep hill, Truth stands, and he that will reach her
> must go about and about, and in that way win what the hill's suddenness
> resists.

The effect is supported by the passage's metrical roughness and irregularity throughout, especially by the forced anapest in line 4:

> Ănd whát | thĕ hĭll's súd|dĕnnéss rĕsísts, wín só

The voice wants to read "hill's" as accented but must push on to the syllable "sud-" before it finds the line's pattern. This rhythmic drag over "hill's" produces a feeling of the steepness or the abruptness of the slope, which cannot be gone up directly but only by a circling sideward path. Throughout the line the voice seems almost literally to be working against gravity.

In "The Frog" the anonymous poet uses syntactical patterning to produce, in spite of the apparent illiteracy, a very subtle formal structure:

> What a wonderful bird the frog are!
> When he stand he sit almost;
> When he hop he fly almost.
> He ain't got no sense hardly;
> He ain't got no tail hardly either.
> When he sit, he sit on what he ain't got almost.

Two sets of parallel sentences ("When . . . almost" in lines 2−3 and "He ain't got . . ." in lines 4−5) adroitly set up the last line which gathers both patterns in its climactic syntax.

Frequently, when someone talks of the speaking "voice" being caught in the words of a poem, it is the syntax that is giving the effect. Robert Frost was a master of coaxing both music and meaning out of syntax. Listen again to the repetitions and emphases of these lines from "An Old Man's Winter Night":

> What kept his eyes from giving back the gaze
> Was the lamp tilted near them in his hand.
> What kept him from remembering what it was
> That brought him to that creaking room was age.
> He stood with barrels round him—at a loss.   5
> And having scared the cellar under him
> In clomping here, he scared it once again
> In clomping off;—and scared the outer night,
> Which has its sounds, familiar, like the roar
> Of trees and crack of branches, common things,   10
> But nothing so like beating on a box.

Even the four *him*'s in lines 3−6—the first three unaccented—work to a minor climax within the turning and returning syntax that gives a rhythm to the old man's habitual, now meaningless, movements in the house.

One of Frost's loveliest poems is a sonnet, "The Silken Tent," written "in one long, versatile sentence" (Robert Francis's description). It is a love poem, in praise of a lady's poise and summery grace. Like all the best miracles, Frost's is a quiet one, not obvious at first glance:

> She is as in a field a silken tent
> At midday when a sunny summer breeze
> Has dried the dew and all its ropes relent,
> So that in guys it gently sways at ease,
> And its supporting central cedar pole,   5

That is its pinnacle to heavenward
And signifies the sureness of the soul,
Seems to owe naught to any single cord,
But strictly held by none, is loosely bound
By countless silken ties of love and thought   10
To everything on earth the compass round,
And only by one's going slightly taut
In the capriciousness of summer air
Is of the slightest bondage made aware.

It is the subtlety of the syntax that makes the comparison possible at all. "She is as in a field a silken tent" focuses the comparison on the qualities of the tent's movement. And it is the ambiguity, the flexibility, of the syntax throughout that presents the poem's central paradox of freedom and control, or freedom *within* control. In just the way the tent is described as being "at ease" and "loosely bound" within the many but unconstricting guy-ropes that allow it to maintain its extent and shape, so is the poem's statement at ease and loosely bound within the many but unconstricting restraints of not only its one sentence but of a properly rhymed sonnet as well! So deftly ambiguous is the poem's syntax that it can refer to tent and lady alternately or simultaneously, and we are hardly aware of or made uncomfortable by the shift of focus as in "countless silken ties of love and thought." The root word hidden in "guys" is "guides," guide-ropes; and "guides" are very different from rules or strictures.

Richard Poirier, in *Robert Frost: The Work of Knowing* (Oxford University Press, 1977, p. xv), tellingly remarks: "The characteristics of litany which can be heard in the first line might of themselves suggest that if the tent belongs in 'a field' it also belongs in 'The Song of Songs,' where the bride says that she is as comely 'as the tents of Kedar, as the curtain of Solomon.'" The biblical allusion, in a poem which says "heavenward" and mentions "the sureness of the soul," is unquestionable. My back-fence neighbor, Phillips Salman, points out that there is something chivalric about the tent, a bit of tourneys, knights, and fair ladies, a whiff of *amour courtois*. But we might encounter a silken tent closer to home, at an elegant lawn- or garden-party, and the suggestions of such a festivity seem equally unquestionable. If we find in "guys" a pun on "fellows" (Frost could have said simply "them"), we may be having a glimpse, impressionistic though it must remain, of the scene from which the poem originates. Is it tent or woman who "gently sways at ease"? Is a young woman, perhaps a bride, enjoying the flirtatious and innocent admiration of such an occasion? "The sexuality is there," Professor Poirier adds, "as naturally as in 'The Song of Songs' and is a necessary ingredient of that blur of sensation where physical and spiritual realities meet in the poem, sharing in the human exigencies of time and space, and in its delights." In a poem so ambiguously wrought, the diction and syntax become the finest and most delicate of instruments.

Alliteration and Assonance

Alliteration is the repetition of consonant sounds in several words in a passage; **assonance,** the repetition of vowel sounds. The *b*'s in these lines of "An Old Man's Winter Night" are alliteration:

> . . . like the *r*oar
> Of trees and crack of *b*ranches, common things,
> But nothing so like *b*eating on a *b*ox.

Also alliterated, less emphatically, are the *r*'s, the hard *c*'s (including of course "box" — "bocks"), and the *n*'s. Assonance appears in the identical vowels of "crack" and "branches," of "common" and "box," and perhaps, muted by the distance of their separation, of "roar" and "so." The *b*'s are clearly onomatopoetic, suggesting the sounds of the old man's clomping about. The *r*'s may suggest the storm, much as in Pope's "But when loud surges lash the sounding shore, / The hoarse, rough verse should like the torrent roar." Other alliteration in the passage functions musically, linking sounds to thread the lines together so that they are tight and harmonious. The close assonance in "crack" and "branches" connects the words with a subtle emphasis. The assonance of "common" and "box," along with the climaxing of the string of *b*'s and hard *c*'s in "box," gives the word something very near the emphatic finality of rhyme. Every element of "box" repeats sounds heard earlier in the lines.

Given the limited number of common sounds in English, both alliteration and assonance would be hard to avoid. Using them is more discovering, or taking advantage of, than imposing them. Their main value, often more subliminal than obvious, is the linking of sounds that give a passage its autonomy or harmony. In Milton's "Men called him Mulciber; and how he fell / From Heaven they fabled" (page 5), the alliterated *m*'s and then *h*'s and *f*'s, and *l*'s throughout, give the clauses a musical unity. The assonance of "Men" and "fell" helps to frame the line. Similarly, in Williams's "The Red Wheelbarrow" (page 37), stanzas 2 and 3 are linked by the *r*'s of "*r*ed" and "*r*ain," stanzas 3 and 4 by the *w*'s of "*w*ater" and "*w*hite." The vowels of "depends" in stanza 1 reappear in "*r*ed wheel" in stanza 2. And stanzas 1, 3, and 4 have internal assonance: "m*u*ch" and "*u*pon," "glazed" and "rain," "beside" and "white." One by one, these assonances and alliterations are trivial; together they provide an aural undertone that helps to unify the poem. The four *b*'s in the last two quatrains of Roethke's "My Papa's Waltz" (page 56) — "*b*attered," "*b*uckle," "*b*eat," and "*b*ed" — thread the poem's climaxing music. The *s*'s frame the poem's last line — "*S*till clinging to your shirt" — and the short *i*'s and internal rhyme of "St*i*ll cl*i*nging" are onomatopoetic.

Alliteration and assonance also serve to emphasize or pair related words or phrases. The *s*'s in Pope's "The sound must seem an echo to the sense" unify and also sharply emphasize the central meaning. Such emphatic pairing under-lines comparison or contrast, as in Francis's "Excellence is millimeters and not miles" or in Nemerov's "That we may lick their *hinder* parts and thump their *heads*." How potent such alliteration may be can be seen by comparing the last two lines of this stanza of Poe's "To Helen"—

> On desperate seas long wont to roam,
>   Thy hyacinth hair, thy classic face,
> Thy Naiad airs have brought me home
>   To the glory that was Greece
>   And the grandeur that was Rome.

—to an earlier version of the same lines, which are flat and insipid:

> To the beauty of fair Greece
> And the grandeur of old Rome.

One last example is a *tour de force.* In "An Austrian Army" by Alaric A. Watts (1797–1864), *every* word is alliterated and, line by line, the alliteration proceeds through the complete alphabet!

> An Austrian army awfully array'd,
> Boldly by battery besieged Belgrade.
> Cossack commanders cannonading come
> Dealing destruction's devastating doom:
> Every endeavour engineers essay,   5
> For fame, for fortune fighting-furious fray!
> Generals 'gainst generals grapple, gracious God!
> How Heaven honours heroic hardihood!
> Infuriate—indiscriminate in ill—
> Kinsmen kill kindred—kindred kinsmen kill: 10
> Labour low levels loftiest, longest lines,
> Men march 'mid mounds, 'mid moles, 'mid murd'rous mines:
> Now noisy noxious numbers notice nought
> Of outward obstacles, opposing ought—
> Poor patriots—partly purchased—partly press'd   15
> Quite quaking, quickly "Quarter! quarter!" quest:
> Reason returns, religious right redounds,
> Suwarrow stops such sanguinary sounds.
> Truce to thee, Turkey, triumph to thy train,
> Unwise, unjust, unmerciful Ukraine!   20
> Vanish, vain victory! Vanish, victory vain!
> Why wish we warfare? Wherefore welcome were

Xerxes, Ximenes, Xanthus, Xavier?
Yield, yield, ye youths, ye yeomen, yield your yell:
Zeno's, Zimmermann's, Zoroaster's zeal,   25
Again attract; arts against arms appeal!

Rhyme

By definition, **rhyme** is an identity in two or more words of vowel sound
and of any following consonants (or syllables in the case of two- or three-sylla-
ble rhymes). Exact rhymes: *gate-late*; *own-bone*; *aware-hair*; *applause-gauze*; *go-
throw*. Rhymes normally fall on accented syllables. Double (or feminine) rhymes
normally fall on an accented and unaccented syllable: *going-throwing*; *merry-
cherry*; *army-harm me*; but they may fall on two accented syllables, as in *ping-
pong*, *sing-song* or *breadbox-head locks*. Triple rhymes are *merrily-warily*;
admonish you — *astonish you*; *head you off* — *instead you scoff*. There are a few
natural four-syllable or perhaps even five-syllable rhymes, like *criticism-witticism*.
For the most part, multiple rhymes seem comic. Clever, show-off rhymes are
obtrusive and, thus, appropriate to light or humorous verse.

English is not an easy language to rhyme. (By contrast, the problem in
Italian is to keep from rhyming.) There are a number of familiar words for
which there are no natural rhymes, like "circle" or "month." For some words
there is only one natural rhyme: "strength-length," "fountain-mountain." And a
word as much used as "love" offers only meager possibilities: *above, dove, glove,
shove, of.* Despite a poet's best contortions, it is hard to make such rhymes fresh;
consequently, *unrhymed* verse is standard, as the much-used blank verse of
Shakespeare's plays and many of Frost's dramatic monologues. Other properties
of sound, like alliteration and assonance, can make unrhymed verse as musical
or effective as need be.

The difficulty of rhyme in English has opened up a wide variety of inexact
rhyme—often termed **off-** or **slant-rhymes**—that the poet may use with consid-
erable freshness. One device is terminal alliteration, as in *love-move*, *bone-
gone*, *what-bat*, or "*chill-full*." Another is consonance (identity of consonants
with different main vowels), as in *bad-bed*, *full-fool*, *fine-faun*, or *summer-
simmer*; or near consonance as in *firm-room*, *past-pressed*, or *shadow-meadow*.
There is assonance, of course, as in *bean-sweet* or *how-cloud*; and Emily Dickinson has even made length of vowel work, as in "*be-fly*" or, fainter, "*day-eter-
nity*."

Rhyming accented with unaccented (or secondarily accented) syllables is
also a frequent method of off-rhyme, as in "*see-pretty*," "*though-fellow*," "*full-
eagle*," "*fish-polish*," "*them-solemn*," "*under-stir*." There is no need to be systematic about the varieties of off-rhyme. Anything will do in the right context.

In the World War I poem "Arms and the Boy" by Wilfred Owen (1893–1918), off-rhyme becomes nearly as formal as exact rhyme. The persistent refusal to rhyme gives a slightly awry sound to the poem in keeping with its highly ironic theme.

> Let the boy try along this bayonet-blade
> How cold steel is, and keen with hunger of blood;
> Blue with all malice, like a madman's flash;
> And thinly drawn with famishing for flesh.
>
> Lend him to stroke these blind, blunt bullet-leads   5
> Which long to nuzzle in the hearts of lads,
> Or give him cartridges of fine zinc teeth,
> Sharp with the sharpness of grief and death.
>
> For his teeth seem for laughing round an apple.
> There lurk no claws behind his fingers supple;   10
> And God will grow no talons at his heels,
> Nor antlers through the thickness of his curls.

In Marianne Moore's syllabic "The Fish," by contrast, the mingling of exact and inexact rhymes, along with the heavily run-on rhythm, gives a feeling of loose shifting, appropriate to its watery underseascape. This effect is reenforced by the surprising lack of rhyme in the last line of each stanza—which may suggest to the ear the openness of the long, yet unsettled, struggle of sea and rock-coast. The title is part of the poem's first sentence:

The Fish

> wade
> through black jade.
>   Of the crow-blue mussel-shells, one keeps
>   adjusting the ash-heaps;
>   open and shutting itself like   5
>
> an
> injured fan.
>   The barnacles which encrust the side
>   of the wave, cannot hide
>   there for the submerged shafts of the   10
>
> sun
> split like spun
>   glass, move themselves with spotlight swiftness

into the crevices—
in and out, illuminating   15

the
turquoise sea
of bodies. The water drives a wedge
of iron through the iron edge
of the cliff; whereupon the stars,   20

pink
rice-grains, ink-
bespattered jelly-fish, crabs like green
lilies, and submarine
toadstools, slide each on the other.   25

All
external
marks of abuse are present on this
defiant edifice—
all the physical features of   30

ac-
cident—lack
of cornice, dynamite grooves, burns, and
hatchet strokes, these things stand
out on it; the chasm-side is   35

dead.
Repeated
evidence has proved that it can live
on what can not revive
its youth. The sea grows old in it.   40

The inventive rhyming is extraordinary. Expectation makes us hear the subtle
double off-rhyme in "swíftnĕss-crévĭcĕs." A slight emphasis on the unaccented
article "an" is achieved by setting it in a line by itself; and this gives the run-on
an awkward, "injured" movement. Similarly, the rhyme on the first syllable of
the broken "ac- / cident" seems ingeniously suggestive. The rhymes may be as
heavy as "wade-jade" in the rhythmically viscous "wade / through black jade,"
or as light and merely touched-on as "the-sea" in the rhythmically shifting and
quick "illuminating // the / turquoise sea / of bodies." The pattern of unrhymed fifth lines is resolved in the last stanza; there by assonance the light *i* of
"it" picks up the light *i* of "live" (which is rhymed with "revive" only by
terminal alliteration of *v*'s) and so brings the poem to a fulfilled musical stop.

The interface of sea and rock is amusingly suggested in the poet's saying that the barnacles "encrust the side / of the *wave*," rather than the side of the rock. The color and suspense of the endless warfare between these entities is deftly presented in every detail of varying line-length, run-on, and rhyme.

Rhyme works in a number of ways. It may serve simply as a formal device: musically pleasurable, part of the poem's tune. It may, in its sharpness and precision, reenforce the poem's "bite," closing the box up tight, as in epigrams. It may be charming and graceful as in Blake's "The Lamb" (page 167), grand and sonorous as in Shakespeare's Sonnet 55 ("Not marble, nor the gilded monuments," page 101), or unremitting and abrasive as the triple rhymes in Frost's sardonic "Provide, Provide" (page 101). Like alliteration, rhyme may be emphatic, underlining comparisons or contrasts. The juxtaposition "chance-dance" almost sums up the opposition in Pope's

> True ease in writing comes from art, not chance,
> As those move easiest who have learned to dance.

So far we have been considering *end*-rhyme, that is, rhyme occurring at line-ends as part of the formal organization of the poem. Rhyme may also be **internal,** occurring anywhere within lines, musically "accidental." Internal rhyme may be as obvious as in the line of the popular song, "the l*azy*, h*azy*, cr*azy*, d*ays* of summer," or as in Algernon Swinburne's "Sister, my sister, O *fleet sweet* swallow," where along with the alliteration it perhaps suggests the quick, darting flight of a swallow. Or it may be as casual as it appears in Howard Nemerov's "Learning by Doing" (page 76), where it works almost secretly among the alliteration and assonance that thread the tight lines:

> Maybe a h*un*dred years in s*un* and sh*ow*er
> Dismantled in a morning and let d*own*
> *Ou*t of itself a finger at a time
> And then an arm . . .

Richard Wilbur's stately "Year's End" (page 102) exemplifies the masterly control of sound. Note the second stanza:

> I've known the wind by water banks to shake
> The late leaves down, which frozen where they fell
> And held in ice as dancers in a spell
> Fluttered all winter long into a lake;
> Graved on the dark in gestures of descent,
> They seemed their own most perfect monument.

The lovely whirling sound within the "which" clause occurs through several features. Mainly it is the result of the internal rhyme of "h*el*d," which attaches to the end-rhyme "*fell*" and unexpectedly hurls the voice toward the end-rhyme "*spell*." That quick movement is intensified by the only technically accented "in" of "ās dáncĕrs ĭn ă spéll," with three essentially unaccented syllables speeding the line toward the emphatic "spell." Although hardly noticeable, the "rhyme" of two *in*'s—one unaccented, the other technically accented, "ĭn ĭce ăs dáncĕrs ĭn ă spéll"—also contributes to the magical feeling of whirling, as does the light, hidden rhyme in "*And*" and "*dan*cers."

Part of the effect, too, comes from syntactical suspension. We wait a line and a half for the clause's subject, "which," to find its verb, "Fluttered." This suspension mirrors the suspended motion of the leaves (dancers) as, in ice, they *seem* to be still turning but are not. The alliterated *f*'s of "*f*rozen," "*f*ell," and "*F*luttered" help mark off this suspension within the continuing *l*'s that begin with "*l*ate *l*eaves" in line 2 and culminate with "*l*ong into a *l*ake" in line 4. The trochaic substitution "Flúttĕred" signals the resumption of reality. There is motion in stasis—leaves in ice, dancers in a spell.

Playing with sounds to see what they can be made to do may be serious work for the poet; it can also be plain fun, especially in comic poems. Rhymes can be both funny and effective, like Richard Armour's "bottle-lot'll." The more outrageous, the better. In *Don Juan* Lord Byron (1788–1824) offered up such rhymes as "fellows-jealous," "the loss of her—philosopher," and

> But—Oh! ye lords of ladies intellectual,
> Inform us truly, have they not hen-peck'd you all?

The twentieth-century master of outlandish rhyme was Ogden Nash (1902–1971), who reported that kids eat spinach "inach by inach," who advised "if called by a panther / Don't anther," and who said of "The Cobra":

> This creature fills its mouth with venum
> And walks upon its duodenum.
> He who attempts to tease the cobra
> Is soon a sadder he, and sobra.

The English Jesuit, Gerard Manley Hopkins, rhymed "Saviour—gave you a" in his serious sonnet "Hurrahing in Harvest" (page 100) and got away with it. But such multiple and contrived rhymes are best avoided in poems that don't intend to be funny.

Too much rhyme is like too much lipstick. Robert Frost's test for rhymes was to see if he could detect which had occurred to the poet first. Both rhyme words had to seem equally natural, equally called for by what was being said. If one or the other seemed dragged in more for rhyme than sense, the rhyming was a failure. This is a good test and a hard one. If you sometimes have to settle for a slightly weak rhyme, always be sure to put the weaker of the pair *first*; then, when the rhyme-bell sounds in the ear with the second, it will be calling attention to the more suitable and natural word. Rhyming is usually easier in couplets, where rhymes come closer together, than in quatrains or other stanzaic forms, where it is more difficult to project ahead and know whether a suitable rhyme may be found or fitted in. At least the poet doesn't have to go back so far if he finds himself in difficulty.

Rhyming a whole poem on one sound, like playing a tune on one note, makes an amusing puzzle for the poet:

Myth, Commerce, and Coffee
on United Flight #622 from
Cleveland to Norfolk

Clouds, like bird-tracked snow,
spread to dawn-sun five miles below,

while businessmen (& poets) flow
on air streams, to and fro.

Now, of course, we know   5
Icarus could have made a go,

formed Attic Airways Co.,
expanded, advertised, and so

have carried Homer and Sappho
from Athens to Ilo   10

on reading tours—with, below,
clouds spread out like bird-tracked snow.

Texture

All of the things this chapter has been about, diction, syntax, alliteration and assonance, and rhyme, function together, along with rhythm, to give a poem its **texture.** As cloth gets its texture or character from the quality of the interwoven strands, so a poem has a texture or "feel" that comes from the interweaving of its technical elements and its meanings. Consider how these elements mingle in Robert Herrick's "Delight in Disorder." (A *lawn* is a fine scarf; a *stomacher,* a bodice; and *ribbands,* ribbons.)

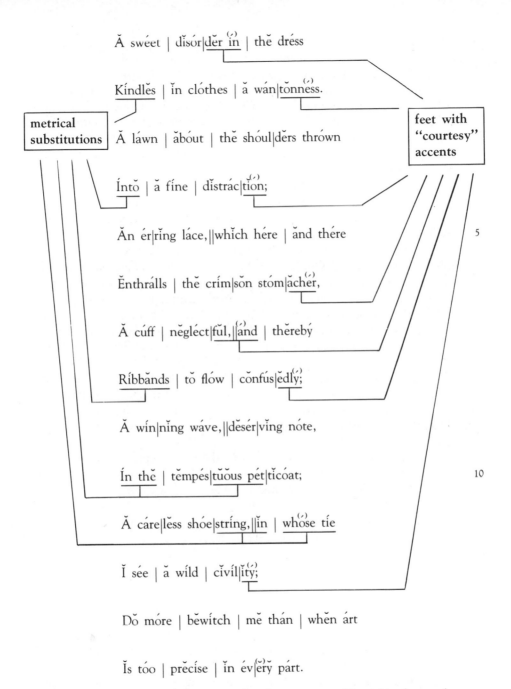

Every formal element of the poem bends to support Herrick's theme that we don't like things too neat, too mechanical, but enjoy a little spontaneity. Regularities and irregularities play against one another throughout. Only in the final couplet—when he mentions the opposite of charming casualness, "too precise in every part"—do the formal elements rigidify, in imitation of the idea.

Before the final couplet, the rhythm varies considerably over the tetrameter base. Seven lines have light, "courtesy" accents, five of them coming at line-ends where full accents would be normal. There are seven metrical substitutions. The little rhythmical flutters in line 10 are particularly imitative. Five lines have strong caesuras, two of which occur in the middle of feet. Five lines (1, 3, 5, 7, and 11) are run-on, so that the sense repeatedly flows and stops in a varied way down the trellis of lines.

Only in the final couplet does the rhythm at last march strictly by meter. The suppressed extra syllable in "every," usually elided in speech, underscores the marchlike effect, as the meter, like Marianne Moore's steam roller, crushes "all the particles down / into close conformity."

Something similar happens in the rhymes. Of the first six couplets, only the fifth is exactly rhymed ("note" and "-coat"). The others are off-rhymed in various ways, the least variation being the rhyme on a secondary accent in "dress" and "wantŏnnéss." The slightly awkward separation of syllables we normally elide in "dis-trac-tĭ-ŏn" increases the irregularity. Then, and only, in the final couplet, the rhyme is at last monosyllabic, hard, and exact: "art-part."

Alliteration and assonance add touches of casual order. The *d*'s of line 1 link the words most essential to the sense: "*d*isorder" and "*d*ress," as do the hard *c*'s in "*K*indles" and "*c*lothes" in line 2. In lines 3—4, "lawn" and "fine" add off-rhyme; and in lines 5—6, "err-" and "there," internal rhyme. Alliterations in lines 6—12 weave a continuous undersong. Noteworthy assonances occur in "sh*ou*lders thr*ow*n," "in the t*e*mp*e*stuous p*e*tticoat," and "in whose t*ie* / *I* s*ee* a wild civility."

By contrast, alliteration and assonance in the final couplet seem to increase its formality. Metrical rigidity comes from the relative evenness of the syllables; there is hardly a truly light unaccented syllable in the two lines:

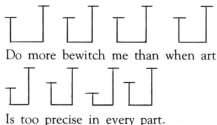

Do more bewitch me than when art

Is too precise in every part.

Packed meaning, long vowels, and consonant-thick words join the effect, as do the internal rhymes ("Do," "too"; "be-," "me," "pre-," "-ry").

The syntax also contributes. After the first couplet, which concisely states the theme, the poem is a single rather disorderly, random sentence. The multiple subjects appear one after another, untidily: a lawn, a lace, a cuff, a wave, a shoestring. Four are garments or parts of garments, but the wave is a property, so even the subjects are not quite parallel. Other parts of garments appear in subsidiary phrases or clauses: a stomacher and ribbands. The subjects are variously modified by prepositional phrases, subordinate clauses, and adjective clauses, which slop over from line to line. Adjectives appear before ("erring lace") and after nouns ("cuff neglectful").

With all the asides (and asides of asides) even the direction of this wandering sentence is not clear until, with the last couplet, it reaches the main verb ("Do more bewitch"). Then the sudden syntactical focus of the sentence reenforces the rhythmical stiffness of the couplet.

Every formal element is working, albeit apparently casually, to mirror meaning. Herrick's point is not wildness but a wild *civility*. A disheveled woman isn't attractive, nor is one who is overly neat. A hint of disorder, a suggestion of wantonness—natural, spontaneous, well-mannered—is what makes a woman's dress delightful. The same quality in its texture makes this poem delightful. "*Ars celare artem*," as Horace's famous dictum says: the art is to hide the art.

QUESTIONS AND SUGGESTIONS

1. In A. E. Housman's "Bredon Hill," one adjective has been omitted, in line 8. Housman himself deliberated long over the choice, trying out a number of words before he found the one he wanted to characterize the English countryside. What possibilities would you suggest? (Housman's successive notions appear in Appendix I.)

> In summertime on Bredon
>   The bells they sound so clear;
> Round both the shires they ring them
>   In steeples far and near,
>   A happy noise to hear.   5
>
> Here of a Sunday morning
>   My love and I would lie,
> And see the _____ counties,
>   And hear the larks so high
>   About us in the sky.   10
>
> The bells would ring to call her
>   In valleys miles away:
> "Come all to church, good people;

Good people, come and pray."
But here my love would stay.   15

And I would turn and answer
  Among the springing thyme,
"Oh, peal upon our wedding,
  And we will hear the chime,
  And come to church in time."   20

But when the snows at Christmas
  On Bredon top were strown,
My love rose up so early
  And stole out unbeknown
  And went to church alone.   25

They tolled the one bell only,
  Groom there was none to see,
The mourners followed after,
  And so to church went she,
  And would not wait for me.   30

The bells they sound on Bredon,
  And still the steeples hum.
"Come all to church, good people,"—
  Oh, noisy bells, be dumb;
  I hear you, I will come.   35

2. Think up some comic rhymes for these hard-to-rhyme words. Consider ways of working them into contexts that would make them seem natural. Then check your versions with those in Appendix I.

circle   *rhinoceros*   *broccoli*   *umbrella*

stop-sign   *evergreen*   *pelican*

3. In "Pitcher," Robert Francis uses rhyme to express the baseball pitcher's art of deception and variation. Like a batter, the reader is tempted to perceive the poem as not really rhymed. In the first couplet, for instance, the way the second line pulls on to "at"—"tŏ ăim át"—not only imitates the sense (passing the rhyme or identity he might have seemed to aim at) but also suggests an uncertainty as to whether the lines are intended to rhyme. Study the way the poet keeps the reader mystified until, in the last couplet, he understands "too late"—when the curve catches the plate.

His art is eccentricity, his aim
How not to hit the mark he seems to aim at,

His passion how to avoid the obvious,
His technique how to vary the avoidance.

The others throw to be comprehended. He   5
Throws to be a moment misunderstood.

Yet not too much. Not errant, arrant, wild,
But every seeming aberration willed.

Not to, yet still, still to communicate
Making the batter understand too late.   10

4. Here is a rough paraphrase of a poem called "The Fourth of July." Following
the development of its general sense as closely as possible, but choosing your
own form, lineation, diction, syntax, images, and elaborations, *write* the poem.
Compare your version with the real poem, by Howard Nemerov, which may be
found in Appendix I.

Having happened to drink too much tonight, I see from a hill the town's
fireworks at a distance, fine rockets exploding slowly and very colorfully over the
harbor. I also happen to be crying, because I remember the various fireworks we
could purchase during my boyhood and use by ourselves—dangerously no doubt.
Now there are laws of course, by means of which we are prevented from the
harms and abuses that former freedom sometimes caused. And now the town's
government can put on an entirely safe display, which can be far more grand
than any single person could afford then (small pinwheels, a few firecrackers—
one of which might have got tied to a dog's tail—and the like). In fact, this
public display is gorgeous: giant rockets bursting in the sky like flowers, or
showers and fountains of precious or semiprecious stones, with huge booms
resounding long afterward. Tears of happiness fill my eyes. On such a night I
fervently hope that God will bless this country of ours and that He will also
bless the town's responsible and well-paid authorities who are in charge of this
celebration of our independence.

5. Consider the structure of the ever-branching sentence of the first twelve lines
of "Catania to Rome" by Richmond Lattimore (b. 1906). What is the effect?
Also, what is the effect of the stanzas? of the single last line? (If line 13 were
prose, wouldn't we expect a comma after "station"?)

The later the train was at every station,
the more people were waiting to get on,
and the fuller the train got, the more time it lost,

and the slower it went, all night, station to station,
the more people were on it, and the more people   5
were on it, the more people wanted to get on it,

waiting at every twilight midnight and half-daylight
station, crouched like runners, with a big suitcase
in each hand, and the corridor was all elbows armpits

knees and hams, permessos and per favores, and a suitcase   10
always blocking half the corridor, and the next station
nobody got off but a great many came aboard.

When we came to our station we had to fight to get off.

6. Using these rhyme words: *box-side-locks-wide,* write a reasonably coherent
quatrain (*a/b/a/b*). Then, reordering, rhyme: *box-locks-side-wide* (*a/a/b/b*).
Could you also do *wide-locks-side-box* and so on? (See Appendix I for possible
versions.)

7. Look back at John Updike's "Player Piano" (page 20). Can you tabulate the
variety of sound devices by which he imitates the tinkly quality of a mechanical
piano?

POEMS TO CONSIDER

Hurrahing in Harvest   1877

GERARD MANLEY HOPKINS   (1844–1889)

Summer ends now; now, barbarous in beauty, the stooks° arise   *stalks of grain*
   Around; up above, what wind-walks! what lovely behaviour
   Of silk-sack clouds! has wilder, wilful-wavier
Meal-drift moulded ever and melted across skies?

I walk, I lift up, I lift up heart, eyes,   5
   Down all that glory in the heavens to glean our Saviour;
   And, éyes, heárt, what looks, what lips yet gave you a
Rapturous love's greeting of realer, of rounder replies?

And the azurous hung hills are his world-wielding shoulder
   Majestic—as a stallion stalwart, very-violet-sweet!—   10
These things, these things were here and but the beholder
   Wanting; which two when they once meet,
The heart réars wíngs bold and bolder
   And hurls for him, O half hurls earth for him off under his feet.

Sonnet 55

WILLIAM SHAKESPEARE   (1564–1616)

Not marble, nor the gilded monuments
Of princes, shall outlive this powerful rhyme;
But you shall shine more bright in these conténts
Than unswept stone°, besmeared with sluttish time.   *gravestone or monument*
When wasteful war shall statues overturn,   5
And broils root out the work of masonry,
Nor Mars° his sword nor war's quick fire shall burn   *Roman god of war*
The living record of your memory.
'Gainst death and all-oblivious enmity
Shall you pace forth; your praise shall still find room   10
Even in the eyes of all posterity
That wear this world out to the ending doom.
So, till the judgment that yourself arise,
You live in this, and dwell in lovers' eyes.

Provide, Provide

ROBERT FROST   (1874–1963)

The witch that came (the withered hag)
To wash the steps with pail and rag,
Was once the beauty Abishag°,

The picture pride of Hollywood.
Too many fall from great and good   5
For you to doubt the likelihood.

Die early and avoid the fate.
Or if predestined to die late,
Make up your mind to die in state.

Make the whole stock exchange your own!   10
If need be occupy a throne,
Where nobody can call *you* crone.

Some have relied on what they knew;
Others on being simply true.
What worked for them might work for you.   15

No memory of having starred
Atones for later disregard,
Or keeps the end from being hard.

Better to go down dignified
With boughten friendship at your side   20
Than none at all. Provide, provide!

3 *Abishag:* the name of a fictional movie star, borrowed from the biblical account of a
beautiful young woman in I Kings, 1:3.

Year's End   1950

RICHARD WILBUR   (b. 1921)

Now winter downs the dying of the year,
And night is all a settlement of snow;
From the soft street the rooms of houses show
A gathered light, a shapen atmosphere,
Like frozen-over lakes whose ice is thin   5
And still allows some stirring down within.

I've known the wind by water banks to shake
The late leaves down, which frozen where they fell
And held in ice as dancers in a spell
Fluttered all winter long into a lake;   10
Graved on the dark in gestures of descent,
They seemed their own most perfect monument.

There was perfection in the death of ferns
Which laid their fragile cheeks against the stone
A million years. Great mammoths overthrown   15
Composedly have made their long sojourns,
Like palaces of patience, in the gray
And changeless lands of ice. And at Pompeii

The little dog lay curled and did not rise
But slept the deeper as the ashes rose
And found the people incomplete, and froze   20
The random hands, the loose unready eyes
Of men expecting yet another sun
To do the shapely thing they had not done.

These sudden ends of time must give us pause.   25
We fray into the future, rarely wrought
Save in the tapestries of afterthought.
More time, more time. Barrages of applause
Come muffled from a buried radio.
The New-year bells are wrangling with the snow.   30

The Universe   1963

MAY SWENSON (b. 1919)

                        What
                            is it about,
                    the universe,
                    the universe about us stretching out?
        We, within our brains,   5
            within it,
                        think
        we must unspin
        the laws that spin it.
                    We think *why*   10
            because we think
            because.
            Because we think,
                we think
                    the universe about us.   15

            But does it think,
                    the universe?
                Then what about?
                            About us?
                    If not,   20

must there be cause
                in the universe?
Must it have laws?
                    And what
            if the universe   25
                    is not about us?
            Then what?
            What
                    is it about?
            And what   30
                        about *us?*

5

Stanzas and Fixed Forms:
Rooms, Houses, and
an Old Man of Nantucket

The etymology of the word **stanza**—a group of lines, usually of a fixed (and repeated) number and pattern of lines—takes us to an Italian word that means, among other things, a room. Stanzas are rooms, and a poem of them, a house. As there are one-room houses, there are one-stanza poems; and there are mansionlike poems of many stanzas. There are small rooms, spacious rooms, narrow rooms, ballrooms, living rooms, sunrooms, and, of course, closets. Stanzas come in all shapes and sizes, and, if need be, the poet can always invent one that fits the poem under construction.

We may distinguish between "closed" and "open" stanzas: between stanzas that are end-stopped, closing with the end of a sentence and a period, and run-on stanzas, those from which a sentence continues across the stanza-break. Closed stanzas, like paragraphs in prose, correspond to units of meaning or segments of an argument. Francis's "Glass" (page 11) and Williams's "The Nightingales" (page 35) use closed stanzas. Frost's "Dust of Snow" (page 14) and Williams's "The Red Wheelbarrow" (page 37) use open stanzas. Marianne Moore's "To a Steam Roller" (page 39) and Cunningham's "For My Contemporaries" (page 56) mix open and closed stanzas. Such choices, made in the writing of a poem, have to do with the flow or structure, poised balance or imbalance of the statement. For a poem like Moore's "The Fish" (page 90), given its fluid and shifting subject matter, open stanzas seem obvious, as does her choice of varying line lengths.

Line-Length and Stanzas

In the main (exceptions pop up like dandelions) verse lines of even length convey more poise than do verse lines of uneven length, which suggest agitation. George Herbert's "The Collar," with its lines of various lengths and its irregular rhymes, shows what can be done. The speaker is a devout but rebellious Christian who is feeling cheated by the life of sacrifice he leads. The food imagery, including the board (table) he strikes, is a metaphorical reference to communion. Notice how, as the internal conflict climaxes, the alternation of long and short lines becomes more pronounced.

I struck the board and cried, "No more;	
I will abroad!	
What? shall I ever sigh and pine?	
My lines and life are free, free as the road,	
Loose as the wind, as large as store°.	*abundance* 5
Shall I be still in suit°?	*in someone's service*
Have I no harvest but a thorn	
To let me blood, and not restore	
What I have lost with cordial fruit?	
Sure there was wine	10
Before my sighs did dry it; there was corn	
Before my tears did drown it.	
Is the year only lost to me?	
Have I no bays° to crown it,	*wreaths*
No flowers, no garlands gay? All blasted?	15
All wasted?	
Not so, my heart; but there is fruit,	
And thou hast hands.	
Recover all thy sigh-blown age	
On double pleasures: leave thy cold dispute	20
Of what is fit and not. Forsake thy cage,	
Thy rope of sands,	
Which petty thoughts have made, and made to thee	
Good cable, to enforce and draw,	
And be thy law,	25
While thou didst wink and wouldst not see.	
Away! take heed;	

I will abroad.
Call in thy death's-head° there; tie up thy fears.   *skull*
    He that forbears   30
      To suit and serve his need,
        Deserves his load."
But as I raved and grew more fierce and wild
    At every word,
Methought I heard one calling, *Child!*   35
    And I replied, *My Lord.*

Something similar happens in the stanzas of "Song" by John Donne
(1572–1631). The indented lines, particularly the two short lines near the end
of each stanza, and the triple rhyming give the poem a rapid, frenetic feeling.

Go and catch a falling star,
    Get with child a mandrake root°,   *forked root*
Tell me where all past years are,
    Or who cleft the Devil's foot,
Teach me to hear mermaids singing,   5
Or to keep off envy's stinging,
        And find
        What wind
Serves to advance an honest mind.

If thou beest born to strange sights,   10
    Things invisible to see,
Ride ten thousand days and nights,
    Till age snow white hairs on thee.
Thou, when thou return'st, wilt tell me
All strange wonders that befell thee,   15
        And swear
        Nowhere
Lives a woman true, and fair.

If thou find'st one, let me know,
    Such a pilgrimage were sweet;   20
Yet do not, I would not go,
    Though at next door we might meet;
Though she were true when you met her,
And last till you write your letter,
        Yet she   25
        Will be
False, ere I come, to two, or three.

The speaker's changeableness—"If thou find'st one . . . Yet do not"—also indicates how upset he is. His statement is bitter and extreme. It is also inaccurate: "Nowhere / Lives a woman true, and fair." Presented with measured calm, such a statement would find little sympathy. But we are able to sympathize because we feel the speaker's agitation. We can guess that he has just been betrayed by a woman, and we may realize how much he really wishes that what he is saying were not so. The poem is a dramatic monologue, belonging to a moment, arising out of an implied dramatic situation, not a considered pronouncement on the nature of women.

In contrast, consider Theodore Roethke's "My Papa's Waltz" (page 56) with its lines of even length. The plight of the boy is surely as upsetting as that of Donne's unhappy lover. Frightened by his father's roughness, divided in feeling between his father's strange gaiety and his mother's frowning disapproval, he is doubtless agitated and upset. Yet the lines are even, the poem's stanzas closed. The difference is that the voice in Donne's poem is inside the situation dramatically, and the voice in Roethke's, recalling the situation, is outside it. Roethke's speaker is not the boy but the man the boy has become, the man who has survived and who can remember with understanding. The voice is at some distance, time, from the event, not (as Donne's speaker is) still within it.

Usually shorter lines lend themselves to lightness, ease, delicacy, speed, intricacy. Remember William Carlos Williams's "Poem" (page 31) about the cat? Longer lines tend toward weight, substance, difficulty, seriousness, like the pentameters of Shakespeare's Sonnet 55 (page 101). Shorter lines also lend themselves to wit. It is difficult to imagine Herrick's tetrameter "Delight in Disorder," which tumbles and falls so freely from line to line, in hexameters. In general, what is true of shorter or longer lines holds for longer or shorter stanzas. Couplets step more quickly than quatrains or nine-line Spenserian stanzas.

In starting a poem, the poet must very soon sense what sort of lines and stanzas it calls for. Here is a poem of mine, "Swimmer in the Rain," about a bay-creek behind one of New Jersey's sand-spit islands. In choosing the length of lines—or letting the poem choose—I was aware of the linear, vertical, staccato nature of rain, so that shorter, quicker lines seemed appropriate. I also wanted a light touch, a fanciful tone. When I began to jot down my earliest impression in the first draft, I began with trimeter lines of six or seven syllables:

> No one but him to see
> the rain begin—a fine scrim
> far down the bay, like smoke,
> smoking and hissing its way

The impulse lasted for only eight or ten lines, and I sensed that the poem was moving too slowly. Noticing the accidental rhyme of "him-scrim," I began the second draft by changing to dimeter lines of four or five syllables. Although I soon abandoned the rhyming, the poem had discovered its form. Because substitutions in dimeter radically vary the norm, I had the quick, jerky movement the poem wanted. The verticality remains in the fairly long stanzas.

No one but him
seeing the rain
start—a fine scrim
far down the bay,
smoking, advancing   5
between two grays
till the salt-grass rustles
and the creek's mirror
in which he stands
to his neck, like clothing   10
cold, green, supple,
begins to ripple.

The drops bounce up,
little fountains
all around him,   15
swift, momentary—
every drop tossed back
in air atop
its tiny column—
glass balls balancing   20
upon glass nipples,
lace of dimples,
a stubble of silver
stars, eye-level,
incessant, wild.   25

White, dripping, tall,
ignoring the rain,
an egret fishes
in the creek's margin,
dips to the minnows'   30
sky, under which,
undisturbed, steady
as faith the tide pulls.
Mussels hang
like grapes on a piling.   35
Wet is wet.

The swimmer settles
to the hissing din—
a glass bombardment,
parade of diamonds,   40
blinks, jacks of light,
wee Brancusi's°, chromes   *modern sculptures*
like grease-beads sizzling,   *like those of Constantin*
myriad—and swims   *Brancusi (1876—1957)*
slowly, elegantly,   45
climbing tide's ladder
hand over hand
toward the distant bay.

Hair and eye-brows
streaming, sleek crystal   50
scarving his throat—
no one but him.

The choice of both line and stanza length has a good deal to do with the
possibilities the poet will be able to exploit in the process of writing a particular
poem.

The poet may elect not to use stanzas at all, but to write the poem, in
effect, as one stanza. Herrick *could* have separated the couplets of "Delight in
Disorder" as Robert Francis did in "Pitcher." Compare this stanza-spaced version:

A sweet disorder in the dress
Kindles in clothes a wantonness.

A lawn° about the shoulders thrown   *fine scarf*
Into a fine distraction;

An erring lace, which here and there   *bodice*
Enthralls the crimson stomacher°,

A cuff neglectful, and thereby   *ribbons*
Ribbands° to flow confusedly;

A winning wave, deserving note,
In the tempestuous petticoat;

A careless shoestring, in whose tie
I see a wild civility;

Do more bewitch me than when art
Is too precise in every part.

In separating the couplets, we weaken the poem, giving it a visual meticulousness that Herrick's flowing version avoids. We also call attention to the paired (rhymed) lines in a way that emphasizes a mechanical feature of the poem.

Consider the little stanza Marianne Moore has invented for "Nevertheless."

Nevertheless

you've seen a strawberry
    that's had a struggle; yet
    was, where the fragments met,

a hedgehog or a star-
    fish for the multitude   5
    of seeds. What better food

than apple-seeds—the fruit
    within the fruit—locked in
    like counter-curved twin

hazel-nuts? Frost that kills   10
    the little rubber-plant-
    leaves of *kok-saghyz*-stalks, can't

harm the roots; they still grow
    in frozen ground. Once where
    there was a prickly-pear-   15

leaf clinging to barbed wire,
    a root shot down to grow
    in earth two feet below;

as carrots form mandrakes
    or a ram's-horn root some-   20
    times. Victory won't come

to me unless I go
    to it; a grape-tendril
    ties a knot in knots till

knotted thirty times,—so   25

the bound twig that's under-
gone and over-gone, can't stir.

The weak overcomes its
menace, the strong over-
comes itself. What is there   30

like fortitude! What sap
went through that little thread
to make the cherry red!

Given Marianne Moore's style, we might expect the meter to be syllabics, and a quick test shows that the lines count out to six syllables. But as we read, an iambic beat quickly establishes itself. Except for "-bérry" (where we expect ˘ ´) the opening lines are normal enough iambic trimeter:

yŏu've séen ă stráwbĕrry̆

   thăt's hád ă strúgglĕ; yét

   wăs, whére thĕ frágmĕnts mét,

ă hédgehóg ŏr ă stár-

   físh fŏr thĕ múltĭtúde

   ŏf séeds. Whăt béttĕr fóod

thăn ápplĕ-séeds—thĕ frúit

   wĭthín thĕ frúit . . .

We may count "-berry" as a trochaic substitution, albeit a very abnormal one (lines usually end with feet of culminating accent: iambs, anapests, or spondees). The metrical difficulty seems appropriate, rhythmically suggesting the "struggle" the misformed strawberry has had; "-berry" may also signal that the poem will not be bound by conventional meter and that other unusual metrical variations will be allowed. This idiosyncrasy is not, of course, irrelevant to the theme. If defining things were as important as understanding, we might decide that the meter of "Nevertheless" is something of a cross between syllabics and iambic trimeter, leaving the poet free to slip out of either and back at need.

    The management of meter and rhythm is very interesting. For the moment, however, notice the stanzas. Although all the lines are of the same length (whether counted iambically or syllabically), Moore has indented the second and third lines of each stanza. Only these lines are rhymed. Not wanting to rhyme all three lines (sonically heavy), she logically chose not to start all three lines at the left margin—to avoid that possible expectation. The individuality of the invented stanza may also be a reason for the choice. "Nevertheless" is, among other things, a poem about individuality.

To have said that hardly explains the full effect of the chosen stanza. In stanza 6 there is perhaps a visual suggestion. After the "longer" (unindented) line, there seems to be a sensation of dropping, as the root drops down from the line of barbed wire:

> leaf clinging to barbed wire,
>> a root shot down to grow
>> in earth two feet below

A similar dropping effect occurs in stanza 5:

> harm the roots; they still grow
>> in frozen ground.

And, in stanzas 8–10, the playfulness about "over" and "under" gathers some of its complexity from the stanza shape. In these stanzas, starting with the word "tendril," the rhythm almost reverses itself; trochees, rather than iambs, become the norm.

> Víctŏry̆ wŏn't cóme
>
>
> tŏ mé ŭnléss Ĭ gó
>
>> tŏ ít; ă grápe-téndrĭl
>>
>> tíes ă knót ĭn knóts tĭll
>
>
> knóttĕd thírty̆ tímes,—sŏ
>
>> thĕ bóund twíg thăt's úndĕr-
>>
>> góne ănd óvĕr-góne, cán't stír.

Thĕ wéak óvĕrcómes ĭts

    ménăce, thĕ stróng óver-

    cómes ĭtsélf. Whăt ĭs thĕre

    lĭke fórtĭtúde!

The sturdy march of the iambs resumes, as the poem comes to its fully resolved conclusion. The "knotting" feeling comes from this succession of "backward" trochees and from the syntactical repetition of the words "knot" three times and "-gone" twice. It also comes from the strongly forced run-ons from "till," "so," and the broken "under-"; from the internal rhymes of "th*ir*-" and "ov*er*," which pick up the end-rhymes of "und*er*" and "st*ir*"; from the adjacent accented syllables of "bóund twíg" and "-góne, cán't stír"; from the extra syllable (and extra accent) of the line "góne ănd óvĕr-góne, cán't stír," which both stiffens and extends the line; and, finally, from the syntactical suspension, reenforced by the comma, between the subject, "bound twig," and its predicate, "can't stir." The trochaic rhythm continues in stanza 10, where only "The weak" and "the strong" are iambic. (The rhetorical emphasis of the exclamation is on "is," since the point is not identity or place.)

It is a dazzling passage and surely would have pleased Pope. (If there were a heaven poets go to, we might find that bewigged eighteenth-century Englishman and Miss Moore, late of Brooklyn, discussing just such matters over watercress sandwiches—her favorite.) The sense of difficulty, of realizing one's nature against difficulties, which we have been shown in a strawberry, apple-seeds, rubber-plants, a prickly-pear-leaf, carrots, and a ram's-horn root, could scarcely be summed up more rhythmically. The poem's last example—the cherry—is no anticlimax, however. That the stanza requires two lines to reach the first rhyme-word may aurally suggest the distance the sap must travel before it makes "the cherry red." This long journey to the fruition of the rhymes may well be a significant function of the stanza pattern throughout the poem. Whatever all of its effects are, the stanza Moore invented (or discovered) and then used so brilliantly is central to the poem's achievement. As she says in "The Past is the Present": "Ecstasy affords / the occasion and expediency determines the form."

Elementary Forms

The mechanics of the usual stanza forms are simple, and their potential variations and uses too many to begin counting. The **couplet** is the most elementary stanza: two lines, and when it is rhymed, *a a.* In any of its variations, the couplet tends to succinctness. Rhymed, it is capable of epigrammatic punch. A flexible form, it has been serviceable, used without stanza spacing, for longer poems or narratives (Pope's "The Rape of the Lock" or Chaucer's *The Canterbury Tales*).

Triplets (tercets) are stanzas of three lines. They may be rhymed *a-a-a* as in Frost's "Provide, Provide" (page 101) or Robert Herrick's lovely "Upon Julia's Clothes":

> Whenas in silks my Julia goes
> Then, then, methinks, how sweetly flows
> That liquefaction of her clothes.
>
> Next, when I cast mine eyes, and see
> That brave vibration, each way free,   5
> O, how that glittering taketh me!

Triple-rhyming can easily become monotonous and is difficult to maintain beyond very short poems. Rhyming *a b a* or *a b b* (Moore's "Nevertheless") are alternatives. The well-known Italian form, **terza rima,** follows the *a b a* scheme *and* uses the unrhymed line in the immediate stanza for the double-rhyme of the next stanza: *a b a, b c b, c d c,* and so on; Shelley's "Ode to the West Wind" is the most familiar example in English.

Quatrains are stanzas of four lines. When they are rhymed, the usual schemes are: *a b c b* (with rhymes on only two of the four lines, the easiest), *a b a b, a a b b,* and *a b b a*. The relative ease of *a b c b* makes it handy in ballads, hymns, and popular songs. An example of the more difficult *a b a b* scheme is the funny and touching "First Confession" by X. J. Kennedy (b. 1929). Note, though, that although he maintains exact rhymes for the second and fourth lines, the poet accepts off-rhymes for the first and third lines.

> Blood thudded in my ears. I scuffed,
>   Steps stubborn, to the telltale booth
> Beyond whose curtained portal coughed
>   The robed repositor of truth.
>
> The slat shot back. The universe   5
>   Bowed down his cratered dome to hear
> Enumerated my each curse,
>   The sip snitched from my old man's beer,
>
> My sloth pride envy lechery,
>   The dime held back from Peter's Pence°   *Catholic offering*   10

With which I'd bribed my girl to pee
  That I might spy her instruments.

Hovering scale-pans when I'd done
  Settled their balance slow as silt
While in the restless dark I burned   15
  Bright as a brimstone in my guilt

Until as one feeds birds he doled
  Seven Our Fathers and a Hail
Which I to double-scrub my soul
  Intoned twice at the altar rail   20

Where Sunday in seraphic light
  I knelt, as full of grace as most,
And stuck my tongue out at the priest:
  A fresh roost for the Holy Ghost.

A further example of rhymed quatrains is Robert Frost's "Stopping by Woods on a Snowy Evening," which uses a difficult *a a b a* rhyme scheme. The difficulty is redoubled by Frost's picking up the unrhymed line for the triple rhymes of the next stanza, and so on.

Whose woods these are I think I know.
His house is in the village though;
He will not see me stopping here
To watch his woods fill up with snow.

My little horse must think it queer   5
To stop without a farmhouse near
Between the woods and frozen lake
The darkest evening of the year.

He gives his harness bells a shake
To ask if there is some mistake.   10
The only other sound's the sweep
Of easy wind and downy flake.

The woods are lovely, dark and deep,
But I have promises to keep,
And miles to go before I sleep,   15
And miles to go before I sleep.

Frost's commentary is illuminating:

> I can have my first line any way I please. But once I say a line I am commit-
> ted. The first line *is* a commitment. *Whose woods these are I think I know.* Eight
> syllables, four beats—a line—we call it iambic. I'm not terribly committed
> there. I can do a great many things. I did not choose the meter. What we
> have in English is mostly iambic anyway. When most of it is iambic, you just
> fall into that. *His house is in the village though*—the second line. I might be
> committed to couplets. If I had made another couplet beside that—a rhyme
> pair—I'd be in for it. I'd have to have couplets all the way. I was dancing
> still. I was free. Then I committed a stanza:
>
> Whose woods these are I think I know.
> His house is in the village though;
> He will not see me stopping here
> To watch his woods fill up with snow.
>
> *He will not see me stopping here* is uncommitted. For the three rhymes in the
> next stanza, I picked up the unrhymed line in the first stanza and rhymed its
> end-rhyme "here" with "queer," "near" and "year," and for the third stanza I
> picked up "lake" from the unrhymed line in the second stanza and rhymed it
> with "shake," "mistake" and "flake." For the fourth stanza I picked up "sweep"
> from the unrhymed line in the third stanza, to rhyme with "deep" and "sleep."
>   Every step you take is a further commitment . . . How was I going to get
> out of that stanza?

He gets out of it brilliantly, resolving the form by keeping the "sweep" rhyme
throughout the last stanza, *d d d d,* and repeating "And miles to go before I
sleep" so that we feel both the weariness and the determination of the man
stopped by the lonely, lovely woods. The monotony of the five rhymes—
"sweep," "deep," "keep," "sleep," "sleep"—gives sound to these feelings.

Complex Forms

Beyond the quatrain, the possibility of stanzaic variation increases so
quickly that there is no point in keeping track. Three longer stanzas have been
employed with some frequency: **rime royal** (seven lines of iambic pentameter, *a
b a b b c c*), **ottava rima** (eight lines of iambic pentameter, *a b a b a b c c*), and
the **Spenserian stanza** (nine lines, eight of iambic pentameter and one of iambic
hexameter, *a b a b b c b c c*). Working with such complex rhyme schemes can
be like putting the pieces into a mosaic. As I worked on the *a b c b a c* stanza

of "A Problem in History," for instance, the rhyme in line 1 required my looking ahead all the way to line 5.

> At morning light the ark lay grounded fast
> On top of Ararat°; and Noah sent out   *mountain in Genesis 8:4*
> The raven flapping on jet-fingered wings
> Unreturning; and thrice to look about
> Sent the timid dove, that returned at last   5
> Fluttering an olive bough. The robin sings
>
> On the spattered rail and the sun shines
> On the steaming earth, that like a bog stank
> Greening at the clear blue sky. Asses bray
> From the hold, the animals come down the plank   10
> By twos and twos, in awkward-footed lines
> Sniffing, while hawks and songbirds spray
>
> Into the new air. Forgetful of the flood,
> In a busy hour all are debarked and gone
> Down from Ararat. By sunfall the voices   15
> Of their going have vanished. The ark alone
> Centers their outward footprints in the mud,
> Settles through the night with creaking noises
>
> Wearied with its long journey. In that repose
> New suns will wreathe it with green-ivy vines,   20
> Shade it with growing oaks and bushes round
> There on the world's top, till it rots with rains
> And snows and suns of time. And no one knows
> What green the unreturning raven found.

Having ended the first line of the third stanza with "flood," I had to aim what followed so that I could hit "mud" at the end of the fifth line. The difficulty of such rhyme schemes isn't in doing them once, but in then having to repeat them in further stanzas. The advantage of such self-imposed difficulty is that it may force the poet to discover words or images he would not have thought of otherwise. Here, I am happiest with the image of the birds' emerging from the ark—"*spray* / Into the new air"—which occurred to me only because I was searching for a word to complete the "bray" rhyme. Had I not painted myself into that corner, I might well have accepted something like "hawks and songbirds fly" (or "soar"), which is less interesting.

One variant on stanzaic form is to use numbered **sections,** as do Mary Oliver in "Strawberry Moon" (page 138) and James Wright in "Before a Cashier's Window in a Department Store" (page 242). Whether the sections are themselves subdivided into stanzas or not, the effect is to slow down and make very deliberate the poem's progression, distinguishing (somewhat as paragraphs do in prose) between the parts of the poem's statement or narrative.

Three complex stanza-poem forms should also be mentioned: sonnet, villanelle, and sestina. The **sonnet** is easily the most familiar and useful: fourteen lines of rhymed iambic pentameter. The **Shakespearean** (or **Elizabethan**) **sonnet** is rhymed in three quatrains and a couplet: *a b a b, c d c d, e f e f, g g.* Shakespeare's Sonnet 73 (page 12) is a good example, in which the sense corresponds to the four divisions. Frost's "The Silken Tent" (page 85) uses the form more fluidly. The **Italian** (or **Petrarchan**) **sonnet** is rhymed: *a b b a a b b a, c d e c d e* (or *c d c d c d*). Harder because of its fewer and more interlocking rhymes, the Italian sonnet falls into only two divisions, of eight and six lines: **octave** and **sestet.** The sense, statement and resolution, usually conforms to this division. Although its "turn" does not come exactly between the octave and the sestet, Milton's sonnet "On His Blindness" typifies the form:

> When I consider how my light is spent,
> Ere half my days, in this dark world and wide,
> And that one talent which is death to hide,
> Lodged with me useless, though my soul more bent
> To serve therewith my Maker, and present   5
> My true account, lest he returning chide;
> Doth God exact day-labor, light denied?
> I fondly ask. But patience to prevent
> That murmur, soon replies, God doth not need
> Either man's work or his own gifts; who best   10
> Bear his mild yoke, they serve him best; his state
> Is kingly. Thousands at his bidding speed
> And post o'er land and ocean without rest:
> They also serve who only stand and wait.

Poets have worked any number of successful variations on the rhyme schemes of both kinds of sonnet. Edmund Spenser used an interlocking *a b a b, b c b c, c d c d, e e.* Frost, who wrote more sonnets than might be supposed, tried numerous variations, including: *a a a b b b c c c d d d e e.* His finest sonnet, "Acquainted with the Night," is a variation on *terza rima,* with the final couplet made by simply "omitting" the unrhymed line in the last "triplet": *a b a, b c b, c d c, d e d, e e.*

> I have been one acquainted with the night.
> I have walked out in rain—and back in rain.
> I have outwalked the furthest city light.

I have looked down the saddest city lane.
I have passed by the watchman on his beat   5
And dropped my eyes, unwilling to explain.

I have stood still and stopped the sound of feet
When far away an interrupted cry
Came over houses from another street,

But not to call me back or say good-by;   10
And further still at an unearthly height,
One luminary clock against the sky

Proclaimed the time was neither wrong nor right.
I have been one acquainted with the night.

How far the sonnet will stretch can be observed in many of E. E. Cummings's sonnets. Here is his satire on patriotic platitudes and a politician's Fourth of July speech. Note how he solved a problem in rhyming lines 9 and 13:

"next to of course god america i
love you land of the pilgrims' and so forth oh
say can you see by the dawn's early my
country 'tis of centuries come and go
and are no more what of it we should worry   5
in every language even deafanddumb
thy sons acclaim your glorious name by gorry
by jingo by gee by gosh by gum
why talk of beauty what could be more beaut-
iful than these heroic happy dead   10
who rushed like lions to the roaring slaughter
they did not stop to think they died instead
then shall the voice of liberty be mute?"

He spoke. And drank rapidly a glass of water

The **villanelle,** borrowed from the French, is a poem of six stanzas—five triplets and a quatrain. It employs only *two* rhymes throughout: *a b a, a b a, a b a, a b a, a b a, a b a a.* Moreover, the first and third lines are repeated entirely, three times, as a refrain. Line 1 appears again as lines 6, 12, and 18. Line 3, as lines 9, 15, 19. Dylan Thomas (1914–1953) casts the masterful elegy for his father, "Do Not Go Gentle into That Good Night," as a villanelle:

Do not go gentle into that good night,
Old age should burn and rave at close of day;
Rage, rage against the dying of the light.

Though wise men at their end know dark is right,
Because their words had forked no lightning they   5
Do not go gentle into that good night.

Good men, the last wave by, crying how bright
Their frail deeds might have danced in a green bay,
Rage, rage against the dying of the light.

Wild men who caught and sang the sun in flight,   10
And learn, too late, they grieved it on its way,
Do not go gentle into that good night.

Grave men, near death, who see with blinding sight
Blind eyes could blaze like meteors and be gay,
Rage, rage against the dying of the light.   15

And you, my father, there on the sad height,
Curse, bless, me now with your fierce tears, I pray.
Do not go gentle into that good night.
Rage, rage against the dying of the light.

There are enough villanelles in English to convince us that poets like to make trouble for themselves.

Incidentally, the device of **refrain**—a phrase, line, or group of lines repeated from stanza to stanza, usually at the end—recalls one of the origins of the short poem: in song. It is a small step from the merry "Hey nonny nonny" of a Shakespearean song to the deliciously somber "Litany for a Time of Plague" by Thomas Nashe (1567–1601), of which this is a stanza:

Beauty is but a flower
Which wrinkles will devour;
Brightness falls from the air;
Queens have died young and fair;
Dust hath closed Helen's eye.
I am sick, I must die.
  Lord, have mercy on us!

Or to the sophistication of "The Mower's Song" by Andrew Marvell (1621–1678):

My mind was once the true survey
Of all these meadows fresh and gay;
And in the greenness of the grass
Did see its hopes as in a glass;
When Juliana came, and she   5
What I do to the grass, does to my thoughts and me.

But these, while I with sorrow pine,
Grew more luxuriant still and fine;
That not one blade of grass you spied,
But had a flower on either side;   10
When Juliana came, and she
What I do to the grass, does to my thoughts and me.

Unthankful meadows, could you so
A fellowship so true forego,
And in your gaudy May-games meet,   15
While I lay trodden under feet?
When Juliana came, and she
What I do to the grass, does to my thoughts and me.

But what you in compassion ought,
Shall now by my revenge be wrought: 20
And flowers, and grass, and I and all,
Will in one common ruin fall.
For Juliana comes, and she
What I do to the grass, does to my thoughts and me.

And thus, ye meadows, which have been   25
Companions of my thoughts more green,
Shall now the heraldry become
With which I shall adorn my tomb;
For Juliana comes, and she
What I do to the grass, does to my thoughts and me.   30

In the twentieth century, Yeats is the master of the refrain; a reader might
usefully search out "Two Songs of a Fool," "For Anne Gregory," or "Long-
Legged Fly."

Borrowed from the French and (if possible) even more difficult than the
villanelle is the **sestina**: six six-line stanzas and one three-line stanza. Instead of
rhyme, the *six words* at the ends of lines in the first stanza are repeated in a
specific, shifting order as line-end words in the other five six-line stanzas. Then
all six words are used again in the final triplet, three of them at line-ends, three

of them in midline. The order of the line-end words in the stanzas may be transcribed this way: 1-2-3-4-5-6, 6-1-5-2-4-3, 3-6-4-1-2-5, 5-3-2-6-1-4, 4-5-1-3-6-2, 2-4-6-5-3-1; and in the triplet, (2)-5-(4)-3-(6)-1. Poets from Sir Philip Sidney until now have used the sestina successfully. In "Hallelujah: A Sestina," how casually and comfortably Robert Francis handles the improbable list of words—*Hallelujah, boy, hair, praise, father, Ebenezer*—yet says what he wants to say! The inevitable round and round, spiraling-in quality of the sestina is beautifully illustrated.

A wind's word, the Hebrew Hallelujah.
I wonder they never give it to a boy
(Hal for short) boy with wind-wild hair.
It means Praise God, as well it should since praise
Is what God's for. Why didn't they call my father   5
Hallelujah instead of Ebenezer?

Eben, of course, but christened Ebenezer,
Product of Nova Scotia (hallelujah).
Daniel, a country doctor, was his father
And my father his tenth and final boy.   10
A baby and last, he had a baby's praise:
Red petticoat, red cheeks, and crow-black hair.

A boy has little say about his hair
And little about a name like Ebenezer
Except that he can shorten either. Praise   15
God for that, for that shout Hallelujah.
Shout Hallelujah for everything a boy
Can be that is not his father or grandfather.

But then, before you know it, he is a father
Too and passing on his brand of hair   20
To one more perfectly defenseless boy,
Dubbing him John or James or Ebenezer
But never, so far as I know, Hallelujah,
As if God didn't need quite that much praise.

But what I'm coming to—Could I ever praise   25
My father half enough for being a father
Who let me be myself? Sing hallelujah.
Preacher he was with a prophet's head of hair
And what but a prophet's name was Ebenezer,
However little I guessed it as a boy?   30

Outlandish names of course are never a boy's
Choice. And it takes time to learn to praise.
Stone of Help is the meaning of Ebenezer.
Stone of Help—what fitter name for my father?
Always the Stone of Help however his hair   35
Might graduate from black to Hallelujah.

Such is the old drama of boy and father.
Praise from a grayhead now with thinning hair.
Sing Ebenezer, Robert, sing Hallelujah!

For the poet who enjoys the challenge of complicated forms, there are
many more, like the French rondeau and rondel, the Malayan pantoum, or the
Welsh cywydd llosgyrnog, all of which have been successfully adapted to English. The place to find these is Lewis Turco's *The Book of Forms* (Dutton, 1968).

Short Forms

The **haiku** (or hokku) is a Japanese form: three lines of five, seven, and
five syllables. The essence of the haiku, however, is less in its syllabic form than
in its tone or touch. Consequently, given the differences in the languages, ob-
serving the five-seven-five syllabification in English isn't particularly valuable.
The essence of the haiku is elusive, very deeply embedded in its culture and
strongly influenced by Zen Buddhism. Haiku are, in general, very brief natural
descriptions or observations that carry some implicit spiritual insight—in short,
meditative nuggets.

The most famous of all haiku is by Matsuo Basho (1644—1694), translated
by Nobuyuki Yuasa (into *four* lines although the original is three):

Breaking the silence
Of an ancient pond,
A frog jumped into water—
A deep resonance.

Nearly as famous is this tender poem by Kobayashi Issa (1763—1827), translated
by Robert Bly:

Cricket, be
careful! I'm rolling
over!

Another by Issa, also translated by Bly:

The old dog bends his head listening . .
I guess the singing
of the earthworms gets to him.

Because of the spiritual, cultural overtone of the form, original haiku in English often seem precious or phony, especially when they call attention to themselves by a title like "Haiku." The lesson of the haiku, though—brevity, pith, the force of an image presented without moralizing—is well taken. Ezra Pound's "In a Station of the Metro," although directly influenced by the haiku, is entirely a Western poem:

The apparition of these faces in the crowd;
Petals on a wet, black bough.

A kindred tradition from Greek and Latin is the **epigram,** a very brief, aphoristic, and usually satiric poem like Pound's "The Bath Tub" (page 353) or Alexander Pope's "Epigram from the French":

Sir, I admit your gen'ral rule
That every poet is a fool.
But you yourself may serve to show it,
That every fool is not a poet.

Samuel Taylor Coleridge (1772–1834) characterized the form:

What is an epigram? a dwarfish whole,
Its body brevity, and wit its soul.

Anonymous described it thus:

Three things must epigrams, like bees, have all,
A sting, and honey, and a body small.

But the term *epigram,* traditionally, may also cover more sober poems like Pound's "In a Station of the Metro." The Greek word *epigramma* meant "inscription," as on a tomb or statue, and primarily implies brevity and pithiness. An **epitaph** (literally, "on a tomb") is a commemoration suitable for inscribing on a gravestone. But epitaphs, especially comic ones, are a literary convention that has little to do with real chisels or real marble—as in "Epitaph, In Case" by Anonymous:

Here, till this silent majority arise,
Richard Nixon for the last time lies.

Technically, a one-line poem can't be verse—it doesn't "turn." One-liners, nonetheless, make a delightful mini-genre. Since poetry is an art of concentration or compression, these tiny poems must be close to the center of it. This one by W. S. Merwin (b. 1927) is startling:

Elegy

Who would I show it to

So swift and fleeting are one-line poems that it often takes a minute for them to sink in. With Merwin's "Elegy," the silence, we may say, completes the poem. The title also provides an essential juxtaposition—and so the gap across which the spark can leap—in this poem by Eric Torgersen (b. 1943):

Wearing Mittens

You remember the sea.

"Frankenstein in the Cemetery" by Mike Finley (b. 1950) has a lovely comic pathos: "Here is where I ought to be. And here. And here. And here. And here. And here." Tiniest of these tiny knots is by Joseph Napora (b. 1944), with a palindromic title, "Sore Eros":

tOUCH

(A **palindrome** is a word, phrase, or sentence that reads the same backward as forward: "Rats live on no evil star" or "Madam, I'm Adam.") A still shorter poem is this by James Wright, which is printed in its entirety:

In Memory of the Horse David, Who Ate One of my Poems

PROSE POEMS

Borrowed from the French, the **prose poem** is a short composition in prose that asks for the concentrated attention usually given to poetry rather than the more discursive attention usually given to prose. It is normally shorter in length than the short story or essay. "Looking at a Dead Wren in My Hand" by Robert Bly (b. 1926), for instance, acts as we expect a poem to act:

Forgive the hours spent listening to radios, and the words of gratitude I did not say to teachers. I love your tiny rice-like legs, that are bars of music played in an empty church, and the feminine tail, where no worms of Empire have ever slept, and the intense yellow chest that makes tears come. Your tail feathers open like a picket fence, and your bill is brown, with the sorrow of an old Jew whose daughter has married an athlete. The black spot on your head is your own mourning cap.

"Oh My God, I'll Never Get Home," by Russell Edson (b. 1935), works in a way somewhat different from the way a short story works:

A piece of a man had broken off in a road. He picked it up and put it in his pocket.

As he stooped to pick up another piece he came apart at the waist.

His bottom half was still standing. He walked over on his elbows and grabbed the seat of his pants and said, legs go home.

But as they were going along his head fell off. His head yelled, legs stop.

And then one of his knees came apart. But meanwhile his heart had dropped out of his trunk.

And his head screamed, legs turn around, his tongue fell out.

Oh my God, he thought, I'll never get home.

LIMERICKS

Easily the most popular verse form in English, the **limerick** is a five-line poem, rhymed *a a b b a.* The first, second, and fifth lines are trimeter; the third and fourth, dimeter. The dominant rhythm is anapestic. The skeleton looks like this:

˘ ˘ ´ ˘ ˘ ´ ˘ ˘ ´

˘ ˘ ´ ˘ ˘ ´ ˘ ˘ ´

˘ ˘ ´ ˘ ˘ ´

˘ ˘ ´ ˘ ˘ ´

˘ ˘ ´ ˘ ˘ ´ ˘ ˘ ´

Fleshed out, and with an occasional iamb substituted for an anapest, the limerick goes like this one by the versatile Anonymous:

There was a young fellow named Hall,
Who fell in the spring in the fall;
    'Twould have been a sad thing
    If he'd died in the spring,
But he didn't—he died in the fall.

Part of the fun often is using a proper name, preferably polysyllabic, to end the first line and then getting the second and fifth lines to rhyme with it. Anonymous also wrote:

There was an old man of Nantucket
Who kept all his cash in a bucket;
    But his daughter, named Nan,
    Ran away with a man,
And as for the bucket, Nantucket.

Punning on names will probably never be cleverer than in this limerick, also by Anonymous, about the distinguished nineteenth-century clergyman, the Reverend Henry Ward Beecher:

Said a great Congregational preacher
To a hen, "You're a beautiful creature."
    And the hen, just for that,
    Laid an egg in his hat,
And thus did the hen reward Beecher.

Titles

Like houses for sale, poems usually have a sign out front—**titles.** Primarily, titles announce the poem's subject or theme, as in "My Papa's Waltz" or "Delight in Disorder." But they may work more obliquely, addressing someone or something, as "To a Steam Roller"; emphasizing a main image, as "Dust of Snow"; or adding a note, as "To Waken an Old Lady." Sometimes titles function as the poem's real first line, as in Moore's "The Fish." Not infrequently, the title is the hardest part of a poem to write. Sometimes a poem seems complete in itself, and the title must be an afterthought. The poet at a loss for a title can often find one by looking back through the poem's worksheets for a good phrase or image or detail he or she had discarded. The title may sometimes be a convenient place to tuck information that will not fit easily *within* a poem, as in "Myth, Commerce, and Coffee on United Flight #622 from Cleveland to Norfolk."

Because the title is the first part of a poem the reader encounters, there is every reason to make it interesting—lest, thumbing through magazine or anthology, the reader just passes it by. Wallace Stevens was a master of the intriguing title. How could a reader resist poems called "Invective Against Swans," "The Emperor of Ice-Cream," or "The Revolutionists Stop for Orangeade"? Notice, moreover, how skillfully he uses a title as an active part of a poem:

A Rabbit as King of the Ghosts

The difficulty to think at the end of day,
When the shapeless shadow covers the sun
And nothing is left except light on your fur—

There was the cat slopping its milk all day,
Fat cat, red tongue, green mind, white milk   5
And August the most peaceful month.

To be, in the grass, in the peacefullest time,
Without that monument of cat,
The cat forgotten in the moon;

And to feel that the light is a rabbit-light,   10
In which everything is meant for you
And nothing need be explained;

Then there is nothing to think of. It comes of itself;
And east rushes west and west rushes down,
No matter. The grass is full   15

And full of yourself. The trees around are for you,
The whole of the wideness of night is for you,
A self that touches all edges,

You become a self that fills the four corners of night.
The red cat hides away in the fur-light   20
And there you are humped high, humped up,

You are humped higher and higher, black as stone—
You sit with your head like a carving in space
And the little green cat is a bug in the grass.

A satiric account of the danger of a subjective view of the world, Stevens's poem is as deliciously colored and witty as a painting by Paul Klee. The speaker is a rabbit, weary of being on guard against a cat, imagining himself safe at twilight, feeling that the light of the moon is "a rabbit-light" and swelling up with his own image of himself, while "the little green cat" seems only "a bug in the grass." The poem stops there, and a reader who didn't recall the title might not understand how this ironic tale of self-delusion ends.

Indentation and Dropped-Line

On the model of the Greek elegaic couplet (hexameter followed by pentameter), a convention of English verse allows the **indentation** of shorter lines, as in the alternating tetrameter and trimeter lines of the **ballad stanza**:

The king sits in Dumferling toune°,	*town*
Drinking the blude-reid° wine:	*blood-red*
"O whar will I get guid° sailor	*good*
To sail this schip of mine?"	

Similarly, the longer and shorter lines of limericks are indicated by indentation. This convention may be observed in metered poems like Herbert's "The Collar" (page 106), in syllabics like Moore's "Critics and Connoisseurs" (page 164), or more arbitrarily, for visual purposes, in free-verse stanzas like Williams's in "Asphodel, That Greeny Flower" (page 35).

Indentation may also be used very flexibly, in free verse, as an open-ended musical notation to indicate subordination or the speeding and bunching of the voice-flow—as in E. E. Cummings's "O sweet spontaneous" (page 50) or in this poem by A. R. Ammons (b. 1926):

First Carolina Said-Song

(as told me by an aunt)

In them days
    they won't hardly no way to know if
      somebody way off
      died
         till they'd be   5
         dead and buried

         and Uncle Jim

hitched up a team of mules to the wagon
and he cracked the whip over them
      and run them their dead-level best   10
the whole thirty miles to your great grandma's funeral

                  down there in
                  Green Sea County

                  and there come up this
awfulest rainstorm   15
                        you ever saw in your whole life
                        and your grandpa
                        was setting
                        in a goat-skin bottomed chair

and them mules a-running   20
and him sloshing round in that chairful of water

                  till he got scalded
                  he said

                        and ev-
ery   25
anch of skin come off his behind:

we got there just in time to see her buried
            in an oak grove up
            back of the field:

it's growed over with soapbushes and huckleberries now.   30

The convention of indentation crosses and mingles with another convention: that of the **dropped-line,** which perhaps originated in dramatic usage. In
printing Shakespeare, for instance, when a single pentameter line is divided
between two speakers, the second part of the line is shown as "dropped":

Brutus: What means this shouting? I do fear, the people
            Choose Caesar for their king.
Cassius: Ay, do you fear it?
            Then must I think you would not have it so.

                    The Tragedy of Julius Caesar, I,ii,79—81

On this model, for rhythmical emphasis, Richard Wilbur uses dropped-lines in
"Love Calls Us to the Things of This World" (page 302); for instance,

And the heaviest nuns walk in a pure floating
Of dark habits,
                  keeping their difficult balance.

Another model for the dropped-line is the Greek stanza called Sapphics, which consisted of—to simplify—three lines of eleven syllables followed by an indented line of five syllables. Ezra Pound imitated this form in an early poem, "Apparuit," and on that model developed the dropped-line as a resilient technique in English. He uses it in "The Garden" (page 19) and in "The Three Poets" (page 27), and it is a major device in both "Homage to Sextus Propertius" (page 386) and *The Cantos*. Here is a passage from *Canto* II, spoken by Acoetes, the pilot of a ship whose crew had kidnapped the slumbering god Bacchus. The ship was whelmed in vines and in the lynxes and panthers that were Bacchus's attendant beasts; and the guilty mariners were changed into dolphins.

> Aye, I, Acœtes, stood there,
> > and the god stood by me,
> Water cutting under the keel,
> Sea-break from stern forrards,
> > wake running off from the bow,   5
> And where was gunwale, there now was vine-trunk,
> And tenthril where cordage had been,
> > grape-leaves on the rowlocks,
> Heavy vine on the oarshafts,
> And, out of nothing, a breathing,   10
> > hot breath on my ankles,
> Beasts like shadows in glass,
> > a furred tail upon nothingness.
> Lynx-purr, and heathery smell of beasts,
> > where tar smell had been,   15
> Sniff and pad-foot of beasts,
> > eye-glitter out of black air.

Both indentation and the dropped-line, in varying forms, open fresh possibilities for rhythmical innovation in our time.

QUESTIONS AND SUGGESTIONS

1. Write a sonnet, selecting all the rhyme words first and arranging them on the page. Then fill it in, keeping the meter. Write *anything*, don't worry

whether it makes much sense. Read it aloud. How does it sound? Are there parts of it you like?

2. Write a *serious* limerick. What problems do you find?

3. Study the stanzas and spacing of E. E. Cummings's "chanson innocente." How has he kept, and varied, the form he chose?

in Just-
spring   when the world is mud-
luscious the little
lame balloonman

whistles   far   and wee   5

and eddieandbill come
running from marbles and
piracies and it's
spring

when the world is puddle-wonderful   10

the queer
old balloonman whistles
far   and   wee
and bettyandisbel come dancing

from hop-scotch and jump-rope and   15

it's
spring
and
        the

                goat-footed   20

balloonMan   whistles
far
and
wee

4. How does the poet, Conrad Hilberry (b. 1928), achieve the feeling of slow-motion in "Storm Window"? What do syntax, repetitions, run-on lines, and the lack of stanzas contribute to the effect?

At the top of the ladder, a gust catches the glass
and he is falling. He and the window topple
backwards like a piece of deception slowly
coming undone. After the instant of terror,

he feels easy, as though he were a boy   5
falling back on his own bed. For years,
he has clamped his hands to railings, balanced
against the pitch of balconies and cliffs
and fire towers. For years, he has feared falling.
At last, he falls. Still holding the frame,   10
he sees the sky and trees come clear
in the wavering glass. In another second
the pane will shatter over his whole length,
but now, he lies back on air, falling.

5. Here are two poems on a common subject. Which do you prefer? Why? How
has each poet used form to present his material? Consider syntax, and choice
and deployment of images. (See Appendix I for the identity of the poets.)

a) *Death of a Soldier*

   All men must pass this way.
   There comes to each a fall
   Of year, impersonal
   And brief as but one day.

   This soldier chose to die   5
   Bravely for honor's gain,
   And did not fall in vain.
   These autumn clouds do fly

   Like flags to sing his death.
   Although he fell like dirt,   10
   His heart is God's, unhurt,
   Who moves clouds with his breath.

b) *Death of a Soldier*

   Life contracts and death is expected,
   As in a season of autumn.
   The soldier falls.

   He does not become a three-days personage,
   Imposing his separation,   5
   Calling for pomp.

   Death is absolute and without memorial,
   As in a season of autumn,
   When the wind stops,

   When the wind stops and, over the heavens,   10
   The clouds go, nevertheless,
   In their direction.

6. Consider, in "The Denial" by George Herbert, the usefulness of the stanza the poet has invented for this poem-prayer. How do metrical effects reenforce the pattern of unrhymed and rhymed fifth lines?

> When my devotions could not pierce
>   Thy silent ears;
> Then was my heart broken, as was my verse:
>   My breast was full of fears
>   And disorder.   5
>
> My bent thoughts, like a brittle bow,
>   Did fly asunder:
> Each took his way; some would to pleasures go,
>   Some to the wars and thunder
>   Of alarms.   10
>
> As good go anywhere, they say,
>   As to benumb
> Both knees and heart, in crying night and day,
>   *Come, come, my God, O come,*
>   But no hearing.   15
>
> Therefore my soul lay out of sight,
>   Untun'd, unstrung:
> My feeble spirit, unable to look right,
>   Like a nipt blossom, hung
>   Discontented.   20
>
> O cheer and tune my heartless breast,
>   Defer no time;
> That so thy favors granting my request,
>   They and my mind may chime,
>   And mend my rhyme.   25

POEMS TO CONSIDER

In Bertram's Garden   1960

DONALD JUSTICE (b. 1925)

Jane looks down at her organdy skirt
As if *it* somehow were the thing disgraced,

For being there, on the floor, in the dirt,
And she catches it up about her waist,
Smooths it out along one hip,   5
And pulls it over the crumpled slip.

On the porch, green-shuttered, cool,
Asleep is Bertram, that bronze boy,
Who, having wound her around a spool,
Sends her spinning like a toy   10
Out to the garden, all alone,
To sit and weep on a bench of stone.

Soon the purple dark will bruise
Lily and bleeding-heart and rose,
And the little Cupid lose   15
Eyes and ears and chin and nose,
And Jane lie down with others soon
Naked to the naked moon.

I Knew a Woman   1954

THEODORE ROETHKE   (1908–1963)

I knew a woman, lovely in her bones,
When small birds sighed, she would sigh back at them;
Ah, when she moved, she moved more ways than one:
The shapes a bright container can contain!
Of her choice virtues only gods should speak,   5
Or English poets who grew up on Greek
(I'd have them sing in chorus, cheek to cheek).

How well her wishes went! She stroked my chin,
She taught me Turn, and Counter-turn, and Stand;
She taught me Touch, that undulant white skin;   10
I nibbled meekly from her proffered hand;
She was the sickle; I, poor I, the rake,
Coming behind her for her pretty sake
(But what prodigious mowing we did make).

Love likes a gander, and adores a goose: 15
Her full lips pursed, the errant note to seize;
She played it quick, she played it light and loose;
My eyes, they dazzled at her flowing knees;
Her several parts could keep a pure repose,
Or one hip quiver with a mobile nose   20
(She moved in circles, and those circles moved).

Let seed be grass, and grass turn into hay:
I'm martyr to a motion not my own;
What's freedom for? To know eternity.
I swear she cast a shadow white as stone.   25
But who would count eternity in days?
These old bones live to learn her wanton ways:
(I measure time by how a body sways).

Nuns Fret Not
at Their Convent's Narrow Room   1807

WILLIAM WORDSWORTH   (1770–1850)

Nuns fret not at their convent's narrow room;
And hermits are contented with their cells;
And students with their pensive citadels;
Maids at the wheel, the weaver at his loom,
Sit blithe and happy; bees that soar for bloom,   5
High as the highest Peak of Furness-fells,
Will murmur by the hour in foxglove bells:
In truth the prison, into which we doom
Ourselves, no prison is: and hence for me,
In sundry moods, 'twas pastime to be bound   10
Within the sonnet's scanty plot of ground;
Pleased if some souls (for such there needs must be)
Who have felt the weight of too much liberty,
Should find brief solace there, as I have found.

The Invention of the Telephone

1971

PETER KLAPPERT   (b. 1942)

The time it took he could have
crawled—on the hairs of his knuckles,
on his eyelids, on his teeth.

He could have chewed his way.
In a place without friction   5
he could have re-invented the wheel.

But he wanted you to be
proud of him, so he invented
the telephone before he called.

Strawberry Moon

1979

MARY OLIVER   (b. 1935)

1

My great-aunt Elizabeth Fortune
stood under the honey locust trees,
the white moon over her and a young man near.
The blossoms fell down like white feathers,
the grass was warm as a bed, and the young man   5
full of promises, and the face of the moon
a white fire.

Later,
when the young man went away and came back with a
          bride,
Elizabeth   10
climbed into the attic.

2

Three women came in the night
to wash the blood away,
and burn the sheets,
and take away the child.   15

Was it a boy or girl?
No one remembers.

3

Elizabeth Fortune was not seen again
for forty years.

Meals were sent up,   20
laundry exchanged.

It was considered a solution
more proper than shame
showing itself to the village.

4

Finally, name by name, the downstairs died   25
or moved away,
and she had to come down,
so she did.

At sixty-one, she took in boarders,

washed their dishes,   30
made their beds,
spoke whatever had to be spoken,
and no more.

5

I asked my mother:
what happened to the man? She answered: 35
Nothing.
They had three children.
He worked in the boatyard.

I asked my mother: did they ever meet again?
No, she said,   40
though sometimes he would come
to the house to visit.
Elizabeth, of course, stayed upstairs.

6
Now the women are gathering
in smoke-filled rooms,   45
rough as politicians,
scrappy as club fighters.
And should anyone be surprised

if sometimes, when the white moon rises,
women want to lash out   50
with a cutting edge?

II

Content:
The Essential Something

6

Subject Matter:
Roses and Fried Shoes

Content, the other half of the indivisible equation that defines poetry, is hard to describe systematically, more so than form. There was a time when certain subjects were thought to be "poetic" and others not. Today it would be hard to think of anything that is off-limits to the poet, unless perhaps it is (every age has its prejudices) being too "poetic." As Louis Simpson (b. 1923) says, in "American Poetry":

Whatever it is, it must have
A stomach that can digest
Rubber, coal, uranium, moons, poems.

Like the shark, it contains a shoe.
It must swim for miles through the desert   5
Uttering cries that are almost human.

Poems can be about anything. If someone says that one can't start a poem with "fried shoes," a poet will almost certainly start a poem with "fried shoes." (Gregory Corso said it, and John Hollander wrote the poem.) In this poem David Wagoner (b. 1926) takes issue with a critic's proscription:

Walking in the Snow

"... if the author had said, 'Let us put
on appropriate galoshes,' there could,
of course, have been no poem ..."

—an analysis of Elinor Wylie's "Velvet Shoes,"
College English, March 1948, p. 319.

Let us put on appropriate galoshes, letting them flap open,
And walk in the snow.
The eyes have fallen out of the nearest snowman;
It slumps in its shadow,
And the slush at the curb is gray as the breasts of gulls.   5
As we slog together
Past arbors and stiff trees, all knocked out cold
At the broken end of winter,
No matter what may be falling out of the sky
Or blowing sideways   10
Against our hearts, we'll make up our own weather.
Love, stamping our galoshes,
Let's say something inappropriate, something flat
As a scholar's ear
And, since this can't be a poem, something loud   15
And pointless, leading nowhere
Like our foot prints ducking and draking in the snow
One after the other.

It is useful to remind the beginning poet, even these days, of this freedom of subject matter. Assuming that things too close to your nose can't be interesting or that poems need to be about the grand and important is a kind of blindness hard to escape. Look at things. Notice. Look at a slice of bread, really look at it, and then write about what you *see*. Forget about the staff of life and shimmering fields of golden grain. Look at the bread. This is one of the secrets hidden in the open. *Look. Notice.*

It is easy to see only what everybody sees, notice only what everybody notices. The result is **clichés**—not only clichés of language, but clichés of observation, of thinking, and even of feeling. We all fall victim to them. But the vision to see something freshly, singularly, is at the center of making good poems. Insights don't have to be on a grand scale. Indeed, most of the original ones are small. (And the only thing more dangerous than not noticing is convincing yourself that everything you notice is interesting just because you noticed it.) In "The Black Snake" (page 170) Mary Oliver mentions that the dead snake in the road "lies looped and useless / as an old bicycle tire." In "In a Prominent Bar in Secaucus One Day" (page 177) X. J. Kennedy mentions "lovely white clover that rusts with its grass." In "A Blessing" (page 353) James Wright describes a pony's "long ear" as being "delicate as the skin over a girl's wrist." These small insights are triumphs of observation. The term **image** (or imagery) is sometimes used to refer to such visual detail and the mental pictures it evokes, even when it is simply literal ("the white diagonal lines in an empty parking lot"). But the term is also, appropriately, used for the interjected comparisons ("like fishbones") which may be described as metaphorical.

A poem must be interesting. Whether or not it elucidates one of the great human truths, it had better be interesting—or we are likely to leave it half-read and turn the page. Poems compete with everything else in the world for our attention. As E. E. Cummings says: "It is with roses and locomotives (not to mention acrobats Spring electricity Coney Island the 4th of July the eyes of mice and Niagara Falls) that my 'poems' are competing. They are also competing with each other, with elephants, and with El Greco."

There is nothing like **subject matter** to make poems interesting. Notice the pleasures of topicality in "At the Bambi Motel" by Elizabeth Spires (b. 1952):

Walls the color of old plums, a "tapestry"
above the bed: 4 dogs playing cards,
smoking cigars. One cheats, aces tucked
in his vest, squints at the schnauzer's
royal flush and sighs. A wall-size mirror   5
doubles the room, doubles the double
bed into something immense, a mattress
for a troupe of acrobats.
Where are we? How did we get here?
And most of all, where's Bambi?   10
I wouldn't, couldn't have dreamed
up this place if I'd read true romance
magazines for a year. In room 12,
someone's having a row with someone
else. *Cow!* he accuses her.   15
Pipsqueak! You call this a honeymoon!
she yells back. Fighting
must have a titillating effect.
Silence for a minute. The pop of a cork.
And then of all things, giggling!   20
I bet somebody's made the front page
of *The National Enquirer* staying here.
What if our room's broken into by mistake?
What if the guy next door is a senator,
the girl Miss Panty Hose of 1968?   25
I chain the door shut, tape the keyhole

under your doubting gaze.
Your eyes glaze over, you begin your
impersonation of a sex maniac
who can't get his clothes undone.   30
Sin makes us blush like innocents
nevertheless. . .
                              I fall asleep
dreaming of Bambi. There's a forest fire!
I must get the dogs out! Intoxicated,
they dive out a window into a snowbank,   35
cards falling out of their clothes.
(Snow? An hour ago it was August!)
Room 12 lends the fire department champagne
to put out the flames. The senator's
distressed—Miss Panty Hose is more   40
undressed than I am. She grabs him
by the nose, makes him say "cheese"
for the photos. Where will we stay now?
The dogs are grateful. One knows
a place down the road, Roxie's.   45
"They treat you real good there," he growls,
"pink lightbulbs and wait till you see
what's on their walls. . ."

Subject matter is up front, obvious, able to draw us into poems, like a story that begins, "He undid her blouse." Subject matter differentiates poems from one another. Especially for a beginning poet, subject matter can do 90 percent of the job.

A good subject, stumbled on at the right moment, becomes a way of expressing our ideas and feelings. It can release, shape, focus them, as we might not be able to do directly. Often enough, it will even reveal ideas and feelings we weren't aware of having. So it was for me when I stumbled on a little story about the French painter Toulouse-Lautrec (1864—1901). The poem the story inspired is called "Ungainly Things."

A regular country toad—pebbly,
     squat,
          shadow-green

as the shade of the spruces
     in the garden   5
          he came from—rode

to Paris in a hatbox
        to Lautrec's
            studio (skylights

on the skies of Paris);   10
        ate
            cutworms from a box,

hopped
        occasionally
            among the furniture and easels,   15

while the clumsy little painter
        studied
            him in charcoal

until he was beautiful.
        One day   20
            he found his way

down stairs toward the world
        again,
            into the streets of Montmartre°,   *district of Paris*

and, missing him, the painter-dwarf   25
        followed,
            peering among cobbles,

laughed at, searching
        until long past dark
            the length of the Avenue Frochot,   30

over and over,
        for the fisted, marble-eyed
            fellow

no one would ever see again
        except   35
            in sketches that make ungainly things beautiful.

I chanced upon this story in the foreword of a small book of Lautrec's drawings
of animals, A Bestiary, published in 1954 by the Fogg Museum at Harvard:

A friend sent him in a hat box, from L'Isle Adam, a large toad (plate 11) which hopped about his apartment for days, becoming quite a pet. At last it escaped into the "wilderness" of the rue Caulaincourt (Montmartre quarter, in Paris). Toulouse-Lautrec, a far more affectionate and soft hearted man than some biographers have represented him, was desolate. When the rumor came later that the toad had been seen on the Avenue Frochot, he spent hours searching for him—the length of that street!

Adding what I knew of toads, Paris, and Lautrec—the painter we associate with can-can dancers and sophisticated scenes of Parisian night life near the turn of the century—I retold the story. It was a way of expressing my feeling about the beauty in the ordinary, which we all too easily accept as dull and boring, and about the role of art in helping us to recapture simple wonder. But in writing the poem I discovered something I didn't know I was thinking, about the role of the artist. There is only one toad in the poem, but the title is plural.

Presenting

Emotions, in themselves, are not subject matter. Being in love, or sad, or lonely, or feeling good because it is spring, are common experiences. Poems that merely say these things, *state* these emotions directly, are unlikely to be very interesting. We may respect such statements, but we can't be moved by them.

The *circumstances* of the emotion, the scene or events out of which it comes, however, are subject matter. Don't tell the emotion. Tell the causes of it, the circumstances. Presented vividly, they will not only convince us of its truth but will also make us dramatically *feel* it. Theodore Roethke doesn't state his feeling about his father in "My Papa's Waltz." He lets us feel it for ourselves by presenting us with the particular scene out of which the feeling came. In "Dust of Snow" Robert Frost communicates the feeling by telling us about the crow, the hemlock, and the chill sprinkling of snow. In "Nevertheless" Marianne Moore presents her theme—admiration for fortitude, overcoming obstacles—by presenting a number of examples that surprise us because we don't usually think of strawberries and grape vines as courageous. Often, as in William Carlos Williams's "Poem" about the cat or in E. E. Cummings's "next to of course god america i," the poet simply gives us the facts and trusts them to elicit the proper feeling. Frequently, presenting the facts will be the only way to describe an emotion adequately. What word, or list of words, that describes the emotions of love, fear, pain, mischief, panic, delight, and helplessness could begin to sum up what the boy (and the grown man) feel in (and about) the little scene in "My Papa's Waltz"?

The key is **presenting**; not to tell about, but to show. Put the spring day or the girl or the father *into* the poem. Put the mountain *into* the poem so that, in the absence of the mountain, the poem can take the place of the mountain. In "The Poem That Took the Place of the Mountain" Wallace Stevens is saying not only that the poem can save and remember experience, but also that it can bring to "exactness," because we can imagine it, the world that is always incomplete and transitory in reality:

There it was, word for word,
The poem that took the place of a mountain.

He breathed its oxygen,
Even when the book lay turned in the dust of his table.

It reminded him how he had needed   5
A place to go in his own direction,

How he had recomposed the pines,
Shifted the rocks and picked his way among clouds,

For the outlook that would be right,
Where he would be complete in an unexplained completion: 10

The exact rock where his inexactnesses
Would discover, at last, the view toward which they had edged,

Where he could lie and, gazing down at the sea,
Recognize his unique and solitary home.

We have already looked at some of the ways in which imitative elements of form (shape, sound, rhythm) help in *presenting*. In chapter 8 we will discuss metaphor. For the moment, let's examine the management of subject matter, some of the ways in which a poet may arrange or dispose it in a poem to make it effective.

It almost goes without saying that subject matter should be presented accurately. Accuracy of information, of detail, of terminology tends to make the presentation convincing. Whether writing about antiques, rocking chairs, leopards, Denver, black holes in space, or the physiology of the grasshopper, the poet should know enough, or find out enough, to be reasonably authoritative. Tulips don't bloom in July. Whales are mammals, not fish. Ernie Banks played shortstop for the Chicago Cubs. Common knowledge and plain observation are usually sufficient, but sometimes the poet will come upon a subject that takes her or him to the library and requires becoming something of a specialist. Ezra Pound notes, in *ABC of Reading,* a physician's claim that the accuracy of medical information in the *Iliad* proved Homer to have been an army doctor!

Particulars

In presenting subject matter, **particulars** in and of themselves are frequently a source of vividness. Here is Gerard Manley Hopkins's "Pied Beauty," which both praises and exemplifies the effect of colorful and idiosyncratic detail:

Glory be to God for dappled things—
  For skies of couple-colour as a brinded° cow;   *brindled, streaked*
   For rose-moles all in stipple° upon trout that swim; *stippled, dotted*
Fresh-firecoal chestnut-falls; finches' wings;
  Landscape plotted and pieced—fold, fallow and plough,   5
   And áll trádes, their gear and tackle and trim.
All things counter, original, spare, strange;
  Whatever is fickle, freckled (who knows how?)
   With swift, slow; sweet, sour; adazzle, dim;
He fathers-forth whose beauty is past change: 10
     Praise him.

Specific details add overtones as well as color. Suppose, in "Dust of Snow," Frost had said merely "tree" instead of "hemlock": the picture is vaguer, and the deadly suggestions of the funereal hemlock are lost. In Roethke's "My Papa's Waltz" the detail about the "pans" sliding from the "kitchen shelf" does more than indicate the rowdiness of the drunken father's dancing. It tells us something about the middle-class or lower-middle-class family—the kitchen described is neither large nor very elegant. More important, it sets the scene in the kitchen. Suggestions abound. The father, who works with his hands ("a palm caked hard by dirt"), has come home late from work, having stopped off for his whiskey. He has come in by the back door, into the kitchen. Dinner is over and the pans back on the shelf, but the boy and his mother are still in the kitchen. That they have not waited dinner, or waited it longer, measures the mother's stored-up anger, as does the word "countenance," which suggests how formidably she has prepared herself. The incongruity of the father's merriment is all the stronger because the waltzing occurs, so inappropriately, in the kitchen.

"Traveling through the Dark" by William Stafford (b. 1914) shows a perfect articulation of details:

Traveling through the dark I found a deer
dead on the edge of the Wilson River road.
It is usually best to roll them into the canyon:
that road is narrow; to swerve might make more dead.

By glow of the tail-light I stumbled back of the car   5
and stood by the heap, a doe, a recent killing;
she had stiffened already, almost cold.
I dragged her off; she was large in the belly.

My fingers touching her side brought me the reason—
her side was warm; her fawn lay there waiting,   10
alive, still, never to be born.
Beside that mountain road I hesitated.

The car aimed ahead its lowered parking lights;
under the hood purred the steady engine.
I stood in the glare of the warm exhaust turning red;   15
around our group I could hear the wilderness listen.

I thought hard for us all—my only swerving—,
then pushed her over the edge into the river.

Some of the details, like "the Wilson River road," attest to the reality of the
incident. The speaker has seen dead deer along the road before and is not
sentimental ("It is usually best to roll them into the canyon"). The most effective detail, perhaps, is the "glow of the tail-light," which bathes the whole
scene an eerie red. Everything about the car is made to participate. The glow is
red, like blood. The parking lights are "lowered," as if in respect or recognition
of the tragedy. The engine "purred" like an animal, and the exhaust is "warm."
The doomed warmth and life of the fawn could not be more ironically emphasized. Stafford has not added these details to the grim tableau—they are all
naturally a part of it—but he has *used* them superbly to illuminate the event.

Absent specifics, left-out particulars that are natural parts of the material
all too often result in missed opportunities. This occurs in this sonnet, submitted in a writing workshop I conducted once upon a time.

To One Who Shed Tears at a Play

Because I hold that fleeting moment dear
I prison it within each shining word
As fragile as the flight of startled bird,
Yet strong as iron bands. I still can hear

The actors speak their lines. The climax near,   5
They find frustration, sorrow, and they gird
Themselves for bitter loss. And you who heard
Pay them the priceless tribute of a tear.

O, gentle heart! May that day never come,
When you are heedless of the sight of grief,   10
Though only grief that mimics. For the sum
Of your vicarious sharing brings relief.
The callous heart is like a broken drum,
A bitter fruit, a sere and withered leaf.

The group concluded that the difficult sonnet form is well managed, though at the price of the rather archaic rhyme-word "gird" and the padded "For the sum / Of your vicarious sharing" instead of simply "For your vicarious sharing." (The fact, not the amount, is the point.) The main problem, however, seemed to be a curious abstractness about its subject matter, someone who cries at a play. A surprising proportion of the poem does not deal directly with the subject at all. The first three and a half lines are about the writing of the poem, and the images in the last two lines are, oddly, about the "callous heart" rather than the "gentle heart" of the person who wept.

Consider the missing particulars, the missed opportunities. About the person who cries, we know nothing: not age, nor sex, nor any other detail, although such information might considerably affect our responses. Nor do we know anything about the speaker's relationship to this person. Was it a stranger who happened to be in the next seat? a friend? a relative? perhaps a son or daughter? Why did that person's sympathetic reaction strike the speaker as valuable? We don't even know what the play was, though that detail might have been useful. We are strangely barred from the very event that is supposed to move us. Its color and convincingness are left out.

Of course, all poems do not need description equally. Some require little or none, such as J. V. Cunningham's "For My Contemporaries." With poems that depend on description, the *selection* of particulars is more to the point than a mere piling up of them. There is no way to include everything about anything. Too many particulars may be as ineffective as too few. Dylan Thomas's lyric evocation of the childhood experience of a farm, "Fern Hill" (page 173), manages its rich profusion of detail without losing its thematic thread. The past tense—"Now as I *was* young and easy under the apple boughs"—is an implicit reminder throughout that the paradise of boyhood ends; and the emphatic fourth lines in stanzas 1 and 2—"Time let me hail and climb" and "Time let me play and be"—keep the poem's dizzyingly lovely detail always in perspective.

In writing, jot down every item that comes to mind. Then, as the poem begins to take shape, pick and choose among them for those that fit and best bear out the poem's developing direction. Most poets' manuscripts are embroidered in the margins with lists of details, adjectives, whatever. A. E. Housman's list of words for "_____ counties" in "Bredon Hill" (page 97)—*sunny, pleasant, checkered, patterned, painted, colored*—show him accumulating such a range of possibilities.

Consider the selection of detail in "First Death in Nova Scotia" by Elizabeth Bishop (1911–1979):

In the cold, cold parlor
my mother laid out Arthur
beneath the chromographs:
Edward, Prince of Wales,
with Princess Alexandra,   5
and King George with Queen Mary.
Below them on the table
stood a stuffed loon
shot and stuffed by Uncle
Arthur, Arthur's father.   10

Since Uncle Arthur fired
a bullet into him,
he hadn't said a word.
He kept his own counsel
on his white, frozen lake,   15
the marble-topped table.
His breast was deep and white,
cold and caressable;
his eyes were red glass,
much to be desired.   20

"Come," said my mother,
"Come and say good-bye
to your little cousin Arthur."
I was lifted up and given
one lily of the valley   25
to put in Arthur's hand.
Arthur's coffin was
a little frosted cake,
and the red-eyed loon eyed it
from his white, frozen lake.   30

Arthur was very small.
He was all white, like a doll

that hadn't been painted yet.
Jack Frost had started to paint him
the way he always painted   35
the Maple Leaf (Forever).
He had just begun on his hair,
a few red strokes, and then
Jack Frost had dropped the brush
and left him white, forever.   40

The gracious royal couples
were warm in red and ermine;
their feet were well wrapped up
in the ladies' ermine trains.
They invited Arthur to be   45
the smallest page at court.
But how could Arthur go,
clutching his tiny lily,
with his eyes shut up so tight
and the roads deep in snow?   50

The poem very selectively presents a child's view of death. Nothing outside the "cold, cold parlor" is mentioned, nor anything before or after the one event, seeing little Arthur in his coffin. Only two details of the parlor are referred to, the color lithographs of the royal family and the stuffed loon on its marble-topped table. Although no other furnishings of the room are mentioned, these two are sufficient to suggest the ornate and rather formal nature of the room, as well as something about the household (its patriotism, its family loyalty, its propriety). We accept the poem as autobiographical and assume the speaker to be a little girl.

The loon and the chromographs of the royal family have several aspects in common. Like Arthur himself and his coffin ("a little frosted cake"), both are studies in white and red. The loon's breast and "frozen lake" of marble-topped table are white, and his glass eyes are red. "The gracious royal couples" are "warm in red and ermine" (a white, thick fur)—the only colors noted. Arthur is "white, forever," except for the "few red strokes" of his hair. Very likely it is the red and white of the loon and the chromographs that make the little girl notice them. And both are connected with death. "Uncle Arthur, Arthur's father" had killed the loon and had it stuffed. And the ermine of the royal family similarly comes from animals that have been killed to provide decorative fur. These particulars give the poem its icy, rich unity: red and white; warm (royal family) and cold (loon). The funeral reminds the little girl of a birthday, the "little frosted cake" of the coffin.

The particulars suggest beautifully the little girl's incomprehension of the death she is witnessing. The loon is not so much dead as silent: "Since Uncle

Arthur fired / a bullet into him, / he hadn't said a word." "He kept his own counsel" and only "eyed" little Arthur's coffin. The girl's fantasy that the royal family had "invited Arthur to be / the smallest page at court" is the only way that she can translate her cousin's death into her experience. ("Jack Frost" suggests the dimensions of her experience.) Her mother's well-meaning but too careful "'Come and say good-bye / to your little cousin Arthur'" invites the fantasy. Although the girl doesn't understand, she is nonetheless aware that the confusion between life (red) and death (white) will resolve itself ominously. "But how could Arthur go, / clutching his tiny lily, / with his eyes shut up so tight / and the roads deep in snow?" (Lily and snow are yet more white.) That question, with which the poem ends, shows how fragile is her defense against the grim truth.

Descriptive Implication

Bishop's handling of the details of "First Death in Nova Scotia" quietly gathers up nuances until they become symbolic. Without ever departing from the realistic scene, the reds and whites of loon and royal family, nonetheless, become symbols of the confusion about life and death in the child's feelings. Like most effective details, they function in more than one way, on more than one level. As Pound comments, "the natural object is always the adequate symbol."

Similarly, in "Cherrylog Road" by James Dickey (b. 1923), in addition to giving the poem its richly colored surface, the details provide a sort of running commentary on the action. The poem does not *state* its evaluation of the meeting of the narrator and Doris Holbrook in the auto junkyard, but *implies* it in the choice of particulars. As you read the poem, weigh carefully the feelings the details evoke, one by one, as they appear.

> Off Highway 106
> At Cherrylog Road I entered
> The '34 Ford without wheels,
> Smothered in kudzu,
> With a seat pulled out to run   5
> Corn whiskey down from the hills,
>
> And then from the other side
> Crept into an Essex
> With a rumble seat of red leather
> And then out again, aboard   10
> A blue Chevrolet, releasing
> The rust from its other color,

Reared up on three building blocks.
None had the same body heat;
I changed with them inward, toward   15
The weedy heart of the junkyard,
For I knew that Doris Holbrook
Would escape from her father at noon

And would come from the farm
To seek parts owned by the sun   20
Among the abandoned chassis,
Sitting in each in turn
As I did, leaning forward
As in a wild stock-car race

In the parking lot of the dead.   25
Time after time, I climbed in
And out the other side, like
An envoy or movie star
Met at the station by crickets.
A radiator cap raised its head,   30

Become a real toad or a kingsnake
As I neared the hub of the yard,
Passing through many states,
Many lives, to reach
Some grandmother's long Pierce-Arrow   35
Sending platters of blindness forth

From its nickel hubcaps
And spilling its tender upholstery
On sleepy roaches,
The glass panel in between   40
Lady and colored driver
Not all the way broken out,

The back-seat phone
Still on its hook.
I got in as though to exclaim,   45
"Let us go to the orphan asylum,
John; I have some old toys
For children who say their prayers."

I popped with sweat as I thought
I heard Doris Holbrook scrape   50

Like a mouse in the southern-state sun
That was eating the paint in blisters
From a hundred car tops and hoods.
She was tapping like code,

Loosening the screws,   55
Carrying off headlights,
Sparkplugs, bumpers,
Cracked mirrors and gear-knobs,
Getting ready, already,
To go back with something to show   60

Other than her lips' new trembling
I would hold to me soon, soon,
Where I sat in the ripped back seat
Talking over the interphone,
Praying for Doris Holbrook   65
To come from her father's farm

And to get back there
With no trace of me on her face
To be seen by her red-haired father
Who would change, in the squalling barn,   70
Her back's pale skin with a strop,
Then lay for me

In a bootlegger's roasting car
With a string-triggered 12-gauge shotgun
To blast the breath from the air.   75
Not cut by the jagged windshields,
Through the acres of wrecks she came
With a wrench in her hand,

Through dust where the blacksnake dies
Of boredom, and the beetle knows   80
The compost has no more life.
Someone outside would have seen
The oldest car's door inexplicably
Close from within:

I held her and held her and held her,   85
Convoyed at terrific speed
By the stalled, dreaming traffic around us,
So the blacksnake, stiff

With inaction, curved back
Into life, and hunted the mouse   90

With deadly overexcitement,
The beetles reclaimed their field
As we clung, glued together,
With the hooks of the seat springs
Working through to catch us red-handed   95
Amidst the gray breathless batting

That burst from the seat at our backs.
We left by separate doors
Into the changed, other bodies
Of cars, she down Cherrylog Road   100
And I to my motorcycle
Parked like the soul of the junkyard

Restored, a bicycle fleshed
With power, and tore off
Up Highway 106, continually   105
Drunk on the wind in my mouth,
Wringing the handlebar for speed,
Wild to be wreckage forever.

As the details of "Cherrylog Road" accumulate, they both give color to the narrative and help reveal the way the narrator feels about it. This is **tone**: the poet's attitude toward his material. Tone may be, for instance, approving, disapproving, pitying, admiring, ironic. Every element in a poem, including diction, imagery, and rhythm, will contribute to its tone, establishing a mood, conveying the poet's sense of his subject. Robert Frost's tone in "An Old Man's Winter Night" might be described as pitying. E. E. Cummings's tone in "next to of course god america i" is satiric. The tone of a poem may be mixed, as Howard Nemerov's "Learning by Doing" mingles the lyrical with the satiric or witty.

The setting in "Cherrylog Road," an auto junkyard, is itself a comment on what happens there. At its most favorable, this field of battered, functionless cars, of rust and ruin and desolation, is an ironic place for a meeting of lovers. The feeling of this "parking lot of the dead" is neither joyful nor pleasurable. "The '34 Ford without wheels" in stanza 1 is "smothered in kudzu" (a creeping vine that can literally bury fields and trees). The heat of the "southern-state sun / That was eating the paint in blisters / From a hundred car tops and hoods," the dust, the weeds, the "ripped" seats and "jagged windshields," the fear of Doris's father with his "strop" and his "string-triggered 12-gauge shotgun," all make the experience uncomfortable. The identification of the lovers with the cars and the place is suggested by the cars' "body heat" and by the junkyard's "weedy heart." The succession of animal images is a series of tonal footnotes: "cricket," "toad," "blacksnake," "beetles."

Most of the poem is devoted to the junkyard and the lovers' approach. Very little is shown of their meeting. We see hardly more than "The oldest car's door inexplicably / Close from within." The few details of the love-making aren't very pleasurable: "we clung, *glued* together, / With the *hooks* of the seat springs / Working through to *catch us red-handed*." There is something grimly static about "I held her and held her and held her." They are "Convoyed at terrific speed / By the stalled, dreaming traffic around us"—that is, at *no* speed. For, as in the pretend "wild stock-car race" of stanza 4, there is in reality no movement.

Doris has already been compared to a mouse in stanza 9: "I thought / I heard Doris Holbrook scrape / Like a mouse." Then, when in stanzas 15–16, in images that suggest sexual arousal, the love-making is compared in this way,

> So the blacksnake, stiff
> With inaction, curved back
> Into life, and hunted the mouse
>
> With deadly overexcitement

we have a pretty clear evaluation of the lovers' relationship. If Doris is the mouse, the narrator is the blacksnake which has earlier (stanza 14) been described as "[dying] of boredom." That "deadly overexcitement" perhaps tells something, too, of the success, or lack of success, of the love-making, as does the "gray breathless batting / That burst from the seat at our backs." Like the poem's title itself, a good many of the poem's details carry a sexual overtone. At the end, when the narrator mounts his motorcycle—"a bicycle *fleshed* / With power"—we may recall that it is a vehicle for one rider, not two. The final emotion seems not joyful or fulfilling, but desperate:

> Drunk on the wind in my mouth,
> Wringing the handlebar for speed,
> Wild to be wreckage forever.

The poem is not condemning this not very attractive "southern state" Romeo and Juliet, who are merely acting out their natures, who have no other models. The fault, it implies, lies with the society itself, which, in other details, the poem takes some care to characterize. It is a world of wealth and caste ("Lady and colored driver"), of stock-car races and fantasies of movie stars, of bootleggers and orphans, of condescending pieties ("some old toys / For children who say their prayers"). Since it seems to be on the narrator's mind, we can probably imagine that he had experienced the charity of some "grandmother" with a "long Pierce-Arrow" in the orphan asylum. The graveyard of abandoned cars seems a sort of underworld mirror of the values of the society in which the cars were once shiny and new. The voice of the poem is, of course, the narrator's, the boy's. But the carefully chosen and deployed details are the poet's implicit commentary.

One useful way of thinking of **visual detail** is as "camera work": camera angle or location, close-up or distant shot, fade-in or fade-out, panning, montage, and so on. Working with only the black squiggles of words on a page, the poet somehow controls what the reader sees with his or her mind's eye. Dickey makes us see the "car's door inexplicably / Close from within"; and in "the squalling barn" he keeps us at a distance, seeing the barn from the outside and only hearing Doris's (imagined) howling; then in "change . . . Her back's pale skin with a strop" he gives us a momentary close-up, not of the beating, but of its result. The poet no doubt manages such things intuitively, but it is good to be aware of the possibilities. Look at Roethke's "My Papa's Waltz" again (page 56), and note how cinematographically it is done. We never glimpse the father's face. We see his *hand* twice, however: close-ups of the hand on the boy's wrist, the battered knuckle; and of the "palm caked hard by dirt." We are also given a close-up of the buckle and the shirt. The camera is *at the boy's eye-level*, sees what he sees; and the man now speaking sees again what he saw as a boy. Note, incidentally, that he says "My right ear scraped a buckle," not the expected reverse: "A buckle scraped my right ear." How perfectly we see that he cannot blame the father for anything!

As another instance of a poet's camera work, consider again Shakespeare's quatrain:

> That time of year thou mayst in me behold
> When yellow leaves, or none, or few, do hang
> Upon those boughs which shake against the cold,
> Bare ruined choirs, where late the sweet birds sang.

Line 2 shows us first the yellow leaves of fall, then the later absence of leaves. It is a distant shot; we don't see a particular tree, simply yellow leaves in the aggregate. But notice how, as the camera seems to pan from "yellow leaves" to "none," it suddenly stops and moves in for a close-up shot: "or few." So close are we to a few leaves, we are probably seeing a single tree. The sense of loss is intensified, and the desolation of the few surviving leaves is greater than that produced by "none." "Boughs" in line 3 seems a close-up still, but we are now looking *up* into the branches of a particular tree. In line 4 the branches are compared to "Bare ruined choirs"; that is, choirlofts of a ruined and roofless church. For a moment we have the impression of standing inside such a church, looking upward through its rafters (like the branches) at the sky. The film word for the effect might be a "dissolve." It is only momentary, however; and in the last half of line 4 we are looking at the early winter boughs again, but this time with a superimposed shot of the same boughs in summer, with birds in them. The musical association between the songbirds and the choirlofts underlies the shift. Good description is not only a matter of choosing effective details but also of visualizing them in the most effective way, from the right angle and the right distance.

Telling a story always involves the projection of scenes into the reader's or hearer's mind. The poet's narrative methods, as in the thirteenth-century Scottish ballad "Sir Patrick Spence," often approximate the film techniques of dissolve, jump-cut, or superimposition. Notice how the anonymous poet, especially in the syntactical leap of lines 11–12, dissolves one scene into another. What the poet chooses to show—or *not* to show—is illuminating.

> The king sits in Dumferling toune,
>   Drinking the blude-reid wine:
> "O whar will I get guid sailor
>   To sail this schip of mine?"
>
> Up and spak an eldern knicht°,   *knight* 5
>   Sat at the kings richt kne:
> "Sir Patrick Spence is the best sailor
>   That sails upon the se."
>
> The king has written a braid° letter,   *broad, forthright*
>   And signed it wi' his hand,   10
> And sent it to Sir Patrick Spence,
>   Was walking on the sand.
>
> The first line that Sir Patrick red,
>   A loud lauch lauchèd° he;   *laugh, laughed*
> The next line that Sir Patrick red,   15
>   The teir° blinded his ee.   *tear*
>
> "O wha° is this has don this deid,   *who*
>   This ill deid don to me,
> To send me out this time o' the yeir,
>   To sail upon the se!   20
>
> "Mak haste, mak haste, my mirry men all,
>   Our guid schip sails the morne."
> "O say na sae°, my master deir,   *not so*
>   For I feir a deadlie storme.
>
> "Late late yestreen I saw the new moone,   25
>   Wi' the auld° moone in hir arme,   *old*

And I feir, I feir, my deir master,
   That we will cum to harme."

O our Scots nobles wer richt laith°   *loath*
   To weet° their cork-heild schoone°;   *wet; cork-heeled shoes* 30
Bot lang owre a'° the play wer playd,   *But long before all*
   Their hats they swam aboone°.   *above them*

O lang, lang may their ladies sit,
   Wi' their fans into their hand,
Or ere° they se Sir Patrick Spence   *before* 35
   Cum sailing to the land.

O lang, lang may the ladies stand,
   Wi' their gold kems° in their hair,   *combs*
Waiting for their ain° deir lords,   *own*
   For they'll se thame na mair.   40

Haf owre°, haf owre to Aberdour,   *halfway over*
   It's fiftie fadom° deip,   *fathom*
And thair lies guid Sir Patrick Spence,
   Wi' the Scots lords at his feit.

The sparks that make poems kindle are their particulars. "Go in fear of abstractions," Pound advises. In too many poems, words like *love, peace, nature, beauty,* or *truth* have the empty, pretentious ring of words in political speeches. Particulars are proof-positive in a way abstractions cannot be. On the other hand, the eighteenth-century critic Samuel Johnson warned the poet not to "count the streaks of the tulip." "Nothing," he said, "can please many, and please long, but just representations of general nature." Whether from particulars or from the merely novel, "the pleasures of sudden wonder are soon exhausted, and the mind can only repose on the stability of truth." Perhaps ours is a more skeptical age or at least an age less certain of the truth. Depending on abstractions to carry the poem with a rhetorical drum-roll—dadadaDA! Love! Truth!—isn't likely to succeed. Such loaded words are cop-outs; being preached at is not what we want from poems. Mere particulars, however, if they are not shaped to some larger meaning or do not illuminate some aspect of human experience, are as Dr. Johnson said "soon exhausted." Robinson Jeffers sums it up this way: "Permanent things, or things forever renewed like the grass and human passions, are the materials of poetry; and whoever speaks across the gap of a thousand years will understand that he has to speak of permanent things, and rather clearly too, or who would hear him?"

The "universality of the local" is William Carlos Williams's resolution of the matter: "all my life I have striven to emphasize it." His famous dictum "No ideas but in things" does not mean *no* ideas; rather, it means ideas arrived at, "universals of general applicability" discovered through particulars, the local. Much depends on his seeing the red wheelbarrow so that others "may the better see, touch, taste, enjoy—their own world *differing as it may* from mine." In that faith he wrote his little, ordinary urban scenes, of a cat, sparrows, an old woman munching plums, the houses of poor workingmen, or a girl who gets her nose busted when she goes out with the wrong bunch of fellows. "The guys from Paterson," Williams says, "beat up / the guys from Newark," and reminds us that once upon a time the guys from Greece beat up the guys from Troy over another beautiful woman, Helen. In the *Iliad* Homer wrote of gods and heroes, not ruffians from New Jersey. But, as Williams suggests in a prose passage in *Kora in Hell,* we should not miss the point.

> Giants in the dirt. The gods, the Greek gods, smothered in filth and ignorance. The race is scattered over the world. Where is its home? Find it if you've the genius. Here Hebe with a sick jaw and a cruel husband,—her mother left no place for a brain to grow. Herakles rowing boats on Berry's Creek! Zeus is a country doctor without a taste for coin jingling. Supper is of a bastard nectar on rare nights for they will come—the rare nights! The ground lifts and out sally the heroes of Sophocles, of Æschylus. They go seeping down into our hearts, they rain upon us and in the bog they sink again down through the white roots, down—to a saloon back of the railroad switch where they have that girl, you know, the one that should have been Venus by the lust that's in her. They've got her down there among the railroad men. A crusade couldn't rescue her. Up to jail—or call it down to Limbo—the Chief of Police our Pluto. It's all of the gods, there's nothing else worth writing of. They are the same men they always were—but fallen. Do they dance now, they that danced beside Helicon? They dance much as they did then, only, few have an eye for it, through the dirt and fumes.

Universals in particulars. Ideas in things. Not the one nor the other exclusively, but the relationship of the two. How would one sort out Robert Herrick's ideas from his things in "Delight in Disorder" without robbing both of their significance? Or Elizabeth Bishop's understanding of the child's experience in "First Death in Nova Scotia" from the objects that exemplify her confusion?

Marianne Moore is the master of mingling abstractions with particulars, to the renewal of both. Observe, in "Critics and Connoisseurs," how carefully she plays particulars and abstractions off each other, distinguishing between the admirable (because unconscious) fastidiousness of the child and the unfortunate (because conscious and self-serving) fastidiousness of the Ming "products," the battleshiplike swan, the foolish ant, and, of course, the critics and connoisseurs whom she addresses.

There is a great amount of poetry in unconscious
    fastidiousness. Certain Ming°   *Chinese dynasty*
        products, imperial floor coverings of coach-
wheel yellow, are well enough in their way but I have seen some-
        thing
            that I like better—a   5
                mere childish attempt to make an imperfectly bal-
                    lasted animal stand up,
                similar determination to make a pup
                    eat his meat from the plate.

I remember a swan under the willows in Oxford,   10
    with flamingo-colored, maple-
        leaflike feet. It reconnoitered like a battle-
ship. Disbelief and conscious fastidiousness were
            ingredients in its
                disinclination to move. Finally its hardihood was   15
                    not proof against its
                proclivity to more fully appraise such bits
                    of food as the stream

bore counter to it; it made away with what I gave it
    to eat. I have seen this swan and   20
        I have seen you; I have seen ambition without
understanding in a variety of forms. Happening to stand
        by an ant-hill, I have
            seen a fastidious ant carrying a stick north, south,
                east, west, till it turned on   25
            itself, struck out from the flower bed into the lawn,
                and returned to the point

from which it had started. Then abandoning the stick as
    useless and overtaxing its
        jaws with a particle of whitewash—pill-like but   30
heavy—it again went through the same course of procedure.
            What is
        there in being able
            to say that one has dominated the stream in an attitude of
                self-defense;
            in proving that one has had the experience   35
                of carrying a stick?

Just as the poem distinguishes between two kinds of fastidiousness, conscious
and unconscious, so it distinguishes (by showing us) two kinds of conscious

fastidiousness: the swan's false and snobbish reserve and the ant's false and pointless activity. Either way it is "ambition without / understanding," which comes as she notes "in a variety of forms." The child's fastidiousness is unconscious, devoted to whatever its object is. The poem's abstractions are thus sharp and useful, not soggy inflations. It is written in 9-line stanzas of approximate syllabics, with lines 1–3 and 8 having always 14, 8, 12, and 12 syllables. The usually slight variations in lines 4–7 and 9—perhaps resulting from revision of an exactly-counted early version—may serve as a formal reminder that there is little point in being too fastidious.

The difference between statement and implication is important. Abstractions *state* a meaning, and particulars may *imply* a meaning. Abstractions also, too easily, overstate, if only by drawing a conclusion and so precluding further consideration. Particulars, on the other hand, may too easily simply remain particulars and not generate a focused meaning. Moore's abstractions very precisely bring the particulars into focus without stopping thought about them. They guide, but do not force, and so leave something for the reader to do. Moore's preference is recorded: "I myself, however, would rather be told too little than too much." Or, as Frost says in "Mending Wall,"

> But it's not elves exactly, and I'd rather
> He said it for himself.

Clarity

A word on **obscurity** is needed. Nobody, I think, is in favor of it. Robert Francis puts it pithily: "It is not difficult to be difficult." If what you are saying is worth saying, nothing can be gained (and everything can be lost) by obscuring it. If what you are saying is not worth saying, no one is going to like you any better for making that fact hard to discover. Obscurity isn't mystery. Clear water, through which the stones on the bottom can be seen in precise detail, is far more mysterious than muddy water. Nor is obscurity the same as **ambiguity.** In the positive sense, ambiguity means that more than one meaning is possible simultaneously; and this can often be enriching, as it is when William Stafford says, in "Traveling through the Dark," "I thought hard for us all." He might mean "for us humans," including even the reader in the group of those concerned. He might also mean "for this little group of man, deer, and fawn." Or he might mean, too, because he has just said that he "could hear the wilderness listen," "the wilderness and the other creatures nearby" or even "all of nature." *And* he might mean, as well, the car with its "lowered parking lights" and its purring engine, which has ironically come to seem almost a living participant in the little red-lit scene. How to take the ambiguous phrase "for us all" is left to the reader. *All* the meanings may be relevant at once, like concentric circles; they are complementary, reenforcing one another. But when such meanings are contradictory—or just point in totally different directions—the result is obscurity. Given several exclusive choices, a reader is like the proverbial ass between two piles of hay. It couldn't make up its mind and so starved to death.

The beginning poet will find that being clear can be a task, for what seems obvious to the poet may be anything but obvious to the reader. I have often watched student poets writhe as class discussions about their poems came to silly conclusions about what they meant. The fault is sometimes the reader's, who isn't paying enough attention and misses a signal. But all too often the poet, in his or her ingenious solitude, has so tangled and hidden the signals in the underbrush that it is no wonder no one sees them. Even trying to be perfectly plain, the poet may, nonetheless, for some odd reason, accidentally end up not being clear.

One of the richnesses of poetry is that, like the circles from a stone dropped in water, its meanings ripple outward. Poems may well mean things the poets didn't intend, along, of course, with those they did intend. This is true so long as those circles of meaning, no matter how far from the poem's center, are concentric: those meanings must complement and not contradict or interfere with the central, literal meanings of the poem. With any poem that works in a personal way, a reader's response will inevitably call up his or her own experience, associations, and feelings. These will never be exactly like the poet's, just as one person can never hope to convey by description the *exact* mental picture of a particular place to another person. (Even pointing out a particular star to someone is hard.) So long as the reader's "poem" doesn't violate the poet's "poem," change its direction or alter its main shape, the transaction is proper. Indeed, it is what any poet hopes for: that a reader will make the poem truly his own or her own.

Visual details, description, are frequently the strengths of poems. They are the touches of color that bring an argument to life (Moore's wonderfully accurate "maple- / leaflike feet" of the swan). They make a scene vivid and circumstantially convincing (Dickey's "A blue Chevrolet, releasing / The rust from its other color, / Reared up on three building blocks"). Such details can be psychological or dramatic symbols (Bishop's loon or Dickey's blacksnake). Notice, however, that none, if any, of the poems we have been discussing is wholly or mainly descriptive. Purely descriptive poems, though we are all tempted to write them, are rare. Description by itself is likely to be boring, like slides of someone's trip to Europe. Description usually needs some dramatic or thematic thrust to carry it. A poem about the yellow iris in the garden will seldom be as interesting as the real yellow iris in the garden. Pound's advice: "Don't be 'viewy' . . . the painter can describe a landscape much better than you can."

Still, like a photograph of something we hope never to forget, description has its force. As William Carlos Williams says in "Poem,"

The rose fades
and is renewed again
by its seed, naturally
but where

save in the poem   5
shall it go
to suffer no diminution
of its splendor

QUESTIONS AND SUGGESTIONS

1. After studying a piece of bread or the sliced-open center of an orange for twenty minutes or so, write a description of it.

2. Write a poem about one of the following (or a similarly dumb thing). Put in a lot of particulars. See what you can make of it.

fried amethysts	*a squirrel's tail*	*hammers*
lion-breath	*hopscotch*	*four oranges*
blue	*counting bricks in a wall*	

3. Compare these poems (one eighteenth-century, one twentieth-century) on a similar subject, a child encountering a lamb. What inferences can be drawn about Starbuck's child?

The Lamb

WILLIAM BLAKE (1757–1827)

   Little Lamb, who made thee?
   Dost thou know who made thee?
Gave thee life, and bid thee feed
By the stream and o'er the mead;
Gave thee clothing of delight,   5
Softest clothing woolly bright;
Gave thee such a tender voice,
Making all the vales rejoice?
   Little Lamb, who made thee?
   Dost thou know who made thee?   10

Little Lamb, I'll tell thee!
Little Lamb, I'll tell thee:
He is calléd by thy name,
For he calls himself a Lamb,
He is meek and he is mild;   15
He became a little child.
I a child and thou a lamb,
We are calléd by his name.
Little Lamb, God bless thee!
Little Lamb, God bless thee!   20

Lamb

GEORGE STARBUCK (b. 1931)

Lamb, what makes you tick?
You got a wind-up, a Battery-Powered,
A flywheel, a plug-in, or what?
You made out of real Reelfur?
You fall out of the window you bust?   5
You shrink? Turn into a No-No?
Zip open and have pups?

I bet you better than that.
I bet you put out by some other outfit.
I bet you don't do nothin.   10
I bet you somethin to eat.

4. "Curse of the Cat Woman," by Edward Field (b. 1924), draws on an old horror movie for its subject. How would you describe the poem's tone? What phrases or images let us know the poem is humorous? Is there also, perhaps, a serious overtone?

It sometimes happens
that the woman you meet and fall in love with
is of that strange Transylvanian people
with an affinity for cats.

You take her to a restaurant, say, or a show,   5
on an ordinary date, being attracted
by the glitter in her slitty eyes and her catlike walk,
and afterwards of course you take her in your arms
and she turns into a black panther
and bites you to death.   10

Or perhaps you are saved in the nick of time
and she is tormented by the knowledge of her tendency:
That she daren't hug a man
unless she wants to risk clawing him up.

This puts you both in a difficult position—   15
panting lovers who are prevented from touching
not by bars but by circumstance:
You have terrible fights and say cruel things
for having the hots does not give you a sweet temper.

One night you are walking down a dark street   20
and hear the pad-pad of a panther following you,
but when you turn around there are only shadows,
or perhaps one shadow too many.

You approach, calling, "Who's there?"
and it leaps on you.   25
Luckily you have brought along your sword
and you stab it to death.

And before your eyes it turns into the woman you love,
her breast impaled on your sword,
her mouth dribbling blood saying she loved you   30
but couldn't help her tendency.

So death released her from the curse at last,
and you knew from the angelic smile on her dead face
that in spite of a life the devil owned,
love had won, and heaven pardoned her.   35

5. John Updike's "Dog's Death" tells a little domestic story. How are the necessary parts of the exposition and narrative arranged, ordered for effect? What details keep the tender subject from seeming sentimental? Does the latitude the poet has allowed himself in rhyming (or not rhyming) help to keep the poem from seeming pat?

She must have been kicked unseen or brushed by a car.
Too young to know much, she was beginning to learn
To use the newspapers spread on the kitchen floor
And to win, wetting there, the words, "Good dog! Good dog!"

We thought her shy malaise was a shot reaction.   5
The autopsy disclosed a rupture in her liver.
As we teased her with play, blood was filling her skin
And her heart was learning to lie down forever.

Monday morning, as the children were noisily fed
And sent to school, she crawled beneath the youngest's bed.   10
We found her twisted and limp but still alive.
In the car to the vet's, on my lap, she tried

To bite my hand and died. I stroked her warm fur
And my wife called in a voice imperious with tears.

Though surrounded by love that would have upheld her,   15
Nevertheless she sank and, stiffening, disappeared.

Back home, we found that in the night her frame,
Drawing near to dissolution, had endured the shame
Of diarrhoea and had dragged across the floor
To a newspaper carelessly left there. *Good dog.*   20

POEMS TO CONSIDER

The Black Snake   1979

MARY OLIVER   (b. 1935)

When the black snake
flashed onto the morning road,
and the truck could not swerve—
death, that is how it happens.

Now he lies looped and useless   5
as an old bicycle tire.
I stop the car
and carry him into the bushes.

He is as cool and gleaming
as a braided whip, he is as beautiful and quiet   10
as a dead brother.
I leave him under the leaves

and drive on, thinking
about *death:* its suddenness,
its terrible weight,   15
its certain coming. Yet under

reason burns a brighter fire, which the bones
have always preferred.
It is the story of endless good fortune.
It says to oblivion: not me!   20

It is the light at the center of every cell.
It is what sent the snake coiling and flowing forward
happily all spring through the green leaves before
he came to the road.

Van Busbeke Discovers the Tulip, 1550   1967

DEBORAH BLISS*

The Dutchman, whistling, paces
past the white mosque, the lapis

lazuli gleaming in its
ceiling. (He's had breakfast,

had time to think fondly of ancient   5
history, of ice-flaked milk

and Dutch buns in his library
looking over Leyden°.)   *city in Holland*

Here in a warmer land,
here in Ancyra°, boys   *Ankara, Turkey*   10

cool the water-skins
in the Paphlagonian° breeze.   *Black Sea province*

RES GESTAE DIVI AUGUSTI°:   *deeds of divine Augustus*
Van Busbeke, bending down

in the marble antechamber,   15
copies the Latin, benignly

nibbling his stylus. He pushes
his spectacles to the bridge

of his nose, sunburnt from the jaunt
up the River Sangarius. And soon   20

he hums absently (like
his daughters' knitting-songs

at home in Holland's watery
spring, by the slow fire).

At noon he discards his gear.   25

Across the muddy bazaars,
the goat pasture, the river,

he and his party, lunch-
bound, discover tulips.

Festival flowers, turbaned,   30
they pass in a green flotilla.

Oh *Proserpina°*—carmine—
Chrysolora°—yellow—

and *Pottebakker°*—white—   *varieties of tulip*
such souvenirs for Holland!   35

A Siding near Chillicothe   1966

RICHMOND LATTIMORE (b. 1906)

From the high deck of Santa Fe's El Capitan
cabs, sand-domes, stacks were seen above the box-car line:
old locomotives parked, antediluvian

in cruel progress, gone before us to that night
toward which we, sacks of memories, slide in blander airs,   5
and streamline our old eyes and thoughts from glass and flight.

Our ears, boys' ears, and eyes and hearts were haunted by
huge hoots of laughter down the dark: the glow: the steam
bulging in black and red up the spark-shot sky.

Now wheels, rails rust together, dews and sunshine eat   10
the iron grace: through silence their corrosion ticks
and drops in red dust, junk of grandeurs obsolete.

So, like old elephants who stumbled off to die
in their known place and rot their bulks from ivory bones,
the locomotives stood against the prairie sky.   15

Fern Hill   1946

DYLAN THOMAS   (1914–1953)

   Now as I was young and easy under the apple boughs
  About the lilting house and happy as the grass was green,
      The night above the dingle° starry,   *wooded valley*
        Time let me hail and climb
      Golden in the heydays of his eyes,   5
  And honoured among wagons I was prince of the apple towns
  And once below a time I lordly had the trees and leaves
        Trail with daisies and barley
  Down the rivers of the windfall light.

   And as I was green and carefree, famous among the barns   10
  About the happy yard and singing as the farm was home,
      In the sun that is young once only,
        Time let me play and be
      Golden in the mercy of his means,
  And green and golden I was huntsman and herdsman, the calves   15
Sang to my horn, the foxes on the hills barked clear and cold,
        And the sabbath rang slowly
      In the pebbles of the holy streams.

All the sun long it was running, it was lovely, the hay
Fields high as the house, the tunes from the chimneys, it was air   20
      And playing, lovely and watery
        And fire green as grass.
      And nightly under the simple stars
As I rode to sleep the owls were bearing the farm away,

All the moon long I heard, blessed among stables, the night-jars°   *birds* 25
    Flying with the ricks°, and the horses   *haystacks*
        Flashing into the dark.

And then to awake, and the farm, like a wanderer white
With the dew, come back, the cock on his shoulder: it was all
    Shining, it was Adam and maiden,   30
        The sky gathered again
    And the sun grew round that very day.
So it must have been after the birth of the simple light
In the first, spinning place, the spellbound horses walking warm
    Out of the whinnying green stable   35
        On to the fields of praise.

And honoured among foxes and pheasants by the gay house
Under the new made clouds and happy as the heart was long,
    In the sun born over and over,
        I ran my heedless ways,   40
    My wishes raced through the house high hay
And nothing I cared, at my sky blue trades, that time allows
In all his tuneful turning so few and such morning songs
    Before the children green and golden
        Follow him out of grace,   45

Nothing I cared, in the lamb white days, that time would take me
Up to the swallow thronged loft by the shadow of my hand,
    In the moon that is always rising,
        Nor that riding to sleep
    I should hear him fly with the high fields   50
And wake to the farm forever fled from the childless land.
Oh as I was young and easy in the mercy of his means,
        Time held me green and dying
    Though I sang in my chains like the sea.

7

Characters:
Dukes and Dying Ladies,
Pigs and Pedestrians

In every poem there is a voice, a **speaker**—someone who *says* whatever it is. Usually it is the poet. Often, however, it is not. In Emily Dickinson's famous "Because I Could Not Stop for Death," the speaker is in fact describing her own death, and so can hardly be the poet. The same is true of the speaker in "The Death of the Ball Turret Gunner" by Randall Jarrell (1914–1965). Jarrell, we know, was a control tower operator in World War II, not a belly gunner in a bomber, and was not killed by flak or fighters during a raid over Germany. In the same way, the Victorian Englishman Robert Browning was not the Renaissance Italian duke who speaks in "My Last Duchess" (page 179); nor is the twentieth-century American, Philip Levine, the brave and dignified pig on his way to market in "Animals Are Passing from Our Lives" (page 201). These speakers are **dramatic characters,** or *personae* (singular: **persona**), and the poems in which they appear are **dramatic monologues.**

More poems than may seem so are dramatic monologues. We understand the novelist's or the playwright's right to invent or imagine. Shakespeare was not an unhappy Danish prince, and the boy Sam Clemens never went down the Mississippi on a raft. The truth of *Hamlet* or *Huckleberry Finn* is not lessened by those facts. The poet's right to invent is equal. Just because a thought has come in the bathtub, the poet need not say so; he or she may well combine that true experience (the thought) with another (a seashore walk) to write a poem. Altering or recombining details of experience in order to make it more accessible is legitimate. Life is not art, and the essential truth of it can sometimes be best translated into art by tinkering.

In a sense *every* poem is a dramatic monologue. As in life we show different faces to different people or in different situations (at the beach, in church), so in writing we always, in some way or to some degree, change or adjust the voice we use. We present ourselves differently, quite naturally adopt somewhat different *personae*, wear different masks in different circumstances. To expect the poet in real life to be the speaker in his or her poems, or in a particular poem, is likely often to be disappointed. The voice in the poems may be gloomy, while the person we meet at a party, with a whiskey sour in hand, may seem cheery and fairly ordinary.

This goes against the grain of a very popular romantic myth of the poet— someone with disheveled hair and wild eyes, who is dying of consumption in a garret. The public likes that sort of image, and *we* like that sort of image. If poets are the lightning rods of the race, we like them to look as if they have been pretty regularly struck by lightning. In reality, though, poets look more or less like everyone else and aren't particularly more desperate persons than, say, surgeons or shipping clerks. If a poet wants to look "like a poet," there is probably no harm in it; but there may be a danger in carrying over a role or mask from art to real life, as perhaps Sylvia Plath did, whose suicide validated the poems in a way probably unnecessary.

It seems worth being aware, critically, that the poet and the speaker may not be identical. Even in a didactic poem like Pope's *An Essay on Criticism,* it is likely that the poet is, as lecturers do, using a voice more authoritative than his real conversational voice. (Pope was in fact only twenty-three when he donned the magisterial robes for this poem.) In such a sense all poems may be usefully thought of as dramatic monologues, as utterances, with an "utterer," a speaker, and an at least implicit circumstance in which the utterance is uttered. The **tone** of a poem may include, as well as the poet's attitude toward the subject, the poet's attitude toward himself or herself (or to the dramatic speaker) and the poet's attitude toward the reader or audience. Recall the confiding nudge—"eh, reader?"—in Louis Simpson's "On the Lawn at the Villa" (page 48). To be aware that these attitudes may alter from poem to poem (now knowing, now naïve, now questioning, now authoritative) is to know what can be controlled. The range of diction, the familiarity or formality, the choice of images, and so on, have much to do with the creation of character for the reader. For readers who do not know the poet personally, *every* poem involves the presentation of a character.

Because people are interesting, putting people into poems is one of the elementary ways of making poems interesting, whether the poet (or someone very like the poet) is the only character or the poet invents a whole cast, as Shakespeare, Browning, and Frost do. As in fiction, a character may be presented either in the first person or in the third person. The old man in Frost's "An Old Man's Winter Night" is presented in the third person ("he"), much as an omniscient novelist might present him. The old man is alone, no one else is there; but like an omniscient camera's eye the reader observes him clomping from room to room. The speaker in Dickey's "Cherrylog Road," however close to or far from Dickey himself, is presented in the first person ("I"); that is, he is allowed to present himself in his "own" words. X. J. Kennedy uses both techniques in presenting the drunken lady in the next poem. The speaker in the first and last stanzas describes her from the outside and recounts the accompanying action, but the lady speaks for herself in the main portion of the poem.

In a Prominent Bar in Secaucus One Day

To the tune of "The Old Orange Flute"
or the tune of "Sweet Betsy from Pike"

In a prominent bar in Secaucus° one day
Rose a lady in skunk with a topheavy sway,
Raised a knobby red finger—all turned from their beer—
While with eyes bright as snowcrust she sang high and clear:

"Now who of you'd think from an eyeload of me   5
That I once was a lady as proud as could be?
Oh I'd never sit down by a tumbledown drunk
If it wasn't, my dears, for the high cost of junk.

"All the gents used to swear that the white of my calf
Beat the down of the swan by a length and a half.   10
In the kerchief of linen I caught to my nose
Ah, there never fell snot, but a little gold rose.

"I had seven gold teeth and a toothpick of gold,
My Virginia cheroot was a leaf of it rolled
And I'd light it each time with a thousand in cash—   15
Why the bums used to fight if I flicked them an ash.

"Once the toast of the Biltmore°, the belle of the Taft°,
I would drink bottle beer at the Drake°, never draft,
And dine at the Astor° on Salisbury steak
With a clean tablecloth for each bite I did take.   20

"In a car like the Roxy° I'd roll to the track,   *movie palace*
A steel-guitar trio, a bar in the back,
And the wheels made no noise, they turned over so fast,
Still it took you ten minutes to see me go past.

"When the horses bowed down to me that I might choose,   25
I bet on them all, for I hated to lose.
Now I'm saddled each night for my butter and eggs
And the broken threads race down the backs of my legs.

"Let you hold in mind, girls, that your beauty must pass
Like a lovely white clover that rusts with its grass.   30
Keep your bottoms off barstools and marry you young
Or be left—an old barrel with many a bung.

"For when time takes you out for a spin in his car
You'll be hard-pressed to stop him from going too far
And be left by the roadside, for all your good deeds,   35
Two toadstools for tits and a face full of weeds."

All the house raised a cheer, but the man at the bar
Made a phonecall and up pulled a red patrol car
And she blew us a kiss as they copped her away
From that prominent bar in Secaucus, N.J.   40

1 *Secaucus:* town in the industrial marsh of New Jersey, near New York City.   17,
18, 19 *Biltmore, Taft, Drake, Astor:* once fashionable hotels in New York.

Part of the fun (and of the pathos) in this portrait comes of our recognizing
that, however much truth is mingled with her exaggeration, she was never quite
so much a lady as she believes. Her language tells us about her world: "All the
gents used to swear that the white of my calf / *Beat* the down of a swan *by a
length and a half.*" Her ideas of elegance fall painfully short: bottle beer in preference to draft and, as an instance of fine dining, the humdrum Salisbury steak.
In this way the poet communicates *around* what she is saying so that we perceive her as he wants us to, not as she perceives herself. The irony on her part
is unintentional; the irony on the poet's part isn't. We end up admiring her less
for the reason she gives (that she was once a grand lady) than for her blarney
and her bravery of spirit. Like Chaucer's not very different Wife of Bath, she is
indomitably human.

Irony

Irony is saying one thing and meaning another, as when you drop a pile of
dishes and someone says, "Beautiful!" Notice how Robert Browning
(1812–1889), who never says a word, uses unintentional irony to characterize

the villainous Duke of Ferrara (who speaks the whole poem) in "My Last Duchess":

That's my last duchess painted on the wall,
Looking as if she were alive. I call
That piece a wonder, now: Frà Pandolf's hands
Worked busily a day, and there she stands.
Will't please you sit and look at her? I said   5
"Frà Pandolf" by design, for never read
Strangers like you that pictured countenance,
The depth and passion of its earnest glance,
But to myself they turned (since none puts by
The curtain I have drawn for you, but I)   10
And seemed as they would ask me, if they durst,
How such a glance came there; so, not the first
Are you to turn and ask thus. Sir, 'twas not
Her husband's presence only, called that spot
Of joy into the Duchess' cheek: perhaps   15
Frà Pandolf chanced to say "Her mantle laps
"Over my lady's wrist too much," or "Paint
"Must never hope to reproduce the faint
"Half-flush that dies along her throat": such stuff
Was courtesy, she thought, and cause enough   20
For calling up that spot of joy. She had
A heart—how shall I say?—too soon made glad,
Too easily impressed; she liked whate'er
She looked on, and her looks went everywhere.
Sir, 'twas all one! My favor at her breast,   25
The dropping of the daylight in the West,
The bough of cherries some officious fool
Broke in the orchard for her, the white mule
She rode with round the terrace—all and each
Would draw from her alike the approving speech,   30
Or blush, at least. She thanked men—good! but thanked
Somehow—I know not how—as if she ranked
My gift of a nine-hundred-years-old name
With anybody's gift. Who'd stoop to blame
This sort of trifling? Even had you skill   35
In speech—which I have not—to make your will
Quite clear to such an one, and say, "Just this
"Or that in you disgusts me; here you miss,
"Or there exceed the mark"—and if she let
Herself be lessoned so, nor plainly set   40

Her wits to yours, forsooth, and made excuse,
—E'en then would be some stooping; and I choose
Never to stoop. Oh sir, she smiled, no doubt,
Whene'er I passed her; but who passed without
Much the same smile? This grew; I gave commands;   45
Then all smiles stopped together. There she stands
As if alive. Will't please you rise? We'll meet
The company below, then. I repeat,
The Count your master's known munificence
Is ample warrant that no just pretense   50
Of mine for dowry will be disallowed;
Though his fair daughter's self, as I avowed
At starting, is my object. Nay, we'll go
Together down, sir. Notice Neptune, though,
Taming a sea-horse, thought a rarity,   55
Which Claus of Innsbruck cast in bronze for me!

The Duke is addressing the agent of a Count, whose daughter he wants to marry and make his next Duchess. He is on his best behavior. Nonetheless, we quickly see his domineering ("since none puts by / The curtain I have drawn for you, but I" or "if they durst"); his pride ("My gift of a nine-hundred-years-old name"); his arrogance ("and I choose / Never to stoop"); his greed ("no just pretense / Of mine for dowry"); and, of course, the falseness of his jealousy, for in fact he can say nothing that does not suggest that his last Duchess was young and innocent and charming. The agent is not his equal, but the Duke declines precedence—"Nay, we'll go / Together down, sir"—in a gesture that is meant to appear democratic and in fact appears calculated and false. He unintentionally sums up his unpleasant purpose: "his fair daughter's self, as I avowed / At starting, is my object." *Object.* Like the painting, and like the little Neptune "cast in bronze for me!" The pun is Browning's, of course, speaking around the Duke's monologue since the Duke means only "my aim, my objective."

Another monologue in which the reader is led to perceive more, or differently, than the speaker is "I Heard a Fly Buzz" by Emily Dickinson (1830–1886):

I heard a Fly buzz—when I died—
The Stillness in the Room
Was like the Stillness in the Air—
Between the Heaves of Storm—

The Eyes around—had wrung them dry—   5
And Breaths were gathering firm
For that last Onset—when the King
Be witnessed—in the Room—

I willed my Keepsakes—Signed away
What portion of me be   10
Assignable—and then it was
There interposed a Fly—

With Blue—uncertain stumbling Buzz—
Between the light—and me—
And then the Windows failed—and then   15
I could not see to see—

The first three stanzas present a typical deathbed scene. The room is quiet with
the ominous silence that sometimes falls between the "Heaves of Storm," an
image that suggests the interrupted agonies of the dying speaker. The dashes and
the emphatic capital letters give an impression of breathless portentousness, and
there is already a curious abstractness about the speaker's perceptions. The rela-
tives and perhaps friends in the room are mentioned impersonally only as "Eyes
around" and "Breaths." They and the speaker alike await the moment of death,
"when the King / Be witnessed—in the Room." Whether the "King" is God or
more simply death, the expectation is a large and dramatic one: "King." But no
majestic event occurs: only a fly appears, that unpleasant insect drawn to carrion.

The confusion of the speaker's senses is suggested by her application of
visual qualities to a sound: "With Blue—uncertain stumbling Buzz." (This is an
example of **synesthesia**: the perception, or description, of one sense modality in
terms of another, as when we describe a voice as velvety or sweet.) Impossibly
for so small a creature, the fly seems to "interpose" "Between the light—and
me." In line 15 the speaker, still trying to account for her loss of sight outside
herself, blames the "Windows," reporting oddly that they "failed." The final
line records the still flickering consciousness inside the already senseless body
before it, too, goes out like the speck of afterlight on a television screen: "I
could not see to see—" The final dash suggests the simple tailing off of awareness, without resolution. The grand expectation of "the King" has been ironically foreclosed by the merely physical, naturalistic collapse of sense and
consciousness. The dying speaker never understood.

Irony comes in as many flavors as ice cream. **Verbal irony** involves a
discrepancy between what is *said* and what is *meant*. To say "Lovely day!" when
the weather is awful is ironic. Irony of this sort may range from poking fun to
sarcasm. Dick's comment, in "A True Maid" by Matthew Prior (1664–1721), is
ironic in this way:

No, no; for my virginity,
    When I lose that, says Rose, I'll die;
Behind the elms, last night, cried Dick,
    Rose, were you not extremely sick?

He seems to express sympathy but is really rebuking her, exposing the false piety of her remark. Verbal irony, when it involves understatement, may also be serious and tender, as in X. J. Kennedy's "Little Elegy" (subtitled "for a child who skipped rope"):

> Here lies resting, out of breath,
> Out of turns, Elizabeth
> Whose quicksilver toes not quite
> Cleared the whirring edge of night.
>
> Earth whose circles round us skim,   5
> Till they catch the lightest limb,
> Shelter now Elizabeth
> And for her sake trip up Death.

Saying that she merely "lies resting, out of breath, / Out of turns," meaning that she is dead, is ironic understatement, touching in its restraint and in its gentle reminder of what death does to such youthful vitality.

Instances of irony may also be distinguished by whether it is deliberate or accidental. As in the last example, the speaker may be quite conscious of it. Or, as in "My Last Duchess" or "I Heard a Fly Buzz," the speaker may be unconscious of the irony. The term **dramatic irony** is used when the speaker or character acts in a certain way because he is unaware of something the reader or audience knows. Hamlet does not kill the King when he is at prayer, lest the King, repentant and thus in a state of grace, go straight to heaven. Hamlet does not know what the audience has been shown: that the King, burdened with guilt because he cannot regret his crime, is unable to pray.

Life itself is often ironic; that is, things turn out in unexpected ways, surprising us by the discrepancy between appearance and reality. "Richard Cory" by E. A. Robinson (1869–1935), exemplifies such **situational irony**:

> Whenever Richard Cory went down town,
> We people on the pavement looked at him;
> He was a gentleman from sole to crown,
> Clean favored, and imperially slim.
>
> And he was always quietly arrayed,   5
> And he was always human when he talked;
> But still he fluttered pulses when he said,
> "Good-morning," and he glittered when he walked.
>
> And he was rich—yes, richer than a king—
> And admirably schooled in every grace;   10

In fine, we thought that he was everything
To make us wish that we were in his place.

So on we worked, and waited for the light,
And went without the meat, and cursed the bread;
And Richard Cory, one calm summer night,   15
Went home and put a bullet through his head.

Robert Frost's "Home Burial" (page 196), a poem rich in irony, has in it perhaps as much about the relationship of a man and a woman as any poem in English does. Like a short story, it presents a complete scene, telling as much about the couple as we could want to know. There is truth on the husband's side, as there is truth on the wife's. His accidentally ironic comment on the "little graveyard" where their dead child is buried—"Not so much larger than a bedroom, is it?"—and her accidentally ironic overtones as she describes him digging the child's grave—

"I saw you from that very window there,
Making the gravel leap and leap in air,
Leap up, like that, like that, and land so lightly
And roll back down the mound beside the hole.
I thought, Who is that man? I didn't know you.
And I crept down the stairs and up the stairs
To look again, and still your spade kept lifting . . ."

—lead to the inexplicable sexuality at the heart of their quarrel. Randall Jarrell's essay on the poem in *The Third Book of Criticism,* as fine as commentary can ever be, shows how Frost has packed every gesture, every word with dramatic significance. Every object in the poem—the stairs, the window, the spade, the mound and hole of the grave-digging, the door—become symbols to help interpret the characters and their action and reaction.

Symbols

A **symbol** is something that stands for or represents something else, like the *x* in an algebraic equation or the stars and stripes in the American flag. In literature a symbol stands for or represents something, usually thematic and intangible, beyond the literal. Symbols may be fairly minor and local to a particular poem, like the mouse and blacksnake in "Cherrylog Road" that symbolize the lovers or the auto junkyard that perhaps symbolizes the society in which they live. Symbols may be more general and open-ended, as the highly specific wheelbarrow in William Carlos Williams's "The Red Wheelbarrow" symbolizes labor, fertility, or even the importance of seeing the world in a certain way. Some things, from frequent use, carry larger symbolic associations. In Williams's "Poem" ("The rose fades . . ."), for instance, we understand that he is not talking specifically about the *rose,* but about all the transitory and beautiful things for which the rose is a traditional symbol, as in Robert Herrick's "Gather ye rosebuds while ye may, / Old time is still a-flying; / And this same flower that smiles today / Tomorrow will be dying," which is addressed "To the Virgins, to Make Much of Time."

The value of symbols lies in their resonance. Because their meaning is not specifically stated, it can spiral out like circles in water; or, like a beam of light, it can illuminate anything that lies in its path, at whatever distance. It may symbolize any number of situations of the same kind. Equally, actions and events may become symbols. Although the poem is entirely particular, the child's mysterious encounter with death in Elizabeth Bishop's "First Death in Nova Scotia" becomes in some sense symbolic of all instances of that common experience. The man and the dead doe in William Stafford's "Traveling through the Dark" perhaps symbolize the ambiguous values of technology as it impinges on the natural world. In this way the "local," in Williams's phrase, the perfectly particular, made vivid enough, becomes universal. Any poem that works, that communicates its excitement, despair, or confusion, does so because it achieves a symbolic resonance. The poet will find that he has symbols aplenty. Things *become* symbolic as he works with them, the less self-consciously, the better. Imposing symbols invariably makes them ring false.

Some poems are deliberately, primarily symbolic, like Robert Frost's familiar "The Road Not Taken."

> Two roads diverged in a yellow wood,
> And sorry I could not travel both
> And be one traveler, long I stood
> And looked down one as far as I could
> To where it bent in the undergrowth;   5
>
> Then took the other, as just as fair,
> And having perhaps the better claim,
> Because it was grassy and wanted wear;
> Though as for that the passing there
> Had worn them really about the same,   10
>
> And both that morning equally lay
> In leaves no step had trodden black.
> Oh, I kept the first for another day!
> Yet knowing how way leads on to way,
> I doubted if I should ever come back.   15

I shall be telling this with a sigh
Somewhere ages and ages hence:
Two roads diverged in a wood, and I—
I took the one less traveled by,
And that has made all the difference.   20

The difference between two paths in a real wood, we understand, isn't likely to
be very important. Certainly it would not have the significance the poem
claims: "And that has made all the difference." Paths in a wood are pretty
much alike, and if the speaker by chance had come upon a pot of gold on this
particular walk, he could have told us. In a real wood it is possible to return
another day and find little changed.

So we sense at once that "The Road Not Taken" is primarily symbolic. It
is a poem about the nature of choice, and the significance claimed ("all the
difference") makes clear that it is about some sort of life-choice. The difference
comes from the speaker's having taken "the one less traveled by." His criterion
in choosing is nonconformity, individuality, an Emersonian self-reliance, "doing
his own thing"—however a reader wants to put it. The poem seems a simple
and proud affirmation.

But Frost is rarely as simple as he seems, and he certainly isn't here. The
last two lines, which contain the poem's very smug summing up, are essentially
untrue. The speaker wanted to choose the less traveled road. But the choice was
not easy ("long I stood"), and the other road was desirable enough ("sorry I
could not travel both"). Seven lines (6–12) are devoted to the difficulty of
making out which of the two was in fact less traveled. In the wood the speaker's
ambivalence was nearly total:

Then took the other, as *just as fair*,
And having *perhaps* the better claim,
Because it was grassy and wanted wear;
Though as for that the passing there

Had worn them *really about the same*,
And both that morning *equally* lay
In leaves no step had trodden black.

If there was any difference at all, it was marginal, and the speaker's best
conclusion was that both "equally lay / In leaves no step had trodden black."
When he says decisively, in the last lines, "Two roads diverged in a wood, and
I— / I took the one less traveled by," we must plainly doubt it.

We must also doubt the last line: "And that has made all the difference."
Since the two roads were nearly indistinguishable, it seems unlikely that the
result could be very different. In any case, the speaker has not traveled the
other road and, as "way leads on to way," he presumably will not. He knows

nothing about "the road not taken"—whether it would finally have been better or worse, or would have made any difference at all. He can't know.

One further peculiarity of the poem is helpful in understanding it. There are three time periods in it: time past, in the wood when the choice was made; time present, in which the poem is "spoken"; and time future, predicted in stanza 4. Why is time future necessary? Why is it not sufficient to report the choice in the past and to affirm in the present the "difference" it made? The poem's last three lines could replace the last three lines of stanza 3, in effect, and that would be that.

The solution to the puzzle, I think, is that the speaker is too close to the present (and to the choice) to make the claim of the last two lines. He knows that the choice was nearly arbitrary and that the principle he wanted to live by was of little use. Like the time in "Acquainted with the Night," the choice was "neither wrong nor right" in a universe that, for good or ill, will not bend to human wishes. But that is a moral relativity no one can bear. The poem's time future reflects, in spite of his experience, the speaker's need to believe that choice makes a difference, that one is responsible for outcomes. The poem is not called "The Road Taken," as we might expect from the assurance of the last two lines, but "The Road *Not* Taken." The sigh is perhaps all that will remain to mark the fact that, like most of us, the speaker truly needs to improve the past in retelling it.

Dramatic Material

The variety available to the poet for handling dramatic material is wide. Consider two poems on essentially the same subject, an automobile accident: "Auto Wreck" by Karl Shapiro (b. 1913) and "The Weather Is Brought to You" by J. D. Reed (b. 1940). In both poems the speaker comes upon the aftermath of an accident at night and reports it vividly. Their themes are, I think, very similar. First, "Auto Wreck":

Its quick soft silver bell beating, beating,
And down the dark one ruby flare
Pulsing out red light like an artery,
The ambulance at top speed floating down
Past beacons and illuminated clocks   5
Wings in a heavy curve, dips down,
And brakes speed, entering the crowd.
The doors leap open, emptying light;
Stretchers are laid out, the mangled lifted
And stowed into the little hospital.   10

Then the bell, breaking the hush, tolls once,
And the ambulance with its terrible cargo
Rocking, slightly rocking, moves away,
As the doors, an afterthought, are closed.

We are deranged, walking among the cops   15
Who sweep glass and are large and composed.
One is still making notes under the light.
One with a bucket douches ponds of blood
Into the street and gutter.
One hangs lanterns on the wrecks that cling,   20
Empty husks of locusts, to iron poles.

Our throats were tight as tourniquets,
Our feet were bound with splints, but now,
Like convalescents intimate and gauche,
We speak through sickly smiles and warn   25
With the stubborn saw of common sense,
The grim joke and the banal resolution.
The traffic moves around with care,
But we remain, touching a wound
That opens to our richest horror.   30
Already old, the question Who shall die?
Becomes unspoken Who is innocent?

For death in war is done by hands;
Suicide has cause and stillbirth, logic;
And cancer, simple as a flower, blooms.   35
But this invites the occult mind,
Cancels our physics with a sneer,
And spatters all we knew of denouement
Across the expedient and wicked stones.

The scene is urban. In the first stanza we see the old-fashioned ambulance
(with a bell instead of a siren) arrive, take on "its terrible cargo," and depart.
Everything is strangely depersonalized. We never see the ambulance's driver or
attendants; the machine itself, rather than the people, seems the actor: "The
doors leap open . . . are closed." Passives only imply the human actions:
"Stretchers are laid out, the mangled lifted / And stowed. . . ." Except for the
one word "mangled," nothing is said of the victims. The grisly life-or-death
reality is suggested only indirectly by images: the ambulance bell is "beating,
beating" like a heart, and the ambulance warning-flasher is "Pulsing out red
light like an artery." The ambulance seems less to drive than to fly—"floating

down," it "Wings in a heavy curve, dips down," which perhaps suggests its angelic function. The hill it descends registers only impressionistically in the "beacons and illuminated clocks" it passes.

In stanza 2 the speaker, one of the crowd of onlookers (for whom he speaks), makes the shock of witnessing the experience explicit: "We are deranged." By contrast, the cops are "large and composed," doing their jobs, apparently impervious to the horror. We learn almost offhandedly that more than one car was involved: "the wrecks that cling, / Empty husks of locusts, to iron poles." In stanza 3 the onlookers' shock is acknowledged in displaced images similar to the "beating, beating" and "red light like an artery" of stanza 1: "Our throats were tight as tourniquets, / Our feet were bound with splints." The onlookers' internalization of what they are seeing is clear. Now, with the worst over, they are "Like convalescents" and begin to speak to one another with the familiarity of survivors: "intimate and gauche." Yet they "remain, touching a wound." The question has become more than the random suddenness of the accidental ("Who shall die?"): it is *why?* Having presented the experience, in stanza 4 the speaker sums up the onlookers' "wound." Other kinds of death have reasons, are logical; but accidental death "Cancels our physics with a sneer," destroying not only our ideas of cause and effect but also our deepest need for appropriate dramatic conclusion ("denouement"). So cruel is accident that the simply amoral stones must seem "wicked." Shapiro's speaker makes the poem's theme explicit.

Here, for contrast, is J. D. Reed's "The Weather Is Brought to You":

It is 64° in Devereaux,
and a volunteer pumper
hoses gas from the expressway.

Troopers with the faces of mandrills
hobnail over crushed metal,   5
using big flashlights like pointers
in a planetarium.

Sprockets dangle in the weeds,
torn radiators gurgle,

and the dead wait under wool blankets,   10
expiring
like tungsten filament
in a hissing, broken headlight.

Reed's speaker, also an onlooker, mainly reports what he sees. Unlike the speaker in "Auto Wreck," he does not describe his feelings; and the poem's theme is never directly stated. The title and first line suggest that he is a driver, listening to his car radio, who comes upon and passes the accident scene slowly. The simple ", / and" of lines 1–2, linking the weather report he has been hearing to the accident scene, suggests how casually and unexpectedly he comes upon it. He sees the fire truck in the highway first, as he approaches; then the wrecks being inspected by the troopers; then, nearer, the sprockets "in the weeds" and the bodies by the side of the highway. The order of the details indicates the succession of the speaker's notice. What he sees is as impressionistic as the first stanza of "Auto Wreck." The verb "hobnail" (of their boots) suggests the unfeeling crudeness of the troopers' job, and the image of their "big flashlights like pointers / in a planetarium" suggests the merely academic precision of their inspection. They seem alien to the human, "with the faces of mandrills," animal and unsympathetic; and presumably the red and blue flashers of the emergency vehicles also give them the colors characteristic of mandrills' faces. Close-ups show the sprockets, which "dangle in the weeds," and then "the dead." Ironically they are covered by "wool blankets," whose warmth is irrelevant.

The report is less factual than it seems. Oddly, the victims are both already "the dead" and "expiring," as if the speaker is unsure. Also oddly, the burning out of the headlight in the last lines—

like tungsten filament
in a hissing, broken headlight

—cannot be part of the scene. This would have occurred much earlier, immediately with the crash and long before the policemen and fire truck arrived. The detail enters the poem as a *comparison* for how the "dead" are "expiring." Even the comparison of the human to the mechanical seems odd, reenforced by the displaced attribution to the "torn" radiators of the throat sound "gurgle." Much of this is no doubt due to the strangeness of suddenly coming upon the scene. But the displacements are not unlike those in "Auto Wreck," and the speaker's feelings—surprise, strangeness, and awe at the least—may be inferred.

The poem's title is, of course, an announcer's tag, to be completed with the name of an advertiser. Isolated here, however, it suggests more: the *weather*, not just the weather report, is brought to us by . . . ? Accidents, like the weather, are things that simply occur, are imposed on us seemingly by forces of which we can have little comprehension. The comparison of the flashlights to "pointers in a planetarium," in this context, implies more than it might otherwise. The universe is inexplicable; we understand it only indirectly and with difficulty. After two sentence-stanzas, even the breaking of the last sentence into two stanzas may suggest the speaker's discomposure, if not hesitation, in coming to the human center of the accident. That he actively imagines the "hissing, broken headlight" implies that his feelings are anything but passive. Unlike the theme of "Auto Wreck," the theme of Reed's poem is left unstated, for the reader to gather as he repeats the experience in his mind's eye.

QUESTIONS AND SUGGESTIONS

1. Consider the dramatic implications in these poems. Who is the speaker? What do we know about him? What is the situation in which we imagine the poem was spoken?

a) *The Flea*

JOHN DONNE (1572–1631)

Mark but this flea, and mark in this
How little that which thou deny'st me is;
It sucked me first, and now sucks thee,
And in this flea our two bloods mingled be;
Thou know'st that this cannot be said   5
A sin, nor shame, nor loss of maidenhead,
   Yet this enjoys before it woo,
    And pampered swells with one blood made of two,
    And this, alas, is more than we would do.

Oh stay, three lives in one flea spare,   10
Where we almost, yea more than, married are.
This flea is you and I, and this
Our marriage bed, and marriage temple is;
Though parents grudge, and you, we're met
And cloistered in these living walls of jet.   15
   Though use° make you apt to kill me,   *habit*
    Let not to that, self-murder added be,
    And sacrilege, three sins in killing three.

Cruel and sudden, hast thou since
Purpled thy nail in blood of innocence?   20
Wherein could this flea guilty be,
Except in that drop which it sucked from thee?
Yet thou triumph'st, and say'st that thou
Find'st not thyself, nor me, the weaker now;
   'Tis true; then learn how false, fears be;   25
    Just so much honor, when thou yield'st to me,
    Will waste, as this flea's death took life from thee.

b) *The Bishop Orders His Tomb at St. Praxed's Church*
Rome, 15—

ROBERT BROWNING (1812–1889)

Vanity, saith the preacher, vanity!°   *reference to* Ecclesiastes 1:2
Draw round my bed: is Anselm keeping back?
Nephews—sons mine . . . ah God, I know not!° Well—   *that is, illegitimate sons*

She, men would have to be your mother once,
Old Gandolf envied me, so fair she was!   5
What's done is done, and she is dead beside,
Dead long ago, and I am Bishop since,
And as she died so must we die ourselves,
And thence ye may perceive the world's a dream.
Life, how and what is it? As here I lie   10
In this state-chamber, dying by degrees,
Hours and long hours in the dead night, I ask
"Do I live, am I dead?" Peace, peace seems all.
Saint Praxed's ever was the church for peace;
And so, about this tomb of mine. I fought   15
With tooth and nail to save my niche, ye know:
—Old Gandolf cozened me, despite my care;
Shrewd was that snatch from out the corner South
He graced his carrion with, God curse the same!
Yet still my niche is not so cramped but thence   20
One sees the pulpit o' the epistle-side°,   *right side of the altar*
And somewhat of the choir, those silent seats,
And up into the aery dome where live
The angels, and a sunbeam's sure to lurk:
And I shall fill my slab of basalt there,   25
And 'neath my tabernacle take my rest,
With those nine columns round me, two and two,
The odd one at my feet where Anselm stands:
Peach-blossom marble all, the rare, the ripe
As fresh-poured red wine of a mighty pulse.   30
—Old Gandolf with his paltry onion-stone°,   *cheap marble*
Put me where I may look at him! True peach,
Rosy and flawless: how I earned the prize!
Draw close: that conflagration of my church
—What then? So much was saved if aught were missed!   35
My sons, ye would not be my death? Go dig
The white-grape vineyard where the oil-press stood,
Drop water gently till the surface sink,
And if ye find . . . Ah God, I know not, I! . . .
Bedded in store of rotten fig-leaves soft,   40
And corded up in a tight olive-frail°,   *basket*
Some lump, ah God, of *lapis lazuli*,
Big as a Jew's head cut off at the nape,
Blue as a vein o'er the Madonna's breast . . .
Sons, all have I bequeathed you, villas, all,   45
That brave Frascati° villa with its bath,   *luxurious suburb of Rome*
So, let the blue lump poise between my knees,
Like God the Father's globe on both his hands
Ye worship in the Jesu Church so gay,
For Gandolf shall not choose but see and burst!   50

Swift as a weaver's shuttle fleet our years:
Man goeth to the grave, and where is he?
Did I say basalt for my slab, sons? Black—
'Twas ever antique-black I meant! How else
Shall ye contrast my frieze to come beneath?   55
The bas-relief in bronze ye promised me,
Those Pans and Nymphs ye wot° of, and perchance   *know*
Some tripod, thyrsus°, with a vase or so,   *staff associated with Bacchus*
The Saviour at his sermon on the mount,
Saint Praxed in a glory, and one Pan   60
Ready to twitch the Nymph's last garment off,
And Moses with the tables . . . but I know
Ye mark me not! What do they whisper thee,
Child of my bowels, Anselm? Ah, ye hope
To revel down my villas while I gasp   65
Bricked o'er with beggar's mouldy travertine°   *cheap stone*
Which Gandolf from his tomb-top chuckles at!
Nay, boys, ye love me—all of jasper, then!
'Tis jasper ye stand pledged to, lest I grieve.
My bath must needs be left behind, alas!   70
One block, pure green as a pistachio-nut,
There's plenty jasper somewhere in the world—
And have I not Saint Praxed's ear to pray
Horses for ye, and brown Greek manuscripts,
And mistresses with great smooth marbly limbs?   75
—That's if ye carve my epitaph aright,
Choice Latin, picked phrase, Tully's° every word,
No gaudy ware like Gandolf's second line—
Tully, my masters? Ulpian° serves his need!
And then how I shall lie through centuries,   80
And hear the blessed mutter of the mass,
And see God made and eaten all day long,
And feel the steady candle-flame, and taste
Good strong thick stupefying incense-smoke!
For as I lie here, hours of the dead night,   85
Dying in state and by such slow degrees,
I fold my arms as if they clasped a crook°,   *a bishop's ceremonial crozier*
And stretch my feet forth straight as stone can point,
And let the bedclothes, for a mortcloth°, drop   *pall*
Into great laps and folds of sculptor's-work: 90
And as yon tapers dwindle, and strange thoughts
Grow, with a certain humming in my ears,
About the life before I lived this life,
And this life too, popes, cardinals and priests,
Saint Praxed° at his sermon on the mount,   95
Your tall pale mother with her talking eyes,
And new-found agate urns as fresh as day,

And marble's language, Latin pure, discreet,
—Aha, ELUCESCEBAT° quoth our friend:
No Tully, said I, Ulpian at the best!   100
Evil and brief hath been my pilgrimage.
All *lapis*, all, sons! Else I give the Pope
My villas! Will ye ever eat my heart?
Ever your eyes were as a lizard's quick,
They glitter like your mother's for my soul,   105
Or ye would heighten my impoverished frieze,
Piece out its starved design, and fill my vase
With grapes, and add a vizor and a Term°,   a bust on a pedestal
And to the tripod ye would tie a lynx
That in his struggle throws the thyrsus down,   110
To comfort me on my entablature
Whereon I am to lie till I must ask
"Do I live, am I dead?" There, leave me, there!
For ye have stabbed me with ingratitude
To death—ye wish it—God, ye wish it! Stone—   115
Gritstone°, a-crumble! Clammy squares which sweat   cheap, crumbly sandstone
As if the corpse they keep were oozing through—
And no more *lapis* to delight the world!
Well go! I bless ye. Fewer tapers there,
But in a row: and, going, turn your backs   120
—Ay, like departing altar-ministrants,
And leave me in my church, the church for peace,
That I may watch at leisure if he leers—
Old Gandolf, at me, from his onion-stone,
As still he envied me, so fair she was!   125

77 *Tully*: Marcus Tullius Cicero, noted for the purity of his Latin.   79 *Ulpian*: Comitius
Ulpianus, a late Latin writer of doubtful style.   95 *Saint Praxed*: confusion of Christ and
Saint Praxed.   99 *elucescebat*: late Latin word meaning "he shone" or "was famous."
Cicero would have written *elucebat*.

c) *Working Men*

BRAD GERMAN*

The man in charge is stealing my wallet
    and the money I made hauling bricks.
Who put him in charge? Who said
    he could have this job?
He was a stranger,   5
    like I was, a moment ago,
now he's my boss:
    a cool authority, a specialist, with
    finger soft tools searching my
    pockets like a hungry spider.   10

Across the faces of the street are
curtains, covering their eyes like cataracts.
    The children on the corner,
    they aren't even looking!
What of those other men in charge,   15
the elected bosses? Will they take charge
    when I'm back hauling bricks,
and protect me? Or,
        did they give this man his job too?
He shoves me aside,   20
            and vanishes in a haze of footsteps.
My eyes are averted to the ground;
in this old neighborhood, I know
        my place.

2. Try writing a poem in the voice of one of the following:

    a suicide

    a major league outfielder

    a widow

    a boy who is proud of a pocket knife he has stolen

    Andrew Jackson

    Count Dracula's housecat

3. Each of these poems presents a woman, speaking in her own voice. Consider
the differences in character and presentation that let the poets define the
women. If you don't recognize the woman in c, look at Appendix I.

a) *Woman's Work*

JILL FRESHLEY*

From the west window
I can see the men
gathered around the calf,
strung up for the butchering
like the crucified Christ.   5
Their breath hangs, like hickory smoke,
in the air for a moment,
and I'm glad to be in my kitchen,
warm and smelling of bread.
They make the first cut   10
down his white belly
and warm their hands
in the steam belching out
as the snow beneath them flushes
a sudden and angry red.   15

I turn my head away,
recalling the many chilly mornings
I'd fed that calf, stroked its muzzle
and called it by name.
I take the loaves from the oven   20
and set them to cool,
then sit down to my knitting again.
I remember the year on my birthday
when we went up in the airplane
and I thought how from there   25
the plowed fields resembled an afghan,
all golden like harvested corn,
like the brown when it's planted
and the green when it's grown.

b) *Portrait: Woman in a Grey House*

MARGARET LALLY*

   I've been here so long
That the voices of children
Are voices of men
And what I remember is
Moving, unmoving,   5
A slow modulation of staying.

I stare at the window,
I cry with the rain,
The boards and the bones
Have protected each other.   10

c) *In 1856 she won second prize in the Bread Division
at the local Cattle Show . . .*

                                        —Ellmann & O'Clair

ALBERT GOLDBARTH (b. 1948)

The poultry pecks its cages like nightmare
clockworks. They're the universe,
maybe, before man thinks up Sequential Time.
Their skins are a first dream of quill pens. And

so the undulant fields about her today,   5
light wheats, and brooding ryes, are raw
tables: schema of home and safety. This
is a County Fair, and here's a choir of strawberry jams

beneath their paraffin halos, and these
are the showcattle being rubbed between   10
brushed flanks so in pleasure they'll
still for the judges . . . She looks down.

A bee is architecting
air around a flower. The judges are here.
The bee see the bee see the bee. And now   15
they've left, with ahems. And now she's writing

We know, by now—the Word was first
And—after—earth, and grain, and grass—
As world to Him—'tis rising, now,
The making of my Second Place.   20

POEMS TO CONSIDER

Home Burial   1914

ROBERT FROST   (1874–1963)

He saw her from the bottom of the stairs
Before she saw him. She was starting down,
Looking back over her shoulder at some fear.
She took a doubtful step and then undid it
To raise herself and look again. He spoke   5
Advancing toward her: 'What is it you see
From up there always—for I want to know.'
She turned and sank upon her skirts at that,
And her face changed from terrified to dull.
He said to gain time: 'What is it you see,'   10
Mounting until she cowered under him.
'I will find out now—you must tell me, dear.'
She, in her place, refused him any help
With the least stiffening of her neck and silence.
She let him look, sure that he wouldn't see,   15
Blind creature; and awhile he didn't see.
But at last he murmured. 'Oh,' and again, 'Oh.'

'What is it—what?' she said.

                           'Just that I see.'

'You don't,' she challenged. 'Tell me what it is.'

'The wonder is I didn't see at once.   20
I never noticed it from here before.
I must be wonted to it—that's the reason.
The little graveyard where my people are!
So small the window frames the whole of it.
Not so much larger than a bedroom, is it?   25
There are three stones of slate and one of marble,
Broad-shouldered little slabs there in the sunlight
On the sidehill. We haven't to mind *those*.
But I understand: it is not the stones,
But the child's mound—'

                    'Don't, don't, don't, don't,' she cried.   30

She withdrew shrinking from beneath his arm
That rested on the bannister, and slid downstairs;
And turned on him with such a daunting look,
He said twice over before he knew himself:
'Can't a man speak of his own child he's lost?'   35

'Not you! Oh, where's my hat? Oh, I don't need it!
I must get out of here. I must get air.
I don't know rightly whether any man can.'

'Amy! Don't go to someone else this time.
Listen to me. I won't come down the stairs.'   40
He sat and fixed his chin between his fists.
'There's something I should like to ask you, dear.'

'You don't know how to ask it.'

                   'Help me, then.'

Her fingers moved the latch for all reply.

'My words are nearly always an offense.   45
I don't know how to speak of anything
So as to please you. But I might be taught
I should suppose. I can't say I see how.
A man must partly give up being a man
With women-folk. We could have some arrangement   50
By which I'd bind myself to keep hands off
Anything special you're a-mind to name.

Though I don't like such things 'twixt those that love.
Two that don't love can't live together without them.
But two that do can't live together with them.'   55
She moved the latch a little. 'Don't—don't go.
Don't carry it to someone else this time.
Tell me about it if it's something human.
Let me into your grief. I'm not so much
Unlike other folks as your standing there   60
Apart would make me out. Give me my chance.
I do think, though, you overdo it a little.
What was it brought you up to think it the thing
To take your mother-loss of a first child
So inconsolably—in the face of love.   65
You'd think his memory might be satisfied—'

'There you go sneering now!'

                              'I'm not, I'm not!
You make me angry. I'll come down to you.
God, what a woman! And it's come to this,
A man can't speak of his own child that's dead.'   70

'You can't because you don't know how to speak.
If you had any feelings, you that dug
With your own hand—how could you?—his little grave;
I saw you from that very window there,
Making the gravel leap and leap in air,   75
Leap up, like that, like that, and land so lightly
And roll back down the mound beside the hole.
I thought, Who is that man? I didn't know you.
And I crept down the stairs and up the stairs
To look again, and still your spade kept lifting.   80
Then you came in. I heard your rumbling voice
Out in the kitchen, and I don't know why,
But I went near to see with my own eyes.
You could sit there with the stains on your shoes
Of the fresh earth from your own baby's grave   85
And talk about your everyday concerns.
You had stood the spade up against the wall
Outside there in the entry, for I saw it.'

'I shall laugh the worst laugh I ever laughed.
I'm cursed. God, if I don't believe I'm cursed.'   90

'I can repeat the very words you were saying.
"Three foggy mornings and one rainy day
Will rot the best birch fence a man can build."
Think of it, talk like that at such a time!
What had how long it takes a birch to rot   95
To do with what was in the darkened parlor.
You *couldn't* care! The nearest friends can go
With anyone to death, comes so far short
They might as well not try to go at all.
No, from the time when one is sick to death,   100
One is alone, and he dies more alone.
Friends make pretense of following to the grave,
But before one is in it, their minds are turned
And making the best of their way back to life
And living people, and things they understand.   105
But the world's evil. I won't have grief so
If I can change it. Oh, I won't, I won't!'

'There, you have said it all and you feel better.
You won't go now. You're crying. Close the door.
The heart's gone out of it: why keep it up?   110
Amy! There's someone coming down the road!'

'You—oh, you think the talk is all. I must go—
Somewhere out of this house. How can I make you—'

'If—you—do!' She was opening the door wider.
'Where do you mean to go? First tell me that.   115
I'll follow and bring you back by force. I *will!*—'

Those Winter Sundays   1966

ROBERT HAYDEN (1913–1980)

Sundays too my father got up early
and put his clothes on in the blueblack cold,
then with cracked hands that ached
from labor in the weekday weather made
banked fires blaze. No one ever thanked him.   5

I'd wake and hear the cold splintering, breaking.
When the rooms were warm, he'd call,
and slowly I would rise and dress,
fearing the chronic angers of that house,

Speaking indifferently to him, 10
who had driven out the cold
and polished my good shoes as well.
What did I know, what did I know
of love's austere and lonely offices?

Fat 1980

CONRAD HILBERRY (b. 1928)

Wait. What you see is another person
hanging here. I am the girl who jumps
the Hodgman's fence so quick they never see me.
Skipping rope, I always do hot peppers.
But once on the way home I got in a strange 5
car. I screamed and beat on the windows,
but they smiled and held me. They said I could go
when I put on the costume, so I climbed
into it, pulled up the huge legs,
globby with veins, around my skinny shins, 10
pulled on this stomach that flops over itself,
I pushed my arm past the hanging elbow fat
down into the hand and fingers, tight
like a doctor's glove stuffed with vaseline.
I hooked the top behind my neck, with these 15
two bladders bulging over my flat chest.
Then I pulled the rubber mask down over
my head and tucked in the cheek and chin
folds at the neck, hiding the seam. I hate
the smell. When they pushed me out of the car, 20
I slipped and staggered as though the street
was wet with fish oil. You see what this costume is.
If you will undo me, if you will loan me a knife,
I will step out the way I got in.
I will run on home in time for supper. 25

Animals Are Passing from Our Lives   1968

PHILIP LEVINE   (b. 1928)

It's wonderful how I jog
on four honed-down ivory toes
my massive buttocks slipping
like oiled parts with each light step.

I'm to market. I can smell   5
the sour, grooved block, I can smell
the blade that opens the hole
and the pudgy white fingers

that shake out the intestines
like a hankie. In my dreams   10
the snouts drool on the marble,
suffering children, suffering flies,

suffering the consumers
who won't meet their steady eyes
for fear they could see. The boy   15
who drives me along believes

that any moment I'll fall
on my side and drum my toes
like a typewriter or squeal
and shit like a new housewife   20

discovering television,
or that I'll turn like a beast
cleverly to hook his teeth
with my teeth. No. Not this pig.

The Bats   1974

BRENDAN GALVIN   (b. 1938)

Somebody said for killing one
you got a five-dollar reward

from Red Farrell the game warden,
because at night they drank cow blood,
dozens of them plastered on the cow
like leaves after a rain,
until she dropped.
If they bit you you'd get paralyzed for life,
and they built their nests
in women's hair, secreting goo
so you couldn't pull them out
and had to shave it off.
That was how Margaret Smith got bald,
though some said it was wine.
But who ever saw one
or could tell a bat from the swifts
they sometimes flew with,
homing on insects those green evenings?
We never climbed the fence of Duffy's orchard
to catch them dog-toothed
sucking on his pears,
and the trouble was, as Duffy always said,
that in the dark you couldn't
recognize them for the leaves
and might reach up and get bit.
So the first time one of us found one
dead and held it open,
it looked like something crucified
to a busted umbrella,
the ribbed wings like a crackpot would make
to try and fly off of a dune.
As if it was made up of parts
of different animals, it had long bird-legs
stuck in lizard wrinkle pants,
and wire feet.
It wasn't even black, but brown and furry
with a puppy nose,
and when we threw it at each other
it wouldn't stick on anyone.
Then someone said his father knew somebody
who used to hunt between town and the back shore.
Coming home one night he ran across
a bat tree in the woods,
must have been hundreds folded upside down
pealing their single bell-notes through the dark.

Metaphor:
To Keep Cows in

Metaphor is the ever-fresh, magical center of poetry. Aristotle declared that "the greatest thing by far is to be a master of metaphor. It is the one thing that cannot be learned from others; and it is also a sign of genius, since a good metaphor implies an intuitive perception of the similarity in dissimilars." Two millennia later Robert Frost remarked, "There are many other things I have found myself saying about poetry, but the chiefest of these is that it is metaphor, saying one thing and meaning another, saying one thing in terms of another." Inextricably entwined both with the ways in which we think and with the origin and nature of language itself, metaphor seems inexhaustibly complex in theory. Fortunately, just as we needn't know much about human musculature to run, we needn't have a theory of metaphor to use it. Asked "What's a metaphor?" the poet, happy to be the one who causes the trouble (not the one who has to straighten it out), may be inclined to answer with the hoary pun that appears in the chapter's title.

Frost's definition is adequate: "*saying one thing in terms of another.*" A **metaphor** is a comparison of whatever is under discussion (the subject, or a part of it) with something that would not normally be a part of that subject. If you say that you are "busy as a bee," the bee enters metaphorically into what you are saying. Conventionally the subject (or part) being compared is called the **tenor**:

the thing to which it is compared, the **vehicle.** Imagine an opera singer being taken in a cart to be burned at the stake—the singer is the important thing, and the cart only a means of transportation. The comparison may be explicit or implicit. When it is explicit, or stated, it is called **simile.** Generally, a simile is syntactically announced by *like* or *as.* "He is busy *as a bee*" is a simile. The similes are italicized in the following:

> The wild tulip, at end of its tube, blows out its great red bell
> *Like a thin clear bubble of blood*
>
> ROBERT BROWNING

> A twitch, a twitter, an elastic shudder in flight
> And serrated wings against the sky,
> *Like a glove, a black glove, thrown up at the light*
> *And falling back*
>
> D. H. LAWRENCE

> I wandered lonely *as a cloud*
>
> WILLIAM WORDSWORTH

Similes are also used extensively by Alfred Lord Tennyson (1809—1892) in "Tears, Idle Tears."

> Tears, idle tears, I know not what they mean,
> Tears from the depth of some divine despair
> Rise in the heart, and gather to the eyes,
> In looking on the happy autumn-fields,
> And thinking of the days that are no more.   5
>
> Fresh *as the first beam glittering on a sail,*
> *That brings our friends up from the underworld,*
> Sad *as the last which reddens over one*
> *That sinks with all we love below the verge;*
> So sad, so fresh, the days that are no more.   10
>
> Ah, sad and strange *as in dark summer dawns*
> *The earliest pipe of half-awakened birds*
> *To dying ears, when unto dying eyes*
> *The casement slowly grows a glimmering square;*
> So sad, so strange, the days that are no more.   15

Dear *as remembered kisses after death,*
And sweet *as those by hopeless fancy feigned*
On lips that are for others; deep *as love,*
Deep *as first love,* and wild with all regret;
O Death in Life, the days that are no more!   20

When the comparison is implicit, or unstated, the term *metaphor* itself is used. A metaphor compresses the comparison, asserting or assuming the identity of tenor and vehicle. "The man *is a busy bee.*" "The waves *were angry.*" "The gun *barked.*" "A ship *ploughs* the sea." The compression can often be untangled into a looser form, where the tenor and vehicle are identifiable. "The waves were like a person who is angry." "The gun made a noise like the bark of a dog." "The ship goes through the sea as a plough goes through the soil." The compression of a metaphor, in effect, suppresses an element or elements of the comparison. Richard Wilbur, in "Year's End," speaks of the "death of ferns / Which laid their fragile *cheeks* against the stone / A million years." We understand something like this: "their fragile *fronds, which are as soft as cheeks.*" I say "something like" because somewhat different "translations" of the metaphor are possible. Because associations and connotations abound, no two readers respond in exactly the same way. "Cheeks" are human attributes; thus, a personification is involved. The ferns are like dying persons who lay their cheeks "against the stone." The delicacy of ferns might even suggest that they are like dying girls. For the sensitive reader a very ephemeral but significant little dramatic scene may be buried in the seemingly simple metaphor, "cheeks."

The tones and overtones of metaphor give it its power and make it elusive. Exact translation is impossible, and in that, of course, lies the suggestive richness of metaphor, its ability not only to compact and compress but also to express the inexpressible. Metaphors are italicized in the following fragments:

The silver *snarling* trumpets 'gan to chide

JOHN KEATS

The *dust* of snow

ROBERT FROST

Life's *but a walking shadow, a poor player*
That struts and frets his hour upon the stage
And then is heard no more. *It is a tale*
Told by an idiot, full of sound and fury,
Signifying nothing.

WILLIAM SHAKESPEARE

Each wight who reads not, and but scans and spells,
Each word-*catcher* that *lives* on syllables,
Ev'n such *small* critics some regard may claim,
Preserved in Milton's or in Shakespeare's name.
Pretty! *in amber to observe the forms*
Of hairs, or straws, or dirt, or grubs, or worms!
The things, we know, are neither rich nor rare,
But wonder how the devil they got there?

ALEXANDER POPE

Here you can see the use of metaphor in a whole poem, "Natural Gas" by Peter Wild (b. 1940):

When you push the lever up
the warm gases *leap* through the house.

All night I lie awake
as beside me you lie *buried* in the dark,
listening to the thermostat click on and off,   5

the ghosts of the fierce creatures
starting, stopping, puzzled in the pipes
all the way from Texas.

The Metaphorical Link

Language itself is deeply metaphorical. We speak of the *eye* of a needle, the *face* of a cliff, the *hands* of a clock, the *heel* of a hand, the *branch* of a river, getting down to *brass tacks, crab* grass, a check that *bounces,* an election won by a *landslide,* a person's going *haywire,* an idea's *dawning* on us, the years *rolling by.* So familiar are such phrases that we usually don't notice that they are metaphorical; we don't actually think of faces, hands, landslides, the tangly wire used for baling hay, or whatever. Such dead metaphors show one of the primary ways in which language changes to accommodate new possibilities. Confronted with something new, for which there is no word, we thriftily adapt an old word as a comparison, and soon the new meaning seems perfectly literal. The part of a car that covers the engine, for instance, became the *hood.* On early cars, it was in fact rounded and looked very like a hood; but the word survives, although now hoods are flat and look nothing like hoods. (They still cover the engines' *heads*.) Sometimes the perfectly literal becomes metaphorical. Actual trunks were strapped to the back of early automobiles, and the word survives, although now the trunks are built-in and we may forget their likeness to trunks in an attic. Such metaphors continue to be useful even after their sense has evaporated. We say someone is "mad as a hatter" although there aren't many hatters around and although the chemical they used (which, in fact, often made them crazy) is no longer used.

The world itself is wordless, and Adam's giving names to the beasts in Eden is one of the great archetypal human activities. There are still many things, actions, feelings, and relationships for which there are no words, or only specialized or technical words. There are no words for the V of the hand be- tween thumb and forefinger, for a single filament of a spider's web, for the strange green of stormlight, or for the many looks and appearances of the sea's surface. Eskimos have, understandably, more than twenty different words for kinds of snow, while we barely distinguish two or three. Translators often find no precise equivalent in the way that two languages notice or measure out the parts of the world. Feelings are particularly inarticulate and almost always need metaphor to get themselves into language. The general words we have—*love, hate, compassion, awe, anger,* and the like—really express little about specific cases. A man may *love* his wife, his dog, a spring day, pistachio ice cream, and Vermont. To verbalize the exact feeling, he may well need metaphor. "O, my luve's like a red, red rose." Different lovers might say a white rose, a daisy, a zinnia, a violet, or almost anything, even pistachio ice cream. In such cases the poet (or any of us) borrows the vocabulary, the mode of discourse, that belongs to something else and uses it to say whatever there are no words for ("ploughs," "a bee," "dust," "a thin clear bubble of blood").

Richard Wilbur's "Praise in Summer" wittily suggests the inescapability of metaphor.

Obscurely yet most surely called to praise,
As sometimes summer calls us all, I said
The hills are heavens full of branching ways
Where star-nosed moles fly overhead the dead;
I said the trees are mines in air, I said   5
See how the sparrow burrows in the sky!
And then I wondered why this mad *instead*
Perverts our praise to uncreation, why
Such savor's in this wrenching things awry.
Does sense so stale that it must needs derange   10
The world to know it? To a praiseful eye
Should it not be enough of fresh and strange
That trees grow green, and moles can course in clay,
And sparrows sweep the ceiling of our day?

Even wanting to dispense with metaphor ("this mad *instead*"), the speaker falls back into it without thinking: "And sparrows *sweep the ceiling of our day*." Notice that metaphor is hidden in aviators' or meteorologists' use of the word "ceiling," and that "sweep" may well not be entirely fanciful if the sparrows are snapping up midges and mosquitoes. The seemingly innocent word "course" is also metaphorical, recalling its Latin source, meaning "to run." "Course" also means "to hunt," and moles do that as well. Is "course" here literal or metaphorical, or both? Does "trees grow green" mean that they grow and are green, or that they produce greenness, as a farmer might grow a crop? Perhaps they "become" ("grow" in the sense of "turn") green? Is the compression of "trees grow leaves that are green" a metaphorical compression? (**Synecdoche** is a type of metaphor in which a part of something stands for the whole, as when someone speaks of an employee as a "hired hand.") Where they join, the seeming simplicity of language and the seeming simplicity of the world take on a magical complexity.

Metaphors work in a bewildering variety of ways (no catalog could be made) and do a bewildering variety of jobs, sometimes so complexly that no conscious analysis can follow them. They may illustrate or explain (the heart is like a pump); emphasize; heighten; communicate information or ideas; carry a tone, feeling, or attitude. They may even work—Dylan Thomas's phrase is the "**logic of metaphor**"—as a mode of discourse, a sort of language of associations, as they do in Thomas's "Twenty-Four Years" (page 236) or in "Sir, Say No More" by Trumbull Stickney (1874–1904):

> Sir, say no more,
> Within me 'tis as if
> The green and climbing eyesight of a cat
> Crawled near my mind's poor birds.

The eerie sensation communicates perfectly, though a critic might work all day to untangle the threads the image knots up so simply.

Though a metaphorical leap may seem inexplicable and arbitrary, the metaphor may communicate clearly, as in "Loan" by Warren Nelson:

> Moon, I am clumsy in these boots.
> Loan me a small bird's feet.

Why the speaker addresses the moon (perhaps the poem's real subject is love?) or why he elects to ask for "a small bird's feet" we do not know. But in the image itself (this is the whole poem) we hear a plaintive human desire that we understand.

So accustomed are we to metaphor that we hardly notice how fully it serves. In Shakespeare's Sonnet 73 ("That time of year thou mayst in me behold"), for instance, metaphors provide almost the whole effect of the poem, translating emotions into vivid and dramatic particulars about winter trees, choirlofts, twilight, embers. The metaphors virtually stand for or present the emotion. Like literal particulars, metaphors enrich the texture and color of a poem, as well as often being the principal means for evoking the feeling.

For practical purposes, the distinction between simile and metaphor is far less important than their similarity. Syntactically, simile is perhaps simpler, closer to the straightforward, logical uses of language. But the evocative functions of metaphor and simile can be measured properly only by the unique force of specific instances. The oddly popular notion that metaphor is stronger than simile, more forceful or evocative, is not really true. Consider the sonnet "Composed upon Westminster Bridge, September 3, 1802" by William Wordsworth:

> Earth has not anything to show more fair:
> Dull would he be of soul who could pass by
> A sight so touching in its majesty:
> This City now doth, like a garment, wear
> The beauty of the morning; silent, bare,   5
> Ships, towers, domes, theatres, and temples lie
> Open unto the fields, and to the sky;
> All bright and glittering in the smokeless air.
> Never did sun more beautifully steep
> In his first splendour, valley, rock, or hill;   10
> Ne'er saw I, never felt, a calm so deep!
> The river glideth at his own sweet will:
> Dear God! the very houses seem asleep;
> And all that mighty heart is lying still!

This fine panorama of early-morning London offers a rare instance of simile and metaphor doing the same job at the same moment. "Like a garment" in line 4 is a simile, "wear" a metaphor. Unquestionably the simile is stronger and more noticeable than the metaphor, which a reader is likely to notice secondarily, if at all. The very general "like a garment" makes the personification of the city vague and keeps it from interfering with the brilliant visual details of the literal scene: "silent, bare, / Ships, towers, domes, theatres, and temples lie." The "beauty of the morning" seems diaphanous, filmy—"bare" suggests almost nothing—and so with exquisite tact the simile establishes the personification of the sleeping city as feminine. This is balanced, with equal tact, by the masculine sun and river of the final lines. The sexual overtones, which give the sonnet a curiously moving loveliness, seem hardly more than a faint "overimage" superimposed on the literal scene with the finest delicacy.

The content and interaction of images, in any poem, is important; and the syntactical distinction between simile and metaphor may be handled to advantage. But "O, my luve's like a red, red rose" and "O, my luve is a red, red rose" are functionally more alike than different. Look again at Browning's lines from "Up at a Villa—Down in the City":

The wild tulip, at end of its tube, blows out its great red bell
Like a thin clear bubble of blood

Again unquestionably, the simile "Like a thin clear bubble of blood" is more startling, more evocative, than either of the metaphors, "tube" for the stem and "great red bell" for the flower. It clearly carries the main, somewhat unpleasant tone of the passage (the speaker is comparing the city and the country to the disadvantage of the latter). The vaguely clinical "tube" (and "bell," which has laboratory overtones) beautifully set up the grimly lovely "Like a thin clear bubble of blood."

In a way, it is surprising that metaphor works at all, much less that it usually works instantly and intuitively. The reader, without analysis, perceives those elements or qualities of tenor and vehicle that are pertinent and ignores those that are irrelevant. Analysis can follow intuition and enumerate the relevant elements or qualities of the comparison. But the sum of the parts of the enumeration, however illuminating, rarely equals the effect of the comparison as a whole. Always, as with the last lines of Wilbur's "Praise in Summer," the nuances and associations of a metaphor go beyond the certainties that analysis, plodding after, can pin down.

Consider the opening image of Robert Burns's familiar "A Red, Red Rose":

O, my luve's like a red, red rose
That's newly sprung in June.

We understand this relatively simple metaphor at once, but what has gone into our understanding? What likenesses justify the comparison? How is a woman like and unlike a rose? A list of likenesses would include such qualities as beautiful, fresh, young, natural, and might go on to sweet-smelling, happy or good-natured (since we connect roses with happy occasions), healthy, lively, and so on. There is really no way of being sure that such a listing is complete. Someone might suggest further qualities—passionate, perhaps, because of the intensity of "red, red" and the traditional linking of roses with physical beauty, red with strong feelings.

On the other hand, a list of *unlikenesses*, which we instantly dismiss or ignore, might include such qualities as having thorns (being prickly), being red (a heavy drinker?), being angry (red is the color of wrath), growing out of the ground, reproducing by pollen, and so on. So experienced and expert are we all at handling metaphor that we make such discriminations effortlessly and without articulating them. Context guides our response. If the line were, say, "O, my mother-in-law's like a red, red rose," we might well reorder the qualities we include and exclude in our response.

Richard Wilbur's comparison of a cricket and a hearse in "Exeunt" is somewhat easier to account for:

> Piecemeal the summer dies;
> At the field's edge a daisy lives alone;
> A last shawl of burning lies
> On a gray field-stone.

> All cries are thin and terse;   5
> The field has droned the summer's final mass;
> A cricket like a dwindled hearse
> Crawls from the dry grass.

Cricket and "dwindled hearse" are both long, dark or black, and shiny. The insect's slow movement ("Crawls") and the solemn speed of a hearse (which might be described as moving at a crawl) correspond. The adjective "dwindled" makes sure that we see the hearse at such a distance or in such reduction that the cricket isn't overshadowed by its mass. Miniaturization suggests fragility. The hearse's associations with death appropriately color the late-summer slow pace of the cricket, whose normal sprightliness and agility are past, and imply its impending death with the coming of cold weather. Differences are muted (size, by "dwindled") or ignored (legs or wheels, for example). Compared to the hearse, · the cricket symbolizes and suggestively pictures the "death" of the summer.

Pattern and Motif

Often metaphors function locally; that is, they have no particular connection to other metaphors or other parts of the poem, as in X. J. Kennedy's "In a Prominent Bar in Secaucus One Day,"

> "In the kerchief of linen I caught to my nose
> Ah, there never fell snot, but *a little gold rose*."

or, later,

> "Now I'm *saddled* each night for my butter and eggs
> And *the broken threads race* down the backs of my legs."

"Gold rose," "saddled," and "broken threads" are essentially separate images.

Metaphors often, however, work in patterns or interactions, as with Browning's "tube" and "thin clear bubble of blood" or, more generally, the male and female personifications in Wordsworth's sonnet about London. In Kennedy's poem, for example, the snot—little gold rose image does form a secondary pattern with other flower/plant images:

> "Let you hold in mind, girls, that your beauty must pass
> *Like a lovely white clover that rusts with its grass*"

and

> "And be left by the roadside, for all your good deeds,
> *Two toadstools* for tits and a face *full of weeds.*

The connection is minimal, but the sequence—gold rose, rusting clover, toadstools, weeds—provides a motif of the poem's theme. (**Motif** is a pattern of recurrent, unifying images or phrases.) Similarly, the various racing references and images form a motif that reveals the lady's experience and character.

In Wilbur's "Exeunt," however, the metaphors make a very tight pattern. In line 1 the metaphorical "the summer dies" links to the metaphorical "hearse" in line 7. In line 2 "lives alone" begins the personification of the flower. That "daisy" is also a feminine name hints further at the personification. The metaphorical "shawl of burning" (late summer sun, or perhaps fallen leaves) in line 3 fits this developing image of an elderly woman, as does the literal "gray" in line 4. The last occasion of the full hum of the summer field is described metaphorically in line 6 as a "final mass," presumably a funeral mass, after which the cricket-hearse appears. Each metaphor is appropriate where it appears; but together, all suggest a comparison to the death of an old woman—a deftly implied little tale that parallels, and evokes feelings for, the literal end of summer. The poem's title, "Exeunt," the plural of the Latin word used in stage directions for the departure of several characters from the stage, suggests that the dramatic implications of the poem are more than accidental.

Such unifying links, patterns, or motifs between and among the metaphors in a poem must, in part, be conscious on the poet's part. But it is probably a matter more of recognizing and developing possibilities than of cold-bloodedly inventing or imposing them. A poem of mine, "In the Field Forever," for example, began with a visual comparison of the sun to a dandelion (color, shape, glowing spokes). The moon's likeness to another sort of flower followed readily, and this developing pattern called for the metaphor for stars, which in turn suggested the rhyme in the fourth line. The changeable moon's occasional likeness to a scythe fits the pattern:

> Sun's a roaring dandelion, hour by hour.
> Sometimes the moon's a scythe, sometimes a silver flower.

But the stars! all night long the stars are clover,
Over, and over, and over!

Often, as here, the poet need only perceive the potential pattern in the material.

When metaphors dominate or organize a passage or even a whole poem, they are called **extended metaphors** or **conceits.** Secondary metaphors spring from a first, controlling metaphor, as does the varied car imagery in Ted Kooser's "Looking for You, Barbara" (page 224). In Mary Oliver's "Music at Night," the extended metaphor controlling the entire poem is a comparison of music to a brother "Who has arrived from a long journey," whose reassuring presence makes the flux and danger of the world—"the maelstrom / Lashing"— seem, for the moment, tamed.

> Especially at night
> It is the best kind of company—
>
> A brother whose dark happiness fills the room,
> Who has arrived from a long journey,
>
> Who stands with his back to the windows   5
> Beyond which the branches full of leaves
>
> Are not trees only, but the maelstrom
> Lashing, attentive and held in thrall
>
> By the brawn in the rippling octaves,
> And the teeth in the smile of the strings.   10

So compelling is the fantasy of the metaphor that it is impossible to say whether the trees outside the windows are part of the metaphorical description of the brother or part of the literal scene. The real and the imagined weave into one picture.

The "distance" between the tenor and the vehicle of a metaphor, or between the tones usually associated with them, controls the effect. "A rose is like a carnation" narrows the gap too closely, and the emotional or intellectual spark is faint and uninteresting. "A rose is like a locomotive" opens the gap too wide, and the spark doesn't get across; we have no idea what qualities of rose and locomotive are being compared. In general, the greater the distance between tenor and vehicle, the greater is our surprise and pleasure, but only if the comparison seems just, accurate, congruent, not merely a wild stab. Burns's "O, my luve's like a red, red rose" seems straightforward because girls and roses are traditionally associated. But X. J. Kennedy's "'Ah, there never fell snot, but a little gold rose'" is shocking, because our feelings about boogers, roses, and gold are worlds apart. The metaphor succeeds (delights us) when we realize how right, after all, the comparison is. In context, a reminder of the speaker's pitiful pretentiousness, it is humorously in character.

John Donne, in "A Valediction: Forbidding Mourning" (page 225), presents the calm parting of true lovers (one of whom is going on a journey) in terms of metaphors from religion, geology, astronomy, and metallurgy. He compares their parting to the unworried death of virtuous men, to the unharmful movements of the heavens ("trepidation of the spheres") in contrast to earthquakes, and to the fineness of gold leaf which, though hammered to "airy thinness," never breaks. The poem's final image is yet more startling: the lovers are likened to a pair of drawing compasses! The whole world seems ransacked and brought to bear, to center, on these lovers, whose parting becomes for us as momentous as the metaphors that express it.

Emily Dickinson's poem "A Route of Evanescence" similarly delights us when we realize what it is about and how evocative its comparisons are. In the first four lines we see something moving rapidly—a wheel, colors (cochineal is a brilliant red dye)—but it is so fast ("Rush") that we cannot identify it.

A Route of Evanescence
With a revolving Wheel—
A Resonance of Emerald—
A Rush of Cochineal—
And every Blossom on the Bush   5
Adjusts its tumbled Head—
The mail from Tunis°, probably,   *North African city*
An easy Morning's Ride—

The mystery clears in lines 5–6 when we gather that, whatever it is, it has to do with disturbing the flowers on a bush—a hummingbird! The mere glimpse of its colors and fan-shape in lines 1–4 evokes the bird's quick and jerky flight ("Resonance," "Rush"). The personification of the blossoms as "tumbled heads" prepares for the metaphorical guess in lines 7–8: "The mail from Tunis, probably." The exaggeration, "An easy Morning's Ride," offhandedly insists on the hummingbird's speed in flight and characterizes the exotic quality of an ordinary back yard that enjoys such colors as emerald and cochineal. If we remember that many of our bird-neighbors winter in Florida or South America (if not North Africa), the metaphor hardly seems farfetched. If we also remember that the hummingbird picks up and delivers pollen from flower to flower—that population of "tumbled Head[s]"—the comparison with the "mail" seems less than outrageous. Even the pun mail/male may not be irrelevant, and we may guess why the news so "tumble[s] Head[s]"! The poem's dazzling metaphors lead not only to a vivid action picture of the hummingbird but also to a fresh experience of how strange and colorful the merely everyday truly is.

Mixed Metaphor

Metaphors may go wrong in several ways; when this happens, they are usually called **mixed metaphors.** The trouble sometimes comes from not shielding out qualities in the comparison that are irrelevant or unintentionally off-key. "Her eyes are lakes, along whose edge a velvet green of scum sparkles with insects like a jeweler's tray," for instance, is a blunder. Too many things are happening at once; and though the jeweler's tray is a lively image, the reader is all too likely to be misdirected into responding to the scum around the eyes. Or the trouble comes when elements of a metaphor are not congruent with one another, as in "The feather of smoke above the cabin slowly flapped its wings and disappeared across the winter sky." A feather doesn't have wings, and it is hard to imagine the flapping of what does not exist. Shielding out the individual feather and making the first part of the image less distinct, however, might make it work: "The feathery smoke above the cabin slowly flapped its wings and disappeared across the winter sky."

In "It Dropped So Low—In My Regard" Emily Dickinson insists on having a metaphor two ways and very nearly, if not completely, spoils a poem:

> It dropped so low—in my Regard—
> I heard it hit the Ground—
> And go to pieces on the Stones
> At bottom of my Mind—
>
> Yet blamed the Fate that flung it—*less*   5
> Than I denounced Myself,
> For entertaining Plated Wares
> Upon my Silver Shelf—

"It" is apparently some idea, illusion, or bit of wishful thinking, which is revealed to be false. In stanza 1 it is compared to something fragile, breakable, like glassware: "And go to pieces on the Stones." But in stanza 2 it is compared to merely "Plated Wares": silver plate rather than sterling silver. Such metal can't fall and break, "go to pieces"; rather, it bends or dents. The poem is left with its central metaphor irreconcilably divided against itself.

Metaphor is predominantly visual. The range, however, is from the sharp and colorful, through a variety of the less distinct, to essentially nonvisual images. Muted, vague, shadowy, partial shots (to return to the film analogy) are possible; soft superimpositions, close-ups, momentary flashes to a different scene. We do, and we do not, *see* something breaking in the first stanza of "It Dropped So Low—In My Regard." The difference between "feather of smoke" and "feathery smoke" is largely one of making the image less distinct. Consider Shakespeare's Sonnet 30:

When to the sessions of sweet silent thought
I summon up remembrance of things past,
I sigh the lack of many a thing I sought,
And with old woes new wail my dear times' waste:
Then can I drown an eye, unused to flow,   5
For precious friends hid in death's dateless night,
And weep afresh love's long since cancelled woe,
And moan the expense of many a vanished sight:
Then can I grieve at grievances foregone,
And heavily from woe to woe tell o'er   10
The sad account of fore-bemoaned moan,
Which I new pay as if not paid before.
    But if the while I think on thee, dear friend,
    All losses are restored and sorrows end.

Muted in puns, the main pattern of images is a series of legal and quasi-legal terms: "sessions," "summon," "dateless," "cancelled," "expense," "grievances," "account," "pay," "losses," "restored," which together suggest a court proceeding over some financial matter. Only the *tone* comes through, however: a certain judicial solemnity, an irrecoverable loss, some technical injustice, which the miraculous appearance of the "dear friend" overturns. This shadowy story exists more as a quality of the sonnet's diction than as metaphor, and yet it is the sum of a number of passing comparisons. We see no courtroom and, so delicately is it written, are hardly aware of the source of the metaphors.

Metaphorical Implication

Even simple metaphors may work with an almost inexhaustible subtlety and often do much more than either poet or reader may be aware. Consider two poems, two girls, two pairs of metaphors in "A Red, Red Rose" by Robert Burns (1759–1796) and "She Dwelt Among the Untrodden Ways" by Wordsworth. First, the Burns:

O, my luve's like a red, red rose
That's newly sprung in June.
O, my luve's like the melodie
That's sweetly played in tune.

As fair art thou, my bonnie lass,   5
So deep in luve am I;
And I will luve thee still, my dear,
Till a'° the seas gang° dry.   *all; go*

Till a' the seas gang dry, my dear,
And the rocks melt wi' the sun;   10
And I will luve thee still, my dear,
While the sands o' life shall run.

And fare thee weel, my only luve,
And fare thee weel a while!
And I will come again, my luve,   15
Though it were ten thousand mile!

Focus on the two metaphors in the first stanza. Read the four lines over and
over until you can say them with your eyes shut. Relax. Let the associations be
visual. Experience them instead of thinking about them.

The metaphors—rose, melody—tell us a good deal about the speaker's affection for, and pleasure in, the girl. They also tell us, I think, more about the
girl herself than we realize. We have mentioned such qualities as beautiful,
fresh, young, natural, and perhaps sweet-smelling, happy or good-natured,
healthy, lively, and maybe passionate. The metaphor of the "melodie" in lines
3—4 might reenforce some of these and incline us to add having a musical voice
or being in harmony with herself and her environment. Let me ask you some
questions about her, however, which may at first seem silly. Don't try to answer
them by thinking, but just see whether an answer comes to you. If one doesn't,
don't worry about it. Go from question to question slowly and don't bear down
on any of them. Every reader's responses will differ a little because we are going
beyond what is really demonstrable to the deep resonances of the images. Most
readers, though, will agree on many of the responses. Hard to define though it
may be, there will be something like a consensus. Look for what you see just
beyond the edge of your field of vision, for what you know just beyond the edge
of your knowledge.

Is the girl a city girl or a country girl?

Is she an indoor girl or an outdoor girl?

Is she an introvert or an extrovert? quiet or fun-loving? shy or fond of company?

What is her complexion? the color of her hair? Is she slight or robust?

Does she like dancing?

*Where is the melody played? indoors or outdoors? by whom? with what instru-
ments?*

This testing of the impressions we carry away from the metaphors is imprecise, and there is surely nothing provable about them; yet we can begin to
trace them from things in the poem. Although the two images—rose, melody—
are separate, there are perhaps interactions between them. Having visualized the

rose outdoors, we may well, lacking anything to prevent it, imagine the melody as played outdoors. The word "melodie" itself suggests that the music is not very sophisticated, so that something like chamber music is unlikely. That it is noteworthy that the melody is "played in tune" (hardly remarkable for really accomplished or professional musicians) suggests amateur players. Something about lines 1–2, probably "newly sprung in June," suggests naturalness of growth, like a wild rose, or may at least shield out the impression of a very formal garden or one deliberately cultivated. "Sweetly" and "newly sprung" imply youth and innocence, and they temper somewhat the passionate color of the "red, red rose," so that an impression of the sexuality of the girl is registered but not made much of. The pun in "sprung" perhaps suggests physicality, vigor, liveliness. "Red, red" may suggest rosiness of cheek; not a pale, indoor girl, she is used to the outdoors and sunshine and physical exercise. Is she likely of a darker complexion, dark-haired? The music implies other people, a gathering, doubtless a happy one; and one at which the girl, like the melody, is not far from the center of attention. She is gregarious, then, active, popular, easy in company, and not shy.

Music outdoors, amateur musicians, a fiddle perhaps. Roses. A sociable occasion. A lively, beautiful girl, a "bonnie lass," fond of company. *A country dance?*

Such are the resonances of Burns's metaphors. The "rightness" he probably felt when he wrote these lines (like the "rightness" we feel when we read them) almost certainly derives from a quick, intuitive apprehension of just such accumulating associations and nearly undetectable nuances.

Turn now to Wordsworth's poem: another country girl, another pair of images.

> She dwelt among the untrodden ways
>   Beside the springs of Dove,
> A maid whom there were none to praise
>   And very few to love:
>
> A violet by a mossy stone   5
>   Half hidden from the eye!
> —Fair as a star, when only one
>   Is shining in the sky.
>
> She lived unknown, and few could know
>   When Lucy ceased to be;   10
> But she is in her grave, and, oh,
>   The difference to me!

Wordsworth tells us, apart from the two metaphors in stanza 2, a good deal more about Lucy than Burns tells about his lass. But the resonance of the metaphors is no less fascinating. Lucy's beauty is of a very different kind. In contrast to a rose, the violet offers quite other qualities: pale, delicate, quiet, shy, very young, fragile, and, in context, sickly. The moss implies shade, trees, moisture, perhaps a moist spot not far from a stream. We don't see these things, of course, but have a sense of them outside the frame of the picture. The camera is in for a close-up shot, for we see the violet clearly. The moss also implies that the stone is imbedded, not movable. The stone's mass and hardness emphasize, by contrast, the violet's smallness and fragility. Its immobility and mossy age emphasize the violet's sensitivity; its permanence, the violet's youth and transience. The stone is very like (and it would not be irrelevant if we are reminded of) a gravestone. ("Her grave" is in fact mentioned in stanza 3.) The stone also, doubtless, symbolizes the harsh, isolating, and indifferent circumstances of her life. The syntax is ambiguous; we can't conclude whether the violet hides itself or the stone hides it. If she is shy and withdrawn, it is perhaps not altogether by choice.

Another ambiguity links the images of violet and star. Is the violet "Fair as a star"? or is it Lucy, directly, who is "Fair as a star"? It matters little, since the comparison necessarily involves all three, but the ambiguity does have the effect of relating violet and star more directly than the images in Burns's first stanza are related. The star is presumably the evening star, at twilight, when it is for a brief time the "only one" before the gathering dark lets other stars be seen. The soft, dusk color of the sky may be pale and violet. And both violet and star are shapes radiating from a center. The fragility of the evening's first star, as it first becomes visible, parallels the delicacy and half-hiddenness of the violet. The transition from violet to star is flawless.

The star adds other qualities to the emotional portrayal of Lucy in these metaphors. Bright, sharp, fine, its beauty is permanent and enduring, though it will soon be "lost" among the many bright stars of the night sky. It is, also, as the violet was not, publicly visible. The transition from violet to star, from close-up to long shot, is itself an image of Lucy's death, her disappearance from earth and reappearance in heaven. So, the poem implies, Lucy's unknown beauty in life was transformed in death to a kind of perfection and permanence. The two couplets seem irreversible (as are Burns's couplets).

Here, at its subtlest, metaphor turns into symbol. The natural object suffices. Things become meanings. Naming creates a world. As John Crowe Ransom noted: "The image cannot be dispossessed of a primordial freshness, which idea can never claim. An idea is derivative and tamed. The image is in the natural or wild state, and it has to be discovered there, not put there, obeying its own law and none of ours."

QUESTIONS AND SUGGESTIONS

1. Make up as many metaphors or similes as you can for a common object (street light, fire plug, telephone pole, daisy, dandelion, floor lamp, or the like). Try to use one or more of the better ones in a poem.

2. A metaphor or simile has been omitted from these passages. What comparisons would you choose? (The originals are in Appendix I.)

a) Raspberries _____, redly in their leaves   [verb]

b) [of a country funeral procession going up a hill road]

       Four cars like _____
behind the hearse, old Chevies and a Ford,
they fluttered up where the land rose out of view

c) A black fly flew slowly up,
   droning, _____-ing the halves of the air

d) In a week or two, forsythia
will shower its peaceful _____
all over the towns.

e) The clarinet, a dark tube
_____ in silver

f) Big as _____ ,
two white launches between water and sky
march down the bay.

g) The green creek whirled by a boat's wash
into _____

h) Dreams are the soul's _____

3. Study the elements of Pound's "In a Station of the Metro" (page 125). Can you decide whether it is day or night outside the subway station? Clear or rainy? What are the people in the station wearing?

4. Another love poem that uses the rose as its central image is the surreal "Rose" by Michael Benedikt (b. 1937). How does the poet play off the traditional image? What do we know, by metaphorical implication, about this girl?

She makes herself a rose by standing around in your mind, growing,
She stands there on one leg and she says thorny things
But every time the sun comes she straightens up and jumps up almost
    another foot
A few more clear days and this rose will be through the roof
Passers-by in every direction will finally understand the secret   5
Of a love that far outran the pace of even the wonders of modern
    horticulture.
How many nights have you dreamt of such sweet cultivation?
Evenings of evil love, lying slyly with your arms around a vegetable
Swept off her feet, yet upset lest you see
A foot, like a root, tumbling down to real ground from between
    these human sheets.   10

5. Each of these poems is centered in its metaphors. As far as possible, itemize the elements that go into each comparison. Don't quit too soon!

a) *"Taking the Hands"*

ROBERT BLY (b. 1926)

Taking the hands of someone you love,
You see they are delicate cages . . .
Tiny birds are singing
In the secluded prairies
And in the deep valleys of the hand.

b) *On Being Served Apples*

BONNIE JACOBSON*

Apples in a deep blue dish
        are the shadows of nuns

Apples in a basket
        are warm red moons on Indian women

Apples in a white bowl   5
        are virgins waiting in snow

Beware of apples on an orange plate:
        they are the anger of wives

c) *Watermelons*

CHARLES SIMIC (b. 1938)

Green Buddhas
On the fruit stand.
We eat the smile
And spit out the teeth.

d) *Waking from Sleep*

ROBERT BLY

Inside the veins there are navies setting forth,
Tiny explosions at the water lines,
And seagulls weaving in the wind of the salty blood.

It is the morning. The country has slept the whole winter.
Window seats were covered with fur skins, the yard was full   5
Of stiff dogs, and hands that clumsily held heavy books.

Now we wake, and rise from bed, and eat breakfast!—
Shouts rise from the harbor of the blood,
Mist, and masts rising, the knock of wooden tackle in the sunlight.

Now we sing, and do tiny dances on the kitchen floor.   10
Our whole body is like a harbor at dawn;
We know that our master has left us for the day.

e) *Outfielder*

STEPHEN DUNN   (b. 1939)

So this is excellence: movement
toward the barely possible—
the puma's dream
of running down a hummingbird
on a grassy plain.

f) *Brief Song*

ELTON GLASER   (b. 1945)

When love carries us
to this altitude
of lean air, our heads
clear, our hearts
open like parachutes.

g) *The Release*

JOSEPH BRUCHAC   (b. 1942)

At sunset
the shadows of all the trees
break free and go running
across the edge of the world.

Sonnet 130   1609

WILLIAM SHAKESPEARE   (1564—1616)

My mistress' eyes are nothing like the sun;
Coral is far more red than her lips' red;
If snow be white, why then her breasts are dun;
If hairs be wires, black wires grow on her head.
I have seen roses damasked, red and white,   5
But no such roses see I in her cheeks;
And in some perfumes is there more delight
Than in the breath that from my mistress reeks.
I love to hear her speak, yet well I know
That music hath a far more pleasing sound;   10
I grant I never saw a goddess go;
My mistress, when she walks, treads on the ground:
  And yet, by heaven, I think my love as rare
  As any she belied with false compare.

Icicles   1978

MARK IRWIN*

Slender beards of light
hang from the railing.

My son shows me
their array of sizes:

one oddly shaped,   5
its queer curve,

a clear walrus tooth,
illumined, tinseled.

We watch crystal cones
against blue sky;   10

suddenly some break loose:
an echo of piano notes.

The sun argues
ice to liquid.

Tiny buds of water,   15
pendent on dropper tips,

push to pear shapes:
prisms that shiver silver

in a slight wind
before falling.   20

Look, he says laughing,
a pinocchio nose,

and grabs one
in his tiny hand,

touching the clear carrot,   25
cold to his lips.

Looking for You, Barbara   1976

TED KOOSER   (b. 1939)

I have been out looking for you,
Barbara, and as I drove around,
the steering wheel turned through my hands
like a clock. The moon
rolled over the rooftops and was gone.   5

I was dead tired; in my arms
they were rolling the tires inside;

in my legs they were locking the pumps.
Yet what was in me for you
flapped as red in my veins   10
as banners strung over a car lot.

Then I came home and got drunk.
Where were you? 2 A.M.
is full of slim manikins
waving their furs from black windows.   15
My bed goes once more around the block,
and my heart keeps on honking its horn.

A Valediction: Forbidding Mourning   1633

JOHN DONNE   (1572−1631)

As virtuous men pass mildly away,
   And whisper to their souls to go,
Whilst some of their sad friends do say
   The breath goes now, and some say, No;

So let us melt, and make no noise,   5
   No tear-floods, nor sigh-tempests move,
'Twere profanation of our joys
   To tell the laity our love.

Moving of th' earth° brings harms and fears,   *earthquakes*
   Men reckon what it did and meant;   10
But trepidation of the spheres°,   *irregular movements in the heavens*
   Though greater far, is innocent.

Dull sublunary° lovers' love   *below the moon; hence,*
   (Whose soul is sense) cannot admit   *subject to change*
Absence, because it doth remove   15
   Those things which elemented° it.   *composed*

But we by a love so much refined
   That our selves know not what it is,
Inter-assuréd of the mind,
   Care less, eyes, lips, and hands to miss.   20

Our two souls therefore, which are one,
　Though I must go, endure not yet
A breach, but an expansion,
　Like gold to airy thinness beat.

If they be two, they are two so   25
　As stiff twin compasses are two;
Thy soul, the fixed foot, makes no show
　To move, but doth, if th' other do.

And though it in the center sit,
　Yet when the other far doth roam,   30
It leans and hearkens after it,
　And grows erect, as that comes home.

Such wilt thou be to me, who must
　Like th' other foot, obliquely run;
Thy firmness makes my circle just,   35
　And makes me end where I begun.

9

The Nonrational:
Burglars and Housedogs

A good poem, read again and again over the years, seems always fresh, saying more each time than we recall, showing itself to us in ever new lights. Passing centuries may not dim this mysteriously self-renewing energy. We are not mistaken in believing that such poetry comes from, and keeps us in touch with, a fundamental power deep within the psyche, where dark rivers from time-beyond-memory carve the stone. The sound, "the musical qualities of verse," which T. S. Eliot (1888–1965) calls the **"auditory imagination,"** may be one source of this power. It is, he says,

> the feeling for syllable and rhythm, penetrating far below the conscious levels of thought and feeling, invigorating every word; sinking to the most primitive and forgotten, returning to the origin and bringing something back, seeking the beginning and the end. It works through meanings, certainly, or not without meanings in the ordinary sense, and fuses the old and obliterated and the trite, the current, and the new and surprising, the most ancient and the most civilised mentality.

Another source of the inexhaustible energy may be images, literal or metaphorical, which reach beneath consciousness to some magical comprehension deep in our personal and racial memories. Freudian symbols and Jungian archetypes, magic talismans, superstitions, and dreams seem outcroppings of this subterranean granite of the human experience. Yet another source of poetry's buried energy may be the age-old forms of language itself, its glacial mass and electrical suddenness, its molds from which every new thought and discovery must take their shapes in our consciousness.

Poets need not, perhaps should not, concern themselves too directly with these issues. It is enough that the energy exists and that they may, when they are writing well, tap it. After all, we flip an electric light switch without thinking of the fossils, eons old, the trees and animals that drew energy from the sun, then dissolved into the black lakes and frozen black rivers, from which we in turn draw through dynamos and copper wires light into the lamp on the desk. Certain kinds of poems, however, particularly in the twentieth century, have depended on this ancient, subliminal power in new ways, especially by suppressing the ordinary conscious working of the mind so that the profound effects of language and images may be more direct. Eliot describes the assumptions:

> The chief use of the "meaning" of a poem, in the ordinary sense, may be (for here again I am speaking of some kinds of poetry and not all) to satisfy one habit of the reader, to keep his mind diverted and quiet, while the poem does its work upon him: much as the imaginary burglar is always provided with a bit of nice meat for the house-dog. This is a normal situation of which I approve. But the minds of all poets do not work that way; some of them, assuming that there are other minds like their own, become impatient of this "meaning" which seems superfluous, and perceive possibilities of intensity through its elimination.

Eliot's The Waste Land is an extreme example of such a poem, in which the "habits" of narrative or argument (in the sense of sequential thinking) have been suppressed in favor of a succession of characters, voices, scenes, fragments of scenes, images, quotations, allusions, snippets.

It seems true enough that we are not merely or exclusively rational creatures, that we often think and feel by leaps and intuitions, and that the subterranean or subconscious levels of our being—that part of the mind that is awake and dreaming even when we sleep—cannot be ignored. Rational control may sometimes be dangerous repression. On the other hand, we are also rational, conscious beings. Order, as much as impulse, is part of our nature. Shaking down our sensations and impressions into some logical or narrative form often has great value.

The danger of what may be loosely called the nonrational in poetry—whether in whole poems or in parts—is obscurity. Giving up or going beyond conscious order, the poet must assume that other sensibilities are enough like his or her own to respond to or follow the kind of irrational "order" it is establishing. If the poet errs in this assumption or fails somehow to accomplish what he or she thinks is being done, the incomprehensible poetry resulting will be private in the worst sense; that is, only the poet will understand it. The risk will often be worth taking, but the poet should not let ego get involved. ("Well, my friend said it makes sense to him.") Later, if not sooner, a reader's conscious mind will want to satisfy itself, in some measure, about the kind of experience the poem is. We must feel convinced of its "rightness." This is perhaps what Wallace Stevens meant when he remarked, "Poetry must resist the intelligence almost successfully."

Nonsense Verse

The value of the nonrational in poetry is in expressing the inexpressible: moods or feelings for which there is no simple rational equivalent, the dream-like quality of experience, or mystical states or beliefs. Immediacy and emotional compression may be intensified. The nonrational may be simply pleasurable, as in **nonsense verse,** nursery rhymes, or the tra-la-la's of song. Even nonsense, however, is not trivial when it is "right." Delight is never trivial. And who knows, in the Age of Freud, what deep feelings (rebellion against authority perhaps) find their expression when we hear "the cow jumped over the moon" and "the dish ran away with the spoon." "Jabberwocky" by Lewis Carroll (1832−1898) is exemplary:

'Twas brillig, and the slithy toves
    Did gyre and gimble in the wabe;
All mimsy were the borogoves,
    And the mome raths outgrabe.

"Beware the Jabberwock, my son!   5
    The jaws that bite, the claws that catch!
Beware the Jubjub bird, and shun
    The frumious Bandersnatch!"

He took his vorpal sword in hand:
    Long time the manxome foe he sought—   10
So rested he by the Tumtum tree,
    And stood awhile in thought.

And as in uffish thought he stood,
    The Jabberwock, with eyes of flame,
Came whiffling through the tulgey wood,   15
    And burbled as it came!

One, two! One, two! And through and through
　　The vorpal blade went snicker-snack!
He left it dead, and with its head
　　He went galumphing back. 20

"And hast thou slain the Jabberwock?
　　Come to my arms, my beamish boy!
O frabjous day! Callooh! Callay!"
　　He chortled in his joy.

'Twas brillig, and the slithy toves 25
　　Did gyre and gimble in the wabe;
All mimsy were the borogoves,
　　And the mome raths outgrabe.

Whatever it is, this is not the recognizable world in which we live. Humpty Dumpty's explanation, "Well, 'slithy' means 'lithe and slimy' . . . there are two meanings packed up in one word," doesn't get ~s very far. Nor does Carroll's explanation of "frumious" as combining "fuming" and "furious." Even if it were possible to satisfactorily explain all the strange, made-up words, we wouldn't be likely to bother, preferring to leave them unsolved and wonderful. *That* is precisely why we like the poem. The story is clear enough. A boy slays the dreaded Jabberwock. Indeed, it is unquestionably archetypal, like David and Goliath. (**Archetype** is a symbol of very general or mythical familiarity.) It doesn't matter much whether we know who the "beamish boy" is, nor what evil fellow the Jabberwock is, nor why the boy searches out the Jabberwock rather than the Jubjub bird or the "frumious Bandersnatch." Neither are we much worried that the Jubjub and Bandersnatch survive. It's rather pleasant and scary to know that there are still some evil fellows out there for another day. John Ciardi's suggestion that "Jabberwocky" is a satire of the pompous bugaboos "of a great deal of Victorian morality and social pretense" is a good one. But the happy nonsense survives its explanations with some irreducible meaning of its own.

"You Were Wearing," by Kenneth Koch (b. 1925), is zany contemporary nonsense:

You were wearing your Edgar Allan Poe printed cotton blouse.
In each divided up square of the blouse was a picture of Edgar Allan
　　Poe.
Your hair was blonde and you were cute. You asked me, "Do most
　　boys think that most girls are bad?"
I smelled the mould of your seaside resort hotel bedroom on your hair
　　held in place by a John Greenleaf Whittier clip.

"No," I said, "it's girls who think that boys are bad." Then we read
 Snowbound together 5
And ran around in an attic, so that a little of the blue enamel was
 scraped off my George Washington, Father of His Country, shoes.

Mother was walking in the living room, her Strauss Waltzes comb in
 her hair.
We waited for a time and then joined her, only to be served tea in
 cups painted with pictures of Herman Melville
As well as with illustrations from his book *Moby Dick* and from his
 novella, *Benito Cereno.*
Father came in wearing his Dick Tracy necktie: "How about a drink,
 everyone?" 10
I said, "Let's go outside a while." Then we went onto the porch and
 sat on the Abraham Lincoln swing.
You sat on the eyes, mouth, and beard part, and I sat on the knees.
In the yard across the street we saw a snowman holding a garbage can
 lid smashed into a likeness of the mad English king, George the
 Third.

We almost recognize this as a scene from the world we live in, but things keep
going wrong with that perception. There are (or were) sweatshirts with the
likeness of Beethoven on them, but the rest? "Edgar Allan Poe printed cotton
blouse," "John Greenleaf Whittier" hair-clip, "George Washington, Father of
His Country, shoes," and "Abraham Lincoln" porch swing? And people don't
sit on porch swings when there are snowmen.

"You Were Wearing" might be a satire on a certain kind of culturally
pretentious American family. We might guess that the girl doesn't really read
Poe or Whittier, nor the mother listen to Strauss and read Melville. But the
speaker and the girl do read Whittier's *Snowbound,* and it's shaky to guess that
the family enjoys only the signs, not the substance, of the cultural tradition the
poem outlines. Perhaps it is the tradition itself that is satirized? *Snowbound* is a
rather idyllic, old-fashioned sort of poem, a bit goody-goody, as Strauss waltzes
are a bit sugary. Dick Tracy isn't profound. The bit of dialogue between the boy
and girl may suggest that they have absorbed, from that tradition, a repressive
notion of sexuality.

But Poe and Melville certainly aren't shallow figures, and it is difficult,
even discounting their popular images, to dismiss Washington and Lincoln. Together, Poe, Whittier, Washington, Strauss, Melville, Dick Tracy, Lincoln, and
the disliked George the Third seem a mixed and representative, but hardly contemptible, group. One can do a great deal worse, in fact, than to read *Snowbound* or to follow the exploits of Dick Tracy in the comic strips.

The poem's oddness resists the reader's intelligence fairly successfully. The unseasonal porch swing and the speaker's morbid as well as unseasonal smelling "the mould of your seaside resort hotel bedroom on your hair," have a peculiar, disconnected quality. He and the girl run around "in *an* attic," not in *the* attic as we might expect. It is all rather dreamlike. The poem seems, to borrow Eliot's phrase, "not without meanings in the ordinary sense," but it nonetheless evades them, returning the reader to its amusing and enigmatic surface. The touch is high Buster Keaton.

The power of language allows the juxtaposition of all sorts of things, from the palpably untrue to the delectably outrageous. "He awoke in the morning, the early sunlight filtering through the locust, and saw a pterodactyl perched on the roof of his neighbor's house." "A dandelion grew out of Mary's ear. It was very pretty but it kept scratching her." "The Jabberwock, with eyes of flame, came whiffling through the tulgey wood." The parts of language are interchangeable. Strung together in predictable ways, they make recognizable sense: "The blue jay flew up to the tree." Strung together in unusual, surprising ways, they make non-sense: "The tree flew up to the blue jay." The habit of language gives such non-sense at least a momentary credibility; it sounds as if it might be true, until we test it. When, for whatever reason, we find we *like* it, such non-sense becomes nonsense. Like the nonsense of dreams, recombining the stuff of our real experience in crazy ways, it may be somehow significant.

Serious Nonsense

Nonsense may be serious as well as comic. "These Lacustrine Cities" by John Ashbery (b. 1927), for example, is serious nonsense. ("Lacustrine" means "of or pertaining to a lake; living or occurring on or in lakes, as various animals and plants; formed at the bottom or along the shore of lakes, as geological strata.")

These lacustrine cities grew out of loathing
Into something forgetful, although angry with history.
They are the product of an idea: that man is horrible, for instance,
Though this is only one example.

They emerged until a tower   5
Controlled the sky, and with artifice dipped back
Into the past for swans and tapering branches,
Burning, until all that hate was transformed into useless love.

Then you are left with an idea of yourself
And the feeling of ascending emptiness of the afternoon   10
Which must be charged to the embarrassment of others
Who fly by you like beacons.

The night is a sentinel.
Much of your time has been occupied by creative games
Until now, but we have all-inclusive plans for you.   15
We had thought, for instance, of sending you to the middle of the
      desert,

To a violent sea, or of having the closeness of the others be air
To you, pressing you back into a startled dream
As sea-breezes greet a child's face.
But the past is already here, and you are nursing some private project.   20

The worst is not over, yet I know
You will be happy here. Because of the logic
Of your situation, which is something no climate can outsmart.
Tender and insouciant by turns, you see

You have built a mountain of something,   25
Thoughtfully pouring all your energy into this single monument,
Whose wind is desire starching a petal,
Whose disappointment broke into a rainbow of tears.

This sounds as if it makes sense. The sentences go on as if confident they are
saying something. The tone is clear and logical: "for instance, / Though this is
only one example." Flickers of recognition or familiarity keep the reader going
forward. But who the apparently trapped "you" is and who the controlling,
apparently malevolent "we" are, or what and where "These lacustrine cities"
are, cannot be inferred from the poem. Like a dream, the closed system of the
poem makes its own kind of sense, if it makes sense at all. Elsewhere, in a poem
called "What Is Poetry," Ashbery speaks of "Trying to avoid / Ideas, as in this
poem." As Paul Carroll notes in a fine essay on Ashbery's "Leaving the Atocha
Station" (in *The Poem in Its Skin*, Big Table, 1968), "multiple combinations of
words and images (islands of significance) continually form, dissolve, and re-
form." The invitation is, Carroll argues, for the reader to become a poet "helping to create" the poem.

   Such poems are analogous to abstract art—words and images, even whole
sentences, used for their tone and feeling rather than for their representation.
Or they are analogous to music. Ashbery has said:

I feel I could express myself best in music. What I like about music is its ability of being convincing, of carrying an argument through successfully to the finish, though the terms of this argument remain unknown quantities. What remains is the structure, the architecture of the argument, scene or story. I would like to do this in poetry.

Often, in such poems, we intuit the intended feeling easily enough but, being unsure of the literal circumstances that cause the feeling, we must remain unsure of its appropriateness. In William Carlos Williams's wonderful "Great Mullen," for instance, we overhear a lively quarrel in a meadow. The antagonists seem to be a mullen (or mullein, a weed of the figwort family), a drop of dew on a blade of grass, and a cricket. But it is impossible to tell exactly which speaker says what.

> One leaves his leaves at home
> being a mullen and sends up a lighthouse
> to peer from: I will have my way,
> yellow—A mast with a lantern, ten
> fifty, a hundred, smaller and smaller   5
> as they grow more—Liar, liar, liar!
> You come from her! I can smell djer-kiss
> on your clothes. Ha, ha! you come to me,
> you—I am a point of dew on a grass-stem.
> Why are you sending heat down on me   10
> from your lantern?—You are cowdung, a
> dead stick with the bark off. She is
> squirting on us both. She has had her
> hand on you!—well?—She has defiled
> ME.—Your leaves are dull, thick   15
> and hairy.—Every hair on my body will
> hold you off from me. You are a
> dungcake, birdlime on a fencerail.—
> I love you, straight, yellow
> finger of God pointing to—her!   20
> Liar, broken weed, dungcake, you have—
> I am a cricket waving his antennae
> and you are high, grey and straight. Ha!

The dashes, which suggest interruptions, and the frequent uncertainty about who is speaking, convey the agitation of the quarrel. In the first few lines the mullen seems to be speaking, defending its uprightness by describing its tall stalk and bubbling of yellow flowers. The sea imagery ("lighthouse," "A mast with a lantern") and the mullen's arch tone in referring to itself ("One leaves his leaves at home / being a mullen") show the aloofness the mullen feels—or pretends to feel—toward the common meadow and its other inhabitants.

Most of the rest of the poem is spoken by the other voices, the drop of dew and the cricket. "Liar, liar, liar!" says the drop of dew. Far from being lofty and pure, these voices insist, the mullen is earthbound and impure. Its light falls not on the vastness of the sea, but on "a point of dew on a grass-stem." And it is not light, but heat, that the mullen sheds: "Why are you sending heat down on me / from your lantern?" The other voices emphasize, not the mullen's stalk and flowers, but the rosette of flat, homely, woolly leaves at its base, which are likened to a pat of "cowdung" and, later, to "dungcake, birdlime on a fence-rail." The insults and mockery of the other voices are intended to reprove the mullen's pretentiousness and to recall the mullen to its base, earthy origin. It is, after all, a weed.

But who is the "She" referred to in the accusations? "You come from her! I can smell djer-kiss / on your clothes." "She has had her / hand on you!—well?—She has defiled / ME." In the context of the meadow she might well be the earth herself, from which the mullen, with its tall stalk and sea imagery, has been trying to dissociate itself. The stalk, of course, points both away from and down to its earthy origins:

I love you, straight, yellow
finger of God pointing to—her!

The other voice expresses, in addition to fiercely ironic reproof ("pointing to—her!"), its affection for the wayward mullen ("I love you").

More, nonetheless, seems involved in the scene than analysis accounts for. The characterization of the mullen as masculine gives the accusations a tone of anger at a sexual betrayal: "You come from her! I can smell djer-kiss / on your clothes." It helps to know that, as Williams explained, "'djer-kiss' was when I wrote the poem, the name of a very popular perfume with which ladies used to scent their lingerie." A feeling of infidelity and jealousy permeates the poem, but analysis can take the matter no further than that. The poem remains a poem about a quarrel in a meadow, comic and, in some untraceable way, also very much more than comic. What it all stands for we might guess, but could never be certain were it not for the poet's having told us, much later. Of "Great Mullen" Williams commented:

It is a poem which technically I treasure as among one of my best though most unusual. . . . The dialogue is correctly assumed to be between a young poet and his wife, with whom he is deeply in love but to whom he has been unfaithful—in the way a man and woman in the modern world often are. The reference to ejecta, "birdlime" etc., is disgust with himself—but he will not evade speaking of it. God be my witness!

Logic of Metaphor

Short of nonsense, many poems avail themselves of the nonrational. Metaphor itself, even at its simplest, always touches it. "The clock has hands" will seem, depending on how we look at it, either plain everyday sense or somewhat frightening surreal nonsense. But metaphor functions as comparison, and common sense or reason quickly justifies it. We perceive the likenesses, the grounds of the comparison—or enough of them—and so assimilate the metaphor as a perfectly comprehensible part of whatever sort of sense the poem is making. When the comparison is extended beyond the ready likenesses, however, or when metaphors multiply one on the other, they may begin to make a kind of sense of their own. For Dylan Thomas, for instance, metaphor sometimes seemed almost a language in itself, a **"logic of metaphor."** And the resulting poems, though comprehensible, seem more nonrational than rational in method. Here is Thomas's description of his process:

> I make one image—though "make" is not the word; I let, perhaps, an image be "made" emotionally in me and then apply to it what intellectual and critical forces I possess; let it breed another, let that image contradict the first, make the third image, bred out of the other two together, a fourth contradictory image, and let them all, within my imposed formal limits, conflict. Each image holds within it the seed of its own destruction, and my dialectical method, as I understand it, is a constant building up and breaking down of the images that comes out of the central seed, which is itself destructive and constructive at the same time. . . . Out of the inevitable conflict of images—inevitable, because of the creative, recreative, destructive and contradictory nature of the motivating centre, the womb of war—I try to make that momentary peace which is a poem.

Thomas is describing a self-breeding series of **associations**—one image suggesting another in memory or imagination—with the images, in their sequence, replacing rational or discursive ways of saying something. The poet's "intellectual and critical forces," notice, are not suspended, but work only beneath the poem's metaphorical surface to control and direct it. When the method fails and the poet has not arranged the images so that a reader's responses follow them naturally, the result is impenetrable obscurity. When it succeeds, it produces poems of great compressive power, like Thomas's "Twenty-Four Years":

> Twenty-four years remind the tears of my eyes.
> (Bury the dead for fear that they walk to the grave in labour.)
> In the groin of the natural doorway I crouched like a tailor
> Sewing a shroud for a journey
> By the light of the meat-eating sun.
> Dressed to die, the sensual strut begun,

5

With my red veins full of money,
In the final direction of the elementary town
I advance for as long as forever is.

This is a birthday poem, and in line 1 the speaker refers to the reminis-
cences such an occasion may initiate. But they are not happy memories
("tears"), and in the parenthetical line 2 he dismisses such losses, perhaps the
loss of persons he loved ("the dead"). Several things are happening at once in
the line, but they can be sorted out. The reason for putting aside the reminis-
cences is to prevent that sadness from troubling "the dead," from making their
deaths a "labour." Perhaps by "the dead" he means only "our dead selves, the
selves we were in the past," and is thinking primarily of his mother. (Thomas's
mother in fact outlived him.) The line might be paraphrased, if so: "Forget the
past and its sadness lest it make those who are aging and dying, that is, walking
to the grave, suffer needlessly." The "walk to the grave," of course, becomes the
poem's central image for life as a journey "In the final direction of the elementary town," which is apparently death (elementary in the sense of simple, re-
duced-to-elements). "Labour" is chosen as the image for distress because it
suggests hardship but also because it suggests the pain of childbirth; hence, the
guess about the speaker's mother.

Line 3 describes the child in the womb, in the fetal position ("crouched
like a tailor"). Thomas reverses the clearer "In the natural doorway of the
groin," making it "In the groin of the natural doorway," in order to recall the
architectural sense of "groin" (the curved line or edge formed by the intersec-
tion of two vaults or arches), a term frequently used of church architecture and
so adding a religious overtone to the line. "Labour" in line 2 makes the image
of the tailor crouched over his sewing appropriate; it also suggests that the fetus
in some sense shared in the "labour" of his own birth. The "shroud" he sews is
perhaps his skin, or more generally the awareness of death (which birth necessarily implies). Hence, in line 6, when the poem returns to the present tense,
he is "Dressed to die." The sun is "meat-eating" in its strength and symbolizes
the natural forces, time or decay, to which life in the flesh is subject.

Nonetheless, in the poem's last four lines, the feeling is the buoyant one of
youth. The journey is a "sensual strut," and "my red veins full of money"
images the excitement of having life and vigor to spend. Death as "the elementary town" seems no longer particularly frightening. "Town" suggests life, a
community; and for the moment, only the "direction" is "final." The bravery of
the last line ("I advance") is muted somewhat by the paradox of "for as long as
forever is," which implies that "forever" has in fact a limited duration—for the
speaker it may be only as long as his life is. The final rhyme, "eyes"—"is,"
closes the circle of the poem in a muted way. The poem's loose pattern of off-
rhymes thoughout, indeed, suggests the speaker's uneasiness in the consolation
with which the poem concludes.

Thomas's language of metaphor—very little in the poem is literal—is essentially traditional (life is a journey), but the force of its jostling images seems more primitive. The landscape is biological. The self is alone. Even the social convention of money seems detached from its everyday uses. The difference I am pointing to may be seen by comparing Thomas's poem of compound metaphors with Shakespeare's compound metaphors in *Macbeth*:

> To-morrow, and to-morrow, and to-morrow
> Creeps in this petty pace from day to day
> To the last syllable of recorded time;
> And all our yesterdays have lighted fools
> The way to dusty death. Out, out, brief candle!   5
> Life's but a walking shadow, a poor player
> That struts and frets his hour upon the stage
> And then is heard no more. It is a tale
> Told by an idiot, full of sound and fury,
> Signifying nothing.   10

For all his isolating guilt, Macbeth seems a man talking to men and women; he is a member of a social fabric which, though stretched, does not tear. By contrast, Thomas's poem seems barbaric, private, dreamlike.

Surreality

Because of psychology's influence, our usual analogy for the nonrational in twentieth-century poetry is the dream. A French movement of the 1920s, **Surrealism,** has given us a word that sums up the artistic applications of the unconscious: **surreal.** The unconscious, free-associative, nonrational modes of thought (intuition, feeling, fantasy, imagination) put us in touch with a *sur*reality, literally, a superreality. It includes both the inner and the outer world, dream and reality, the flux of sensations or feelings and the hard, daylight facts of experience. In theory the rational is not so much dismissed as transcended, or absorbed, as in this prose poem by Michael Benedikt, "The Atmosphere of Amphitheatre":

> Whenever we turn on a faucet, the celebrated tube of water appears.
> We say "tube" because it appears not to be moving, it appears as likely
> to have been produced from the porcelain upwards as from the spigot
> downwards, as is the usual case. As for me, whenever I turn on any
> faucet, I satisfy my curiosity regarding its nature and character by sim-   5
> ply telling myself that "a column is coming." This is why a person in a

bathroom with both sink faucets running and the bathtub faucets dripping may be reminded of standing on a plantation veranda; and why it
may be enough to walk through the laundryroom in the basement to
experience a feeling reminiscent of standing among the ruins of Greek   10
Temple architecture.

The tone is both reasonable and good-natured ("Whenever we turn on a
faucet," "As for me"). In part for that reason, the careful observation leads
easily to the conjectural double-images of "plantation veranda" and "ruins of
Greek temple architecture," which seem psychologically convincing as well as
amusing.

    The term *surreal* has been used so widely and so loosely that it means little
more than, in some positive sense, nonrational; in any event, the poet is less
interested in definitions than in the fresh possibilities for handling experience or
feeling in poems. The twentieth-century reader is habituated to taking the nonrational seriously, and is not likely to be put off by it. Consider "Eating Poetry"
by Mark Strand (b. 1934):

Ink runs from the corners of my mouth.
There is no happiness like mine.
I have been eating poetry.

The librarian does not believe what she sees.
Her eyes are sad   5
and she walks with her hands in her dress.

The poems are gone.
The light is dim.
The dogs are on the basement stairs and coming up.

Their eyeballs roll,   10
their blond legs burn like brush.
The poor librarian begins to stamp her feet and weep.

She does not understand.
When I get on my knees and lick her hand,
she screams.   15

I am a new man.
I snarl at her and bark.
I romp with joy in the bookish dark.

Almost without thinking, the reader knows what is happening. The speaker has been delightedly reading poems in a library—"eating" them, that is, literally taking them into himself as one ingests food, turning them into his own substance. They make him happy. The librarian, by contrast, is a figure of disapproval, sad, uncomprehending, repressed ("her hands in her dress"). Having been "eaten," the poems are "gone." But the dogs—the feelings or meanings freed by the poems—"are on the basement stairs and coming up," presumably from the *sub*conscious. They are emotional, excited, beautiful. The librarian is angry and frustrated by their rowdy intrusion. Trying to appease her, the speaker tries to communicate his joy and fellow feeling, to make her understand. Freed himself, doglike happy with released feelings, he only scares her: "When I get on my knees and lick her hand, / she screams." He snarls and barks and romps with joy: "I am a new man." The poem affirms the transforming power of poems.

The poem is clearly a metaphorical fantasy. The point is not what literally occurred between the speaker and the librarian—probably nothing much, perhaps no more than his sensing or imagining her disapproval—but the feeling of the experience. The individual happiness of reading poems is somehow at odds with the impersonal, overdisciplined effect of a library. The poem's dreamlike, arbitrary fantasy (why dogs?) will not bother the reader for whom it is simply "right."

The nonrational poem can register that edge of consciousness where the mind plays tricks on us. The leaves, idle stems, and flowers of a curtain suddenly seem to be faces—one, then another, and so on. At a concert we suddenly find ourselves fantasizing that we are the conductor or the soprano anxious about the moment when we shall begin to sing. In a strange room we suddenly have the feeling that we have been there before—*déjà vu.* In "The Prisoner" by Charles Simic (b. 1938) the speaker is taking a nap with a woman he loves. It is after lunch, and the "lazy rustle" of leaves has made them sleepy. For no particular reason, or for no reason in the poem at least, the speaker finds himself imagining a prisoner, who is imagining them.

> He is thinking of us.
> These leaves, their lazy rustle
> That made us sleepy after lunch
> So we had to lie down.
>
> He considers my hand on her breast,   5
> Her closed eyelids, her moist lips
> Against my forehead, and the shadows of trees
> Hovering on the ceiling.
>
> It's been so long. He has trouble
> Deciding what else is there.   10

And all along the suspicion
That we do not exist.

The imaginary prisoner is perhaps the dozy speaker's awareness of his good fortune—lunch, summery trees, a woman he loves, which, for a prisoner, would be something like paradise—and his awareness of the precariousness of such happiness. In stanza 1 the lovers are "us," "we." But in stanza 2, possibly as she has drifted off to sleep, it becomes "my hand on her breast," not on "your breast." The lovers have drifted apart into separate consciousnesses, and in his unease and isolation, the half-awake speaker responds to his own immediate experience at a distance, in the perspective of the imaginary prisoner: "He considers my hand on her breast, / Her closed eyelids. . . ."

In stanza 3 the speaker almost becomes the prisoner: "It's been so long" is the prisoner's awareness, duplicating in some way the speaker's own deep disbelief in the good fortune of his happiness. As he slips toward sleep, the speaker's loosening sense of his surroundings becomes the prisoner's difficulty in imagining the background of his fantasy of the lovers: "He has trouble / Deciding what else is there." And the speaker's inner distrust of his reality becomes the imaginary prisoner's suspicion of *his* imaginary lovers: "And all along the suspicion / That we do not exist." The communal "we" reappears in the last line only to negate its reality: "That we do not exist."

The prisoner, we realize, has been all along a projection of the speaker himself, of some deep fear or self-doubt that will not allow him to accept his real experience for what it is. Isolated in his own consciousness (or subconsciousness) and in his own history, he is "The Prisoner" of the title. In his dim, unguarded moments between wakefulness and sleep, we know the truth about him and, in some measure, about ourselves.

The strangeness in the commonplace, or the strangeness in us sometimes as we observe the commonplace, makes the world more mysterious. Looking into a shoe-repair shop window at night, the poet may begin to be aware of the strange travels and history that bring the shoes to this place (W. S. Merwin, "Shoe Repairs," page 245). Looking at an iris, the poet may see the dark curve of the anther as tracks, as a train driving "deep into the damp heart of its stem." And he may then recall a train journey he took as a boy with his grandmother and (perhaps from a film or who knows where) the image of a boy on a French railway platform holding an iris and "waving goodbye to a grandmother"—until reality is lost in the connections the mind makes (David St. John, "Iris," page 249). Imagining what it must be like inside a stone, "cool and quiet / Even though a cow steps on it full weight," the poet remembers that "sparks fly out / When two stones are rubbed" and thinks that "perhaps it is not dark inside after all; / Perhaps there is a moon shining" (Charles Simic, "Stone," page 21). The poet may find in old "Chevrolet wheels . . . / Lying on their backs in the cindery dirt," in "shredded inner tubes abandoned on the shoulders of thruways," in "curly steel shavings . . . on garage benches," and in the "roads in South Dakota that feel around in the darkness . . .," personifications of his despair about the America of the Vietnam War years (Robert Bly, "Come with Me," page 248). Walking in a "neon fruit supermarket," the poet may fantasize an encounter with Walt Whitman, "childless, lonely old grubber, poking among the meats in the refrigerator and eyeing the grocery boys" (Allen Ginsberg, "A Supermarket in California," page 251). Like talking to ourselves, such a fantasy may be self-conscious. Writing the poem, Ginsberg notes in a parenthetical aside, "(I touch your book and dream of our odyssey in the supermarket and feel absurd.)" But, like talking to ourselves, such a fantasy may express the deepest and most serious feeling; we may reveal ourselves in daydreams no less than in sleeping dreams. Ginsberg is nowhere more earnest than in this affinity for Whitman—both poets, homosexuals, outsiders with a visionary dream of America.

Mysticism

The nonrational in poetry frequently comes close to being a secular mysticism. In "Before a Cashier's Window in a Department Store" by James Wright (1927–1980) a simple and probably ordinary enough experience generates a complex and extraordinary human empathy. The speaker's confrontation with the "beautiful cashier" and the "young manager" produces in him the feelings of several kinds of extreme human suffering: war, poverty, degeneracy, death. (In line 7, with the poet's permission, I have corrected the misprint, "driving," which appears both in *Shall We Gather at the River* and *Collected Poems*.)

1.

The beautiful cashier's white face has risen once more
Behind a young manager's shoulder.
They whisper together, and stare
Straight into my face.
I feel like grabbing a stray child   5
Or a skinny old woman
And diving into a cellar, crouching
Under a stone bridge, praying myself sick,
Till the troops pass.

2.

Why should he care? He goes.   10
I slump deeper.
In my frayed coat, I am pinned down
By debt. He nods,
Commending my flesh to the pity of the daws of God.

3.

Am I dead? And, if not, why not?   15
For she sails there, alone, looming in the heaven of the beautiful.
She knows
The bulldozers will scrape me up
After dark, behind
The officers' club.   20
Beneath her terrible blaze, my skeleton
Glitters out. I am the dark. I am the dark
Bone I was born to be.

4.

Tu Fu° woke shuddering on a battlefield   *poet of the Tang dynasty*
Once, in the dead of night, and made out   25
The mangled women, sorting
The haggard slant-eyes.
The moon was up.

5.

I am hungry. In two more days
It will be spring. So this   30
Is what it feels like.

It is crucial that the speaker's plight is not nearly so desperate as he feels. Department stores are prosperous places, and whatever brings him to the cashier's window can hardly be more awful than a little difficulty with some installment debt. The poem, therefore, risks sentimentality—feelings in excess of the cause. In part it overcomes this danger if we also recognize that the cold and unfeeling bureaucracy of the department store, though different in degree, is not really different in kind from the cold and unfeeling bureaucracies that carry out wars or inquisitions or produce poverty. The manager and the cashier are not monsters. Her moonlike face— "risen once more," "in the heaven of the beautiful"—is cold, blank and indifferent, but also without malice, beautiful. The manager "nods, / Commending my flesh to the pity of the daws of God." Not they, but the system, makes him a victim.

In part the poem overcomes the danger of sentimentality by implicitly acknowledging as irrational the excessive feelings of fear and humiliation and degradation. "I feel like . . .," the speaker says in line 5; and at the end, only "So this / Is what it feels like." "I am pinned down / By debt" may be true without implying real poverty, just as "I am hungry" need not imply that he won't have the price of lunch. The nadir of the experience occurs in the middle of the poem, not at its climax:

Beneath her terrible blaze, my skeleton
Glitters out. I am the dark. I am the dark
Bone I was born to be.

This is metaphorical, just as the cashier's moonlikeness is metaphorical. But the metaphor carries the truth of his fragile mortality—"the dark / Bone I was born to be"—which is true of every human being, rich or poor, and which justifies the compassion for the "stray child," the "skinny old woman," and the Chinese women sorting through the corpses on an eighth-century battlefield. The fact of the department store and the fact that "In two more days / It will be spring" equally place human misery, great or small, in an ironic context, as does the moon above the ancient battlefield. The cashier's moonlikeness (though the word is never used) very precisely but delicately connects with the fourth section's utter simplicity: "The moon was up." The speaker's confrontation with and defeat by authority at a cashier's window in a department store becomes, by an involuntary intuition, a vision of the common plight of the helpless. "So this," the troubled, bourgeois speaker understands, "Is what it feels like."

In such poems the poet must have the articulation of the poem under careful control. The line between convincing significance and silliness is a fine one. When such poems become too easy, they are likely to turn into mere mannerism, like Shelley's embarrassing "I fall on the thorns of life. I bleed." No one can have epiphanies every day, and the poet should be aware that he is courting absurdity, as Ginsberg is in "A Supermarket in California." Here, Wright's use of numbered sections works to hold the temperature of the poem down. "Technique," as Pound said, is "the test of a man's sincerity."

From the delightful nonsense of "Jabberwocky" to the abstract formalism of "These Lacustrine Cities" and to the dreadful earnestness of "Before a Cashier's Window in a Department Store," the poet in our psychological age has an enormous range of the nonrational to draw upon. Poetry has always been in some deep way nonrational. The subliminal powers of rhythm and image are as ancient as language itself; the poet-shaman is a traditional figure. But, after Freud, it is possible again to see the woods of fantasy and the Alps of dream as neither more nor less than parts of the everyday world in which we have our lives.

QUESTIONS AND SUGGESTIONS

1. Imagine that you are a blade of grass, an oak leaf, a daisy by an alley, a brick in a sidewalk, a mountain, or a basketball. What might it *feel* like (specific sensations like the touch of air, ground, a hand)? What has its experience been?

What might it be aware of? Write a poem in the first person, pretending to be that object.

2. Write down a column of arbitrary rhyme words. Fill in the poem with images and sentences, saying anything at all that pops into your head. Don't try to make sense, but make it sound good. *Now* read it over and over aloud, think about it. Does it make any sense? Does it have anything to do with whatever else you have been thinking and feeling?

3. In "Shoe Repairs" how does W. S. Merwin deftly prepare the reader for the poem's leap from the picture of the nighttime shoe repair shop (stanzas 1–2) to the image of it as an "Ark" into which "in another life" we will step down (stanza 3)? Do such initially surprising phrases as "scheduled deaths," "couples," "eyes of masks / from a culture lost forever," and "Ark," seem ultimately justified? (Recall, for instance, that the lace-holes of shoes are called "eyes.") How does the poem's lack of punctuation affect its tone? its theme?

Long after the scheduled deaths of animals
their skins made up into couples
have arrived here
empty
from many turnings   5
between the ways of men
and men

In a side street
by brown walls over a small light
the infinite routes   10
which they follow a little way
come together
to wait in rows in twos
soles
eyes of masks   15
from a culture lost forever

We will know the smell
in another life
stepping down
barefoot into this Ark   20
seeing it lit up but empty
the destined racks
done with the saved pairs
that went out to die each alone

4. In both of these poems, the speakers make statements which seem at first to be enigmatic, but which turn out to have reasonably clear symbolic meaning. In "The Trapper," does the comparison to "the size of a very small boy" suggest an

interpretation? Or, in "Encounter," the image of grass "whispering of its native land"? Using one or the other of these poems as a model, create a character for whom a trade or a landscape provides the elements of a fantasy.

a) *The Trapper*

PETER KLAPPERT (b. 1942)

I am digging a pit
deeper than I will need.

Already
on the other side of this mountain
something is crying in a small hoarse voice.   5

It is breaking its teeth on my teeth.

Some shy animal is taking its paw
apart in the darkness.
Some poor animal is looking through its bones.

When I grab at my lungs they contract   10
like an old leather bellows.

Something the size of a very small boy
is kicking against that trap.

b) *Encounter*

RICHARD SHELTON (b. 1933)

In some small flatland town
a stranger waits for me to arrive by train
and when I step down not knowing
where I am or why I have come
I will recognize him and give him my hand   5
He will fold my pain like a newspaper
and tuck it under his arm
He will take charge of everything

He will open a car door
I will get in and he will drive   10
expertly down Main Street out of town
toward open country where the sky
is half the world

As night comes on
we will hear grass beside the road   15
whispering of its native land
and when the stars bear down like music
I will begin to understand how things
that have never happened before
can happen again   20

from *A Midsummer-Night's Dream (V, i)*   1600

WILLIAM SHAKESPEARE   (1564–1616)

Lovers and madmen have such seething brains,
Such shaping fantasies, that apprehend
More than cool reason ever comprehends.
The lunatic, the lover, and the poet
Are of imagination all compact.   5
One sees more devils than vast hell can hold;
That is, the madman. The lover, all as frantic,
Sees Helen's beauty in a brow of Egypt.
The poet's eye, in a fine frenzy rolling,
Doth glance from heaven to earth, from earth to heaven;   10
And as imagination bodies forth
The forms of things unknown, the poet's pen
Turns them to shapes and gives to airy nothing
A local habitation and a name.
Such tricks hath strong imagination,   15
That, if it would but apprehend some joy,
It comprehends some bringer of that joy;
Or in the night, imagining some fear,
How easy is a bush supposed a bear!

Spider Crystal Ascension   1977

CHARLES WRIGHT   (b. 1935)

The spider, juiced crystal and Milky Way, drifts on his web through the
     night sky
And looks down, waiting for us to ascend . . .

At dawn he is still there, invisible, short of breath, mending his net.

All morning we look for the white face to rise from the lake like a tiny
     star.
And when it does, we lie back in our watery hair and rock.   5

Poem 1950

FRANK O'HARA   (1926–1966)

The eager note on my door said "Call me,
call when you get in!" so I quickly threw
a few tangerines into my overnight bag,
straightened my eyelids and shoulders, and

headed straight for the door. It was autumn   5
by the time I got around the corner, oh all
unwilling to be either pertinent or bemused, but
the leaves were brighter than grass on the sidewalk!

Funny, I thought, that the lights are on this late
and the hall door open; still up at this hour, a   10
champion jai-alai player like himself? Oh fie!
for shame! What a host, so zealous! And he was

there in the hall, flat on a sheet of blood that
ran down the stairs. I did appreciate it. There are few
hosts who so thoroughly prepare to greet a guest   15
only casually invited, and that several months ago.

Come with Me 1964

ROBERT BLY   (b. 1926)

Come with me into those things that have felt this despair for so long—
Those removed Chevrolet wheels that howl with a terrible loneliness,
Lying on their backs in the cindery dirt, like men drunk, and naked,
Staggering off down a hill at night to drown at last in the pond.
Those shredded inner tubes abandoned on the shoulders of thruways,   5
Black and collapsed bodies, that tried and burst,
And were left behind;
And the curly steel shavings, scattered about on garage benches,
Sometimes still warm, gritty when we hold them,
Who have given up, and blame everything on the government,   10
And those roads in South Dakota that feel around in the darkness . . .

Iris   1976

DAVID ST. JOHN   (b. 1949)

There is a train inside this iris:

You think I'm crazy, & like to say boyish
& outrageous things. No, there is

A train inside this iris.

It's a child's finger bearded in black banners.   5
A single window like a child's nail,

A darkened porthole lit by the white, angular face

Of an old woman, or perhaps the boy beside her in the stuffy,
Hot compartment. Her hair is silver, & sweeps

Back off her forehead, onto her cold & bruised shoulders.   10

The prairies fail along Chicago. Past the five
Lakes. Into the black woods of her New York; & as I bend

Close above the iris, I see the train

Drive deep into the damp heart of its stem, & the gravel   .
Of the garden path   15

Cracks under my feet as I walk this long corridor

Of elms, arched
Like the ceiling of a French railway pier where a boy

With pale curls holding

A fresh iris is waving goodbye to a grandmother, gazing   20
A long time

Into the flower, as if he were looking some great

Distance, or down an empty garden path & he believes a man
Is walking toward him, working

Dull shears in one hand; & now believe me: The train   25

Is gone. The old woman is dead, & the boy. The iris curls,
On its stalk, in the shade

Of those elms: Where something like the icy & bitter fragrance

In the wake of a woman who's just swept past you on her way
Home   30

& you remain.

A Band of Poets Desert
from the Red Army, Forever   1977

TIM CALHOUN*

All day our horses ran away with us.
Suddenly the edge vanished.
Stars emerged in the heavens,
Halving themselves infinitely
To make new night flowers.   5

As we galloped near the river without color,
Our minds let go of the reins.
A few individual men
Were lost permanently.
We did not mourn the passing there.   10

By dawn an absolute candle
Gilded the tiny mushroom towns silver,
And smeared gold behind my eyes.
I could not distinguish my comrades
From the one anothers of my being.   15

Clearly the war was over now.
Though a cannon toiled in the distance
And church bells thudded in their rims,
All this behind us became forgotten country.
For what we discovered is never lost.   20

A Supermarket in California   1956

ALLEN GINSBERG   (b. 1926)

What thoughts I have of you tonight, Walt Whitman, for I walked down the sidestreets under the trees with a headache self-conscious looking at the full moon.

In my hungry fatigue, and shopping for images, I went into the neon fruit supermarket, dreaming of your enumerations.

What peaches and what penumbras! Whole families shopping at night! Aisles full of husbands! Wives in the avocados, babies in the tomatoes!— and you, García Lorca°, what were you doing down by the watermelons?

I saw you, Walt Whitman, childless, lonely old grubber, poking among the meats in the refrigerator and eyeing the grocery boys.

I heard you asking questions of each: Who killed the pork chops? What price bananas? Are you my Angel?   5

I wandered in and out of the brilliant stacks of cans following you, and followed in my imagination by the store detective.

We strode down the open corridors together in our solitary fancy tasting artichokes, possessing every frozen delicacy, and never passing the cashier.

Where are we going, Walt Whitman? The doors close in an hour. Which way does your beard point tonight?

(I touch your book and dream of our odyssey in the supermarket and feel absurd.)

Will we walk all night through solitary streets? The trees add shade to shade, lights out in the houses, we'll both be lonely.   10

Will we stroll dreaming of the lost America of love past blue automobiles in driveways, home to our silent cottage?

Ah, dear father, graybeard, lonely old courage-teacher, what America did you have when Charon° quit poling his ferry and you got out on a smoking bank and stood watching the boat disappear on the black waters of Lethe°?

3 *García Lorca:* Spanish poet (1898– 1936).   12 *Charon:* god of Hades who ferried the dead across the rivers Styx and Acheron; *Lethe:* river of forgetfulness in Hades.

Tradition and Feeling:
Aphrodite and the Mouse

The ancient and the new mingle in poetry. The road on which the contemporary poet stands disappears into the past, where it once wound in the rain forest, across the dusty savannah, or out of ice-age mountains. In a two-line poem, "Memory of Spring," W. S. Merwin recalls this antiquity:

The first composer
could hear only what he could write

Civilizations have risen and fallen. The traditions of the arts, even though the works and sometimes the artists' names are forgotten, have been passed along from living hand to living hand. Only one work survives of Praxiteles, the greatest of the Greek sculptors (fourth century B.C.). His famous statue of Aphrodite is lost, and, as Robert Francis notes in "Aphrodite as History," all that is left is a copy of a copy:

Though the marble is ancient
It is only an ancient
Copy and though the lost
Original was still more ancient

Still it was not Praxiteles   5
Only a follower of Praxiteles
And Praxiteles was not first.

Stone falls from stone; paint flakes; languages alter or disappear. "We write
in sand," Edmund Waller wrote in the seventeenth century; "our language
grows / And, like the tide, our work o'erflows." Even the great and sophisticated Chaucer grows irretrievably quaint, and Shakespeare must begin to be
read with the magnifying glass of history. Shakespeare's boast—

Not marble, nor the gilded monuments
Of princes, shall outlive this powerful rhyme

—is perhaps less realistic than the boast of his contemporary, Samuel Daniel:

I know I shall be read, among the rest,
So long as men speak English

Five hundred years? At most, an inch in the long journey of the race.
    Because old poems fade, we always need new poems, just as we need new
sculptures, new paintings, and new music. However durable the human truth
may be, it must always be reimagined and made new. The poet lives "in a
spring still not written of." "All things fall and are built again," William Butler
Yeats says in "Lapis Lazuli." "And those that build them again are gay." Writing in his old age and in the shadow of World War II, Yeats took his theme
from a little scene of Chinamen climbing a mountain path, carved in lapis
lazuli, a deep-blue semiprecious stone. ("King Billy" is the English King William
III, whose cannon won the Battle of Boyne in Ireland in 1690.)

I have heard that hysterical women say
They are sick of the palette and fiddle-bow,
Of poets that are always gay,
For everybody knows or else should know
That if nothing drastic is done   5
Aeroplane and Zeppelin will come out,
Pitch like King Billy bomb-balls in
Until the town lie beaten flat.

All perform their tragic play,
There struts Hamlet, there is Lear,   10
That's Ophelia, that Cordelia;
Yet they, should the last scene be there,
The great stage curtain about to drop,

If worthy their prominent part in the play,
Do not break up their lines to weep.   15
They know that Hamlet and Lear are gay;
Gaiety transfiguring all that dread.
All men have aimed at, found and lost;
Black out; Heaven blazing into the head:
Tragedy wrought to its uttermost.   20
Though Hamlet rambles and Lear rages,
And all the drop-scenes drop at once
Upon a hundred thousand stages,
It cannot grow by an inch or an ounce.

On their own feet they came, or on shipboard,   25
Camelback, horseback, ass-back, mule-back,
Old civilizations put to the sword.
Then they and their wisdom went to rack:
No handiwork of Callimachus°,   *Greek sculptor, 5th c.* B.C.
Who handled marble as if it were bronze,   30
Made draperies that seemed to rise
When sea-wind swept the corner, stands;
His long lamp-chimney shaped like the stem
Of a slender palm, stood but a day;
All things fall and are built again,   35
And those that build them again are gay.

Two Chinamen, behind them a third,
Are carved in lapis lazuli,
Over them flies a long-legged bird,
A symbol of longevity;   40
The third, doubtless a serving-man,
Carries a musical instrument.
Every discoloration of the stone,
Every accidental crack or dent,
Seems a water-course or an avalanche,   45
Or lofty slope where it still snows
Though doubtless plum or cherry-branch
Sweetens the little half-way house
Those Chinamen climb towards, and I
Delight to imagine them seated there;   50
There, on the mountain and the sky,
On all the tragic scene they stare.
One asks for mournful melodies;
Accomplished fingers begin to play.

Their eyes mid many wrinkles, their eyes,
Their ancient, glittering eyes, are gay.

Tradition is the long handle that gives force to the blow of the new, sharp head of the axe. The beginning poet will do well to heed Pound's "Make it new." Without change, art stagnates. But the poet will also do well to remember the ancient calling he or she follows and its perdurable truths. As T. S. Eliot points out in "Tradition and the Individual Talent," the poet "is not likely to know what is to be done, unless he lives in what is not merely the present, but the present moment of the past, unless he is conscious, not of what is dead, but of what is already living." Mere fashion and false lights mislead. John Dryden (1631–1700) has suggested the fate of those rash poets who

Puffed with vain pride, presume they understand,
And boldly take the trumpet in their hand. . . .
With impudence the laurel they invade,
Resolved to like the monsters they have made.
Virgil, compared to them, is flat and dry;   5
And Homer understood not poetry:
Against their merit if this age rebel,
To future times for justice they appeal.
But waiting till mankind shall do them right,
And bring their works triumphantly to light,   10
Neglected heaps we in bye-corners lay,
Where they become to worms and moths a prey.

Magic

Hard as it may be to accept in our scientific age, at the center of the poetic tradition is the fact that poetry, like all arts, is magical. For there is always something in art that cannot be controlled or contrived, something beyond the artist's own powers, something magical. Labor at it as the artist may, the best is always something that just "comes," that is unpredictable and unexpected. "No surprise for the writer," Robert Frost says, "no surprise for the reader."

The classical explanation of the magic was the **Muse,** one of nine goddesses, the daughters of Zeus and Mnemosyne, whose aid and inspiration poets and musicians invoked. Calliope, Enterpe, Erato, and Polyhymnia were the muses of epic, lyric, love, and sacred poetry. Often enough, the Muses were fickle and difficult to please; hence we hear even today the phrase "courting the muse." The Christian explanation was similar: **inspiration** (literally, from Latin, "to be breathed into"). The divine wind blows where it will. The Romantic explanation was **genius,** some freak of nature or of soul. And the modern explanation is the **subconscious,** a bubbling up from the irrational parts of the mind. Whether the source be seen as outside or within the poet, these are all explanations that do not explain. Sociology proves equally unsatisfactory: that poets are somehow the "antennae of the race," alert to the intellectual currents of the time, gathering something from the air. "Creative man," C. G. Jung says, "is a riddle that we may try to answer in various ways, but always in vain." The power remains unexpected and mysterious. Randall Jarrell likens it to being struck by lightning. The poet may stand on high ground in a thunderstorm, but nothing guarantees that he or she will be struck.

Explanations probably do not matter so long as the poet gets on with writing the poems. Poems come, or don't; are good, or not. In practice X. J. Kennedy's punning "Ars Poetica" is good advice:

The goose that laid the golden egg
Died looking up its crotch
To find out how its sphincter worked.

Would you lay well? Don't watch.

Being self-conscious or following some jimcrack theory has probably spoiled more poems than just taking things as they come. The poet's technical experience, his technical readiness, is like a finely tuned radio apparatus that is activated by the message, wherever it comes from.

It should not be surprising that the arts are magical, for they are very primitive and, in their origins, no doubt occult. The oldest paintings known are those on the walls of caves during the stone age. Cave dwellers drew the beasts that they hunted in order, through whatever ceremony, to gain some mysterious mastery over them. The oldest poems were the charms, spells, incantations, curses, and prayers that accompanied the magical rites of preliterate cultures. Their function was to ward off evil or to cure a toothache or to invoke the gods. In the most recent account of such things, Julian Jaynes (*The Origin of Consciousness in the Breakdown of the Bicameral Mind,* 1976) argues that poetry was originally the "divine knowledge" or "divine hallucinations" of primitive man before the dawn of individual consciousness. "The god-side of our ancient mentality . . . usually, or perhaps always, spoke in verse." "Poetry then," he adds, "was the language of the gods."

Children are the most accessible primitives we have, and the old **word magic** still functions among them. "King's X"—though no modern child has the faintest inkling of its meaning—establishes a truce. "Sticks and stones may break my bones / But words don't hurt a bit" remains a magical incantation against insult. Name magic, primitive man's reluctance to have his name known lest it be used in spells against him, still continues as in "Puddentane, / Ask me again and I'll tell you the same." Children even use poetry as a form of government. "Eenee, meenee, mynee, moe. . . ." Remember? Or "One potato, two potato, three potato, four. . . ." Such charms are part of an oral subculture that children pass along from generation to generation because, like all preliterate peoples, children delight in words, find them powerful, and fear them.

Though we don't admit it, adults aren't much different. There are certain words that everybody knows but can't use in public (and that I can't write here); they are taboo. We use magical words in court and in church and when we quarrel. Toilet walls, like walls of ancient caves, are covered with drawings and runes and rhymes, as Edward Field reports in a poem called "Graffiti":

> . . . that whole wall, the size of a school blackboard,
> figured over as it was like an oriental temple,
> the work of a people, a folk artifact,
> the record of lifetimes of secret desires,
> the forbidden and real history of man.

Like graffiti, dirty jokes are an ineradicable, subliterary folk art. Not necessarily funnier than clean jokes, they are a way of handling subjects otherwise too hot to handle—to pass on taboo information or to find out things we are too serious about to discuss openly. Safe behind the defensive leer of jokes we can communicate boldly about what we most fear and most desire. Something like this is happening when we avoid the words for dying by using **euphemism,** that is, evasive circumlocutions like "pass on" or (again hiding behind a leer) "kick the bucket."

Feelings and Self-Discovery

Like those primitive genres, graffiti and dirty jokes, poetry too deals with "hot" subjects. Love and death are its themes. The poem that matters begins always where we are most vulnerable, where we care the most; and it comes, as Richmond Lattimore says in "Verse," "Of some oyster's-irritant, some cinder promoting / iris and spangle." Like whistling in the dark, or talking to yourself, poetry has to do with what troubles us. For the poet, writing is often a process of self-discovery.

Several years ago, when I was living in a farmhouse, a small event made a commotion in my life. Reading one night, I heard the thwack of a mousetrap in the kitchen. Investigating, I found that the trap had struck the mouse only a glancing blow. His head a bloody mess, he was staggering across the floor. I grabbed an empty tin can and chased him through several rooms before I could capture him. Then I considered how to put him out of his misery. There was a pile of concrete blocks behind the house, and I thought of putting him on one and using another to crush him. I thought of putting him in the toilet and flushing him down. What I chose to do was perhaps sillier, though it seemed reasonable enough then.

A friend had moved not long before and, in the process of ridding up things he didn't want, had sold me a Wyatt Earp-looking .22 caliber target pistol for five dollars. So I fetched and loaded the gun and, by using a shirt cardboard under the can, got the mouse onto the grass in the back yard (on which a yellow bug-light shone eerily from the porch). I blasted away—and missed with every shot. In the deep country silence, which I suddenly heard, I reloaded. The second volley hit the mouse.

Never having killed a fellow creature at close range, I was more shaken than I could admit. The indignity made it worse: there I stood in my yard, after midnight, crying over killing a mouse. I knew that my nearest neighbor, who had certainly heard the shots, would ask me about them in the morning. He did, and I lied. I told him that I had just happened to remember the pistol and decided to try it out on a beer can.

Feelings can be embarrassing when they haven't been assimilated into our lives, when we haven't had a chance to test them. I was afraid that my friend would laugh if I told him the truth. The last thing in my mind was writing a poem about the incident. A year or so later, however, in the drift of my inner life, I was able to accept the way I had felt and began to write a poem, "Ballad of the Mouse." I didn't mind then allowing anyone to know what I hadn't earlier been able to tell a single friend.

> A mouse the trap had slapped on, but not caught,
> stood in the floor—
> bloody whiskered—in the curious light
> snapped on from the kitchen door:
>
> grooved in the gray skull-fur   5
> where the steel spring banged him,
> blood from his ears, and one of two bead-black eyes
> popped almost out, and hanging,
>
> looking his bad luck, he skeered through doors,
> halls, waddled along walls,   10
> was exposed behind dressers,
> hobbling with the load of his pain through falls,
>
> bumps, skids, until the portable (peaches
> can) prison (from the trash sack) fell
> into place, changing the hellishly lighted chambers   15
> to a pleasurably blackened cell

as comfortable as his hole, but showing
a scar of light around the rim.
A shirt cardboard slid under—moving floor—
and gathered him   20

into the lurch and claw-slipping tilt and
ride of air, and bore
him giddy, sloping and scratching
out the back door

to the yellow-porch-lit and midnight lawn,   25
and slid free his small terror
into the matty, spiny grass that held him like rails.
Shadowy, his executioner,

choosing (over drowning or crushing)
the doubtful love of a gun,   30
loomed over him, unready, tall. Unsteadily
he tried to run and the world blurred, un-

til he sat gathering his shakes in the grass-blades.
The long-barreled (.22, target) revolver lowered
to arm's length   35
toward the panting, furred bird-ribs not yet dead,

and aimed, and fired.
Six irregular shots
drove deep their thunderous metal seeds
flashing into the earth in spots   40

all around the tiny breath
they were meant for, spurting up yellow-brown
fountains of dirt
as before some palace, circus: forest, pillars, a kind of crown

in the noise and light of the murdering storm.   45
That poor marksman, love,
clicked, quietly
ticked, reloading, far, far, far above

the withered and dumb and dirt-daubled mouse.
Then light and leaden rain   50
stomped down again; and one blind iron tear
flooded all the sap of his pain

into the earth along with it, leaving—
indistinguishable in the churned-up lawn—
a flattened and sucked-out pelt   55
of half-buried once-mouse, now mouse-gone.

In the yellow-gloomed arena, death's main drag, beyond
which stars still leaked
the light of heaven onto woods
and hills the echoes had crashed and streaked   60

and rolled across from farm to farm,
in the ochre fungus of death, gun-handed, stone,
stood the hunter, victor—
tall, furious, foolish; alone.

The poet tests his feeling in the poem. Feelings come in all sizes and
shapes, all shades and colors, twenty-four hours a day. They are all, in a sense,
genuine, since we have them. But many of them are not "true" feelings; that is,
feelings that we can accept, affirm, and live with. For example, rage at an old
lady driving twenty miles per hour in a thirty-five mile zone (and taking up two
lanes) when you are in a hurry is not a "true" feeling. Nor is envy of a friend
who has come into some good fortune. Nor is self-pity. We have such feelings,
but we don't approve them or act on them. At crucial moments we often don't
know what we feel, or have contradictory feelings. As with a delicately balanced mobile, the slightest influence can set feelings in motion. It would be
easy, in a different mood, to feel compassionate toward the old lady in that
car—for the anger to subside as suddenly as it had gathered. We are extremely
changeable. Sorting out the multiplicity of our feelings, understanding them,
editing them, coming to terms with them (whether in action or in art) is as
much a moral process as it is an aesthetic one. How we do this is related to
what kind of person we choose to be. For the poet, as later for the right reader,
the poem (in Frost's words) "ends in a clarification of life—not necessarily a
great clarification, such as sects and cults are founded on, but in a momentary
stay against confusion."

The danger to the poet in relying on what we may call "false" feelings is
sentimentality: feelings in excess of, unjustified by, their specific cause. Who
hasn't stood alone, late on a rainy night, looking out the window at a deserted
street; then, feeling desolate, written a poem about the dark tragedy of everything? In the morning, however, with the sun out and the birds chittering,
these gloomy pronouncements seem silly and empty. Self-pity is emotionally like
taking a bath in warm syrup—"poor me"—and can be destructive when we let
ourselves believe it. Hamlet is credible when he says, suicidally, in context, "To
be or not to be: that is the question"; a beaming undergraduate, girlfriend on
his arm, is not.

For the poet, writing the poem and then the poem itself measure her or his feelings, provide ways of exploring, testing, and weighing them. This is, in part, what Wordsworth meant in saying that poetry "takes its origin from emotion recollected in tranquillity."

> All good poetry is the spontaneous overflow of powerful feelings: and though this be true, poems to which any value can be attached were never produced on any variety of subjects but by a man who, being possessed of more than usual organic sensibility, had also thought long and deeply. For our continued influxes of feeling are modified and directed by our thoughts, which are indeed the representatives of all our past feelings.

Every poet has a deep drawer full of "busted" poems. Some the poet just lost interest in. Some the poet couldn't bring off technically. And more than the poet would like to admit simply melted away because the feeling—sappy, soppy, soupy—couldn't bear the weight of attention that a good poem demands. As Pound notes, "In depicting the motions of the 'human heart' the durability of the writing depends on the exactitude. It is the thing that is true and stays true that keeps fresh for the new reader."

Close kin to sentimentality, **overstatement** is to the ideas of a poem what sentimentality is to feelings. Like the used-car salesman's hard sell, overstatement, claiming too much, asserting something beyond what seems justified, makes a reader uncomfortable, then resistant. One fraction of an ounce over and the scale tips. **Understatement,** on the other hand, is always safe, and its calm usually carries a reassuring air of conviction. Your best reader won't miss anything. Consider a poem by Philip Larkin (b. 1922), "Talking in Bed":

> Talking in bed ought to be easiest,
> Lying together there goes back so far,
> An emblem of two people being honest.
>
> Yet more and more time passes silently.
> Outside, the wind's incomplete unrest   5
> Builds and disperses clouds about the sky,
>
> And dark towns heap up on the horizon.
> None of this cares for us. Nothing shows why
> At this unique distance from isolation
>
> It becomes still more difficult to find   10
> Words at once true and kind,
> Or not untrue and not unkind.

How quietly, carefully, Larkin picks his words. The couple's mutual loss is subtle. It is only "more difficult to find / Words at once true and kind." The couple is still at a "unique distance from isolation"—still together, still close. "Or not untrue and not unkind" is still not "untrue and unkind." Yet the implication of the last line is that words "untrue and unkind" would be all too easy to find. Moreover, the sense that the malaise is progressive, accumulating, is unmistakable ("more and more time passes silently"), although the poem refuses to predict or to draw the conclusions of its evidence. The speaker's feeling comes through indirectly in the image of "the wind's incomplete unrest." Like the wind's, his unrest, his uneasiness remains "incomplete." If the reader senses that, like the clouds, marriages are built and dispersed by unrest, it is the reader's conclusion. "Nothing shows why" is the simple assertion on which the poem's painful awareness turns.

Overstatement may have dramatic uses, as in George Herbert's "The Collar" (page 106) where the speaker's sentimental exaggerations characterize his unstable state of mind:

> I struck the board and cried, "No more;
> I will abroad!
> What? shall I ever sigh and pine?"

Bold, deliberate overstatement—**hyperbole**—can be effective in the appropriate context. We are familiar with everyday hyperbole like "I'd give my right arm for a piece of that pie." We know that the statement isn't to be taken literally. This sort of understood overstatement appears in Dylan Thomas's "Fern Hill" (page 173)—"I was prince of the apple towns"—or in "The Sun Rising" by John Donne (1573–1631). Here the morning sun is shining in on another pair of lovers in bed:

> Busy old fool, unruly sun,
>   Why dost thou thus,
> Through windows and through curtains call on us?
> Must to thy motions lovers' seasons run?
>   Saucy pedantic wretch, go chide   5
>   Late school boys and sour prentices°,   *apprentices*
>   Go tell court huntsmen that the king will ride,
>   Call country ants to harvest offices;
> Love, all alike, no season knows nor clime,
> Nor hours, days, months, which are the rags of time.   10
>
>   Thy beams, so reverend and strong
>   Why shouldst thou think?
> I could eclipse and cloud them with a wink,
> But that I would not lose her sight so long;
>   If her eyes have not blinded thine,   15
>   Look, and tomorrow late tell me,

Whether both th' Indias of spice and mine
   Be where thou leftst them, or lie here with me.
Ask for those kings whom thou saw'st yesterday,
   And thou shalt hear, All here in one bed lay.   20

   She's all states, and all princes, I,
      Nothing else is.
Princes do put play us; compared to this,
All honor's mimic, all wealth alchemy.
      Thou, sun, art half as happy as we,   25
         In that the world's contracted thus;
      Thine age asks ease, and since thy duties be
      To warm the world, that's done in warming us.
Shine here to us, and thou art everywhere;
This bed thy center is, these walls, thy sphere.   30

Angry at being disturbed by the morning light, the speaker tells the sun to go
wake others instead: schoolboys, apprentices, the king's huntsmen, farmers.
Stanzas 2 and 3 are almost nothing but hyperbole. The speaker could "eclipse
and cloud" the sun (by closing his eyes), unless the beauty of the lady's eyes has
already blinded the sun. He asserts that the "Indias of spice and mine" are in
fact here, in the person of the lady; and all kings in himself. "She's all states,
and all princes, I, / Nothing else is." The lovers are, he says, in fact the whole
world, their bed the center of the sun's orbit. The deliberate exaggeration is
playful but not unserious; the self-absorbed lovers are a world in themselves.

The Function of Poetry

Poetry is feeling, the expression of feeling, and the exploration and discipline of feeling. This is a socializing function. As an afternoon in the Metro-
politan Museum of Art looking at paintings like Brueghel's *The Corn Harvest*,
Vermeer's *Young Woman with a Water Jug*, Pieter De Hooch's *Scene in a Court-
yard*, and Frans Hals's *The Merry Company* can make the faces in the Fifth
Avenue bus, afterward, seem beautiful Dutch faces, so all the arts have much to
do with the way we see the world, other people, ourselves. "Poetry is indispen-
sable," said the French poet Jean Cocteau, "—if I only knew what for." But it
seems clear that all the arts have a moral and, in the largest sense, a political
dimension. "The arts," notes Pound in his essay "The Serious Artist," "give us
a great percentage of the lasting and unassailable data regarding the nature of
man." "Literature," he remarks elsewhere, "is news that STAYS news."
   Pound also contends that literature "has to do with the clarity and vigor of
'any and every' thought and opinion":

It has to do with maintaining the very cleanliness of the tools . . . the individual cannot think and communicate his thought, the governor and legislator cannot act effectively or frame his laws, without words, and the solidity and validity of these words is in the care of the damned and despised *litterati*. When their work goes rotten—by that I do not mean when they express indecorous thoughts—but when their very medium, the very essence of their work, the application of word to thing goes rotten, i.e., becomes slushy and inexact, or excessive and bloated, the whole machinery of social and of individual thought and order goes to pot. This is the lesson of history, and a lesson not yet half learned.

Always—though in fashions we may not wholly understand—the arts "help us to live our lives," as Wallace Stevens says. For Stevens, the central event of recent centuries is the disappearance of the gods. "To speak of the origin and end of gods is not a light matter. It is to speak of the origin and end of eras of human belief." In "Two or Three Ideas" he writes:

> To see the gods dispelled in mid-air and dissolve like clouds is one of the great human experiences. It is not as if they had gone over the horizon to disappear for a time; nor as if they had been overcome by other gods of greater power and profounder knowledge. It is simply that they came to nothing. Since we have always shared all things with them and have always had a part of their strength and, certainly, all of their knowledge, we shared likewise this experience of annihilation. It was their annihilation, not ours, and yet it left us feeling that in a measure, we, too, had been annihilated. It left us feeling dispossessed and alone in a solitude, like children without parents, in a home that seemed deserted, in which the amical rooms and halls had taken on a look of hardness and emptiness. What was most extraordinary is that they left no mementoes behind, no thrones, no mystic rings, no texts either of the soil or of the soul. It was as if they had never inhabited the earth. There was no crying out for their return. They were not forgotten because they had been a part of the glory of the earth. At the same time, no man ever muttered a petition in his heart for the restoration of those unreal shapes. There was always in every man the increasingly human self, which instead of remaining the observer, the non-participant, the delinquent, became constantly more and more all there was or so it seemed; and whether it was so or merely seemed so still left it for him to resolve life and the world in his own terms.

We are left, in Stevens's view, in a reality without values, without coherence, alienated, in a time "spiritually violent, it may be said, for everyone alive." It is left to the "increasingly human self" to constantly reimagine the world so as to give it meaning and nobility, as that human self once imagined the gods ("the gods of China are always Chinese"). In the largest sense, the **imagination** is the image-making, and so creative, mind. For Stevens it includes the imaginations of "the philosopher, the artist, the teacher, the moralist and other figures, including the poet," and it is central, as it always was. "We live in the mind," he argues, and there can be no reality, no view of reality, even the bleakest, which is not imagined. It remains possible, therefore, he concludes in the essay "The Noble Rider and the Sound of Words," for the imagination to re-create the world in terms of nobility:

> But as a wave is a force and not the water of which it is composed, which is never the same, so nobility is a force and not the manifestations of which it is composed, which are never the same. . . . It is not an artifice that the mind has added to human nature. The mind has added nothing to human nature. It is a violence from within that protects us from a violence without. It is the imagination pressing back against the pressure of reality. It seems, in the last analysis, to have something to do with our self-preservation; and that, no doubt, is why the expression of it, the sound of its words, helps us to live our lives.

Different as William Carlos Williams's poems may seem from Stevens's, his vision of the function of poetry is essentially the same. "The birth of the imagination," Williams says in the prologue to *Kora in Hell*, "is like waking from a nightmare." In the prose of *Spring and All* he asserts:

> To refine, to clarify, to intensify that eternal moment in which we alone live there is but a single force—the imagination . . . an actual force comparable to electricity or steam, it is not a plaything but a power that has been used from the first to raise the understanding.

Confronted by the vastness, multiplicity, and apparent intractability of the world the senses perceive and "cling to in despair, not knowing which way to turn," alienated from it and from his fellows, the individual cannot escape "crushing humiliation" unless he is able to somehow "raise himself to some approximate co-extension with the universe." "This," Williams declares, "is possible by aid of the imagination." Works of art come to "stand between man and nature as saints once stood between man and the sky." The world, grasped within the poem—its red wheelbarrows, cats, roses, plums, men and women—becomes bearable and beautiful with imagination. "So much depends."

In the prologue to *Kora in Hell*, Williams describes the poetic process:

> A poet witnessing the chicory flower and realizing its virtues of form and color so constructs his praise as to borrow no particle from right or left. He gives his poem over to the flower and its plant themselves, that they may benefit by those cooling winds of the imagination which thus returned upon them will refresh them at their task of saving the world. But what does it mean, re-marked his friends?

Williams's syntax is hard to follow but is exact. Imagination and reality are equal and interacting. Both give, both receive. Without the imagination, reality

is "unrefreshed." Without reality, its colors and minute particulars, the imagination is empty. Finally, however, it is reality that saves us. "This is the generosity also of art. It closes up the ranks of understanding. It shows the world at
one with itself." It is not hyperbole when Williams writes, in "Asphodel, That
Greeny Flower":

> My heart rouses
>> thinking to bring you news
>>> of something
> that concerns you
>> and concerns many men. Look at   5
>>> what passes for the new.
> You will not find it there but in
>> despised poems.
>>> It is difficult
> to get the news from poems   10
>> yet men die miserably every day
>>> for lack
> of what is found there.
>> Hear me out
>>> for I too am concerned   15
> and every man
>> who wants to die at peace in his bed
>>> besides.

QUESTIONS AND SUGGESTIONS

1. Is this a poem or a graffito?

    Born a virgin.
    Died a virgin.
    Laid in her grave.

2. Consider the themes in these poems by students:

a) RON LOUIE*

    A man I met in Cincinnati
    who drove his Volkswagen

from Motown
brought his boy
to the stadium where   5
I sat next to him

Went every year to
one of baseball's parks
driving honestly
to see the country   10
and its baseball
waiting, buying tickets
and not smoking

watching baseballs
spinning circles in   15
Cincinnati's sky
the sky in Riverfront Stadium
the sky in Three Rivers and Shea
like the sky in Yankee and Wrigley
those arcs spinning threads   20
stringing stadium beads

The boy will have seen
every baseball park and
of course, every team
those men   25
There's a new baseball park
next year, being built—
New Orleans
and by the time that
they're through, the boy   30
will have grown
and the teams
will have changed.

b) *Planting*

RUCKY SELIGMAN*

Saints stand
in back gardens
of the houses on the hill
blessing the beanplants
asleep on their vines.   5
Windows open,
April night
mingles with talk
left over from supper
and prayers by bedsides.   10
Families fill the houses

on the hill;
their children are darkhaired,
their women plump,
their sauces rich   15
with fresh vegetables.

c) *The Lament of an Old Eskimo Woman*

TIM CALHOUN*

I say to them, my children
That the old ways are gone.

That motor-boat, rifle, down-jacket
have usurped
Eskimo kyak, harpoon and seal.   5

They do not hear me, my children.

When I lift the map
of my face
before white man's reflecting glass
the snow   10
in my being gathers
and I cry
and mourn the lost world of my mother.

3. How do these poems use *history* to refresh contemporary experience? Consider the way each poet states or implies his theme. Richmond Lattimore's "Hiroshima" is a "found" poem, one of a series called "Sonnets from the Encyclopaedia Britannica"—using information from the edition of 1936. Suppose Estrid the Conqueror in John Ciardi's "Thematic" were imaginary and couldn't be found in any encyclopedia: would that change the poem? Try your hand at a poem using a historical subject, real or fictional. Perhaps choose as your speaker a private soldier in the army of Alexander the Great at the Battle of Granicus—and when you are done, search out the fine little poem "How We Heard the Name" by Alan Dugan (b. 1923).

a) *Hiroshima*

RICHMOND LATTIMORE (b. 1906)

Fortunate in its lovely situation
beside the waters of the Inland Sea,
Hiroshima has raised its population
from about a hundred thousand (1903)
to a quarter of a million souls today.   5
The city stands on a small plain, between
hills and the islands scattered on the bay.

Its fame is partly due to the serene
and nearby presence of divine Bentin
on her small island, and to the belief   10
that she bestows an influence from heaven,
for she is god of radiance, and has been
adored by pilgrims, constantly.

                              The chief
temple dates from the year 587.

b) *Thematic*

JOHN CIARDI (b. 1916)

Estrid the Conqueror raised seven red-handed
sons, all lopped in the Conquest, and he bloodlet
too pale to recruit such captains again.

It was a famous grief and long in the practice
of ethnic tragedians, though Estrid ruled   5
less than a six month's rage, the throne

gone to an idiot nephew whose reign ground on
through so dull a peace, three generations of poet
tick-tocked time without recording his name.

So much for the great emotions. All art knows   10
frenzy matters, of course. Yet one may ask:
whose? to whom? in which of the lost kingdoms?

c) *Waiting for the Barbarians*

CONSTANTINE CAVAFIS (1863–1933)

Translated from the Greek by Richmond Lattimore

Why are we all assembled and waiting in the market place?

It is the barbarians; they will be here today.

Why is there nothing being done in the senate house?
Why are the senators in session but are not passing laws?

Because the barbarians are coming today.   5
Why should the senators make laws any more?
The barbarians will make the laws when they get here.

Why has our emperor got up so early
and sits there at the biggest gate of the city
high on his throne, in state, and with his crown on?   10

Because the barbarians are coming today
and the emperor is waiting to receive them

and their general. And he has even made ready
a parchment to present them, and thereon
he has written many names and many titles.   15

Why have our two consuls and our praetors
come out today in their red embroidered togas?
Why have they put on their bracelets with all those amethysts

and rings shining with the glitter of emeralds?
Why will they carry their precious staves today   20
which are decorated with figures of gold and silver?

Because the barbarians are coming today
and things like that impress the barbarians.

Why do our good orators not put in any appearance
and make public speeches and do what they generally do?   25

Because the barbarians are coming today
and they get bored with eloquent public speeches.

Why is everybody beginning to be so uneasy?
Why so disordered? (See how grave all the faces
have become!) Why do the streets and squares empty so quickly,   30
and they are all anxiously going home to their houses?

Because it is night, and the barbarians have not got here,
and some people have come in from the frontier
and say that there aren't any more barbarians.

What are we going to do now without the barbarians?   35
In a way, those people, they were a solution.

4. Here is a poem of mine with several words or images omitted. In the
context, what words or images would *you* insert if it were your poem? Compare
your suggestions with the original in Appendix I. What gains or losses do you
see?

In a Spring Still Not Written Of

ROBERT WALLACE (b. 1932)

This morning
with a class of girls outdoors, I saw
how frail poems are
in a world   with flowers,   *participle or adjective*
in which, overhead,   5
the great elms
—green, and tall—
stood   leaves in their arms.   *participle*

The girls listened equally
to my drone, reading, and to the bees'   10

ricocheting
among them for the   on the bone,   *noun*
or gazed off at a distant mower's
            of green   *noun*
and clover, flashing,   15
threshing in the new,   sunlight.   *adjective*

And all the while, dwindling,
tinier, the voices—Yeats, Marvell, Donne—
sank drowning
in a spring still not written of,   20
as only the sky
clear above the brick bell-tower
—blue, and white—
was shifting toward the hour.

Calm, indifferent, cross-legged   25
or on elbows half-lying in the grass—
how should the great dead
tell them of dying?
They will come to time for poems at last,
when they have found they are no more   30
the beautiful and young
all poems are for.

POEMS TO CONSIDER

Musée des Beaux Arts°   1940

WYSTAN HUGH AUDEN   (1907–1973)

About suffering they were never wrong,
The Old Masters: how well they understood
Its human position; how it takes place
While someone else is eating or opening a window or just walking dully
        along;
How, when the aged are reverently, passionately waiting   5
For the miraculous birth, there always must be
Children who did not specially want it to happen, skating
On a pond at the edge of the wood:
They never forgot
That even the dreadful martyrdom must run its course   10

Anyhow in a corner, some untidy spot
Where the dogs go on with their doggy life and the torturer's horse
Scratches its innocent behind on a tree.

In Brueghel's Icarus°, for instance: how everything turns away
Quite leisurely from the disaster; the plowman may   15
Have heard the splash, the forsaken cry,
But for him it was not an important failure; the sun shone
As it had to on the white legs disappearing into the green
Water; and the expensive delicate ship that must have seen
Something amazing, a boy falling out of the sky,   20
Had somewhere to get to and sailed calmly on.

Musée des Beaux Arts: Museum of Fine Arts (Belgium).   14 *Brueghel's Icarus:*
"Landscape with the Fall of Icarus," painting by Pieter Brueghel the Elder. Using
homemade wings with feathers fastened with wax, Icarus flew too near the sun. When
the wax melted, he fell into the sea and drowned.

from *Song of the Exposition*   1871

WALT WHITMAN   (1819–1892)

Come, Muse, migrate from Greece and Ionia,
Cross out please those immensely overpaid accounts,
That matter of Troy and Achilles' wrath, and Aeneas', Odysseus' wander-
        ings,
Placard "Removed" and "To Let" on the rocks of your snowy Parnassus,
Repeat at Jerusalem, place the notice high on Jaffa's° gate and on Mount
        Moriah°,   5
The same on the walls of your German, French and Spanish castles, and
        Italian collections,
For know a better, fresher, busier sphere, a wide, untried, domain awaits,
        demands you.

Responsive to our summons,
Or rather to her long-nursed inclination,
Joined with an irresistible, natural gravitation,   10
She comes! I hear the rustling of her gown,
I scent the odor of her breath's delicious fragrance,
I mark her step divine, her curious eyes a-turning, rolling,
Upon this very scene.

I say I see, my friends, if you do not, the illustrious émigré, (having it is
    true in her day, although the same, changed, journeyed considerable,)   15
Making directly for this rendezvous, vigorously clearing a path for herself,
    striding through the confusion,
By thud of machinery, and shrill steam-whistle undismayed,
Bluffed not a bit by drain-pipe, gasometers, artificial fertilizers,
Smiling and pleased with palpable intent to stay,
She's here, installed amid the kitchen ware!   20

5 *Jaffa, Mount Moriah:* places in the Old Testament. Moriah was the mountain on
which Abraham was commanded to sacrifice Isaac.

The Plain Sense of Things   1952

WALLACE STEVENS   (1879–1955)

After the leaves have fallen, we return
To a plain sense of things. It is as if
We had come to an end of the imagination,
Inanimate in an inert savoir.

It is difficult even to choose the adjective   5
For this blank cold, this sadness without cause.
The great structure has become a minor house.
No turban walks across the lessened floors.

The greenhouse never so badly needed paint.
The chimney is fifty years old and slants to one side.   10
A fantastic effort has failed, a repetition
In a repetitiousness of men and flies.

Yet the absence of the imagination had
Itself to be imagined. The great pond,
The plain sense of it, without reflections, leaves,   15
Mud, water like dirty glass, expressing silence

Of a sort, silence of a rat come out to see,
The great pond and its waste of the lilies, all this
Had to be imagined as an inevitable knowledge,
Required, as a necessity requires.   20

To Paint a Water Lily

1959

TED HUGHES   (b. 1930)

A green level of lily leaves
Roofs the pond's chamber and paves

The flies' furious arena: study
These, the two minds of this lady.

First observe the air's dragonfly   5
That eats meat, that bullets by

Or stands in space to take aim;
Others as dangerous comb the hum

Under the trees. There are battle-shouts
And death-cries everywhere hereabouts   10

But inaudible, so the eyes praise
To see the colours of these flies

Rainbow their arcs, spark, or settle
Cooling like beads of molten metal

Through the spectrum. Think what worse   15
Is the pond-bed's matter of course;

Prehistoric bedragonned times
Crawl that darkness with Latin names,

Have evolved no improvements there,
Jaws for heads, the set stare,   20

Ignorant of age as of hour—
Now paint the long-necked lily-flower

Which, deep in both worlds, can be still
As a painting, trembling hardly at all

Though the dragonfly alight,   25
Whatever horror nudge her root.

The Tree That Became a House

JOHN HAINES   (b. 1924)

They came to live in me
who never lived in the woods before.

They kindled a fire
in my roots and branches,
held out their hands   5
never cramped by the weight of an axe.

The flames lighted a clearing
in the dark overhead, a sky of wood;
they burned in me a little hollow
like a moon of ash.   10

I stand here fastened in a living box,
half in my dream life
with finches, wind and fog—

an endless swaying,
divided in the walls that keep them,   15
in the floors that hold them up,
in the sills they lean upon.

The children look out in wonder
at trees shouldering
black against the starlight;   20
they speak in whispers,
searching the forest of sleep.

My split heart creaks in the night
around them,
my dead cones drop in silence.   25

III

Process:
Making the Poem Happen

11

Starting a Poem:
Wind, Sail, and Rigging

Writing a poem is an exciting and chancy business. It is, as A. E. Housman said, "either easy or impossible." When the magic happens, it is easy. When the muses are silent, it is impossible. Usually it is both at once. Ideas well up, words appear, images offer themselves, and the poem begins to materialize on the page. But this is not the whole poem, perfect, complete. Only a shadowy version appears at first: fragments, phrases, an unfinished rhythm—and a luminous sense of the poem-to-be. What Dylan Thomas calls the poet's "craft or sullen art" must finish the job. Edgar Degas's comment about a painting is perhaps true of a poem: "A painting . . . requires as much cunning, rascality, and viciousness as the perpetration of a crime."

Craft isn't just cold-blooded carpentry, though good carpentry is part of it. It is the ability to keep the poem moving, to tease or coax more of the poem out of the shadows, to hold onto the wave-length from which the flickering signals are coming. It is something like the skill with which a good fisherman plays a fish, knowing when to reel in, when to give slack, in order finally to bring it to the boat. All poets must learn, as best they can, from their own experience, how to court their muse, how to draw the most from the mysterious source, whatever it is, deep within themselves. Poets tend to be as superstitious as baseball players, with little rituals, recipes, and tricks: a favorite pen, a preferred place, a lucky time of day or night. Silence or jazz. Pencil or typewriter. Walking or at the desk. Coffee or chartreuse.

Stirrings

It is impossible to say just when, how, or why the first stirrings of a poem appear. Noticing, keeping antennae out, listening for that first transmission, *wanting* to write a poem, are all part of it. An experience that doesn't seem at the time the least bit like a poem may begin, later, to produce one—like watching a double play at a night baseball game. Like the novelist, the poet is, in this sense, always on duty. As James Thurber noted, "I never quite know when I'm not writing. Sometimes my wife comes up to me at a party and says, 'Dammit, Thurber, stop writing.'" The habit of turning experience into words, of trying it out in phrases or images, is fundamental.

One way to do this is to keep a **notebook.** Many poets do, jotting down ideas, observations, images, phrases, bits from reading, and so on. Gerard Manley Hopkins meticulously recorded things he saw and occasionally even made drawings; years later, a phrase or bit of description would appear in a poem. The value of a notebook is, however, probably less as a reference (though it may be useful in that way) than to sharpen the poet's attention and to imprint something on the memory. Poets who don't keep a proper notebook nonetheless tend to accumulate bits and pieces of poems on scraps of paper or the backs of envelopes. The probable fate of a poetic impulse is a few sputterings and then nothing. Most poets have drawers or file boxes of such leftover, half-written poems. Few come to life again, but Thomas Hardy sometimes wrote poems forty years after the fact, using "old notes."

Almost anything can be the start of a poem: something noticed, something read, a scene, an idea, a dream, an image, two words rubbing together into a phrase. Realizing that it is, or might be, the beginning of a poem is the first step. The second is letting the associations flow, the free currents of the mind and feelings pour around that first nub. Frequently the poet has the sensation of a discovery toward which he has been traveling for years. There is about it a kind of inevitability. "Swimmer in the Rain" (page 109) began with the subject, the realization that there might be a poem in it, but without any actual verbalization. I have always loved swimming in the rain. When I was a boy, lifeguards at the park pool herded us out of the water whenever it began to rain, even when there was no thunder or lightning. I couldn't see that a little rain made any difference. So, later on, for many summers on a bay-creek at the New Jersey shore, I went swimming in the rain. One day in the creek several summers ago, I suddenly knew that I was going to write a poem. For a week or so nothing happened. Then the phrase "no one but him" popped into my head.

Somehow that was the key, and the poem—drawing on a very long sequence of physical memories—virtually wrote itself one *sunny* noon! The poem had obviously been gathering unnoticed for years.

Wordsworth noted that poetry

> takes its origin from emotion recollected in tranquillity; the emotion is contemplated till, by a species of re-action, the tranquillity gradually disappears, and an emotion, kindred to that which was before the subject of contemplation, is gradually produced, and does itself actually exist in the mind. In this mood successful composition generally begins.

The stronger and more confusing the emotion, perhaps, the longer the subconscious gestation necessary for it to begin to organize itself into a poem. Several years passed between the event and the writing of "Ballad of the Mouse" (page 258), years during which I had no idea that a poem was coming.

One of the things a poet learns is how to "play" a poem, how not to force it, how to hold off from trying to write it until it is ready. Richard Wilbur reports that he waited fourteen years, occasionally jotting down a phrase "that might belong to a poem," before he started to write "The Mind-Reader"; and he took another three years to finish the poem. Asked how long he was likely to work on a poem, he said, "Long enough." In forcing a poem, trying to write it too soon, the poet is likely to make a hash of it—which may explain not only the poor quality of many poems one sees, but also those broken poems in the drawer. Trying to write in the heat of an emotion, rather than recollecting it later in tranquillity, after the subconscious has had a chance to work, is all too likely to produce posturing, self-pity, overstatement, or sentimentality, those spoilers of genuine feeling. It is like trying to sing while someone is pounding on your finger with a hammer; although it can be done, it won't be done well.

Whatever it is, wherever it originates, the poem always begins with a *given*, in which the poet is aware of the possibility of a poem. Like keeping a notebook, talking to yourself (silently or aloud) is a way of looking for those gifts. Walking and driving are fairly boring activities that leave the mind free to wander and are particularly conducive to poems. So, too, are the trancelike states of listening to music, drifting off to sleep, and insomnia. The poet is, in Freud's phrase, a "professional daydreamer." The conscious mind relaxes its control; thoughts, images, and memories drift in and out of consciousness—and suddenly sometimes, as if glimpsed in peripheral vision, there is the beginning of a poem. Prolonging that state, drawing as much as possible of the poem into words, is the aim. Wordsworth "wrote" all 159 lines of "Tintern Abbey" in his head, on a four- or five-day walking tour. "Not a line of it was altered, and not any part of it written down till I reached Bristol." In the fourth book of *The Prelude*, recalling a favorite dog, Wordsworth describes how he composed poems during idle walking and talking to himself:

Among the favourites whom it pleased me well
To see again, was one by ancient right
Our inmate, a rough terrier of the hills;
By birth and call of nature pre-ordained
To hunt the badger and unearth the fox   5
Among the impervious crags, but having been
From youth our own adopted, he had passed
Into a gentler service. And when first
The boyish spirit flagged, and day by day
Along my veins I kindled with the stir,   10
The fermentation, and the vernal heat
Of poesy, affecting private shades
Like a sick Lover, then this dog was used
To watch me, an attendant and a friend,
Obsequious to my steps early and late,   15
Though often of such dilatory walk
Tired, and uneasy at the halts I made.
A hundred times when, roving high and low,
I have been harassed with the toil of verse,
Much pains and little progress, and at once   20
Some lovely Image in the song rose up
Full-formed, like Venus rising from the sea;
Then have I darted forwards to let loose
My hand upon his back with stormy joy,
Caressing him again and yet again.   25
And when at evening on the public way
I sauntered, like a river murmuring
And talking to itself when all things else
Are still, the creature trotted on before;
Such was his custom; but whene'er he met   30
A passenger approaching, he would turn
To give me timely notice, and straightway,
Grateful for that admonishment, I hushed
My voice, composed my gait, and, with the air
And mien of one whose thoughts are free, advanced   35
To give and take a greeting that might save
My name from piteous rumours, such as wait
On men suspected to be crazed in brain.

A charming picture, the poet spared the embarrassment of being caught talking
to himself by his faithful terrier!

What William Stafford calls "**random writing**"—free associating, just putting anything down, however nonsequential or silly, like talking to oneself on paper—may also work to discover the beginning of a poem. Here, for instance, is his poem "Ask Me":

Some time when the river is ice ask me
mistakes I have made. Ask me whether
what I have done is my life. Others
have come in their slow way into
my thought, and some have tried to help   5
or to hurt—ask me what difference
their strongest love or hate has made.

I will listen to what you say.
You and I can turn and look
at the silent river and wait. We know   10
the current is there, hidden; and there
are comings and goings from miles away
that hold the stillness exactly before us.
What the river says, that is what I say.

Of "Ask Me," Stafford reports:

> My poem started from amid random writing I was doing in my usual morning attempts to scare up something by putting anything down that came to mind. I was at a country place; it was early morning; I was all alone, and feeling that way—in a pleasant way, with a fire in the Franklin stove, the dark outside. It was winter, and I guess the cold made me launch in the way I did, "Some time when the river is ice . . . ."

Like the less mechanical wool-gathering of walking or driving or falling to sleep, random writing is a valuable tactic, especially when the poet is stuck and not writing, when he or she is waiting (in Nemerov's phrase) "for what would come next to come next," or when he or she has an assignment due.

Keeping the poem moving, finishing it, is the harder part of the process. Even when the inspiration holds, when the wind is in the sail (the image is Ben Jonson's), more is required than luck or following an impulse. Just as the quality of the sail and rigging is important, so is the quality of the training and equipment the poet can bring to bear. Also vital is the poet's seamanship: the ability to handle the craft, to tack and steer a course, and to take advantage of the wind so as to arrive somewhere rather than merely to be blown this way and that. It is too late, in a gale, to learn. Being lucky is often knowing *how* to be lucky. Like the good tennis player or the expert sailor, the poet uses accumulated experience in every new situation without being aware that he or she is doing so. Choosing words, images, rhythm, line division for best effect, and whether or not to rhyme may be an instinctive process but is also a result of training. Skill is experience brought to bear on the present.

Even in that rare case when a whole poem simply comes without any conscious effort on the poet's part—the most famous case is Samuel Taylor Coleridge's "Kubla Khan"—it can do so only for the trained sensibility. Here is Coleridge's account:

> In the summer of the year 1797, the Author, then in ill health, had retired to a lonely farm-house between Porlock and Linton, on the Exmoor confines of Somerset and Devonshire. In consequence of a slight indisposition, an anodyne had been prescribed, from the effects of which he fell asleep in his chair at the moment that he was reading the following sentence, or words of the same substance, in "Purchas's Pilgrimage": "Here the Khan Kubla commanded a palace to be built, and a stately garden thereunto. And thus ten miles of fertile ground were inclosed within a wall." The Author continued for about three hours in a profound sleep, at least of the external senses, during which time he has the most vivid confidence, that he could not have composed less than from two to three hundred lines; if that indeed can be called composition in which all the images rose up before him as *things*, with a parallel production of the correspondent expressions, without any sensation or consciousness of effort. On awaking he appeared to himself to have a distinct recollection of the whole, and taking his pen, ink, and paper, instantly and eagerly wrote down the lines that are here preserved. At this moment he was unfortunately called out by a person from Porlock, and detained by him above an hour, and on his return to his room, found, to his no small surprise and mortification, that though he still retained some vague and dim recollection of the general purport of the vision, yet, with the exception of some eight or ten scattered lines and images, all the rest had passed away like the images on the surface of a stream into which a stone has been cast, but, alas! without the after restoration of the latter.

In *The Road to Xanadu* John Livingston Lowes has traced, with fine psychological insight, the sources of the poem's content in Coleridge's reading and experience. The poet's imagination was assimilating and sorting and combining its materials without any apparent intervention by his conscious mind. His technical skills were also, necessarily, at work, rhyming, metering, dividing lines. For a person not a poet the same dream or vision might have been equally marvelous, but it would not have produced a *poem*.

Not infrequently, *parts* of a poem—lines, images—will come to any poet in this mysterious way. Indeed, it wouldn't be rash to say that in every good poem, parts at least will appear unbidden and unaccountably. "No surprise for the poet, no surprise for the reader." But it is rare for a poem to appear whole in this fashion.

When inspiration is up, when the poem is coming, when the wind is in the sail, the poet must go with it. "And the secret of it all is," Walt Whitman reported, to write in the gush, the throb, the flood, of the moment—to put things down without deliberation—without worrying about their style—without waiting for a fit time and place. . . . You want to catch its first spirit—to tally its truth. By writing at the instant the very heartbeat of life is caught.

Put down everything, however odd. The scrawl and chaos of many a poet's manuscripts result from the haste of following out an impulse, of trying to keep up with the speed of the muse. As Ben Jonson notes in his "commonplace book" *Timber, or Discoveries* (1640—41):

> If we have a fair gale of wind, I forbid not the steering out of our sail, so the favor of the gale deceive us not. For all that we invent doth please us in the conception of birth, else we would never set it down. But the safest is to return to our judgment, and handle over again those things the easiness of which might make them justly suspected.

The warning is fitting. Put everything down, but *judge* it later. Not everything the muse dictates or the poet writes is valuable. Much may be wasteful, corny, sloppy, or worse. Many of the unfinished poems in the drawer or file box are just embarrassing, pompous or silly, and it is easy in retrospect to see why they disintegrated in the effort to finish them. The last act in the writing of any poem is always a critical one: the judgment that it is finished. Everything should be there that needs to be, but no more than is needed. And whatever it is, it must seem worth saying.

"The Principle of Decision"

In truth, every creative act in the process of writing the poem, every word, image, or line-break, is also a critical act. Every possibility that comes to mind for what might come next in the poem must be approved or tossed aside. The approval or rejection may be tentative; and very often parallel possibilities may, for a time, be held in mind, bracketed in the body of the poem or jotted down in the margin. It may help to list possible words for a spot in the poem some-where in the vicinity. Is the rose to be, for example,

red	incarnadine	blood-red
crimson	fluffy	sunset
scarlet	red, red	leafy

or any number of thousands of other possibilities? The intention here seems to be color, but "fluffy" and "leafy" show other temptations. Early on, every choice is likely to be tentative, especially when the poet is unsure of the poem's subject or direction. At this stage the writing will properly be trial-and-error blundering. The standard against which possibilities may be tested can hardly be more than a vague or shadowy idea of the poem. But as the tentative choices begin to accumulate, as the idea of the poem clarifies, as the poem in effect materializes on the page, more and more it imposes its own demands and necessities. The direction revealing itself, the poet begins to rule out alternate routes, and choices become more decisive. The writing of even a few lines may be a mingling of a hundred creative and critical acts in rapid, almost invisible succession. Inspiration and evaluation work together like two hands trying to untangle a snarl of fishing line. "Style," Susan Sontag has noted, "is the principle of decision in a work of art, the signature of the artist's will."

Fairly soon the poet must make a commitment to form. Again it may be a tentative commitment, with the first formal decisions provisional, but it will be a commitment nonetheless. Sometimes the poet will have a preconception about the form he or she wants to use, as Pope habitually turned to rhymed and end-stopped pentameter couplets. Sometimes, when the poet is more open, the very first line written (which need not be the first line of the poem) will *feel* like a line that fits the coming poem. Sometimes the initial jottings will be more notelike and the poem will seem, for a while, more like a random assortment of jigsaw puzzle pieces. Early on, in any event, the poet will be looking to discover what sort of form the poem will develop. Length of line? Free verse? Meter? Rhyme? Stanza? Among the possibilities that begin to arise, the poet will be trying to sort out the ones he or she wants. A thin poem? A fat poem? Solid or skeletony? Tight? Loose? Long? Short? Both the sound and the look of the poem, like its subject and direction and tone, may be open for a time. Gradually, as the first shadowy choices are made, the commitment increases; and the tentative formal qualities of the poem become, themselves, standards by which to measure fresh possibilities, blanks into which newly arriving inspirations must be fitted. Some poems reveal their formal qualities clearly and definitely. More often, they don't, and the poet has little but instinct to go on.

Every small choice is, of course, important, and each narrows the possibilities that follow. The most crucial one is probably **line.** The poet's sense of line—what makes a line, how much a line can hold or how little it can manage with, the balance or imbalance of a line, the weight or lightness of a line—may be his or her most valuable piece of equipment, the compass or gyroscope. In action, this sense may seem an instinct, an intuition, but it will have been learned in the reading and writing of many lines. Working in a fixed meter is perhaps the best training in line because trying to fit a flexible content to a rigid pattern requires great dexterity. In meter the poet is constantly testing how much a given line can carry before it begins to feel crowded and clogged, or how little before it begins to feel empty and too thin. When a poet smooths into lines of something like the same weight a content that tends to bunch and spread accordion-like, she or he develops a keen sense of line and of the use of run-ons and end-stops. The best free verse may well be written by poets who, like William Carlos Williams, have done an apprenticeship in pentameter. All too often, free verse by poets with little experience in meter has all the liveliness and energy of piled dishes.

William Stafford's "Ask Me" (page 283) was written in three drafts. A comparison of the first draft with the finished poem shows Stafford's skill in handling lines and in discovering the line-breaks in the nearly seamless material. Here is the draft, without the changes he made:

> Some time when the river is ice, ask me
> the mistakes, ask me whether what I have
> done is my life. Others have come
> in their slow way into the thoughts. And
> some have tried to help or to hurt.   5
> Ask me what differences their strongest efforts
> have made. You and I can then turn
> and look at the silent river and wait.
> We will know the current is there,
> hidden, and there are comings and goings   10
> miles away that hold the stillness
> exactly before us. If the river says anything,
> whatever it says is my answer.

Major changes in substance are few: "the mistakes" in line 2 is to become "mistakes I have made," which is clarifying and emphatic (though "my mistakes" would have been clear enough); "their strongest efforts / have made" in lines 6−7 is to become "their strongest love or hate has made," replacing a flat phrase with a sharp one and underlining the ironic leveling of the effect of "help" or "hurt." The sentence "I will listen to what you say" is to be added, focusing the imagined dramatic dialogue and sharpening the sense that what the speaker would say is different from what the "you" might say about such things. The merely conditional "If the river says anything, / whatever it says is my answer" is to become the ambiguously definite "What the river says, that is what I say," which is tighter and more highly charged.

All these alterations strengthen the poem, as do a number of smaller changes: making a separate sentence of the second "ask me" in line 2, making a continuing sentence of the "And/some have tried" and of the third "ask me" in lines 4−6, for instance, or using the more dramatic dash in line 6 of the final version. Simultaneously, Stafford is almost completely relining the poem. Only the first line remains the same and keeps its line-break. These changes, along with breaking the poem into two equal stanzas (questions and response), also strengthen it. Both the verbal and the rhythmic changes are being made at the same time, each making room for or requiring the other. In sum, the rhythmic changes seem the more significant in giving the poem its ultimate character. Asked about the principles of technique he consciously used, Stafford replied:

My impulse is to say that I had no principles of technique at all in mind. As I look back over the first draft, I do realize, though, that I was getting satisfaction out of syncopating along in the sentences; that is, I find some pleasure in just opening and closing sentences—starting and then holding before myself a feeling that the measure and flow of utterance will lend itself to an easy forwarding of what I am saying.

He added:

My lines are generally just about equal; where a line breaks, though, means something to me, and some of the juggling was meant to preserve how definite the slash [run-on] line is in such changeover sequences as me/mistakes, have/ done, and/some, etc.

The syncopation, this laying of sentences across the line-ends, occurs in both draft and final version. In the final version, however, it has taken on a structural quality. The invitations to "ask me" flow through the first seven lines, all of which are run-on except the seventh; thus, the falling momentum comes to rest only, and properly, with the end-stopped line 7. In the first draft line 5 is end-stopped, and the end of the poem's thematic first half falls indecisively in the middle of a line. By contrast, the rhythmic management in the final version is superb.

The poem turns on line 8, which is properly end-stopped and establishes the speaker's balance in the face of what the imaginary interlocutor would say. The lines then run-on through line 13, which is end-stopped to prepare for the decisive final statement, now complete and taut in its own line. In the draft, by contrast, the end-stopping of "and look at the silent river and wait" seems a false pause; and the line-and-a-half of the final statement seems rhythmically somewhat open-ended as well as substantially conditional. Flow and stasis, movement and poise are not only a central part of the poem's theme but also its essential rhythmic quality. The equal stanzas suggest, structurally, both the tension and the poise in the poem's feeling.

Interestingly, "Ask Me" seems to be free verse. The lines are "generally just about equal." But most of the lines approximate iambic tetrameter. Several, like line 7 ("thĕir stróngĕst lóve ŏr háte hăs máde"), are exactly metrical. In an intermediate version, the poem's last line would have been very strongly metrical as well: "Whát thĕ rívĕr sáys ĭs whát Ĭ sáy." Stafford's final alteration of the line to "What the river says, that is what I say," though still approximately countable as tetrameter, hardens the rhythm away from the temptingly pat iambs—*and* suggests, dramatically, that the speaker's final poise is not smooth nor too easy. "Ask Me" is, in its unintentional nearness to a metrical norm, a perfect example of a poet's unerring instinct for the handling of line.

Determining the line and form may unlock the rest of a poem, allowing it to spread and fill like water into a design. What follows is my entire first draft of

"Swimmer in the Rain" (p. 109). Having got this far, I bogged down, and the
rest of the page is covered with doodles.

```
    No one but him to see
                        a
    the rain begin—∧fine scrim
                   slow
    far down the bay, ~~like~~ smoke,

    smoking and hissing its way
              Then    (into    marsh
    toward, ~~and then~~{up the ∧creek

    where he ~~drifted~~swam, waited

              ~~a suit~~   clad in
  cold,
oo ∧   Thin
    ∧supple, ~~green~~ glass

      to his neck.
```

The minor tinkerings on this first draft are not so important as the accidental rhymes ("him-scrim," "bay-way") that I noticed and underlined; they pro-
vided the new start on the second draft. The rhymes suggested, in order to set
up the "him" rhyme, switching from a three-beat line to a two-beat line. The
second draft, after a fitful try, dropped the rhyming; but with the two-beat line
established, the poem *flowed* out onto the page, reaching fifty-two lines in an
hour or so. Here, slightly simplified, is the first part of the second draft:

```
                No one but him
   to see/      seeing the rain
                           , ~~like~~ smoke,
   start/       ~~begin~~, a scrim ∧

                far down the bay,
                             in a line
                          ing
                ~~and~~ advances ~~till~~∧
                ←——————————————— between two grays
             Till
               ∧the salt-grass rustles

                and the ~~marsh~~ creek's mirror

                  → in which he stood--
            ?
           ( green;
              gr ∧cold, ~~gr~~ and supple/∧

                to his neck, like clothing--
   ripple/      begins to dimple.
```

Several alternative words are noted (with slashes) in the left margin. Other changes are made by crossing out and inserting. The rhyme peters out after the first few lines, though "rustles-supple-dimple" keeps the possibility open. It was obvious, as the poem grew longer, that trying even intermittent rhyming with such short lines would be obtrusive. To avoid repeating "begin" (it appears in the last line of the passage), I scratched it out in line 3 and let "start" stand. This change made room for the insertion of "like smoke," a detail from the first draft that had been crowded out in the two-beat lines. I then scratched "like," making lines 3–4 read: "start, a scrim, smoke / far down the bay." In further drafts the smoke image moves, and "scrim" returns to the end of line 3. The rhymes in lines 1–4 remain, a hint of initial formality that, dissolved by the pace of events, perhaps mirrors the accelerating and overcoming sensation of the rain. In a somewhat different way, the formality of the poem's ending with the same line with which it began reestablishes the control and presents the speaker's resteadied ability to submit to, and so command, the unexpected and majestic. As with the reappearance of the clothing image in the last lines, the poem just turned out that way—I certainly didn't have any rationalizations in mind.

The crucial decision, which in effect released the poem, was the choice of the two-beat line. On the first draft I was stuck because the three-beat lines were simply too *horizontal*—too slow, too paced for the excitement, the fast-changing, the movement, the multiplicity of the rain. The verticality, the speed of the two-beat lines were the *poem's* choice, something I learned from the developing poem, not something I imposed on it. The norm is iambic; but in lines so short, simple substitutions produce a varied, shifting rhythm without seeming uncontrolled or loose:

> Thĕ dróps | bóunce úp,
>
> líttlĕ | fóuntăins
>
> áll ă|róund hĭm,
>
> swíft, mó|mĕntá|rў̆—
>
> ĕverў̆ dróp | tóssed báck
>
> ĭn áir | ătóp
>
> ĭts tí|nў̆ cól|ŭmn—

That quick, two-beat rhythmic pattern and the quick, balancing, piling-up, syntactical elaborations of the multiplying images, I believe, were the necessary technical discoveries.

Over several months "Swimmer in the Rain" went through seven complete drafts. Unusually the poem grew with each, accumulating and adding rather than excluding and compressing. With every critical cut, new images sprang up. Typically, the second draft's

> a glass bombardment,
> tossed, tumbled jacks of light
> everywhere blinding,
> like grease drops sizzling
> in a pan

successively dropped the adverb "everywhere" and the adjectives "tossed, tumbled" and "blinding," as well as the unnecessary pan; and added "glints," then "blinks" in its place; changed "grease drops" to "grease-beads"; and added the line "wee Brancusi's, chromes," and then the line "parade of diamonds." The metal jacks, children's toys, by association led to the "Brancusi's." Here is the final version of the same lines:

> a glass bombardment,
> parade of diamonds,
> blinks, jacks of light,
> wee Brancusi's, chromes
> like grease-beads sizzling,
> myriad—

All in all, the process mainly involved replacing vague, generalizing epithets with additional images. One nagging problem resolved itself only on the seventh draft. From the third draft onward, I kept trying to decide what (in stanza 3) the tide pulled as steady as. At first the best I could do was "wind," with the idea that tide is to water what wind is to air; no doubt I was connecting it with the "minnows' / sky." But steadiness isn't the wind's quality, and only in the final draft did the thematically pertinent suggest itself: "steady / as faith the tide pulls."

Tactics

Several considerations or tactics may help the poet keep the poem going in the process of writing. One is simply to be very delicate about the moment he first commits a line to paper. Poems begin in the head, and often they will continue to develop there, in the relatively free-floating mixture of thought, better than on paper. Putting something on paper tends to fix it; and there is a time, early on, when the shoots of a poem are still too frail for transplanting.

Words that feel full and grand in the mind sometimes look skinny and naked on paper. All that blankness can be intimidating, swallowing up the small handful of words that try to break the silence. Every poet must carefully select the moment to jerk the line and try to set the hook.

On the other hand, at a certain point in the process of writing, seeing the poem becomes important. The lines in the poet's head will inevitably feel somewhat different on paper, and that difference can prompt fresh ideas and directions. The appearance of a poem on the page is part of its total effect. Early enough for the poem not to have "jelled" too much, it is a good idea to use a typewriter. Because we are accustomed to reading poems in print, the poet will see much more clearly how the poem *looks* in a typewriter's approximation of print. Lines will be longer or shorter than the poet imagined, for instance, and the poem thinner or chubbier or more graceful.

The beginning poet will want to experiment with using typewriter, pencil, and pen; with different colors of ink; with script or printing; with lined or unlined paper; with single sheets, tablets, and notebooks. Such things may not be important, or they may. Poems have been written by night-light on an army footlocker after lights-out, and in worse places. But the poet is entitled to prefer working at a desk or (like Frost) with a lapboard in an easy chair. Ernest Hemingway liked to stand at a dresser on which his typewriter sat.

Another trick that may keep the poem going is to say it over aloud, as far as it has gone. As the look of a poem matters, so does its sound; and the poet should keep testing its sound in his ear. Both the awkward and the good things about it will become more obvious with repetition. Starting at the beginning and reading aloud will improve the continuity of the rhythm as well as of the sense. Sometimes the poet will find, when he or she is stuck, that such going back provides the momentum for getting across the hard spot. Ben Jonson said:

> Repeat often what we have formerly written; which besides that it helps the consequence, and makes the juncture better, it quickens the heat of imagination, that often cools in the time of setting down, and gives it new strength, as if it grew lustier by the going back. As we see in the contention of leaping, they jump farthest that fetch their race longest; or, as in throwing a dart or javelin, we force back our arms to make our loose the stronger.

Enjoying the sound of his or her own voice, testing, sculpting, relishing, caressing the unfinished poem is part of the poet's job, one of the tools.

Writing out the poem *in prose*—that is, sketching it or outlining it—is a device some poets, including Yeats, have found useful, particularly for organizing argumentative or longer poems. Note-taking on a possible subject is a variant. When a poet is stuck, either of these may be a way of getting distance and perspective.

Frequently a single inspiration will result in a tangle of possibilities, which may in fact become several poems. A poem might well go in any number of directions, or have in it the potential for making any number of points. The poet may need to untwine some of these, putting them aside before the poem at hand can proceed coherently, as Walter Savage Landor advises:

In every poem train the leading shoot;
Break off the suckers. Thought erases thought,
As numerous sheep erase each other's print
When spongy moss they press or sterile sand.
Blades thickly sown want nutriment and droop,
Although the seed be sound, and rich the soil;
Thus healthy-born ideas, bedded close,
By dreaming fondness perish overlain.

To "train the leading shoot," then, will occasionally help the poet who arrives at an impasse. The trouble may be that two or more intentions, ideas, feelings, images, approaches, or even whole poems have grown and twisted on a single stem, and none can really flourish without being separated from the others. The mixed image of china and silver in Emily Dickinson's "It Dropped So Low—In My Regard" (page 215) is an example of how such inconsistent elements can find their way into a poem. The same thing can happen with ideas. "Purple passages" are especially good at concealing this kind of problem.

Always be clear. Clarity for the poet, which precedes clarity for the reader, is as great an aid as anything in the ambiguous and shadowy early stages of a poem. The stronger the wind in the sail, the greater the need for alert and clear-headed seamanship. As Quintilian observed, "One should not aim at being possible to understand, but at being impossible to misunderstand." Such clarity, like a strong light, will often show the way to the necessary next phrase or idea or image. Seeing clearly what is going right, or going wrong, is not easy. But the poet who doesn't bother to straighten things out for himself or herself can't hope that the reader will care to do any better.

Finally, there can be no advice better than Richmond Lattimore's: "Do it, then."

QUESTIONS AND SUGGESTIONS

1. Try "random writing." Put a first phrase down; then keep going.

2. All the words in Robert Francis's poem "Swimmer" have been sorted out,

arbitrarily, into columns according to their parts of speech. (Repetitions are omitted.) Using these words or some of them, or at least beginning with them and adding words of your own, write your own poem called "Swimmer." After you have had a try, look at Francis's poem in Appendix I.

nouns	verbs	adjectives	adverbs	pronouns	prepositions
stranger	is	least	how	he	on
way	have	powerful	indolently	that	between
depth	lie	dark	always	what	by
lover	hold	drowning	mutually	some	with
arms	support	green	strongly	his	from
water	observe	smooth	now	him	in
enemy	make	more	gently	himself	
danger	stroke		ever	all	
caress	rest				
trust	float				
sea	negotiate				
ally	can			*conjunctions*	*article*
beloved	turn				
love	drown			as	the
swimmer	reach			and	
drowning	defend				
friend	sleep				
violence	lean				
	destroy				

3. On a long walk or drive, keep trying to turn things you see into words—and see if you don't find a poem like this student's "Salvation":

PAMELA AZUSENIS*

Driving past a red brick church
on a back road
in a rocky, hunger-stricken stretch
of Pennsylvania at dusk,
at the moment   5
the red neon cross clicks on
and faltering
blinks
with twisted tubes below spelling
"Jesus Saves."   10
Against the cold black hills
the buzzing sign hangs
in desperate conviction
with distant, dimly lit houses

buried in tree covered blackness   15
like misplaced stars.
Inside them the people emulate their saviour
carefully saving
mismatched buttons and bits of twine
for corporeal repairs,   20
and old Sears catalogues
and wrinkled trading stamps
for their children
on the approaching Christmas,
taking care to insure   25
the only redemption in this land.

4. Here are the title and first line or lines of several poems. Choose one that is intriguing and write the poem this beginning suggests to you. (The poems are in Appendix I.)

a) *The Opening*

   Down its length the rifle barrel

b) *The Passionate Shepherd to His Love*

   Come live with me and be my love,
   And we will all the pleasures prove

c) *The Lark and the Emperor*

   Strangle the Lark.
   Place its pink tongue under glass

d) *For One Moment*

   You take the dollar
   and hand it to the fellow beside you

e) *Autumn Begins in Martins Ferry, Ohio*

   In the Shreve High football stadium

5. In these roughly contemporary poems, "The Eagle" by Alfred Lord Tennyson (1851) and "Ye Who Have Toiled" by Walter Savage Landor (1863), similar elements—high and low, mountainous and sea-level, godlike and ordinary, and birds or beasts of prey—yield quite dissimilar details, symbolic resonances, and themes. In "The Eagle" the vantage point is looking down; in "Ye Who Have Toiled," looking up. What implications arise from the metaphors in "The

Eagle"—"hands," "crawls," "walls," "like a thunderbolt"? How do the rhymed triplets reenforce the tone? In "Ye Who Have Toiled," the lofty, ancient "ruins of a citadel" or of a domestic "chamber" may symbolize the past, the accomplishments of a civilization, or even art ("song"). Who are those "who have toiled" to reach these heights? What "treasure" have they found and why do they not tell? How does the speaker, who also knows but will tell, differ from these "friends"? Does he really prefer the happy delusion ("Thinking it must be gold") to the "glistening" of the bitter truth? Do similar views of nature, finally, underlie both poems?

The Eagle

He clasps the crag with crooked hands;
Close to the sun in lonely lands,
Ringed with the azure world, he stands.

The wrinkled sea beneath him crawls;
He watches from his mountain walls,
And like a thunderbolt he falls.

Ye Who Have Toiled

Ye who have toiled uphill to reach the haunt
Of other men who lived in other days,
Whether the ruins of a citadel
Raised on the summit by Pelasgic° hands,
Or chamber of the distaff and the song . . .   5
Ye will not tell what treasure there ye found,
But I will.
             Ye found there the viper laid
Full-length, flat-headed, on a sunny slab,
Nor loth to hiss at ye while crawling down.
Ye saw the owl flap the loose ivy leaves   10
And, hooting, shake the berries on your heads.
   Now, was it worth your while to mount so high
Merely to say ye did it, and to ask
If those about ye ever did the like?
Believe me, O my friends, 'twere better far   15
To stretch your limbs along the level sand
As they do, where small children scoop the drift,
Thinking it must be gold, where curlews soar
And scales drop glistening from the prey above.

4 *Pelasgic:* the Pelasgians, a prehistoric people who inhabited Greece before the Hellenes.
Some of their crudely hewn stonework survives.

Fable

1847

RALPH WALDO EMERSON   (1803–1882)

The mountain and the squirrel
Had a quarrel;
And the former called the latter "little Prig."
Bun replied,
"You are doubtless very big;   5
But all sorts of things and weather
Must be taken in together
To make up a year
And a sphere.
And I think it no disgrace   10
To occupy my place.
If I'm not so large as you,
You are not so small as I,
And not half so spry.
I'll not deny you make   15
A very pretty squirrel track;
Talents differ: all is well and wisely put;
If I cannot carry forests on my back,
Neither can you crack a nut."

Abandoned Farmhouse

1974

TED KOOSER   (b. 1939)

He was a big man, says the size of his shoes
on a pile of broken dishes by the house;
a tall man too, says the length of the bed
in an upstairs room; and a good, God-fearing man,
says the Bible with a broken back   5
on the floor below the window, dusty with sun;
but not a man for farming, say the fields
cluttered with boulders and the leaky barn.

A woman lived with him, says the bedroom wall
papered with lilacs and the kitchen shelves
covered with oilcloth, and they had a child,
says the sandbox made from a tractor tire.
Money was scarce, say the jars of plum preserves
and canned tomatoes sealed in the cellar hole.
And the winters cold, say the rags in the window frames.
It was lonely here, says the narrow country road.

Something went wrong, says the empty house
in the weed-choked yard. Stones in the fields
say he was not a farmer; the still-sealed jars
in the cellar say she left in a nervous haste.
And the child? Its toys are strewn in the yard
like branches after a storm—a rubber cow,
a rusty tractor with a broken plow,
a doll in overalls. Something went wrong, they say.

Make Big Money at Home! Write Poems in Spare Time!

Make Big Money at Home!
Write Poems in Spare Time!   1962

HOWARD NEMEROV   (b.1920)

Oliver wanted to write about reality.
He sat before a wooden table,
He poised his wooden pencil
Above his pad of wooden paper,
And attempted to think about agony
And history, and the meaning of history,
And all stuff like that there.

Suddenly this wooden thought got in his head:
A Tree. That's all, no more than that,
Just one tree, not even a note
As to whether it was deciduous
Or evergreen, or even where it stood.
Still, because it came unbidden,
It was inspiration, and had to be dealt with.

Oliver hoped that this particular tree   15
Would turn out to be fashionable,
The axle of the universe, maybe,
Or some other mythologically
Respectable tree-contraption
With dryads, or having to do   20
With the knowledge of Good and Evil, and the Fall.

"A Tree," he wrote down with his wooden pencil
Upon his pad of wooden paper
Supported by the wooden table.
And while he sat there waiting   25
For what would come next to come next,
The whole wooden house began to become
Silent, particularly silent, sinisterly so.

It   *1957*

(FOR S.L. AND A.L., WHO THINK OF WRITING)

RICHMOND LATTIMORE   (b.1906)

Do it, then. If you do,
incontrovertibly know
the worst thing you have done
is the best thing under the sun
if it was written true,   5
if it was meant to be so.

Never write to please.

A poem is a not-yet.
Then, as you make it, forget
what you imagine to be   10
the critic who can't read,
the reader who can't see.

Make it alone for you
and yourself.

Choose
what you mean to do.   15
But it will be no use.
It will choose you.

You took no life of ease.

Think of the world when you
are in the world. If it will   20
the world will judge. When you write,
a blind maker, alone
in your individual night,
be steel, be stone.
The world may tear it from you   25
in its day, when you are through.
If not, you have made it still.

Despise temperament.
Beyond all else despise
the trick of lineament,   30
the look of the hair and eyes,
the professional veneer,
the Needs of your Career.
Poets as such are dull.
The poem is all.   35

Live only to understand
only the thing in your hand,
the sight that sticks in your eye,
the wish that sticks in your heart
and will not let you be   40
until it is made art.

12

Revising (I):
Both Ends of the Pencil

Craft completes magic; technique carries out inspiration. It is sometimes fashionable for poets to claim otherwise, to pretend that making poems is all too arcane and mysterious a process to be explicable. But, as Edmund Waller (1606–1687) put it wittily:

> Poets lose half the praise they should have got,
> Could it be known what they discreetly blot.

His contemporary, John Dryden, translating Boileau's *L'Art Poétique* (1674), offered advice on revising as exactly as it can be given:

> Gently make haste, of labor not afraid;
> A hundred times consider what you've said:
> Polish, repolish, every color lay,
> And sometimes add, but oftener take away.
> 'Tis not enough, when swarming faults are writ,
> That here and there are scattered sparks of wit.

Technique is knowing how to use, to focus, to deploy what comes magically. As every creative act calls for a critical one, an evaluation, so it also requires a technical act: shaping, placing, incorporating. Inspiration and technique are like the two legs of a long-distance runner; first one and then the other carries him forward. As each inspiration shows technique how to do the next thing, technique opens the way for the next inspiration.

The secret of writing is rewriting. As W. H. Auden noted, "Literary composition in the twentieth century A.D. is pretty much what it was in the twentieth century B.C.: nearly everything has still to be done by hand." Rewriting is exploring, trying out. The poet uses both ends of the pencil. Luckily, unlike the sculptor or the painter, the poet can go back to earlier versions if he or she makes a mistake. A typical way is to scratch out and add, scratch out and add, scribbling alternatives in the margin, until the sheet is embroidered with corrections—and then to recopy the best version that can be sorted out of it. Then the poet goes on scratching out and adding on that draft. There are 175 worksheets for a poem by E. E. Cummings ("rosetree, rosetree"), and Donald Hall reports that "The Town of Hill" (page 322) went through fifty or sixty drafts; "three years of intensive work, with lots and lots of changes." The poem's deceptive simplicity is a result of labor, fusing Hall's boyhood memories of the town that was later abandoned and flooded to make a lake, with his present vision of the underwater town. Like simplicity, spontaneity and naturalness are usually the result of hard work. Easy writing tends to produce hard reading; hard writing, to produce easy reading. As one beginning poet, Sharon Lillevig, observed:

Effortless

The fluid
dancer sweats.

Leaps and Carpentry

This chapter will look at a number of poets' actual revisions, as examples of the creative process, of the lucky leaps and the careful carpentry. Consider first Richard Wilbur's "Love Calls Us to the Things of This World":

> The eyes open to a cry of pulleys,
> And spirited from sleep, the astounded soul
> Hangs for a moment bodiless and simple
> As false dawn.
>   Outside the open window
> The morning air is all awash with angels.   5
>
> Some are in bed-sheets, some are in blouses,

Some are in smocks: but truly there they are.
Now they are rising together in calm swells
Of halcyon feeling, filling whatever they wear
With the deep joy of their impersonal breathing;   10

    Now they are flying in place, conveying
The terrible speed of their omnipresence, moving
And staying like white water; and now of a sudden
They swoon down into so rapt a quiet
That nobody seems to be there.
                        The soul shrinks   15

    From all that it is about to remember,
From the punctual rape of every blesséd day,
And cries,
        "Oh, let there be nothing on earth but laundry,
Nothing but rosy hands in the rising steam
And clear dances done in the sight of heaven."   20

    Yet, as the sun acknowledges
With a warm look the world's hunks and colors,
The soul descends once more in bitter love
To accept the waking body, saying now
In a changed voice as the man yawns and rises,   25

    "Bring them down from their ruddy gallows;
Let there be clean linen for the backs of thieves;
Let lovers go fresh and sweet to be undone,
And the heaviest nuns walk in a pure floating
Of dark habits,
            keeping their difficult balance."   30

This is a superb, passionate poem. The sight of laundry being drawn into
the morning air between two buildings becomes first a vision of wished-for angelic purity; and then, with accepting insight, of the mingled purity and im-
purity of the human condition. Seeing the pieces of laundry billowing in the
breeze, the waking person momentarily mistakes them for angels. Not fully
awake, he is an "astounded soul," "for a moment bodiless and simple." He
"shrinks" from facing the dirtying reality of the world. As if answering the "cry
of pulleys," the soul "cries":

    "Oh, let there be nothing on earth but laundry,
Nothing but rosy hands in the rising steam
And clear dances done in the sight of heaven."

But in stanza 5, reminded by the sun's "warm look," "The soul descends once more in bitter love / To accept the waking body"—its own inescapable attachment to dirtying reality—and, in the last stanza, to accept the dirtying world itself. The wish for purity is replaced by compassion for the ambiguities and precariousness of the human condition.

The poem's trajectory is psychological, dramatic; its theme, deeply Christian, though not in a doctrinal way; its title, from Saint Augustine. The initial mistaking of laundry for angels seems natural enough for the half-awakened consciousness; the whimsicality of the mistake is recognized soon enough, as the breeze slackens: "nobody seems to be there." But the universal desire for purity, the wish to avoid the inevitable sullying of "every blesséd day," is, however accidentally raised and fancifully expressed, real and in no way whimsical. The colloquial emphatic "blesséd" accidentally carries on the religious imagery. The poem's always useful puns ("spirited from sleep," "awash with angels," "The soul shrinks") culminate in the nuns' "dark habits." Even "the heaviest" (most tempted and worldly) of them, nonetheless, walk "in a pure floating," "keeping their difficult balance," *in* but not *of* the world. With the somewhat biblical word "linen," the "ruddy gallows" suggests the crucifixion, and the "thieves" the two thieves on crosses on either side of Christ. Christ, the poem subtly reminds us, also descended in love into the world and the flesh. The soul's two speeches are, of course, prayers, recognizing that, although the world is often less ideal than we might wish, we must nonetheless live in it and love it.

Richard Wilbur has generously published the first six drafts of the poem's opening lines. In them it is possible to follow the developing poem as it searches for both its language and its form.

DRAFT 1

My eyes came open to the squeak of pulleys
My spirit, shocked from the brothel of itself

Lack of punctuation after the first line suggests that this draft is notational, trying out possibilities for opening the poem. The lines are iambic pentameter, and we can guess that the poet has been mulling them over in his head until they have taken on a distinct metrical shape before trying them on paper. The oddity in the lines is the image "brothel." Sleep, the withdrawal of the soul from the body, is seen very forcefully as a sort of self-indulgence on the soul's part. The implicit rebuke, which will be softened in the final poem to an awareness of the soul's natural but mistaken repugnance for the "things of this world," shows that the thematic direction of the poem is already given. The paradox (or confusion) of a fleshly image for the soul's self-indulgence is striking. That the poet distrusts "brothel," however, is clear from the second draft, where the image is altered.

DRAFT 2

My eyes came open to the shriek of pulleys,
And the soul, spirited from its proper wallow,
Hung in the air as bodiless and hollow

In place of the literal but uninteresting "squeak" of pulleys, the poet tries "shriek," which personifies them. The fairly straightforward "shocked" is replaced by the pun "spirited"—in the sense of something's being carried away mysteriously or secretly. Punctuated, the lines begin to be a sentence. Whichever word came first, a rhyme has suggested itself: "wallow-hollow," and so a further formal possibility has been engaged. In the third draft, perhaps foreseeing trouble in rhyming "pulleys," the poet reverses the word order and replaces "shriek" with "cry."

DRAFT 3

My eyes came open to the pulleys' cry.
The soul, spirited from its proper wallow,
Hung in the air as bodiless and hollow
As light that frothed upon the wall opposing;
But what most caught my eyes at their unclosing
Was two gray ropes that yanked across the sky.
One after one into the window frame
. . . the hosts of laundry came

Propelled, no doubt, by a desire to get on with it, and apparently released by the possibility of rhyming, the poem makes a spurt forward. Without the negative connotations of "shriek" (and its too attention-getting personification), "cry" seems right, meaning ambiguously both to call out in grief or suffering, and to announce. While "pulleys' cry" is awkward, it sets up the very usable rhyme of "sky"—which the poet may not yet know how he will use but which provides an easy target for a subsequent line. Again, whichever came first, the rhyme-pairs "opposing-unclosing" and "frame-came" allow the draft to move forward to the completion of its exposition and what sounds like the end of a stanza. The dots in line 8 indicate a blank the poet leaves to be filled later.

Rhyming has got the poem this far. But the poet is plainly unsatisfied, as the unfinished and unpunctuated line 8 shows. In the fourth draft *all* the rhyme-words except "cry" disappear from the poem, and "cry" moves back to a less clumsy place in its line. The causes, if not the order, of the poet's dissatisfactions can be guessed. "Wallow" muted somewhat the comparison of the soul's weakness to fleshliness, but the confusion is still there, along with an unfortunate animal connotation. Because "hollow" suggests the vacant interior of something solid, it isn't really accurate for the soul. Saying "the wall opposing," to set up the rhyme, is rather stagy—the normal phrase would be "the opposite wall." Saying "at their unclosing" is mere padding. Lines 5—6 seem inaccurate or, at least, a needless digression, for the laundry, not the "two gray ropes," is surely what "most caught my eyes." I suspect it caused the poet some pain to give up the nice detail of the ropes, and especially the word "yanked," which is the first word in the poem to strike naturally and unaffectedly the colloquial tone that the final version values in "awash," "shrinks," "blesséd," "hunks," and "ruddy" (an English colloquialism meaning reddish, and suggesting "bloody"). The window "frame" distracts from what is seen through the window, and line 7 as a whole is open to the misreading of coming *into* the room through the window. "One by one" also limits the view of the laundry and, if allowed to stand, would preclude the panoramic view in the final version's second and third stanzas.

DRAFT 4

The eyes open to a cry of pulleys,
And the soul, so suddenly spirited from sleep,
Hangs in the air as bodiless and simple
As morning sunlight frothing on the floor,
While just outside the window
The air is solid with a dance of angels.

Freedom from rhyme now permits the poem to do in six lines what it had done in eight, and the first line has reached its final form. In line 2 the soul is now spirited merely from "sleep" instead of brothel or wallow. "Hollow" is replaced with the apt "simple" ("bodiless and simple"); that is, simply itself, uncomplicated, in its own nature. But "simple" also means ignorant or foolish, as in "simple-minded"; and the pun looks forward to the poem's ultimate judgment on the soul's natural but foolish desire to avoid the dirtying world. Lines 5—6 of this draft focus quickly and unceremoniously on the laundry/angels. The housecleaning between the third and fourth drafts sweeps away "the hosts of laundry," which was obviously an attempt to sneak up on the word "angels." The fourth draft is direct: "The air is solid with a dance of angels." The explanatory "laundry" is dropped. The bed-sheets, blouses, smocks of the second stanza will make the exposition perfectly clear; and the first stanza can end without apology on the startling appearance of "angels."

The tightening of this draft includes the tentative dropping of iambic pentameter. For the moment the lines will be left not only without rhymes but also free to determine their own length. The possibility is a stanza of lines of differing lengths, such as the poet has used in other poems. If the indentations indicate equal line-length (as they conventionally do), the poet is reading lines 1 and 5 as three feet, line 2 as five feet, and lines 3–4 and 6 as four feet. He is counting loosely, I think, waiting to see how things fall out before being more decisive. For instance, line 1 might be scanned: "Thĕ éyes | ópĕn | tŏ ă crý | ŏf púl|lĕys"—four feet. But, apparently, the poet is scanning it as three feet: "Thĕ ĕyes óp|ĕn tŏ ă crý | ŏf púl|lĕys." This line and the efficient line 5 ("While just outside the window") are the main beneficiaries of dropping the pentameter requirement.

Suggested by this metrical concession (or suggesting it), one of the major changes in the poem occurs: the shift from past to present tense, with a consequent increase in immediacy, appropriate to the Keatsian impressionism of the poem. "Hangs" now looks forward to the "ruddy gallows" of the last stanza, as "hung" could not. The other major change is from the first to the third person: "My eyes" become only "The eyes," opening the way to "the man yawns and rises" in stanza 5. The soul, rather than a first-person speaker, becomes the poem's protagonist. This change provides an important, measuring distance between the voice of the poem and the soul, whose fantasies and recognitions make up the central action. Having this central action occur entirely within the soul, at some remove from the man, who seems almost unaware of this drama, avoids any thorny questions about the relationship of body, mind, and soul—or who/what corrects the soul's mistaken wish for untainted purity. The poem's psychology is, thus, allegorized, simplified. The initial punitive tone toward the soul ("brothel") disappears, and it is the soul itself that, recognizing its understandable desire to disentangle itself from them, "descends in bitter love / To accept the waking body" and the world. The soul's deflection from its true compassion is only momentary, occurring in those few instants of waking before "the man yawns and rises." In the next draft the poet underlines this revision by altering line 3 from "hangs in the air as bodiless and simple" to "Hangs for a moment bodiless and simple." Everything—vision of laundry as angels, the two prayers—in a moment; and the soul's momentary error is not sinful lapse but a *simple* foolishness which it corrects quickly. (This change from first to third person was already implicit in the second draft's "My eyes . . . *the* soul," but it took two further drafts for the poet to respond to the cue.) Significant advance as the fourth draft is, the stanza is not finished.

DRAFT 5

The eyes open to a cry of pulleys,
And spirited from sleep, the astounded soul
Hangs for a moment bodiless and simple
As dawn light in the moment of its breaking:

> Outside the open window
> The air is crowded with a

The unnecessary "so suddenly" in line 2 vanishes (being spirited away is always sudden to the victim); and its space in the line is given to "astounded," which conveys the dramatic excitement one would feel at perceiving angels outside the bedroom window. It also, of course, prepares the way for making allowances for the soul's momentary error. With "for a moment" substituted in line 3, the poem's first three lines are complete. Line 4 gets rid of the "frothed" and "frothing" of the third and fourth drafts. The idea of froth's bubbly airiness, whether on "wall opposing" or on the floor, may picture flickery early sunlight; but the connotations are so negative—foam, frothing at the mouth—that the possibility is discarded. The floor seems as irrelevant and digressive as the wall opposing had been. Line 5 is sharpened: the rather empty "While just" is dropped and the window is made "open," which conveys the immediacy of the angels, as if they might indeed enter the room. Picking up the "open" (verb) of line 1, "the open window" (adjective) here makes the vision doubly close and surprising. In line 6 the poet discards the too static and dense adjective "solid"—"The air is solid with a dance of angels"—in favor of the plainer but more active "crowded." But, before he can add either "dance of angels" or "host of angels," the pending possibilities, the draft breaks off.

The most decisive thing the poet does in the fifth draft is to firm the meter. The four lines that begin with the left margin are iambic pentameter, which is to become again the norm of the poem; the half indentation of line 1 indicates that it is now being scanned as tetrameter, the full indentation of line 5 that it is now being scanned as trimeter.

DRAFT 6

> The eyes open to a cry of pulleys,
> And spirited from sleep, the astounded soul
> Hangs for a moment bodiless and simple
> As false dawn.
> > Outside the open window,
> The air is leaping with a rout of angels.
> > Some are in bedsheets, some are in dresses,
> > > it does not seem to matter

The weakest line in the fifth draft was line 4: "As dawn light in the moment of its breaking." "in the moment" is niggling and lamely repeats "for a moment" in line 3; "of its breaking" is essentially empty. At a stroke in the sixth draft, the poet drops those phrases and alters "As dawn light" to "as false dawn"—period. The economy is complete. False dawn, that early light before sunrise, is itself "bodiless and simple," a vague, incomplete stage, eerie and somehow nonphysical. Like the soul's fanciful vision and its wish for utter and untested purity, it is "false dawn"; the soul's truer prayer is saved, like the sun's "warm look" itself, for the fifth and sixth stanzas. As the progression from false dawn to sunrise is natural, so, by implication, is the soul's from false prayer to true.

The other troublesome line in the fifth draft is line 6: "The air is crowded with a"—which is left unfinished. As "solid" was too heavy and static, so "crowded" is too flat. In the sixth draft the poet tries again for liveliness and surprise: "The air is leaping with a rout of angels." "Rout," which suggests unruliness, suitably describes the free-blowing laundry and adds the unexpected pleasure of imagining a boisterous and disorderly crowd of angels. Heavenly fun, the word implies, needn't be dull. But the word is hardly serious enough for the variety of angelic attitudes and meanings that are to follow in stanzas 2 and 3 ("calm swells of halcyon feeling," "the terrible speed of their omnipresence," for example). And "The air is leaping" seems dyslexic, though perfectly clear. Presumably on the next try, the poet hits the mark of the line exactly: "The morning air is all awash with angels," with its vividly descriptive and explanatory pun.

Presumably, too, in the final draft, the next two lines are properly put forward to stanza 2. (Why the poet alters "dresses" to "blouses" in the first line of stanza 2 is a puzzle the reader may solve.) With the poet's recognition that the two short lines, 4 and 5, together make a single pentameter line, the essential form of the poem's first stanza is set: one line of tetrameter, five of pentameter. Problems in maintaining that pattern in subsequent stanzas might have, but didn't, sent the poet back to rework stanza 1. The decision whether to print "As false dawn. Outside the open window" as a continuous line or a dropped-line was presumably deferred. It was made only when other stanzas showed places where a dropped-line could be effective, especially in stanza 3 ("That nobody seems to be there. / The soul shrinks") and stanza 6 ("Of dark habits, / keeping their difficult balance"), where the dropped-line, along with the metrical irregularities, beautifully illustrates the precariousness in the line's meaning. Not incidentally, the drafts show the poet writing with practiced ease in metered lines, deftly using the trochaic "open" in line 1 for its surprise and positioning (after the first draft) the word "hangs" at the beginning of its line.

The poem is developing in several ways simultaneously. Its main idea, at first fuzzy and uncertain, clarifies with each successive draft. As the details of the scene are considered, then accepted or dropped, the visual impression sharpens. The diction becomes exact; tone and nuance focus with precision. And, by no means least important, after several trials the form settles into a pattern that is appropriate and comfortable. From so sure and carefully modulated a beginning, the poet can continue with confidence.

Trial-and-Error

Similar trial-and-error appears in four successive versions of three lines of "Hyperion" by John Keats (1795–1821). The crux is the image in lines 8–9. Here is the entire opening passage of the poem, with the first of Keats's four versions in italics:

> Deep in the shady sadness of a vale
> Far sunken from the healthy breath of morn,
> Far from the fiery noon, and eve's one star,
> Sat gray-haired Saturn°, quiet as a stone,   *an ancient Titan*
> Still as the silence round about his lair;   5
> Forest on forest hung about his head
> Like cloud on cloud. *No stir of air was there,*
> *Not so much life as what an eagle's wing*
> *Would spread upon a field of green eared corn,*
> But where the dead leaf fell, there did it rest.   10
> A stream went voiceless by, still deadened more
> By reason of his fallen divinity
> Spreading a shade: the Naiad 'mid her reeds
> Pressed her cold finger closer to her lips.

It is a melancholy scene. Saturn sits motionless in the silent, shading forest. The first phrase of the passage is exactly descriptive with its static internal off-rhyme: "stir-air-there." The trouble that Keats senses is in the image for this stillness in the next two lines. From his next version we can see what particularly bothered him. The clumsy and unnecessary "what" was obviously used merely to keep the meter. An easy solution would have been to remove the word in favor of an adjective describing the eagle. He might then have written: "Not so much life as a young eagle's wing." But Keats was also unsatisfied with the eagle. Probably he sensed that it was too positive and vigorous an image of power to be appropriate to the "fallen divinity" he was depicting. In the second version of the lines he exchanges the eagle for the tonally more relevant vulture.

> No stir of air was there,
> Not so much life as a young vulture's wing
> Would spread upon a field of green eared corn

The image that Keats intends is apparently of a large, powerful bird of prey circling high in the sky, probably gliding rather than flapping; and the point is that its wing causes absolutely *no motion* in the field of easily swayed grain far below. (In British usage *corn* indicates wheat or some other edible grain, not

American corn.) Perhaps Keats has in mind the shadow of the bird's wing passing over, but not moving, the limber stalks. The vulture might suit the picture of Saturn in his vale, and even its youth might provide a useful contrast to Saturn's age and weakness.

As the third version reveals, however, Keats discards the entire image. Possibly, carrion or no, the youthful, powerful bird spoils the unvarying tone of the mournful passage. Certainly, the "field of green eared corn"—sunny, spacious, and vital—does not fit the enclosed, "shady" forest scene of defeated Saturn. Interesting though the image is in itself, it seems a wrong choice.

So, in the third version, dropping the bird image altogether, Keats tries again:

> No stir of air was there,
> Not so much life as on a summer's day
> Robs not at all the dandelion's fleece

The substitution of the untended weed for the "green eared corn" strikes the right note; and the light, easily dislodged, white-tufted seeds of the dandelion provide a good measure for the absolute stillness of air as well as, in their color and implicit ruin, a vivid parallel to the "gray-haired," ruined Titan. The image has a literal rightness and consistent, useful overtones. The double negatives, "Not . . . not . . .," may feel awkward at first, but they follow "No stir of air was there" with an emphatic absoluteness. Even the awkwardness seems, rhythmically, to mirror the uselessness of the utterly still air with its inability to dislodge even a seed. For some months Keats let the lines stand so.

Several problems must have bothered him into another, final, revision. Possibly the very choice of the lowly, common, near-comic dandelion came to seem inappropriate to so lofty a poem on a classical subject. More significantly, Keats must have recognized that "fleece," though visually accurate and fluffy enough for a head of dandelion seeds, is a poor image in the context. For one thing, fleece is really quite oily and rather heavy. For another, a fleece is not easily robbed (it would require taking the sheep whole or at least clipping him). Pieces of wool might be snagged from a fleece, but not by the wind—and ease of dislodgement is essential to the image. In any event, robbing a bit of wool from a fleece makes no sense. One other aspect of the image may have concerned Keats: the picture he has given is of a single dandelion, close-up. Having the camera farther away, so as to suggest the extent of the breezelessness, seems to have been a consideration in the revision Keats made:

> No stir of air was there,
> Not so much life as on a summer's day
> Robs not one light seed from the feathered grass

As the psychologist Rudolf Arnheim comments in *Poets at Work*, "The precision of the botanist suggested by practical language ('dandelion') is given up in favor of a description which omits the identifications of the plant but specifies the expressive perceptual features of weight and movement." Like the dead leaf in the next line, the identity of the "seed from the feathered grass" is left abstract, generic. Visually, nothing is allowed to compete with the main pictorial presentation of Saturn. The rhythm of the revised line is masterful: "Róbs nót óne líght séed fröm the féathéred gráss." The five utterly even, accented syllables at the beginning of the line suggest an evenly light, precarious balance without movement. After this, the slightly enhanced speed of "from the feathered grass" seems to pass like the looked-for, but nonexistent, breath of air. Not the least of Keats's mastery is using spondees to convey an impression of lightness! Trying and erring, waiting for the right touch, the poet carefully works beyond the initial impulse.

William Butler Yeats also approached the process of rewriting seriously:

> The friends that have it I do wrong
> Whenever I remake a song,
> Should know what issue is at stake:
> It is myself that I remake.

He sometimes rewrote, years later, poems that had already been published in book form. (W. H. Auden and Marianne Moore also continued to revise earlier poems throughout their careers.) Here, for example, as Yeats published it in 1892, is "The Sorrow of Love":

> The quarrel of the sparrows in the eaves,
> The full round moon and the star-laden sky,
> And the loud song of the ever-singing leaves
> Had hid away earth's old and weary cry.
>
> And then you came with those red mournful lips,   5
> And with you came the whole of the world's tears,
> And all the sorrows of her labouring ships,
> And all burden of her myriad years.
>
> And now the sparrows warring in the eaves,
> The crumbling moon, the white stars in the sky,   10
> And the loud chanting of the unquiet leaves,
> Are shaken with earth's old and weary cry.

Grave, languorous, and lovely, "The Sorrow of Love" shows the effect on the speaker of the woman "with those red mournful lips." Before her, he was unaware of "earth's old and weary cry"; and sparrows, moon, stars, and leaves had seemed only themselves. The quarreling sparrows keep this picture from seeming overpretty. After the woman, all these things of the world are, for him, "shaken with earth's old and weary cry." The positive images become now negative: "the full round moon" decays and is "crumbling," "the ever-singing leaves" are now "unquiet." Even the sparrows' quarreling is worse, "warring."

With "those red mournful lips," the woman herself seems already to have suffered "the sorrow of love" and to bring with her, from the speaker's point of view, "the whole of the world's tears." Presumably because she rejects him, she is his induction into the "sorrow of love." It isn't quite clear what the "labouring ships" have to do with the sorrow of love, but like the sparrows, moon, stars, and leaves, they reflect the speaker's feelings about everything after the sad and beautiful woman.

When Yeats revised the poem in 1925, although only one of the rhymewords is altered ("years" to "peers"), the poem is transformed:

> The brawling of a sparrow in the eaves,
> The brilliant moon and all the milky sky,
> And all that famous harmony of leaves,
> Had blotted out man's image and his cry.
>
> A girl arose that had red mournful lips   5
> And seemed the greatness of the world in tears,
> Doomed like Odysseus and the labouring ships
> And proud as Priam murdered with his peers;
>
> Arose, and on the instant clamorous eaves,
> A climbing moon upon an empty sky,   10
> And all that lamentation of the leaves,
> Could but compose man's image and his cry.

In discussing the 1892 version, I have (somewhat self-consciously) used the word "woman." Although it does not appear in the text and there is nothing directly indicative of age, it seems more accurate to the history implied by her sorrowful experience of love than the word "girl" might. One of the major changes in the 1925 version, then, is the description of her as a "girl," which, at a single touch, increases the poem's pathos: so much sorrow in one so young is profoundly moving. Another major change is the depersonalization of the relationship in the poem. With the use of the third person—"girl" instead of "you"—the speaker's relationship to her (having been rejected or whatever) becomes irrelevant. In the later version, only his experience of her sorrow causes his darkened attitude. The poem loses much less in this playing down of the personal than it gains in poignancy. That gain is intensified by a third major change, in which "earth's old and weary cry" becomes "man's image and his cry." At best, the sorrow of love could have been associated only vaguely with the personified "earth." Dropping this rather weak elegance, Yeats accurately focuses the poem's tragic vision on the human. The natural details of sparrow, moon, stars, leaves (which, after all, exist apart from the human) seemed in stanza 1 to be sufficiently absorbing in themselves. After the girl has appeared, in stanza 3, their clamor, emptiness, and "lamentation" are felt by the speaker to express his feeling. The fourth major change, in lines 7–8, makes powerful use of the ships, which in the first version were a fuzzy image:

> Doomed like Odysseus and the labouring ships
> And proud as Priam murdered with his peers

Both epics of Homer, *Odyssey* and *Iliad,* are called into evidence. Though Odysseus and Priam are mentioned, and though these comparisons characterize the doomed, proud girl, the effect is also to imply a comparison to the two heroic women of these epics, the beautiful and doomed Helen and the proud and faithful Penelope. The "labouring ships" suggest Agamemnon's fleet as much as Odysseus's hard travels. The image of the "murdered" Priam, last king of Troy, encompasses the destruction of Troy. Thus, in their allusive fashion, these two lines gather into Yeats's poem the whole of the heroic and amorous weight of *Iliad* and *Odyssey.* The poem's claim that the sorrow of love centers "man's image and his cry" thus gathers a convincing historical density.

The "And...And...And..." construction of the first version is replaced by more muscular syntax. Details in the first version that were somewhat misty or romantic, like "the ever-singing leaves," are hardened and sharpened. The plural quarreling and warring sparrows—which might now distract from the distinction between the natural and the human and offer a competing miniature to the vision of the Trojan War—become only a single brawling and clamorous sparrow. Yeats here accepts a small loss in order to clarify the shape of the whole poem, as perhaps he also does in letting go the image of the "crumbling" moon.

The reduction of the number of words in the poem makes it seem cleaner and more direct; compare the effect of "The full round moon and the star-laden sky" with the effect of "The brilliant moon and all the milky sky"; or the elimination of the redundant "song" and "singing" in line 3. Dropping the somewhat fussy indentation of lines increases the poem's directness visually. The sound of the final version is everywhere more resonant. Consider the alliteration of the last two lines of the two versions:

> And the loud chanting of the unquiet leaves,
>   Are shaken with earth's old and weary cry

and

> And all that lamentation of the leaves,
> Could but compose man's image and his cry.

The diction in general becomes more dramatic: "you came" in the first version becomes the powerful "A girl arose" in the final version; and the dramatic repetition of "Arose" at the beginning of the third stanza gives a dynamic impetus to the poem's climax, which the flat "And now" did not. Though it may be a subjective response, "arose" and "red mournful lips" also seem somehow to exchange colors in a subtle resonance.

"The Sorrow of Love" is a case of masterful rewriting. The not very clearly incorporated ships in the 1892 version show that only in the final version did Yeats accomplish what he had intended more than thirty years earlier. Yeats perhaps assumed in 1892 that the Homeric allusion was sufficiently clear.

Testing

One of a poet's most difficult jobs is assessing whether the words on the page, which seem right, will convey to a reader a feeling or impression identical to his or her own. If I describe for you the house in which my family lived when I was five years old, for instance, I have in my mind a picture of it, indeed, a whole set of pictures. I can close my eyes and see it. But when I describe it to you, do the words call up exactly the same picture? Obviously, they cannot. If I have chosen the right words, the significant details, the best that can be hoped is that you will visualize a house much *like* the house I am describing, on a street much like the street, and so on. Unless I am describing a building you have also seen (the Empire State Building, say) there is no way we can have identical images in our minds. (Films made from novels we like often disappoint because they rarely reproduce things as we imagined them.)

As writers, we deal at best in impressions of visual scenes, people, ideas, or feelings. The poet's words will always call up, for her or him, the precise scene or feeling. But the poet must consider accurately the effect the words will have on a reader, if they are to evoke in the reader something sufficiently like. Rewriting, insisting on clarity, will help; so will honest friends or a workshop.

Poets tend to become almost insatiable testers and tinkerers. The old saw has it that no poet ever finishes a poem but merely abandons it. With good reason the poet learns to put a new poem away in a drawer for a time, then to have another look. What may seem a stroke of genius at midnight in the first flush of composition may appear quite otherwise in the morning or the following week. In this, poets are like manic depressives—up, down, up—about what they are doing. Because the poem that seems great today can seem dumb tomorrow and wonderful again the day after, poets need friends, other members of a writing class, and eventually editors. What may be obvious to someone else, though not to the poet, may very well start him or her going again on the poem, or provide the clue to patching a thin spot or avoiding a clunker.

Friends are handy but are sometimes too well-meaning. Praise is always nice, but the poet wants (or should want in that heart of hearts) the unvarnished truth. Dryden's seventeenth-century advice still fits:

> . . . to yourself be critic most severe.
> Fantastic wits their darling follies love;
> But find you faithful friends that will reprove,
> That on your works may look with careful eyes,
> And of your faults be zealous enemies: 5
> Lay by an author's pride and vanity,
> And from a friend a flatterer descry,
> Who seems to like, but means not what he says:
> Embrace true counsel, but suspect false praise.
> A sycophant will every thing admire;   10
> Each verse, each sentence sets his soul on fire:
> All is divine! there's not a word amiss!
> He shakes with joy, and weeps with tenderness;
> He overpowers you with his mighty praise.
> Truth never moves in those impetuous ways;   15
> A faithful friend is careful of your fame,
> And freely will your heedless errors blame;
> He cannot pardon a neglected line. . . .
> No fool can want a sot to praise his rhymes.
> The flattest work has ever in the court   20
> Met with some zealous ass for its support;
> And in all times a forward scribbling fop
> Has found some greater fool to cry him up.

Find those, as Pope says, "Who to a friend his faults can freely show."

A writing class or workshop may be helpful. Like off-Broadway audiences, their reactions and understanding (or lack of it) give you a chance to test the poem. Often, because they have the same technical interest in poetry, they will be sharp critics, able to put a finger on problems. When a formal workshop isn't available, you can gather a small group of poets to meet occasionally for exchanging and discussing poems. Even experienced poets find such advice valuable. Groups will, of course, be uneven in the quality of comment. Sometimes, having got into the critical habit, they will tend to niggle at every poem that appears. As always with advice, the poet should listen openly, not defensively, and make up his or her own mind afterward.

Editors can be useful critics, especially when they are poets themselves and when the poems in their magazines are of the sort the submitting poet likes. Objective and genuinely seeking good poems, they rarely comment on poems they reject (some do, some do!); but even a simple no may be worth getting.

Editors seldom reject masterpieces. Although one rejection slip means little, when a group of poems comes back from four, five, or six editors whose judgment one trusts, it is time to have another hard look at the poems. Don't feel, when an editor rejects poems, that he or she is necessarily being unfriendly. Preventing a poet's publishing a poem that isn't very good (or is embarrassing) is in fact a kindly service. Because most magazines receive more good poems than they have space to print, there may occasionally be a scrawl on the rejection slip: "Try us again," or "Fine work," or "Liked 'Apples.'" Occasionally, when an editor accepts a poem—now that is helpful criticism!—he or she will append a question or suggestion. An alert editor can spare the poet many a boner.

It must also be said that poets have spoiled good poems by one revision too many, as Keats did in this stanza from his ballad "La Belle Dame Sans Merci." He altered the wonderfully particular and so mysterious—

> She took me to her elfin grot,
>   And there she wept and sighed full sore,
> And there I shut her wild wild eyes
>   With kisses four . . .

to the lame—

> She took me to her elfin grot,
>   And there she gazed and sighed deep,
> And there I shut her wild sad eyes—
>   So kissed to sleep.

Nonetheless, the dangers of not being sufficiently self-critical are immeasurably greater. "A hundred times consider what you've said."

QUESTIONS AND SUGGESTIONS

1. Here are Yeats's initial sketches of the poem "After Long Silence" (page 325) and a number of lines and alternatives from advancing drafts. Study them, noting the poem's growth, and compare them with the final version.

a) Recording a visit to Olivia Shakespear in October 1929 as a proposed "Subject":

Your hair is white
My hair is white
Come let us talk of love
What other theme do we know
When we were young
We were in love with one another
And then were ignorant.

b) Notes:

1) Your other lovers being dead and gone
2) Those other lovers being dead and gone

friendly light
hair is white

1) Upon the sole theme of art and song
2) Upon the supreme theme of art and song
3) Upon that theme so fitting for the aged; young
   We loved each other and were ignorant

Once more I have kissed your hand and it is right
All other lovers being estranged or dead

The heavy curtains drawn—the candle light
Waging a doubtful battle with the shade

1) We call our wisdom up and descant
2) We call upon wisdom and descant
   Upon the supreme theme of art and song
   Decrepitude increases wisdom—young
   We loved each other and were ignorant

The candle hidden by its friendly shade
The curtain drawn on the unfriendly night
That we descant and yet again descant
Upon the supreme theme of art and song

1) The friendly lamp light hidden by its shade
2) Unfriendly lamp light hidden by its shade

1) And shutters clipped upon the deepening night
2) Those curtains drawn upon the deepening night

That we descant and yet again descant
Upon the supreme theme of art and song—
Bodily decrepitude is wisdom—young

Once more I have kissed your hand and it is right
All other lovers being estranged or dead
Unfriendly lamplight hidden by its shade
The curtains drawn upon the deepening night—

2. Here are drafts and revisions of lines by William Wordsworth and Rupert
Brooke (1887—1915), and of a poem by Robert Frost. Consider why the poets
made the changes and whether they involve gains or losses.

a) from Wordsworth's *The Prelude*:

> Magnificent
> The morning was, in memorable pomp,
> More glorious than I ever had beheld.
> The sea was laughing at a distance; all
> The solid mountains were as bright as clouds.

> Magnificent
> The morning rose, in memorable pomp,
> Glorious as e'er I had beheld—in front
> The sea lay laughing at a distance; near,
> The solid mountains shone, bright as the clouds.

b) from Wordsworth's "The Green Linnet":

> The May is come again:—how sweet
> To sit upon my orchard-seat!
> And birds and flowers once more to greet,
>   My last year's friends together:
> My thoughts they all by turns employ;
> A whispering leaf is now my joy,
> And then a bird will be the toy
>   That doth my fancy tether.

> Beneath these fruit-tree boughs that shed
> Their snow-white blossoms on my head,
> With brightest sunshine round me spread
>   Of spring's unclouded weather,
> In this sequestered nook how sweet
> To sit upon my orchard-seat!
> And birds and flowers once more to greet,
>   My last year's friends together.

c) from Rupert Brooke's "The Soldier":

If I should die think of me
That in some corner of a foreign field
Something of England lies.

If I should die, think only this of me:
That there's some corner of a foreign field
That is forever England. There shall be
In that rich earth a richer dust concealed

d) Robert Frost:

In White   1912

A dented spider like a snowdrop white
On a white Heal-all, holding up a moth
Like a white piece of lifeless satin cloth—
Saw ever curious eye so strange a sight?
Portent in little, assorted death and blight   5
Like the ingredients of a witches' broth?
The beady spider, the flower like a froth,
And the moth carried like a paper kite.

What had that flower to do with being white,
The blue Brunella every child's delight?   10
What brought the kindred spider to that height?
(Make we no thesis of the miller's° plight.)   miller-moth
What but design of darkness and of night?
Design, design! Do I use the word aright?

Design   1936

I found a dimpled spider, fat and white,
On a white heal-all, holding up a moth
Like a white piece of rigid satin cloth—
Assorted characters of death and blight
Mixed ready to begin the morning right,   5
Like the ingredients of a witches' broth—
A snow-drop spider, a flower like a froth,
And dead wings carried like a paper kite.

What had that flower to do with being white,
The wayside blue and innocent heal-all?   10
What brought the kindred spider to that height,
Then steered the white moth thither in the night?
What but design of darkness to appall?—
If design govern in a thing so small.

3. Choose a completed but somehow still unsatisfactory poem of your own, and

have another try at revising it. Read it aloud several times. Does anything make you wince—something you'd be embarrassed to show? (Maybe that's where the trouble is.) Try taking out one or two words (the least effective) or, if the poem is metered, a foot out of each line; does that open it up? Look back through the drafts for a lost word, image, or detail that might start the poem moving again. Type it over, varying the stanzas or breaking it into stanzas.

4. In "Apologies to Creston" Richmond Lattimore uses a very loose hexameter line. How is it appropriate to the poem's subject and mood? What is the effect of the three-line stanzas? One of the ways of testing a poem is to see whether, without loss, any of the words can be made to come loose and drift away. Try tampering with "Apologies to Creston." In spite of its formal leisureliness, is it in fact tight?

As I remember there were other travelers, too,
but no communication. At 2 P.M. and about 102°
there was a Burlington transcontinental in the station,

stainless steel, gleaming under noon gold. We, there alighting
from our tired Chevrolet, as at the wellside in the antique desert,   5
sought the oasis shade and the water; we, carrying

enough money to feed us and our car and get home
and no more; carrying the fragments of prairie travel, of last night
slept on the sidewalk in front of the church, next the weed patch,

somewhere nameless in Nebraska on US 6; now ventured   10
the little metropolis, and in the shining drugstore assimilated
glutinous malts and sundaes; and all about us the sweet-and-pretty

of a model town freshened, pressed starched and crisp, as for a wedding
or garden party; and we, shabby at the eyes from little sleep, not well
shaved, dry and hairy, foreign matter in their green lettuce.   15

How can we pick the towns and stops in the passage
of our life, stick each one like a bug on a pin, assemble
a string, and show them to our dinner guests? Yet of these stuffs are we made.

And even of ours, they; despite disapprovals; and if only
as something once under a fingernail, or combed out   20
of an eyebrow. No communication. But there we are.

Forward then toward evening, and the meal in the wayside weeds,
and the horse opera from the dashboard into late hours, which finally
tumbled us into the camp ground tented with boy scouts, somewhere near
    Keokuk,

and another day gone, and in the middle of it the unshared oasis.   25
Now on the map, unequivocally between Red Oak
and Chariton, find the name: Creston, Iowa: and hope we have not been rude.

The Town of Hill   1971

DONALD HALL   (b. 1928)

Back of the dam, under
a flat pad

of water, church
bells ring

in the ears of lilies,   5
a child's swing

curls in the current
of a yard, horned

pout sleep
in a green   10

mailbox, and
a boy walks

from a screened
porch beneath

the man-shaped   15
leaves of an oak

down the street looking
at the town

of Hill that water
covered forty   20

years ago,
and the screen

door shuts
under dream water.

from *The Task*   1785

WILLIAM COWPER   (1731–1800)

> There is a pleasure in poetic pains
> Which only poets know. The shifts and turns,
> Th' expedients and inventions, multiform,
> To which the mind resorts, in chase of terms
> Though apt, yet coy, and difficult to win—   5
> T'arrest the fleeting images that fill
> The mirror of the mind, and hold them fast,
> And force them sit till he has pencil'd off
> A faithful likeness of the forms he views;
> Then to dispose his copies with such art,   10
> That each may find its most propitious light,
> And shine by situation, hardly less
> Than by the labour and the skill it cost;
> Are occupations of the poet's mind
> So pleasing, and that steal away the thought   15
> With such address from themes of sad import,
> That, lost in his own musings, happy man!
> He feels th' anxieties of life, denied
> Their wonted entertainment, all retire.
> Such joys has he that sings. But ah! not such,   20
> Or seldom such, the hearers of his song.
> Fastidious, or else listless, or perhaps
> Aware of nothing arduous in a task
> They never undertook, they little note
> His dangers or escapes, and haply find   25
> There least amusement where he found the most.

My Father in the Night Commanding No   1963

LOUIS SIMPSON   (b. 1923)

> My father in the night commanding No
> Has work to do. Smoke issues from his lips;
> > He reads in silence.
> The frogs are croaking and the streetlamps glow.

And then my mother winds the gramophone;   5
The Bride of Lammermoor begins to shriek—
        Or reads a story
About a prince, a castle, and a dragon.

The moon is glittering above the hill.
I stand before the gateposts of the King—   10
        So runs the story—
Of Thule, at midnight when the mice are still.

And I have been in Thule! It has come true—
The journey and the danger of the world,
        All that there is   15
To bear and to enjoy, endure and do.

Landscapes, seascapes . . . where have I been led?
The names of cities—Paris, Venice, Rome—
        Held out their arms.
A feathered god, seductive, went ahead.   20'

Here is my house. Under a red rose tree
A child is swinging; another gravely plays.
        They are not surprised
That I am here; they were expecting me.

And yet my father sits and reads in silence,   25
My mother sheds a tear, the moon is still,
        And the dark wind
Is murmuring that nothing ever happens.

Beyond his jurisdiction as I move
Do I not prove him wrong? And yet, it's true   30
        They will not change
There, on the stage of terror and of love.

The actors in that playhouse always sit
In fixed positions—father, mother, child
        With painted eyes.   35
How sad it is to be a little puppet!

Their heads are wooden. And you once pretended
To understand them! Shake them as you will,
        They cannot speak.
Do what you will, the comedy is ended.   40

Father, why did you work? Why did you weep,
Mother? Was the story so important?
    "Listen!" the wind
Said to the children, and they fell asleep.

After Long Silence   1933

WILLIAM BUTLER YEATS   (1865–1939)

Speech after long silence; it is right,
All other lovers being estranged or dead,
Unfriendly lamplight hid under its shade,
The curtains drawn upon unfriendly night,
That we descant and yet again descant   5
Upon the supreme theme of Art and Song:
Bodily decrepitude is wisdom; young
We loved each other and were ignorant.

13

Revising (II):
Seven-Eighths of the Iceberg

Tightening and shaping, two operations that are continuous in rewriting, have almost the force of principles. Both are exemplified in chapter 12. When the poet perceived (between drafts 5 and 6 of "Love Calls Us to the Things of This World") that the last six words of the line "As dawn light in the moment of its breaking" were empty and unnecessary, he was tightening. Clarified by this excision, the line could be refocused from the rather uncertain "As dawn light" into the incisive "As false dawn." Similarly, the poet's constant, early tinkering with rhyme, line-length, and indentation, as later with stanza and dropped-line, exemplifies shaping. Rarely is a poem's exact form a given before the process of writing begins.

Tightening

A good rule of thumb is that a poem (or any writing) should be only as long as is necessary to do its job. There is leeway, of course, but as Shakespeare put it, "It is better to be brief than tedious." Writing is linear: it takes time to read words. Any idea expressed in a hundred words that could have been said fully in fifty must be *less intense* because it is spread over a longer reading time. Redundancies, vague or empty epithets, and rhetorical roundabouts cause, second by second in the reading, a loss in impact; they inevitably lower interest and blur focus. Unnecessary words clutter, confuse, and distract. In his funny and very practical essay on "Fenimore Cooper's Literary Offenses"—in the form of "mock" lectures to the Veterinary College of Arizona—Mark Twain (Samuel L. Clemens, 1835–1910) shows how several inflated passages from Cooper's novels might have been advantageously tightened. One he reduces from three hundred twenty words to two hundred twenty, without loss in content. Another he reduces from eighty words to forty. Although Twain is discussing prose, his account is worth quoting:

> In studying Cooper you will find it profitable to study him in detail—word by word, sentence by sentence. For every sentence of his is interesting. Interesting because of its make-up; its peculiar make-up, its original make-up. Let us examine a sentence or two, and see. Here is a passage from Chapter XI of *The Last of the Mohicans*, one of the most famous and most admired of Cooper's books:
>
> > Notwithstanding the swiftness of their flight, one of the Indians had found an opportunity to strike a straggling fawn with an arrow, and had borne the more preferable fragments of the victim, patiently on his shoulders, to the stopping-place. Without any aid from the science of cookery, he was immediately employed, in common with his fellows, in gorging himself with this digestible sustenance. Magua alone sat apart, without participating in the revolting meal, and apparently buried in the deepest thought.
>
> This little paragraph is full of matter for reflection and inquiry. The remark about the swiftness of the flight was unnecessary, as it was merely put in to forestall the possible objection of some overparticular reader that the Indian couldn't have found the needed "opportunity" while fleeing swiftly. The reader would not have made that objection. He would care nothing about having that small matter explained and justified. But that is Cooper's way; frequently he will explain and justify little things that do not need it and then make up for this by as frequently failing to explain important ones that do need it. . . .
>
> No, the remark about the swiftness of their flight was not necessary; neither was the one which said that the Indian found an opportunity; neither was the one which said he *struck* the fawn; neither was the one which explained that it was a "straggling" fawn; neither was the one which said the striking was done with an arrow; neither was the one which said the Indian bore the "fragments"; nor the remark that they were preferable fragments; nor the remark that they were *more* preferable fragments; nor the explanation that they were fragments of the "victim"; nor the overparticular explanation that specifies the Indian's "shoulders" as the part of him that supported the fragments; nor the statement that the Indian bore the fragments patiently. None of those details has any value. We don't care what the Indian struck the fawn with; we don't care whether it was a straggling fawn or an unstraggling one; we don't

care which fragments the Indian saved; we don't care why he saved the "more" preferable ones when the merely preferable ones would have amounted to just the same thing and couldn't have been told from the more preferable ones by anybody, dead or alive; we don't care whether the Indian carried them on his shoulders or in his handkerchief; and finally, we don't care whether he carried them patiently or struck for higher pay and shorter hours. We are indifferent to that Indian and all his affairs.

There was only one fact in that long sentence that was worth stating, and it could have been squeezed into these few words—and with advantage to the narrative, too: "During the flight one of the Indians had killed a fawn and he brought it into camp."

You will notice that "During the flight one of the Indians had killed a fawn and he brought it into camp," is more straightforward and businesslike, and less mincing and smirky, than it is to say, "Notwithstanding the swiftness of their flight, one of the Indians had found an opportunity to strike a straggling fawn with an arrow, and had borne the more preferable fragments of the victim, patiently on his shoulders, to the stopping-place." You will notice that the form "During the flight one of the Indians had killed a fawn and he brought it into camp" holds up its chin and moves to the front with the steady stride of a grenadier, whereas the form "Notwithstanding the swiftness of their flight, one of the Indians had found an opportunity to strike a straggling fawn with an arrow, and had borne the more preferable fragments of the victim, patiently on his shoulders, to the stopping-place" simpers along with an airy, complacent, monkey-with-a-parasol gait which is not suited to the transportation of raw meat.

I beg to remind you that an author's way of setting forth a matter is called his Style, and that an author's style is a main part of his equipment for business. The style of some authors has variety in it, but Cooper's style is remarkable for the absence of this feature. Cooper's style is always grand and stately and noble. Style may be likened to an army, the author to its general, the book to the campaign. Some authors proportion an attacking force to the strength or weakness, the importance or unimportance, of the object to be attacked; but Cooper doesn't. It doesn't make any difference to Cooper whether the object of attack is a hundred thousand men or a cow; he hurls his entire force against it. He comes thundering down with all his battalions at his back, cavalry in the van, artillery on the flanks, infantry massed in the middle, forty bands braying, a thousand banners streaming in the wind; and whether the object be an army or a cow you will see him come marching sublimely in, at the end of the engagement, bearing the more preferable fragments of the victim patiently on his shoulders, to the stopping-place. Cooper's style is grand, awful, beautiful; but it is sacred to Cooper, it is his very own, and no student of the Veterinary College of Arizona will be allowed to filch it from him.

In one of his chapters Cooper throws an ungentle slur at one Gamut because he is not exact enough in his choice of words. But Cooper has that failing himself. If the Indian had "struck" the fawn with a brick, or with a club, or with his fist, no one could find fault with the word used. And one cannot find much fault when he strikes it with an arrow; still it sounds affected, and it might have been a little better to lean to simplicity and say he shot it with an arrow.

"Fragments" is well enough, perhaps, when one is speaking of the parts of a dismembered deer, yet it hasn't just exactly the right sound—and sound is something; in fact sound is a good deal. It makes the difference between good music and poor music, and it can sometimes make the difference between good literature and indifferent literature. "Fragments" sounds all right when we are talking about the wreckage of a breakable thing that has been smashed; it also sounds all right when applied to cat's meat; but when we use it to describe large hunks and chunks like the fore- and hindquarters of a fawn, it grates upon the fastidious ear.

"Without any aid from the science of cookery, he was immediately employed, in common with his fellows, in gorging himsef with this digestible sustenance."

This was a mere statistic; just a mere cold, colorless statistic; yet you see Cooper has made a chromo out of it. To use another figure, he has clothed a humble statistic in flowing, voluminous and costly raiment, whereas both good taste and economy suggest that he ought to have saved these splendors for a king, and dressed the humble statistic in a simple breech-clout. Cooper spent twenty-four words here on a thing not really worth more than eight. We will reduce the statistic to its proper proportions and state it in this way:

"He and the others ate the meat raw."

"Digestible sustenance" is a handsome phrase, but it was out of place there, because we do not know these Indians or care for them; and so it cannot interest us to know whether the meat was going to agree with them or not. Details which do not assist a story are better left out.

"Magua alone sat apart, without participating in the revolting meal" is a statement which we understand, but that is our merit, not Cooper's. Cooper is not clear. He does not say who it is that is revolted by the meal. It is really Cooper himself, but there is nothing in the statement to indicate that it isn't Magua. Magua is an Indian and likes raw meat.

The word "alone" could have been left out and space saved. It has no value where it is.

Here is Mark Twain's reduction of the passage, cut by 50 percent!

During the flight one of the Indians had killed a fawn and he brought it into camp. He and the others ate the meat raw. Magua sat apart, without participating in the meal, and apparently buried in the deepest thought.

Poetry is especially an art of compression. That does not mean that all poems should be epigrams; nor that, at the expense of clarity or good manners, a poem should be clogged, crammed, or written in telegramese. But the poet should follow William Strunk's rule not to use two words when one will do and must continually weigh the effect of every word she or he uses. Padding a line to keep the form, instead of finding a necessary detail, results in slackness. Richard Wilbur could have padded the first lines of the stanzas in "Love Calls Us to the Things of This World" to make five feet—"The eyes come open to a cry of pulleys," for example—but he chose the shorter, precise "The eyes open to a cry of pulleys."

Reconciling form and content isn't always easy. Where they are irreconcilable, there is no doubt that a poet should ease the formal demands. But the effort to meet the requirements of a tentative form often leads the poet to discover possible words, ideas, images he or she would not otherwise have considered. Form *tests* content. A possibly helpful tactic for the poet writing in meter is to try at some late stage to shorten every line by one foot. Sometimes this test leads to wrenching or distortion and only confirms the lines as written, but sometimes a word comes out of a line easily, revealing a soft spot in the poem. When a word doesn't matter much to the poem, the poet should find one that does.

In poetry every word should be doing more than one job. Its sound, as well as its sense, matters. Moreover, the feeling of mysterious depth in a good poem frequently comes from the implicit, from nuances and connotations, as in Burns's "red, red rose" and "melodie." Everything need not be *said*. Ernest Hemingway's counsel is pertinent:

> If a writer of prose knows enough about what he is writing about, he may omit things that he knows and the reader, if the writer is writing truly enough, will have a feeling of these things as strongly as though the writer had stated them. The dignity of movement of an iceberg is due to only one-eighth of it being above water.

Hemingway says elsewhere that this is a kind of writing "with nothing that will go bad afterwards." What is *not* there—the implicit, the merely intimated, the nuance—will have its effect.

Tighten, then. Consider this draft of "Moorings" by a student, D. A. Fantauzzi:

> A collection of white, yellow, red
> hulks of sailboats—
> bugs with wings
> folded down their backs,
> tucked out of the wind,
> sitting still.
>
> Through the heart
> a tall pin
> sticks each to the blue-green mat.

Sharply observed, the poem presents a colorful scene. Still, a good instinct would test the poem. Here is the text again, with possible excisions shown by brackets:

> [A collection of] white, yellow, red
> [hulks of] sailboats—
> bugs with wings
> folded down their backs,
> [tucked out of the wind,]
> [sitting still.]
>
> [Through the heart]
> a tall pin
> sticks each to the blue-green mat.

The plural "sailboats" might be sufficient without "A collection of." Though the comparison between sailboats and a display of pinned insects makes the word relevant, it has little force where it is, before the comparison is indicated. In line 2 "hulks of" seems unnecessary and misleading. "Hulks" both feels too large and clumsy for sailboats *and* suggests abandoned or battered vessels. The comparison of sails to wings is precise (both are means of propulsion by air) and necessary; the sails are literally "folded down their backs," as might also be the case of insects' wings. "Tucked out of the wind" seems needlessly explanatory, and the action seems too volitional because in the comparison the insects are obviously dead. Line 6 seems wasted as well as somewhat inaccurate. "Sitting" seems too flat and motionless for sailboats on open water, especially if there is wind; and it applies poorly to the lifeless, impaled insects. The feeling of "Through the heart" is right, but since neither sailboats nor insects have hearts, the line seems imprecise, almost a cliché.

Each of these potential deletions raises a question the poet should consider. How necessary is this word, or detail, to the poem I am trying to write? Here is the poem as it might be arranged, with the cuts made:

> White, yellow, red sailboats—
> bugs with wings
> folded down their backs.
>
> A tall pin
> sticks each to the blue-green mat.

Perhaps the unbalanced, low, flat shapes of the poem suggest the folded-down sails. Perhaps, at this stage, some other phrase or detail or other order will occur to the poet. Might the word "collection" go somehow into stanza 2? Might "away from the wind"—a slight alteration of "tucked out of the wind"—make a good final line and recover some of the pathos of "Through the heart"? How would that affect the rhythm? Asking and answering such questions is the process of writing a poem.

The poet's revision adds a detail—"in rows"—that both helps the picture and reenforces the comparison. He decided to keep the phrase "A collection of," which sets up the comparison and prevents a reader's imagining the sailboats as dispersed.

> A collection of white, yellow, red
> sailboats—bugs with wings
> folded down their backs,
> in rows.
>
> A tall pin
> sticks each to the blue-green mat.

Slackness (wasted words, wasted motions) goes against Chekhov's belief, expressed in a letter to Gorki, that "when a person expends the least possible movement on a certain act, that is grace." A remark of Ezra Pound's in 1914 is tongue-in-cheek but not without point: "A Chinaman said long ago that if a man can't say what he has to say in twelve lines he had better keep quiet." Not all poems should be short, of course, nor as short as Pound's "In a Station of the Metro" (page 125), which from a thirty-five line draft became a two-line poem! But every poem should be as short as it can be.

Our century's most remarkable excision occurs in Marianne Moore's famous and often anthologized "Poetry," which was first published in 1921. Moore tinkered with this poem from time to time over the years. This is its most familiar version (1935):

> I, too, dislike it: there are things that are important beyond all this
>   fiddle.
>   Reading it, however, with a perfect contempt for it, one discovers
>   in
>   it after all, a place for the genuine.
>   Hands that can grasp, eyes
>   that can dilate, hair that can rise   5
>   if it must, these things are important not because a
>
> high-sounding interpretation can be put upon them but because they
>   are
>   useful. When they become so derivative as to become unintelligible,
>   the same thing may be said for all of us, that we

```
do not admire what                                                          10
   we cannot understand: the bat
      holding on upside down or in quest of something to

eat, elephants pushing, a wild horse taking a roll, a tireless wolf under
   a tree, the immovable critic twitching his skin like a horse that feels
         a flea, the base-
   ball fan, the statistician—                                              15
      nor is it valid
         to discriminate against 'business documents and

school-books'; all these phenomena are important. One must make a
         distinction
   however: when dragged into prominence by half poets, the result is
         not poetry,
   nor till the poets among us can be                                       20
      'literalists of
      the imagination'—above
         insolence and triviality and can present

for inspection, 'imaginary gardens with real toads in them', shall we
         have
   it. In the meantime, if you demand on the one hand,                      25
   the raw material of poetry in
      all its rawness and
      that which is on the other hand
         genuine, you are interested in poetry.
```

In 1967, almost a half century after the poem was written, she revised it for *Complete Poems*. This is her final version:

```
I, too, dislike it.
   Reading it, however, with a perfect contempt for it, one discovers
         in
   it, after all, a place for the genuine.
```

Everything, *everything*, after the first two sentences has been deleted!—all the marvelous details and the endlessly quoted statement of the ideal in poetry, "'imaginary gardens with real toads in them.'" Moore's admirers were dumb-founded. The 1935 text was printed in one of the notes at the back of *Complete Poems*, perhaps because, as T. S. Eliot said of the famous notes to "The Waste Land," anyone who bought the book and found the poem missing "would demand his money back." But Moore was absolute. The *entire* "Author's Note" at the beginning of *Complete Poems* asserted unremittingly: "Omissions are not accidents."

Critical opinion at present holds that this astonishing revision was a mistake, and editors of anthologies have continued to reprint the familiar version of "Poetry." Fond as we may be of that version, however, disagreeing with any poetic judgment of Marianne Moore's, especially one that she took fifty years to reach, must be rash. And it seems important, for the beginning poet as well as for Moore's most devoted fans, to take pains to understand her long-deliberated revision. We need not doubt that it was as much a sacrifice for her as it seems for us. That she felt impelled to make it, nonetheless, argues for the seriousness of her reasons.

In both reading and teaching the 1935 version of the poem, I have often felt a fuzziness at its center. I always assumed that the poem was right and that my feeling was somehow in error. Now, Moore's unforgiving omission makes the question pertinent. The extraordinary catalog of the bat, elephants, wild horse, wolf, critic, baseball fan, and statistician, along with "'business documents and / school-books,'" is clearly offered as examples of the "genuine." They are the "things that are important" for which there is in poetry "a place." When they are "dragged into prominence by half poets"—misused in some way—"the result is not poetry." As the 1924 version of the poem makes plain, the misuse occurs in making them "unintelligible." Here is that version, entire:

> I too, dislike it:
> there are things that are important
> beyond all this fiddle.
> The bat, upside down; the elephant pushing,
> the tireless wolf under a tree,
> the base-ball fan, the statistician—
> "business documents and schoolbooks"—
> these phenomena are pleasing,
> but when they have been fashioned
> into that which is unknowable,
> we are not entertained.
> It may be said of all of us
> that we do not admire what we cannot
> understand;
> enigmas are not poetry.

In the critically favored 1935 version, the unintelligibility is said to result from these things having become "derivative" (line 9). Subject matter, handled from poem to fashionable poem with decreasing reference to plain reality, might be said to become "derivative" and so "unintelligible"—poetic stage property like the rose or spring. But the catalog given hardly supports such an interpretation:

the bat, elephants, wild horse, and so on, are hardly instances of overused and, thus, derivatively handled subject matter. Just what "half poets" she refers to as having "dragged into prominence" these things, or how, is totally unclear.

The 1935 version, which is only slightly altered from the original 1921 version, seems fatally ambiguous. The pronoun "they" in "When they become so derivative as to become unintelligible" plainly refers, not to the catalog that will shortly follow, but *back* to the "Hands that can grasp, eyes that can dilate, hair that can rise / if it must" of the preceding stanza. A sensible reading of the catalog makes it a list of examples of what "we / do not admire" because "we cannot understand." The oddities in the catalog—the bat's "holding on upside down," the elephants' "pushing," the wild horse's "taking a roll," and especially the "immovable" critic's "twitching his skin like a horse that feels / a flea"— obviously embody this satiric intention, making the catalog not a list of the "genuine" but of the "unintelligible."

In his *Marianne Moore*, published in 1964 (Moore may have seen it before making her final revision of the poem in 1967), Bernard F. Engel innocently assumes yet another reading of the catalog, seeing it as referring to the "all of us" who "do not admire what we cannot understand." He writes: "The 'us' is delightfully and pointedly represented as creatures engaged in a variety of activities"! Engel tries to recenter his reading by adding, "All of 'us' are possible subjects; even the business and schoolroom documents sometimes excluded from the canon of literary material may be used for poetry." Implausible as such an interpretation may seem, it underlines some central ambiguity in the poem, which Engel is trying to straddle. The two catalogs that begin with "Hands that can grasp" and "the bat" are only roughly parallel and seem imperfectly, confusingly related.

The original 1921 version differs in only a few words from the familiar 1935 version. Clearly, Moore was unhappy with the original version when she exchanged it for the simplified 1924 version, whose weakness in turn led her to replace it in 1935 with a version only slightly modified from the original. Whatever had bothered her about that version obviously still bothered her in 1967 when she struck out all of it except the first three lines. The excision followed a long-standing dissatisfaction with the poem. Unless there is material not yet published, we can only guess at the dissatisfaction, but it was clearly neither sudden nor impulsive.

Donald Hall's acute questions—"What poetry is she referring to? All poetry? Some particular kind?"—seem to me as relevant to the 1935 version as to the 1967; and one might add, "What half poets?" The questions are easier to answer for the 1967 version: yes, all poetry, any poetry. Fiddle though it all is, "one discovers in / it, after all, a place for the genuine." And that, Moore seems to be telling us in 1967, is that.

If we miss the catalog with its delicious exemplifications, we may remember that there are wonderful examples all around, on every page of the ·Complete Poems. If we miss the incisive conclusion,

> In the meantime, if you demand on the one hand,
>   the raw material of poetry in
>   all its rawness and
>   that which is on the other hand
>   genuine, you are interested in poetry.

at least we need not worry over the poem's indecisive pronouns: "I," "one," "we," and finally "you." If we miss the righteous condemnation of those unspecified "half poets," whose poems have already vanished, we may come to prefer Marianne Moore's final fairness to them in letting the matter drop. If we miss the splendid phrase, "imaginary gardens with real toads in them," we may recall that we still have it, along with her unquenchable passion for precision and her unqualified witness on behalf of tightening. It is a tough league to play in. "Omissions," she says, "are not accidents."

Shaping

The other essential operation in composition is **shaping.** As the words of a poem come, they must be displayed in lines. Sometimes the earliest verbalization carries with it an intuitive sense of how the poem might be broken into lines, but often the earliest phrases are accompanied by no particular feeling of lineation. They may even be a scattering of disconnected phrases with no certainty even as to which should come first. One of the poet's tasks as the poem develops is opting for some possible form, however tentative, which can be tested and altered as draft leads to draft. Meter? Rhyme? Free verse? Longer lines? Stanzas? The initial preference may be habitual, and often comes from a deeply ingrained and successfully practiced feeling—as Williams instinctively worked in very short lines, or Whitman in very long lines. But a given poem may call for a different sort of form. For instance, in "Yachts" William Carlos Williams elected to work in much longer lines than was his custom: "Today no race. Then the wind comes again. The yachts / move, jockeying for a start, the signal is set . . ." Both the tentative choice of form and the experimental sculpting or fitting of further parts to the poem are shaping. Once a poem begins in one way, in short free verse lines, say, it is usually better for the rest of it to follow in that way—not to change into long lines, for instance, toward the end. Every poem should be formally a whole. A poem *can* mix forms, especially a longer, sectioned poem; but unless there is a clear thematic reason, such mixed-form poems may seem merely half-baked.

In writing stanzaic poems, whether in free verse or in meter, the poet should repeat the established pattern in subsequent stanzas and use it fully so that there is no falling off or slackening. Consider A. E. Housman's "I Hoed and Trenched and Weeded":

I hoed and trenched and weeded,
    And took the flowers to fair;
I brought them home unheeded;
    The hue was not the wear.

So up and down I sow them   5
    For lads like me to find,
When I shall lie below them,
    A dead man out of mind.

Some seed the birds devour,
    And some the season mars,   10
But here and there will flower
    The solitary stars,

And fields will yearly bear them
    As light-leaved spring comes on,
And luckless lads will wear them   15
    When I am dead and gone.

Of its composition, Housman commented: "Two of the stanzas, I do not say which, came into my head, just as they are printed. . . . A third stanza came with a little coaxing after tea. One more was needed, but it did not come: I had to turn to and compose it myself, and that was a laborious business. I wrote it thirteen times, and it was more than a twelvemonth before I got it right." Poems don't always unwind from the top. Robert Lowell recalls that his well-known "Skunk Hour" was "written backwards," the last two stanzas first, then the next-to-last two, and finally the first four in reverse order. It is sometimes useful to scribble out with scanning marks the base meter of a stanza to be written, or to show the holes in a passage that are left to be filled when the inspiration carries the poem further:

The boys met by the bridge, and climbed

beneath it where the gray owls were:

ˇ ´ ˇ ´ ˇ ´   the nest

in which, in feathers more like fur,

two little owls . . .

Such marks hold open the passage and let the poet see clearly what is missing.
    Working in free verse is little different. Lack of a firm rubric allows more freedom, but that makes choices among various possibilities more arbitrary and, for a careful poet, uncertain. Thus, the whole poem is likely to remain in suspension longer in free verse. Line-breaks may want a lot of testing; the poet needs to juggle run-on and end-stopped lines for variety and rhythm. If a stanza

pattern has appeared, fitting further material into it becomes a measuring and shaping of that material. Good free verse has a tight surface tension on which the poet's seemingly trivial vacillations and tinkerings with line or word-placement work like the delicate feet of a water-strider on water.

Worksheets

So far, in these chapters about rewriting, we have been examining fair copies or transcriptions from poets' manuscripts, not actual working manuscripts with their scribbles and scrawls, scratchings out and interlinings, arrows, notations, jottings, marginal lists, and even phone numbers, doodles, or coffee stains. For the poet's own use, often set down in haste, actual manuscripts are usually a mess and often indecipherable. The seven worksheets of "The Girl Writing Her English Paper," however, are fairly legible; and the facsimiles reproduced here (on pages 339–348) will illustrate some of the twists and turns I took in rewriting this poem.

WORKSHEET 1

The first draft of the poem is an unusually complete version. The first five and one-half lines, along with several other phrases, had been composed in my head; as I wrote, most of the rest of the draft came cleanly. The four-line first sentence set a tentative stanza pattern, into which everything that followed fell readily. The only gap was line 3 of the second stanza, which I left to be filled in, sensing that the details of the girl's mess would finish the stanza and could be sorted out later. (Line 4 of that stanza immediately got too long, so I noted, with a slash, details that I would probably push back up to fill line 3.) I made a false start on stanza 4, "wondering at," but quickly scratched it out and the stanza wrote itself straightforwardly. At this stage the poem felt metrical, and without paying much attention I let the lines fall out roughly four, five, or six feet. Like the four-line stanzas, it seemed to want to happen.

The inserted image of "petals" filled out line 2 of stanza 2, and I arrowed "Open books, notebooks," etc., down to line 3. Other tinkerings suggested exchanging the vague "pretty" for the further detail of "in blond jeans" in line 1, replacing the clinical "inspects" with the gesture "bends to" or "bending to," and shortening the very long next-to-last line. I wasn't sure whether to leave the lover *in* the scene, and tried "somewhere" and the less direct "thinking of" instead of "watching." Wanting to see what the poem looked like, so revised, I copied it on worksheet 2. (Since the appearance of a poem on the page is important, I always single-space. Double-spacing would allow more room to work, but I want to see the shape of the poem as it would appear in print.)

A Girl Writing ~~Her~~ [a] Paper for her English Class

in (blond) jeans
She curls, sprawls on one [pretty] hip
and elbows on the floor before the fire
in ~~a~~ [the] fire-lit, lamp-lit, light-sodden room
while all dark circles around outside.

The wreckage of her labor-elegant as Eden—
                    -like petals dropped in the storm
surrounds her, open books, notebooks, sheets {penciling
                                              {notes,
                                    loose
a cup, cigarets/the little tobacco farm (house, pond),
                                              drift of smoke.

                    and writes~~a~~
She bites a nail, scratches (& unscratches) a ~~line~~ [word],
a (frail) watch (silver) on her wrist, her hair
like a shaken waterfall hiding her face
          bends to   text
as she ~~inspects~~ the ~~poem~~. Her lover waits/
    bending to

            ~~wondering at~~
somewhere second ~~to~~ a poem; watches, pretending to read,
          thinking of
but watchin~~g~~her. So fine an attention   had done.
         a   [lost] sleep
to what ~~another~~ man [dead centuries) [to make.]
If all the lights were out, starlight would come in.
                              v
                             the

The poem "stuck" here for some time. I studied this version on at least four occasions over several days (there are indications of three different pens and a pencil). Only two verbal changes are suggested ("breakage" for "wreckage" in line 5, "sun-woven" for "shaken" in line 11), but neither is accepted. In line 8 "*tobacco* farm" is wrong, since the point is not a farm that grows tobacco; and I arrowed "tobacco" over to modify and explain the "smoke-string." By "house" I meant the girl's book, by "pond" the clear-glass ashtray; obviously the image is awkwardly handled. Mainly, I felt, the poem was puffy, mushy, in need of tightening. With pencil lines I tried crossing out one line in each stanza: the overly rhetorical "in the fire-lit, lamp-lit, light-sodden room" in stanza 1; the whole line with the farm image in stanza 2; the rather prosy "She bites a nail, scratches (and unscratches) a word" in stanza 3; and the first halves of the first two lines in stanza 4. At another time I tried underlining in ink the parts of the poem that seemed important; I then copied them out in longhand at the bottom of the page. The result, without stanzas at all, felt dull.

At a third time, with another pen, I also underlined the sentence "So fine an attention . . ." and added the suggestion for another image—"The stars still nailed into the sky"—at the bottom of the sheet. (I did nothing further with the image, probably because it seemed static and emphasized the stars' distance rather than their closeness.) In considering ways of tightening the poem, the crucial decision was to abandon the fairly heavy stanzas and the possibility of meter, both of which made the poem feel stuffy and more literary than it wanted to be.

Going on to worksheet 3, I left behind the melodramatically ominous "while all dark circles around outside" (my feelings about the girl and the scene were mainly cheerful), the needlessly specific details about her watch and hair, and the lover. In the scene he was a distraction and his rather self-pitying jealousy of being "second to a poem" seemed falsely dramatic, and "somewhere," he wasn't usable because he could at most be guessing about her at work. I wanted to concentrate on the picture of the girl, absorbed in a poem.

A GIRL WRITING A PAPER FOR HER ENGLISH CLASS

She curls in blond jeans, sprawls on one hip
[and elbows on the floor) before the fire
~~in the fire-lit, lamp-lit, light-sodden room~~
while all dark circles around outside.

breakage? The wreckage of her labor—elegant as Eden—
surrounds her like petals dropped in a storm—
open books, notebooks, a cup, sheets, pencilings,
~~the little tobacco farm (smoke-string, house, pond).~~

~~She bites a nail, scratches (and unscratches) a word,~~ : ?
a silver watch frail on her wrist, her hair
sun-woven like a shaken waterfall hiding her face
bending to the text. Her lover waits

~~somewhere, second to a poem;~~ pretending to read,
~~but thinking of her.~~ So fine an attention
to what a man dead centuries had done.
If all the lights were out, the starlight would come in.

In jeans, ~~sprawling~~ on one hip,
(before the fire)
The wreckage of her labor-elegant as Eden,
as petals dropped in a storm :
open books, notebooks, cup, sheets, pencilings,
the little farm (tobacco, smoke-string, house, and pond).
If all the lights were out, the starlight would come in.

The stars still nailed into the sky

Having tested the possibility of metered stanzas, however loosely, I could now test the possibilities of free (more exactly, *freed*) verse. There are now stanzas of one, three, four, three, and two lines. After looking at stanzaless free verse at the bottom of worksheet 2, I wanted the greater sharpness and distinctness of a poem in stanzas.

The chief advance in this draft is the relatively clean sorting out of the farm image. House and pond have vanished. The smoke is now rising, literally, from the ashtray. The "fields" have been added, appropriately, next to "papers," whose rectangular shapes make the comparison clear. And the fields have suggested (drawing on the Latin *versus,* meaning both furrows and lines) the phrase "the poem's furrows," which brings the comparison to a focus. Although neither fields nor furrows appear in the earlier versions of the image, I believe I was half-aware of where the farm image was headed.

The untidy "open books, notebooks, a cup, sheets, pencilings" has become succinctly only "books, notebooks, papers" and of course "ashtray." With the lover out of the way, the poem can now draw its moral directly, addressing the reader:

> Consider the fine attention she gives
> to words of a man long dead.

An alternative, typed in the margin, "Reflect, you who do not write poems," awkwardly identified the speaker as a poet, though not the author of the poem about which the girl is so absorbedly writing. The flatness of the moral as stated called up the livelier insertion: "you lunkheads who don't write poems."

In the one-line stanza 1, "on one hip" is first struck out and then rescued to follow "lying." Perhaps because a one-line stanza seemed to stop the flow of the poem almost before it had started, a slash indicates a proposed line break before "by the fire." Stanza 2 is tightened by exchanging "as" for "or" and deleting the comma after "Eden." Stanza 3 is tightened by the excision of the empty "It is" and the needless "She follows." Thus, stanza 2 can lead directly into stanza 3, and the period is crossed out and a dash, then a colon (too formal), and then a dash again is inserted. Also for flow, a period in stanza 4 is deleted in favor of a comma. There is one other noteworthy change: the clumsier nine-word title is replaced by a six-word version.

THE GIRL WRITING HER ENGLISH PAPER

is in jeans, ~~on one hip~~ *lying* by the fire.

The wreckage of her labor, elegant as Eden,
or ~~as~~ petals from a tree,
surrounds her/ ╪ /–

~~It is~~ a little farm╪, smoke
~~smoke~~ rises *ing* from the ashtray/,
books, notebooks, papers, fields/ ;
~~She follows~~ the poem's furrows.

Consider, ~~If~~ the lights went out,
there would be stars overhead/ ,
t ~~The~~ starlight would come in.
    you lunkheads who don't write poems)
Consider, the fine attention she gives   Reflect,
to words of a man long dead.   you who do
                                      not write
                                      poems

Typing this draft, I noticed that three of the five stanzas now had three lines. The first two lines of stanza 3 could easily be combined into a single line, giving it three lines as well. The stanza shape—long, shorter, and still shorter lines—was already there in stanza 2 and almost there in stanzas 4 and 5; and, with the combining of lines 1 and 2, there in stanza 3. Changes in stanzas 4 and 5 were made both to clarify the substance and to bring out the stanza shape. The first preachy "Consider" in stanza 4 is dropped, the proper subjunctive "were to go out" inserted for "went out," and the sense of surprise increased with "suddenly." After considering moving "she gives" to the next line, I struck it out and (a poor change) made the line read: "this fine, slow attention." Either way, it is a weak line and will be much improved in the typing of worksheet 5.

The only stanza not essentially conforming to the shape, stanza 1, is the focus of major tinkering. The copulative "is" gives way to the more active "lies" as main verb, and three additional details are considered: pencil to lip, slimness, blondness. "Slim" is considered, then rejected as the least useful of the three. The draft's last intention is:

> lies on one hip by the fire,
> in jeans, pencil to her lip.
> She's very blond.

In the retyping on worksheet 5, however, the adjective "still" is added to line 1, the "pencil" turns into a "pen," and "She's" reduced to "is"—all in the interests of stanza-shape. (And the elements in line 2 will be reversed.)

THE GIRL WRITING HER ENGLISH PAPER

is (in jeans,) ~~lying~~ lies on one hip   she's very blond.
by the fire., ∧ ~~she's slim, and very~~   , pencil to her lip.

The wreckage of her labor, elegant as Eden
or petals from a tree,
surrounds her—

a little farm, smoke
rising from the ashtray,
book$, notebooks, papers, fields;
and the poem's furrows.
                    I
~~Consider,~~ if the lights ~~went~~ were to go out, suddenly,
there would be stars overhead,
~~the~~ starlight would come in.

Consider, you lunkheads who don't write poems,
This ~~the~~ fine attention ~~she gives~~
to words, slow of a man long dead.

The poem is nearing its final form. Stanza 1 seems messy, a not very rhythmical collection of fragmentary details. Since the title is now treated as part of the poem's opening sentence and is the right length, the idea of counting it as the first line of stanza 1 came easily. Brackets indicate deletion of the less important details, and "blond" is arrowed up to precede "in jeans." Problem solved.

Stanza 5 remains troublesome. The slangy brusqueness of "lunkheads" was clearly out of tone with the rest of the poem. People who don't write poems aren't necessarily lunkheads. Trying out two more polite versions of the line, I chose the less assertive: "Consider, if you don't believe in poems." In copying this draft, I had stumbled on a much improved version of the second line: "how pensively she attends," with its accidental pun on "pen"; and the only problem seemed to be that the last line was not shorter. Dropping the unnecessary "to" made it fit, albeit barely.

THE GIRL WRITING HER ENGLISH PAPER

lies on one hip by the fire, [still,]
[pen to cheek,] in jeans/ .   } 2 ll?
[is very] blond,}   Is blond

The wreckage of her labor, elegant as Eden
or petals from a tree,
surrounds her—

a little farm, smoke rising from the ashtray,
book, notebooks, papers, fields;
the poem's furrows.

If the lights were to go out suddenly,
stars would be overhead,
starlight come in.
                        if you
                        all you who } don't believe
                                in poems,
Consider, you lunkheads who don't write poems,/
how pensively she attends
to words of a man long dead.

I made two tiny alterations—substituting the indefinite for the definite article in line 8 and avoiding the repetition of the word "star" in line 11—and the poem seemed finished. In this version it was accepted and printed.

THE GIRL WRITING HER ENGLISH PAPER

lies on one hip by the fire,
blond, in jeans.

The wreckage of her labor, elegant as Eden
or petals from a tree,
surrounds her—

a little farm, smoke rising from the ashtray,
book, notebooks, papers, fields;
a ~~the~~ poem's furrows.

If the lights were to go out suddenly,
stars would be overhead,
their ~~star~~light come in.

Consider, if you don't believe in poems,
how pensively she attends
words of a man long dead.

NY Times

Reading the poem to an audience over a year later, I found myself wishing that the last stanza wasn't there. The point of the poem was not to club anybody for not liking poetry, but to express all my feelings of awe and astonishment at the girl's utterly absorbed love of a poem. With her lover long gone from the poem, it hardly mattered that the poet might be "long dead." I realized, too, that I could trust the stanza about the starlight. So real was her love for the poem, so real was her concentration that (as stanza 4 said) the factual room with its firelight and lamplight might simply vanish and the reality of the poem and of her culturing labor would continue to exist. The little farm of poem and concentration would merely lie open to the real stars. The metaphorical "petals" of stanza 2 were already leading to this totally natural sense of her role as reader in the completion of the poem she was studying.

I saw that although the storm that had dropped the petals in an early draft had disappeared from the poem (along with the ominously circling "dark"), the fallen petals themselves carried a feeling for the girl's perishable beauty, which is part of the poem's emotion. And I came to understand why, though I had never really thought about it, it had been important to mention "Eden" in the poem. The labor of reading poems, like the labor of writing poems, had something to do with our mortality and our imperfection. Without having meant to, I had alluded to Yeats's "Adam's Curse" (page 77), where he says, "It's certain there is no fine thing / Since Adam's fall but needs much labouring."

So I dropped the last stanza. And the poem was as short as Pound's Chinese had said a poem should be.

THE GIRL WRITING HER ENGLISH PAPER

lies on one hip by the fire,
blond, in jeans.

The wreckage of her labor, elegant as Eden
or petals from a tree,
surrounds her—

a little farm, smoke rising from the ashtray,
book, notebooks, papers, fields;
a poem's furrows.

If the lights were to go out suddenly,
stars would be overhead,
their light come in.

QUESTIONS AND SUGGESTIONS

1. If Ezra Pound was correct in saying that poetry should be at least as well written as prose, Ernest Hemingway revising Ernest Hemingway is worth study. As a war correspondent in 1922, Hemingway cabled the first version to the Toronto *Daily Star*. The second version appeared as a vignette in his collection of stories, *In Our Time*, in 1925. Compare the two versions.

a) In a never-ending, staggering march the Christian population of Eastern Thrace is jamming the roads towards Macedonia. The main column crossing the Maritza River at Adrianople is twenty miles long. Twenty miles of carts drawn by cows, bullocks and muddy-flanked water buffalo, with exhausted, staggering men, women and children, blankets over their heads, walking blindly in the rain beside their worldly goods.

   This main stream is being swelled from all the back country. They don't know where they are going. They left their farms, villages and ripe, brown fields and joined the main stream of refugees when they heard the Turk was coming. Now they can only keep their places in the ghastly procession while mud-splashed Greek cavalry herd them along like cow-punchers driving steers.

   It is a silent procession. Nobody even grunts. It is all they can do to keep moving. Their brilliant peasant costumes are soaked and draggled. Chickens dangle by their feet from the carts. Calves nuzzle at the draught cattle wherever a jam halts the stream. An old man marches bent under a young pig, a scythe and a gun, with a chicken tied to his scythe. A husband spreads a blanket over a woman in labor in one of the carts to keep off the driving rain. She is the only person making a sound. Her little daughter looks at her in horror and begins to cry. And the procession keeps moving.

b) Minarets stuck up in the rain out of Adrianople across the mud flats. The carts were jammed for thirty miles along the Karagatch road. Water buffalo and cattle were hauling carts through the mud. No end and no beginning. Just carts loaded with everything they owned. The old men and women, soaked through, walked along keeping the cattle moving. The Maritza was running yellow almost up to the bridge. Carts were jammed solid on the bridge with camels bobbing along through them. Greek cavalry herded along the procession. Women and kids were in the carts crouched with mattresses, mirrors, sewing machines, bundles. There was a woman having a kid with a young girl holding a blanket over her and crying. Scared sick looking at it. It rained all through the evacuation.

2. Here is the first draft of a poem called "In One Place." If it were your poem, how would you revise it? (The poet's final version appears in Appendix I.)

In One Place

The tree grows in one place.

A seed goes down, and something
holds up two or three leaves
the first year.

           Then the spindling
goes on climbing, branching,
up, up, up,

           until birds
live in it and no one can
remember it wasn't there.

The tree stands always here.

3. Consider these two versions of a poem by D. H. Lawrence (1885–1930), called "The Piano" in the early version, "Piano" in the later. What effects do the omissions have in the much shorter version, in which the speaker's experience is significantly reinterpreted? How is the poem's theme changed? How does the sharpening of the focus on the two women clarify the sexuality of the speaker's inner conflict?

a) Somewhere beneath that piano's superb sleek black
  Must hide my mother's piano, little and brown, with the back
  That stood close to the wall, and the front's faded silk both torn,
  And the keys with little hollows, that my mother's fingers had worn.

  Softly, in the shadows, a woman is singing to me   5
  Quietly, through the years I have crept back to see
  A child sitting under the piano, in the boom of the shaking strings
  Pressing the little poised feet of the mother who smiles as she sings.

  The full throated woman has chosen a winning, living song
  And surely the heart that is in me must belong   10
  To the old Sunday evenings, when darkness wandered outside
  And hymns gleamed on our warm lips, as we watched mother's fingers glide.

  Or this is my sister at home in the old front room
  Singing love's first surprised gladness, alone in the gloom.
  She will start when she sees me, and blushing, spread out her hands   15
  To cover my mouth's raillery, till I'm bound in her shame's heartspun bands.

A woman is singing me a wild Hungarian air
And her arms, and her bosom, and the whole of her soul is bare,
And the great black piano is clamouring as my mother's never could clamour
And my mother's tunes are devoured of this music's ravaging glamour.   20

b) Softly, in the dusk, a woman is singing to me;
   Taking me back down the vista of years, till I see
   A child sitting under the piano, in the boom of the tingling strings
   And pressing the small, poised feet of a mother who smiles as she sings.

   In spite of myself, the insidious mastery of song   5
   Betrays me back, till the heart of me weeps to belong
   To the old Sunday evenings at home, with winter outside
   And hymns in the cosy parlour, the tinkling piano our guide.

   So now it is vain for the singer to burst into clamour
   With the great black piano appassionato. The glamour   10
   Of childish days is upon me, my manhood is cast
   Down in the flood of remembrance, I weep like a child for the past.

4. By its shape "The Snowfall" by Donald Justice might seem to be a sonnet
(octave / sestet). Although the poem is unrhymed and in tetrameter, is this
structural similarity to sonnet form revealing? Had the poet wanted to add a
foot and make the lines pentameter throughout, what words or images might he
have changed or added? (The adjective "misty" might go in line 1, for instance.
Line 3 might have become "Would seem to *demonstrate* that a people once," or
line 14, "In childhood, *which we* never believed till now.") Would you prefer
the pentameter version?

   The classic landscapes of dreams are not
   More pathless, though footprints leading nowhere
   Would seem to prove that a people once
   Survived for a little even here.

   Fragments of a pathetic culture   5
   Remain, the lost mittens of children,
   And a single, bright, detasseled snow-cap,
   Evidence of some frantic migration.

   The landmarks are gone. Nevertheless
   There is something familiar about this country.   10
   Slowly now we begin to recall

   The terrible whispers of our elders
   Falling softly about our ears
   In childhood, never believed till now.

Lion & Honeycomb   1962

HOWARD NEMEROV   (b. 1920)

He didn't want to do it with skill,
He'd had enough of skill. If he never saw
Another villanelle, it would be too soon;
And the same went for sonnets. If it had been
Hard work learning to rime, it would be much   5
Harder learning not to. The time came
He had to ask himself, what did he want?
What did he want when he began
That idiot fiddling with the sounds of things.

He asked himself, poor moron, because he had   10
Nobody else to ask. The others went right on
Talking about form, talking about myth
And the (so help us) need for a modern idiom;
The verseballs among them kept counting syllables.

So there he was, this forty-year-old teen-ager   15
Dreaming preposterous mergers and divisions
Of vowels like water, consonants like rock
(While everybody kept discussing values
And the need for values), for words that would
Enter the silence and be there as a light.   20
So much coffee and so many cigarettes
Gone down the drain, gone up in smoke,
Just for the sake of getting something right
Once in a while, something that could stand
On its own flat feet to keep out windy time   25
And the worm, something that might simply be,
Not as the monument in the smoky rain
Grimly endures, but that would be
Only a moment's inviolable presence,
The moment before disaster, before the storm,   30
In its peculiar silence, an integer
Fixed in the middle of the fall of things,
Perfected and casual as to a child's eye
Soap bubbles are, and skipping stones.

A Blessing

1961

JAMES WRIGHT (1927–1980)

Just off the highway to Rochester, Minnesota,
Twilight bounds softly forth on the grass.
And the eyes of those two Indian ponies
Darken with kindness.
They have come gladly out of the willows   5
To welcome my friend and me.
We step over the barbed wire into the pasture
Where they have been grazing all day, alone.
They ripple tensely, they can hardly contain their happiness
That we have come.   10
They bow shyly as wet swans. They love each other.
There is no loneliness like theirs.
At home once more,
They begin munching the young tufts of spring in the darkness.
I would like to hold the slenderer one in my arms,   15
For she has walked over to me
And nuzzled my left hand.
She is black and white,
Her mane falls wild on her forehead,
And the light breeze moves me to caress her long ear   20
That is delicate as the skin over a girl's wrist.
Suddenly I realize
That if I stepped out of my body I would break
Into blossom.

The Bath Tub

1916

EZRA POUND (1885–1972)

As a bathtub lined with white porcelain,
When the hot water gives out or goes tepid,
So is the slow cooling of our chivalrous passion,
O my much praised but-not-altogether-satisfactory
    lady.

The Mill Back Home   1978

VERN RUTSALA   (b. 1934)

Logs drowse in the pond
Dreaming of their heroes
Alligator and crocodile

I Learn I'm 96% Water   1976

ALBERT GOLDBARTH   (b. 1948)

and stare out over the edge of this little
dinghy I've named The 4 Percent. Such
a large sea . . . ! Such a tiny
motor: this spermtail whipping like crazy . . . !
"The sailor *is* the sea." How   5
Zen! I float in my floating.
The body bobs in its life.

Sentimental Poem   1978

for Woody

MARGE PIERCY   (b. 1936)

You are such a good cook.
I am such a good cook.
If we get involved
we'll both get fat.
Then nobody else will have us.   5
We'll be stuck, two
mounds of wet dough
baking high and fine
in the bed's slow oven.

14

Oddments:
From the Green Cloth Bag

When I was an undergraduate, an elderly and thoroughly eccentric professor allegedly composed his lectures in the following manner. As he thought of ideas he might use, he wrote them on scraps of paper that he stuffed into a green cloth bag hanging from the right arm of his wooden study chair. When the time came to prepare the lecture, he would sit naked in the chair, draw the bits of paper out of the bag, study them, and put those he wanted for the lecture into a second green cloth bag hanging from the left arm of the chair. This he took to the classroom, emptied onto the lectern, and, from the notes thus assembled, discoursed with his customary aplomb.

Such, roughly, is the method by which the notes that make up this chapter have been brought together.

Reading, Masters, Models, Imitation, and So Forth. If I could give only one word of counsel to the beginning poet, unhesitatingly I would say: *Read.* Nothing that anybody knows or can tell you about poetry is as important or will be as useful as what you discover, firsthand, yourself. Read what is fashionable and read what is unfashionable. Know what is happening in poetry now, since there is little point in writing in the manner of 1920 or 1820; and know what Chaucer has done, what Donne, Milton, Pope, Wordsworth, Hardy, and Eliot have done, so as not to be isolated in the mere fashions and prejudices of the moment, imitating an imitator of an imitator. Read poems in any language you know; read translations. Recent American poetry has been deeply enriched by the examples and achievements of, among others, the Chilean Pablo Neruda (1904–1973), the Greek George Seferis (1900–1971), the Mexican Octavio Paz (b. 1914), the French Francis Ponge (b. 1899), the German Georg Trakl (1887–1914), the Yugoslav Vasko Popa (b. 1922), the Czech Miroslav Holub (b. 1923), and the Russian Andrei Voznesensky (b. 1933).

The more poetry you know of all kinds, old and new, good and bad, the more possibilities open for your own writing. Be systematic, be unsystematic. Haunt the poetry sections of bookstores, prowl the poetry shelves in libraries. Stick your nose in the glossiest new paperback and in the mustiest old leather-bound.

None of us ever wants to write a poem in the first place unless we have read a poem that truly takes us, and the poem we write will inevitably be like, or at least try to be like, that poem. What else can it be? The poet's notions of what poetry is, of what poems can do, come from the poems she or he reads and admires. For the poet *all* poems are about poetry—its range, its limits, its possibilities. The undisguised admiration "*I can do that*" is the seed from which every poet sprouts and grows.

Read widely, read *narrowly*. When you find a poem that utterly attracts you, reread, read aloud; get inside it and see how it works. When you come across a poet on your wave-length, find her or his books and read them to the ground. Buy them with your lunch money. These poems will be your models, after which you will, willy-nilly, fashion your own. These poets who speak to you will be your "masters." The poet's secrets are hidden in the open, in the poems, and it isn't necessary to clean his brushes or cook her dinner to apprentice yourself to the best poet writing.

Imitation isn't a problem. It is the only and inescapable route toward becoming a poet. As a student, you may write Donne poems, Yeats poems, Frost poems, Cummings poems, Moore poems, and any number of other poets' poems. Every role you like, you will try out—not always consciously of course. As you discover and absorb admiration after admiration, the influences begin to neutralize each other and naturally disappear. The poems you write will begin to be in your own voice, not in Lowell's or Ginsberg's or Plath's. Even deliberate imitation can be a good exercise. The danger is not in being too much influenced but in being too little influenced—fixing too early or fanatically on a single master and clinging to that one voice, or finding the whole *truth* in one cranky theory or another. Nothing is sadder (or less promising) than the beginner who, having read almost nothing, knows everything.

If you come across the phrase "finding your own voice," don't worry. It is a false scare. There is no disgrace in having learned something from somebody. In any case, no one knows what her or his own voice really sounds like, and the conscious effort to develop an "individual voice" is likely to result only in strain, staginess, and mannerism. If Buffon's famous pronouncement is correct, "Le style c'est l'homme même"—"Style is the man himself"—then its converse is also reassuringly true: "The man himself is his style." There is no point in trying to fake it. Like fingerprints, it is inescapable. When poets no longer sound like anyone else, they sound like themselves.

"Le style c'est l'homme même." If the poet is a beery and blustery fellow, then his style will be and should be beery and blustery. If the poet is a dark and depressive lady, then her style will be and should be dark and depressive. The poet who is neither, however, should be wary of finding himself or herself with someone else's hangover or in somebody else's hairshirt. Don't strike poses. Liars have to keep track of more than one version of everything. Being natural makes life a lot simpler.

"Professional Poet." One of the great pleasures is Robert Francis's book of tiny essays, *The Satirical Rogue on Poetry.* Here, entire, is his essay "Professional Poet":

> Someone the other day called me a professional poet to my face.
> "Don't call me that," I cried. "Don't call anybody that. As well talk about a professional friend."
> "Oh!" he said.
> "Or a professional lover."
> "Oh!"

Cap. and Punc. Trivial matters, **capitalization** and **punctuation.** Once upon a time the convention was that every line began with a capital letter. Now the poet has a choice. Poets may follow that convention, or, like Cummings, write entirely in lower case (or anything in between). My own rule is to capitalize exactly as I would in prose—first word in a sentence, proper nouns, and so on. The trouble with anything too far from the norm, unless one has a very good reason, is that it may seem self-conscious and pretentious.

The same goes for the norms of punctuation. Like every other part of a poem, its commas and semicolons and dashes and periods are important. They help control the flow of the poem for the eye and guide the pauses and emphases of the voice. A lowly comma may, as in Creeley's "I Know a Man" (page 36), play a crucial part in the poem's meaning.

Poems may be written without punctuation, however, for special effect—as in W. S. Merwin's "Shoe Repairs" (page 245), where the voice seems more of inner meditation or thought than of speech. The poet using such a convention, however, must control, with line-breaks, spacing, and especially careful syntax, the flow of the poem so that a reader doesn't become uncertain or confused and stumble over the ideas or rhythm. Merwin's control in "For the Anniversary of My Death" is perfect; and the meaning properly flows out into silence.

Every year without knowing it I have passed the day
When the last fires will wave to me
And the silence will set out
Tireless traveller
Like the beam of a lightless star

Then I will no longer
Find myself in life as in a strange garment
Surprised at the earth
And the love of one woman
And the shamelessness of men
As today writing after three days of rain
Hearing the wren sing and the falling cease
And bowing not knowing to what

Interestingly, Merwin has varied his conventions slightly from book to book. In *The Lice* (1967), from which "For the Anniversary of My Death" is taken, he capitalizes the first letter of each line. In *The Carrier of Ladders* (1970), he capitalizes only the first letter of each stanza, as in "Shoe Repairs," or—the practice in all subsequent books—only the first letter of the opening line of each poem. But he maintains, throughout, the convention of the capital for the first person singular pronoun, "I," no doubt to avoid the self-consciousness that the lower case, "i," would convey.

Cummings's eccentric and delightful use of capital letters and punctuation is well known ("chanson innocente," page 133, or "O sweet spontaneous," page 50) and almost always has a thematic point. In "O sweet spontaneous," for instance, the saucily misplaced comma and period function less as punctuation (they aren't needed) than as a sort of visual satire of the mechanically correct, distortingly rational mind that is the poem's target. Cummings is a hard act to follow, however, and his nose-thumbing tricks usually seem secondhand in another poet's hands.

The Law of Distraction. The "Law of Distraction" says that, in a poem, any stylistic feature that draws attention to *itself* and so away from the subject and feeling, is risky. Even though it allows a reader to be distracted for only the tiniest flicker of a second, a flashy word, an odd (or missing) comma, an ambiguous bit of syntax, an accidental misspelling, or the like, risks a dangerous, albeit subliminal, loss of full attention. Don't leave clamps inside the patient.

Bad Poems, Finicky Ways, Psychic Energy, Excellence, and the Poem Population. William Stafford has remarked: "Writing is a reckless encounter with whatever comes along. . . . A writer must write bad poems, as they come, amongst the better—and not scorn the 'bad' ones. Finicky ways can dry up the sources."

Every poet must forgive himself his failures, his bad poems. The very best poet can write bad poems, though a bad poet is unlikely ever to write a good poem.

Not every poem can be an "Ode to the Nightingale." Some poems are properly modest because their subject or feeling is modest. Not all emotions are grand and dramatic; the price of pretending otherwise is the grandiose or the melodramatic. Major and minor are notions best left to fatuous critics. A major poem (or poet) can nonetheless be gravely flawed; and a minor poem (or poet) may be exquisite. Poets themselves can't do much but write the next poem they have to write. They may not be able to do much about the limitations of their interests and experiences or the size of their emotions, but they can try always to write well.

Most poets start a lot of poems they never finish. Sometimes a poem is unfixable because it is so personal or private that it could not work without explanations or information that would, if included, spoil its shape or wreck its tone. Sometimes a poem is unfixable because the poet started out with something that couldn't make much of a poem in any case. Sometimes, though the poem is plainly not finished, the poet doesn't know what to do next. Sometimes, in the clear light of day, the poem just seems dumb or corny or too full of crossed wires to untangle. Such unfinishable poems go in the poet's file box or drawer to await the resurrection. If the impulse was an important one, it will bubble up again from the dark springs of psychic energy in the subconscious. And, looking through the drawer on rainy days, a poet may turn up a "busted" poem that comes to life again. I found "In the Field Forever" (page 212) scrawled on the back of a torn envelope in the drawer. One of several short poems meant for children, the poem had been forgotten when I gave up the project. The other poems were lousy, but "In the Field Forever" shone like an emerald lost in a bowl of peas.

Write good poems rather than many poems. Let go of poems that are going bad, that would be only fair-to-middling (or worse). There are plenty of poems fair-to-middling. The poem population grows enormously each year—in literally hundreds and hundreds of books and chapbooks, in nearly seven hundred little magazines. No one working round the clock could read even half the poems published in a year. At last count *The New Yorker* was getting submissions of some forty thousand poems per year and printing only two or three per week. The literary magazine *Antaeus* was getting as many, or more. And no doubt thousands and thousands of poems each year, very good ones among them, are not sent to *The New Yorker* or *Antaeus*. Poets & Writers' *Directory of American Poets and Fiction Writers* (1980–1981 edition) lists more than 3536 publishing poets. Creative writing classes are full. Even trying to count all the poems being written would be like counting drops in a waterfall.

Excellence, however, isn't democratic. The poem the poet wants each time she or he sets pen to paper is the one out of the four thousand, or the one out of the four hundred thousand. The poet will write many fair-to-middling poems and many bad poems, but that is the one he or she wants. No one should expect to achieve easily what others work hard for.

Poetic Fashions. Ignore them. Go on doing what you are doing. Or, if that is impossible, go as hard as you can in the opposite direction, away from what is fashionable. When in doubt, ask yourself what Andrew Marvell would have thought of it, or Marianne Moore, or whichever poet you believe in.

"Ars Celare Artem." Horace's dictum is worth repeating. The art is to hide the art. It would be a good afternoon's work if you made a sign to nail up in front of your desk. "Ars celare artem." The art is to hide the art.

On Reading Criticism. Criticism is just talk about poetry (or whatever). Good criticism is just good talk about poetry, and that has value. Pound was probably too fierce: "Pay no attention to the criticism of men who have never themselves written a notable work." A good critic himself, C. S. Lewis was at once fairer and fiercer: "It is always better to read Chaucer again than to read the critics."
Critics who write about criticism die and go to Yale.

"Defense of Poetry." Robert Francis: "I would say that a poem worth defending needs no defense and a poem needing defense is not worth defending. I would say it is not our business to defend poetry but the business of poetry to defend us."

"The Indecipherable Poem." Robert Francis again:

> I have no love for the indecipherable poem, but for the indecipherable poet I have often a warm friendly feeling. He is usually a bright chap, perhaps brilliant, a good talker, someone worth knowing and worth watching. He is also often a college undergraduate majoring in English and in love with writing.
>
> In his literature and writing courses it is taken for granted that the significant poets are the difficult ones. So, what less can an undergraduate poet do than be difficult himself?
>
> Difficulty, of course, is not the only virtue of great poets. They give us passion, vision, originality. None of these the undergraduate poet probably has, but he *can* be difficult. He can be as difficult as he wants to be. He can be as difficult as anybody else. He need only give the words he uses a private set of meanings. It is not difficult to be difficult.
>
> What I mean is, a poem that is very difficult to read may not have been at all difficult to write.
>
> One poem sufficiently difficult can keep a creative writing class busy a whole hour. If its young author feels pleased with himself, can we blame him? He is

human. He has produced something as difficult as anything by Ezra Pound. Why shouldn't he be pleased?

If he wants to, he can let his classmates pick away at his poem indefinitely and never set them straight. If his teacher ventures to criticize a phrase or a line, the author can say that the passage is exactly as he wants it. Is it awkward? Well, he intended it to be awkward since awkwardness was needed at that point. This would be clear, he murmurs, to anyone who understood the poem.

Nobody can touch him. Nobody at all. He is safe. In an ever-threatening world full of old perils and new, such security is to be envied. To be able to sit tight and pretty on top of your poem, impregnable like a little castle perched on a steep rock.

Drugs, Drink, Luck, Inspiration, Work, and the Great Moment. Forget about trying to write when your best friend wouldn't trust you to drive. The roads on Parnassus are steep. Get high on what you are writing. "Nothing goes by luck in composition," Thoreau said. "It allows of no tricks." And Baudelaire defined inspiration as "working every day." "Then," as Robert Lowell notes, "the great moment comes when there's enough resolution of your technical equipment, your way of constructing things, and what you can make a poem out of, to hit something you really want to say. You may not know you have it to say."

"Poetry Makes Nothing Happen." In his elegy "In Memory of W. B. Yeats" W. H. Auden says in passing that "poetry makes nothing happen." Let's hope he is wrong.

Allusions. Explain whatever is necessary, *in* the poem. Avoid referring to things or people no one will remember in a year or so, like senators.

Rules. Break any of the rules when you have to.

Teaching Poetry. Should you ever find yourself in a classroom teaching poetry, which is a hazard few poets avoid, try to *teach* as little as possible. It is better, and not much harder, to let students learn.

Poetry and Politics. Anything at all is worth trying, in a leaky boat, in deep water.

Portability. Poetry is the cheapest and most portable of the arts. Even a pencil and paper aren't necessary. You can make poems in your head, anywhere, any time.

Earning a Living. The poet's aim may be, like Frost's in "Two Tramps in

Mud Time," to join vocation and avocation—"As my two eyes make one in sight." But few poets earn a living by poetry. Williams was a doctor, Stevens was an attorney for an insurance firm, and Frost himself did a lot of teaching. The money, like the honors, if they come, are likely to come too late to do the poet much good. Get a job.

A Hand in the Back of the Room. The owner of the hand in the back always wants to know: "How does one become a poet?" The answer is that it is almost always an accident. Liking poems turns into the habit of writing poems, and the habit of writing poems becomes second nature, a passion. All poets begin as—and if they are wise and lucky, remain—*amateurs.* (The word means *lovers.*)

Somewhere along the way, the beginner shows poems to friends, a teacher, the other members of a writing class; and if they are encouraging, he or she takes a chance and sends some of them off to the editor of a magazine. Probably the editor sends them back because it is likely that they aren't really very good—yet. Perhaps the beginner publishes a few in the school or college literary magazine. He or she reads more poems and writes more poems. And sometimes—only sometimes—despite all the discouragements, despite graduating from college and having a job, the beginner goes on.

Only a few of the poets who begin do not drop out somewhere along the way. Perhaps, probably, they are lucky (an editor accepts a poem at the right moment), but perhaps the need to write poems is, for some reason, just stronger in them. For some poets, like Milton and Keats, poetry seems to become a determination, a consuming ambition. Who knows whether it is excellence or fame or wealth or even some less reputable motive that drives them? Or simply the fascination of words, images, ideas? Poets might well be hard-put to tell us themselves. Maybe Eudora Welty's reply to a student's asking "Why do you write?" is best. She replied, "Because I am good at it."

Had there been creative writing classes in the latter part of the sixteenth century, who knows, the owner of the hand at the back of the room might have been a sophomore named Will Shakespeare.

QUESTIONS AND SUGGESTIONS

1. In the library browse among the poetry in magazines like *Poetry, Atlantic, Hudson Review, The Nation, Antaeus, Poetry Northwest, Poetry Now, Cutbank, Southern Review, Ploughshares, Open Places, Field, American Poetry Review, Black Warrior Review, North American Review, New Republic, Three Rivers Poetry Jour-*

nal, *Iowa Review, Ohio Review, Georgia Review, Carolina Quarterly, Kayak, Nimrod, Prairie Schooner, Epoch, Bitterroot, Hanging Loose, New Letters,* or (criticism) *Parnassus.*

2. Buy a book of poems.

3. Write a deliberate imitation of a poet as a way of exploring his or her technique. What qualities of subject, form, diction, and so on, are most telling? Here is a student's imitation of Alexander Pope. Compare it to the passages by Pope on pages 74 and 366. Is it a fair likeness?

Essay on Pope

The poet's proper study is his kind,
Both to instruct, and to inspire the mind;
Nor least of all the rhyming breed is Pope,
Who springs eternal in the muses' scope.
In Homer first he found the poet's chart,   5
The rules of Nature are the rules of Art;
And whither Homer went, went Pope in stride,
Both followed Nature, and avoided Pride.
His meters danced the dainty minuet,
The partners, speech and accent, finely met,   10
Or swiftly stomped along the printed ways
With steps as thund'rous as his scorn, or praise.
He taught the lowly urchin couplet skill
To use the common tongue, yet not speak ill,
To preach philosophy, or sing a strain   15
Of sylvan song, or curse in Horace' vein;
And drilled his eager pupil in the rules
Of poise, precision, grace. O best of schools:
A poet skilled in craft, oft filled with fire,
None better to instruct, or to inspire!   20

4. In "Second Sheet," the poet Jared Carter (b. 1939) has chosen his central idea from the repeated use of a padding sheet to protect the platen of his typewriter. Study the way he has developed this idea in images ("like leaves," then "like snow"). Choosing a similar mechanical detail of writing—typewriter ribbon or bell or keys, the long line of ink or lead stored inside a pen or pencil, eraser, and so on—write your own poem on the model of "Second Sheet."

Everything I've typed
Trying to write this poem
Sinks into a second sheet—
Piles up there like leaves.

Words pass from one dim
Indecipherable matrix
To another; even now
They fall through what

My heart would say to you
Like snow coming down
Straight, in no wind,
And covering itself.

5. Strictly, **parody** is the exaggerated imitation of a work of art. Following the mannerisms of style (like Whitman's catalogs or Dickinson's breathless dashes) and of subject matter (like Frost's country matters), the parodist pokes fun at, and sometimes holes in, the original. More loosely, parody may be a satiric commentary on the original, as "The Dover Bitch" (1959) by Anthony Hecht (b. 1923) comments on the famous Victorian poem "Dover Beach," written around 1851 by Matthew Arnold (1822–1888). Is Hecht's point insightful? fair? Is there a poet or poem you would like to parody?

Dover Beach

The sea is calm tonight.
The tide is full, the moon lies fair
Upon the straits;—on the French coast the light
Gleams and is gone; the cliffs of England stand,
Glimmering and vast, out in the tranquil bay.
Come to the window, sweet is the night-air!
Only, from the long line of spray
Where the sea meets the moon-blanched land,
Listen! you hear the grating roar
Of pebbles which the waves draw back, and fling,
At their return, up the high strand,
Begin, and cease, and then again begin,
With tremulous cadence slow, and bring
The eternal note of sadness in.

Sophocles long ago
Heard it on the Aegean, and it brought
Into his mind the turbid ebb and flow
Of human misery; we
Find also in the sound a thought,
Hearing it by this distant northern sea.

The Sea of Faith
Was once, too, at the full, and round earth's shore
Lay like the folds of a bright girdle furled.
But now I only hear
Its melancholy, long, withdrawing roar,

Retreating, to the breath
Of the night-wind, down the vast edges drear
And naked shingles° of the world.   gravel beaches

Ah, love, let us be true
To one another! for the world, which seems   30
To lie before us like a land of dreams,
So various, so beautiful, so new,
Hath really neither joy, nor love, nor light,
Nor certitude, nor peace, nor help for pain;
And we are here as on a darkling plain   35
Swept with confused alarms of struggle and flight,
Where ignorant armies clash by night.

The Dover Bitch

(A CRITICISM OF LIFE)

So there stood Matthew Arnold and this girl
With the cliffs of England crumbling away behind them,
And he said to her, "Try to be true to me,
And I'll do the same for you, for things are bad
All over, etc., etc."   5
Well now, I knew this girl. It's true she had read
Sophocles in a fairly good translation
And caught that bitter allusion to the sea,
But all the time he was talking she had in mind
The notion of what his whiskers would feel like   10
On the back of her neck. She told me later on
That after a while she got to looking out
At the lights across the channel, and really felt sad,
Thinking of all the wine and enormous beds
And blandishments in French and the perfumes.   15
And then she really got angry. To have been brought
All the way down from London, and then be addressed
As a sort of mournful cosmic last resort
Is really tough on a girl, and she was pretty.
Anyway, she watched him pace the room   20
And finger his watch-chain and seem to sweat a bit,
And then she said one or two unprintable things.
But you mustn't judge her by that. What I mean to say is,
She's really all right. I still see her once in a while
And she always treats me right. We have a drink   25
And I give her a good time, and perhaps it's a year
Before I see her again, but there she is,
Running to fat, but dependable as they come.
And sometimes I bring her a bottle of *Nuit d'Amour*.

from *An Essay on Criticism*   1711

ALEXANDER POPE   (1688–1744)

'Tis hard to say, if greater want of skill
Appear in writing or in judging ill;
But, of the two, less dangerous is the offense
To tire our patience, than mislead our sense.
Some few in that, but numbers err in this,   5
Ten censure wrong, for one who writes amiss;
A fool might once himself alone expose,
Now one in verse makes many more in prose.
    'Tis with our judgments as our watches, none
Go just alike, yet each believes his own.   10
In poets as true genius is but rare,
True taste as seldom is the critic's share;
Both must alike from Heaven derive their light,
These born to judge, as well as those to write.
Let such teach others who themselves excel,   15
And censure freely who have written well.
Authors are partial to their wit, 'tis true,
But are not critics to their judgment too?

Poets   1969

X. J. KENNEDY   (b. 1929)

These people are . . . quenched. I mean the natives.
    D. H. Lawrence, letter of 14 August 1923 from Dover, New Jersey.

Le vierge, le vivace, et le bel aujourd'hui . . .

    What were they like as schoolboys? Long on themes
And short of wind, perpetually outclassed,
Breaking their glasses, always chosen last
    When everyone was sorted out in teams,

Moody, a little dull, the kind that squirmed   5
At hurt cats, shrank from touching cracked-up birds,
With all but plain girls at a loss for words,
    Having to ask to have their fishhooks wormed,

    Snuffers of candles every priest thought nice,
Quenchers of their own wicks, their eyes turned down   10
And smoldering. In Dover, my home town,
    No winter passed but we had swans in ice,

    Birds of their quill: so beautiful, so dumb,
They'd let a window glaze about their feet,
Not seeing through their dreams till time to eat.   15
    A fireman with a blowtorch had to come

    Thaw the dopes loose. Sun-silvered, plumes aflap,
Weren't they grand, though?—not that you'd notice it,
Crawling along a ladder, getting bit,
    Numb to the bone, enduring all their crap.   20

America   1956

ALLEN GINSBERG (b. 1926)

America I've given you all and now I'm nothing.
America two dollars and twentyseven cents January 17, 1956.
I can't stand my own mind.
America when will we end the human war?
Go fuck yourself with your atom bomb.   5
I don't feel good don't bother me.
I won't write my poem till I'm in my right mind.
America when will you be angelic?
When will you take off your clothes?
When will you look at yourself through the grave?   10
When will you be worthy of your million Trotskyites?
America why are your libraries full of tears?
America when will you send your eggs to India?
I'm sick of your insane demands.

When can I go into the supermarket and buy what I need with my good
 looks? 15
America after all it is you and I who are perfect not the next world.
Your machinery is too much for me.
You made me want to be a saint.
There must be some other way to settle this argument.
Burroughs° is in Tangiers I don't think he'll come back it's sinister. 20
Are you being sinister or is this some form of practical joke?
I'm trying to come to the point.
I refuse to give up my obsession.
America stop pushing I know what I'm doing.
America the plum blossoms are falling. 25

I haven't read the newspapers for months, everyday somebody goes on trial
 for murder.
America I feel sentimental about the Wobblies.
America I used to be a communist when I was a kid I'm not sorry.
I smoke marijuana every chance I get.
I sit in my house for days on end and stare at the roses in the closet. 30
When I go to Chinatown I get drunk and never get laid.
My mind is made up there's going to be trouble.
You should have seen me reading Marx.
My psychoanalyst thinks I'm perfectly right.
I won't say the Lord's Prayer. 35
I have mystical visions and cosmic vibrations.
America I still haven't told you what you did to Uncle Max after he came
 over from Russia.

I'm addressing you.
Are you going to let your emotional life be run by Time Magazine?
I'm obsessed by Time Magazine. 40
I read it every week.
Its cover stares at me every time I slink past the corner candystore.
I read it in the basement of the Berkeley Public Library.
It's always telling me about responsibility. Businessmen are serious. Movie
 producers are serious. Everybody's serious but me.
It occurs to me that I am America. 45
I am talking to myself again.

Asia is rising against me.
I haven't got a chinaman's chance.
I'd better consider my national resources.
My national resources consist of two joints of marijuana millions of genitals

an unpublished private literature that goes 1400 miles an hour and
twentyfive-thousand mental institutions.   50
I say nothing about my prisons nor the millions of underprivileged who live
in my flowerpots under the light of five hundred suns.
I have abolished the whorehouses of France, Tangiers is the next to go.
My ambition is to be President despite the fact that I'm a Catholic.

America how can I write a holy litany in your silly mood?
I will continue like Henry Ford my strophes are as individual as his auto-
mobiles more so they're all different sexes   55
America I will sell you strophes $2500 apiece $500 down on your old
strophe
America free Tom Mooney
America save the Spanish Loyalists
America Sacco & Vanzetti must not die
America I am the Scottsboro boys.   60
America when I was seven momma took me to Communist Cell meetings
they sold us garbanzos a handful per ticket a ticket costs a nickel and
the speeches were free everybody was angelic and sentimental about
the workers it was all so sincere you have no idea what a good thing
the party was in 1835 Scott Nearing was a grand old man a real
mensch Mother Bloor made me cry I once saw Israel Amter plain.
Everybody must have been a spy.
America you don't really want to go to war.
America it's them bad Russians.
Them Russians them Russians and them Chinamen. And them Russians.
The Russia wants to eat us alive. The Russia's power mad. She wants to
take our cars from out our garages.   65
Her wants to grab Chicago. Her needs a Red Readers' Digest. Her wants
our auto plants in Siberia. Him big bureaucracy running our fillingsta-
tions.
That no good. Ugh. Him make Indians learn read. Him need big black
niggers. Hah. Her make us all work sixteen hours a day. Help.
America this is quite serious.
America this is the impression I get from looking in the television set.
America is this correct?   70
I'd better get right down to the job.
It's true I don't want to join the Army or turn lathes in precision parts
factories, I'm nearsighted and psychopathic anyway.
America I'm putting my queer shoulder to the wheel.

20 *Burroughs:* novelist William Burroughs (1914–1981), who fled to Tangiers to avoid
prosecution on drug charges.

The Perfect Suicide   1977

ROGER PFINGSTON   (b. 1940)

In his despair he made a poem
with a gun in it. He shot himself
again and again until he got it right.

Why I Am Not a Painter   1957

FRANK O'HARA   (1926–1966)

I am not a painter, I am a poet.
Why? I think I would rather be
a painter, but I am not. Well,

for instance, Mike Goldberg
is starting a painting. I drop in.   5
"Sit down and have a drink" he
says. I drink; we drink. I look
up. "You have SARDINES in it."
"Yes, it needed something there."
"Oh." I go and the days go by   10
and I drop in again. The painting
is going on, and I go, and the days
go by. I drop in. The painting is
finished. "Where's SARDINES?"
All that's left is just   15
letters, "It was too much," Mike says.

But me? One day I am thinking of
a color: orange. I write a line
about orange. Pretty soon it is a
whole page of words, not lines.   20
Then another page. There should be
so much more, not of orange, of
words, of how terrible orange is
and life. Days go by. It is even in
prose, I am a real poet. My poem   25

is finished and I haven't mentioned
orange yet. It's twelve poems, I call
it ORANGES. And one day in a gallery
I see Mike's painting, called SARDINES.

Teaching Poetry at a Country School in Florida

*Teaching Poetry at
a Country School in Florida*   1977

PETER MEINKE   (b. 1932)

It ain't there. Come off it, Rousseau.
The eyes roll inward, the brain coughs
like a motor at ten below

and doesn't start: they're not bad kids.
Too dumb for poetry, and smart enough to know   5
they don't need it: no one needs it:
not their teachers, nor principal, nor coach
who equates it with queers
and public masturbation
which unfortunately it sometimes resembles   10
particularly the iambic

But we have to do it because
in the midst of that tangible boredom—
from that stack of pathetic papers—
there is always one you come across   15
just before turning to drink
with thoughts of murder or suicide—
there is always one who writes
My wings are invisible but brilliant;
they carry me to the dark forest   20
where the unicorns kneel in prayer. . . .

So. You go on, after a while.
But still, all that effort, so little to show
like that royal palm outside my window going up & up
and up, with a small green *poof* at the top.   25

15

Business:
Scents, Sents, Cents, Sense

There is a practical, business side to being a poet, and this chapter is about that: sending poems to magazines, keeping records, obtaining copyrights, assembling a book, being reviewed and reviewing, giving readings, and such odd matters as dealing with the Internal Revenue Service.

Getting Organized

Keep the drafts of a poem. With the papers clipped together, latest version on top, you can add any correspondence (like an editor's letter of acceptance) to the pile, along with the printed version when it comes along. A complete record of the poem will always be in one place. Some poets date the drafts of a poem.

As time goes on and poems multiply, a system of manila folders will keep them straight: a folder labeled NEW POEMS for poems currently being written, a folder labeled POEMS OUT for poems that are finished and out to magazines, and a folder labeled PUBLISHED POEMS. Perhaps, also, a folder labeled OLD POEM

MSS, for poems from the NEW POEMS folder that no longer seem likely to go anywhere and for poems withdrawn from POEMS OUT when it seems unlikely that they will be published. In time OLD POEM MSS will grow to be the biggest collection, a Sargasso Sea of shipwrecked poems at the back of the drawer. (Typewriter-paper boxes make good storage and can be kept on a shelf out of the way.) Some such system will let you keep the decks clear for action and will provide a ready sense of where everything is.

A heavy clamp binder is also useful for an up-to-date set of good, finished poems. (Make an extra carbon when poems are sent out to magazines.) This binder is handy for carrying to poetry readings and also provides a loose draft of the book you are working toward. As it fills, shuffle the poems around toward what might be a final book order, grouping and separating. A ring binder would do as well but is less satisfyingly booklike. (Books with blank pages can be obtained at reasonable prices from bookstores, but they have the disadvantages of not allowing the growing MS to be typed and of not allowing for insertions, deletions, or shuffling of pages.)

Submitting to Magazines

When should a beginning poet start sending poems out to magazines? As soon as she or he has three or four good, finished poems. It costs very little and is exciting. A poet with several groups of poems in the mail to several magazines can look forward with suspense to the postman. Sending poems out may also be a stimulus to finishing poems. Horace's classical advice—to wait nine years before publishing—might keep the poet from making a mistake (and of course, nothing will come of sending out sloppy, unfinished poems), but learning from mistakes may be more useful in the long run than trying not to make them.

The probability, of course, is rejection. Rejection slips will pile up, and even a very good poet will soon have enough of them to wallpaper his study. *Don't be discouraged.* Poems may be rejected for a hundred reasons that have nothing to do with their quality. The magazine is currently overstocked (most magazines are); it gets more good poems than it can possibly use (most magazines do); it has just accepted another poem about octopuses and doesn't want to publish anything similar; or the editor just had a phone call from his wife about their child's orthodontist's bill and is feeling owlish. Have a look at the rejected poems; if they still look pretty sound to you, put them in another envelope and ship them off again to another magazine. Robert Francis's way of thinking about rejections, which he reports in an essay called "Weighed in the Balance," is tonic:

> "I didn't feel settled quite firmly enough on a choice among these poems," writes the editor of *Poetry*.
>
> An appropriate statement, surely. Honest. Also tactful. I have no complaint.
>
> I am entirely reconciled. Indeed, I am more reconciled than an editor might suppose possible. If there is the least doubt in the editorial mind of the worthiness or suitability of my poem, I much prefer he send it back. I don't want to squeak by. I don't want to creep into the fold.
>
> Perhaps it is pride, but I prefer not to have a poem accepted for any other reason than love. Having known love, now and then, I cannot be content with anything less. Now and again an editor has loved a poem of mine before it was in print, and a reader has loved it afterwards. On such love, on the memory of it, I can live for a while.
>
> Perhaps it is pride, perhaps it is conceit, but I can't keep out of mind the possibility that the poem the editor rejects may have turned the tables on him. While he was judging the poem, the poem may have quietly been judging him. In the eyes of eternity it may be the editor and not the little poem that was weighed in the balance and found wanting.

At some point, after a group of poems has been to six, eight, or ten magazines, the poet should have a really hard look and consider taking them out of circulation (to the OLD POEM MSS folder or, for reworking, back to the NEW POEMS folder). If they still look sound, put them into another envelope and send them off on yet another round of magazines. Inexplicably, even a very good poem may go to twenty or thirty magazines before finding a home. (Even more inexplicably, an editor who has already rejected a poem may sometimes accept it on a second trip around, though I wouldn't recommend wasting postage on the chance.) Nonetheless, for more poems than not, the OLD POEM MSS folder (or file box) is the ultimate destination. A steady pressure of no's from editors, especially editors whose judgment the poet has reason to trust, is saying something he or she needs to know. It is better for the poet to get on to writing new poems than to cling painfully to every word she or he ever put on paper.

Editors *do* read poems submitted to them, and they *do* buy poems from unknown poets. On the other side of the editorial desk, there is a real pleasure in recognizing a fine poem by a newcomer and perhaps being the first to print her or him. Like all of us, editors make mistakes and have off days. While it is true that a "name" makes editors perk up and pay attention, very few editors will prefer a lousy poem by a poet with a reputation to a fine poem by someone they have never heard of. Even in large shops, where incoming poems are likely to be read by subeditors or sub-subeditors, most poems get a fair reading. The subbest-editor has far more reason to hope to find a really good poem that will go all the way to the top than to try to set records for using up rejection slips.

Sooner or later, a rejection slip will carry a little scribbled note from an editor: "Sorry" or "Very close call!" Sooner or later, there will appear a letter of acceptance and perhaps a small check (checks for poems are usually small checks). The next hundred poems you submit may be rejected, but one acceptance will outweigh a thousand rejection slips.

To which magazines should you submit poems? Each poet will make and keep revising a personal list. One good rule of thumb is to stick to magazines you have seen and know. If you like the poems in a magazine, the odds are that you and the editor are on approximately the same wave-length and, therefore, that your poems will get the best possible consideration. Conversely, if you don't much like the poems in a magazine, the odds are that you are wasting stamps. Knowing the magazine will also keep you from sending sonnets to a magazine that prints only free verse, or poems with cuss words to a magazine that is prissy, and so on. As poets we are privileged to write exactly as we want and not to please an editor, but it is sensible to try to find the right market for poems, once written.

Poetry makes very little money, and since agents live by taking a small percentage (usually 10 percent) of the income from a writer's sales, they aren't interested in poetry. The poet must learn to be his or her own agent—knowing markets, sending work around, reading the small print in contracts.

Both *The Writer* and *Writer's Digest* publish a useful list of "poetry markets" in one issue each year. *The International Directory of Little Magazines and Small Presses*, published annually by Dustbooks (P. O. Box 100, Paradise, California 95969; currently $13.95 paperbound), provides an indispensable list. All three offer detailed information about the magazines' needs or peculiarities. If you can't find a magazine in your library, write for a sample copy (enclosing the single copy price).

Another valuable resource is Poets & Writers, Inc. (201 West 54th Street, New York, New York 10019), a publicly supported information center for writers. Its publication *Coda* (five times a year, subscription currently $10.00) provides lively, practical information about the literary and publishing scene; announcements and deadlines for prizes and grants; news of magazines seeking MSS or of poets hunting jobs or readings; and articles about such matters as copyright or the problems of little magazines. A poet may be included in the Poets & Writers' *Directory of American Poets* after he or she has published a minimum of ten poems (in at least three different literary magazines). Being listed gets the poet slightly lowered rates for *Coda* and Poets & Writers' other publications.

Submitting poems, start at the top. If *The New Yorker* or *Atlantic* or *Poetry* is where you wish to be published, by all means send poems there first. The odds may be horrendous, but for the price of two envelopes and two stamps it is worth a try. Then send the poems to the other magazines on your list, in descending order of your preference. How long your list is, and how quickly it slopes to magazines of modest prestige, depends on your patience, your conviction, and perhaps your supply of stamps. When you bump into a new magazine you like, add it to your list. When a magazine takes six months to reply or sends the MS back misfolded or with a shoe-print (it's happened), delete it. Magazines that pay should be higher on the list than ones that don't. (Dr. Samuel Johnson: "Sir, no man but a blockhead ever wrote except for money.") A very important criterion is the quality of the editor. Since one of the things a poet gets from submitting a MS is criticism (even if it is only a rejection slip), send your poems to the best editors you know, who are probably also poets you admire and whose judgment you tend to trust.

The mechanics of submitting poems are simple. Type each poem cleanly, single-spaced, in the center of a sheet of regular 8½″ × 11″ bond paper, allowing a space or two between title and poem, and putting your name and address near the upper left-hand corner. Should a poem require more than one page, a heading near the top right corner of the second and each subsequent page should show your name, short title, and page number. Also, for poems of more than one page, indicate whether there is, or is not, a stanza-break between pages—[#] or [no#].

A polite but useless convention, which you should ignore, is accompanying the submission with a cover letter stating that the enclosed poems are being submitted for publication and that the editor's consideration will be gratefully appreciated, and so forth. Since all that is perfectly obvious, don't bother with a cover letter unless there is in fact something out of the way about the submission that needs explaining. Nor is there much use in a list of the poet's "credits," as it is sometimes crassly called (poems published or accepted by *This Review* and *That Quarterly* and *The Other Journal*) or in enclosing biographical data. An editor is going to take, or not take, one of the poems on the desk. And he or she is likely to be faintly resentful of all such nudging, shoving, and elbowing. Let the poems speak for themselves, neatly typed (use a fresh ribbon), carefully proofread, one to a page.

Never submit a reproduced manuscript. It takes only a few minutes to type or retype a batch of poems. No matter how rude one editor may have been, rumpling or spilling coffee on the MS, a sharp MS is a courtesy due to the next editor. Photocopies suggest that the poet may be submitting the same poems to more than one magazine at the same time, a practice that is flatly improper. Many magazines are unfairly slow in replying to submissions, and at three or four or six months apiece, it can take a long time to circulate a MS. The proper response to such editorial rudeness, which leaves the poet in a dither over whether a MS has been lost or is getting special consideration, is simply not to send poems to that magazine again. In general, with mail time considered, a month is fairly prompt; six weeks, reasonable. But if an editor keeps a MS more than two months, the poet should send the editor a postcard wondering whether his poems have been lost in the mail and, if they still happen to be on the editor's desk, asking for their return.

In no event, however, send poems to two magazines at the same time. If your poems are lousy, the practice will work like a charm—they will all come back. But if there is a good poem among them, it is all too likely that, sooner or later, more than one editor will accept the same poem. You won't be able to explain to either of them convincingly, and you will have lost at least one sympathetic friend in power and made a good start on a bad reputation.

How many poems should you send at a time? Three or four usually makes a batch worth an editor's time. Don't send more than seven or eight; a batch larger than that is confusing and makes the poet seem undiscriminating. Fold the sheets together, like a business letter, and use regular business-size envelopes. Manila envelopes of larger size can be used, with the sheets folded in half or sent flat; it costs slightly more, is niftier, and makes no difference. Address the editor by name if you know it, or simply "Poetry Editor."

Always make carbon copies, which may be useful for later checking and which can be clipped to the drafts.

Always enclose a self-addressed, stamped envelope (SASE) or, if the MS is going abroad, International Reply Coupons (which can be bought at any post office). Fold the return envelope in thirds and tuck it in with the poems.

Keep a log or record of submissions. For instance, use a giant paperclip to clip together copies of the poems (with drafts) of a submitted group, along with a 5" × 8" card for listing the poems in the group. As the group goes and comes, enter on the card the date sent and the magazine, then the date returned and any acceptance or comment. A small notebook will do as well. Dates and other particulars of publication should also be recorded, which may help keep track of copyrights when the time comes to gather a book MS.

One recent, and I hope passing, development is worth note. Following the example of several presses, which have introduced the policy of requiring a "reading fee" to accompany all unsolicited book MSS, several little magazines have announced the policy of requiring that potential contributors also be subscribers. The financial perch of little magazines is often precarious—and ironic. It isn't unusual for a magazine to be offered poems by three or four times as many poets as it sells copies. An odd kind of success! Obviously, more people write (and want to publish) poetry than are willing to pay to read it. Undoubtedly, even impecunious poets ought to subscribe to more magazines and buy more books than they do, but reading fees and required subscriptions won't solve the problem. No really genuine magazine or publisher can afford philosophically to cut itself off from an inglorious Keats who may not happen to have ten dollars to spare. And editors whose salaries are paid by writers are, or will soon become, charlatans. The old rule is a good rule: if anyone wants money to publish or consider your poems, duck.

Copyright

On 1 January 1978, a major new **copyright** law (Title 17, USC, Copyrights) went into effect, both improving and simplifying the protection of an author's rights in his or her work. Going by the rule that wherever there are legalities there are complications, I offer the following, not as a summary of the law, but only as a working writer's understanding of it as it affects him. Full information and forms can be obtained on inquiry from the Copyright Office, Library of Congress, Washington, D.C. 20559. A useful pamphlet, *A Writer's Guide to Copyright,* is available from Poets & Writers, Inc. (201 West 54th Street, New York, New York 10019; $4.95).

A significant provision of the new law extends the copyright protection of a work to the author's lifetime plus fifty years. That protection begins with the creation of the work, so the MSS in your desk are included. An author *may* register unpublished work himself (Form TX, one copy of the work, and a ten-dollar fee), but there is no need to go to this trouble. The publisher of any reputable periodical or of a book will register the work on publication. Even though the registration is made in the publisher's name, the copyright belongs to the author—*unless there is a written agreement to the contrary.* In the absence of such a written agreement, a magazine acquires only the right to initial publication of a work in one of its issues (first North American serial rights). Since magazines are interested in one-time publication of a work, the author retains copyright and full control. Some magazines, however, may want a written agreement transferring other rights (for instance, the right to include a poem in an anthology of poems originally published in that magazine). The author should be wary. Theoretically, such an agreement can require the poet to obtain the magazine's permission to reprint the work elsewhere and can even entitle the magazine to a share of whatever fees or royalties the work may earn. Such agreements are not normally abused (reputable magazines by and large don't do disreputable things), but the writer ought to read the fine print in any contract she or he is invited to sign.

Ideally, the new law simplifies things. Unless she or he explicitly assigns it in writing, the author intrinsically holds copyright in his works. But there is a complication. Although registration *by the author* (as distinct from, and in addition to, registration by the publishers of magazines or books) is not necessary for a work to be protected by copyright, such registration—it appears—*is* necessary for him to bring suit for copyright infringement. This requirement, it would seem, makes nonsense of the rest of the law; it apparently deprives authors of the copyright protection the law otherwise assures unless they register the work in their own name and within a specified time, since it deprives them of the possibility of enforcing that protection. Section 408 (17 USC 408) states: "such registration is not a condition of copyright protection." *But* Section 411 (17

USC 411) states: "no action for infringement of the copyright in any work shall be instituted until registration of the copyright claim has been made." As there can hardly be a right that is not enforceable, requiring such registration is plainly contradictory to the thrust of the law as a whole; and the courts may be expected ultimately to hold the requirement invalid. Meanwhile, to be safe, the writer apparently must register works *himself or herself*, preferably within three months of publication and absolutely within one year of publication. Form TX (along with a ten-dollar fee and two copies of the periodical or book) is appropriate for a single poem. Several poems in one or in several periodicals can be registered as a group; Form GR/CP (in addition to the TX's and along with a single ten-dollar fee and two complete copies of each periodical) is appropriate. Obviously, careful record-keeping is called for, and sufficient copies of each magazine should be salted away for this purpose. Litigious writers will enjoy all of this. Others may well feel, as the monetary value of a poem seems unlikely to make lawsuits a practical use of time or energy, merely annoyed and depressed.

Book publication is always by contract—written agreement—and it is standard for the publisher to control the copyright even though it may be registered in the author's name. The publisher grants permissions for reprints in anthologies or elsewhere, also setting and collecting the fees, which are usually split on a 50% basis: in short, the publisher provides the services of an agent. Also standard in the contract is a provision for the automatic return of control of the copyright to the author when the publisher allows the book to go out of print. This clause is particularly important to the writer. Without it the publisher could legitimately hold the rights to the book indefinitely without keeping it in print, thus leaving the book in limbo. No book contract should be signed that does not have a provision for automatically letting the rights revert to the author, usually six months after the publisher has allowed the book to go out of print. (The publisher may not be required to give notice of this nonevent, and its permissions department may go on collecting and splitting fees, innocently but improperly, unless the author exercises his or her contractual rights.)

Terms of publication, like royalties, are variable: 10 percent of the list price as royalty is normal. Since, however, poetry is unlikely to sell well, even trade publishers may suggest a lower percentage (or even a flat payment) on the first printing, with escalation agreed upon should the book go to further printings. Small presses often pay royalties only in the form of copies—10 or 15 percent of the books printed, which the author may sell when he or she gives readings or the like. In any event, read a book contract carefully and ask questions; if in doubt, consult someone who knows about such things.

Reprinting of poems in anthologies is also usually by contract or written agreement (which a simple exchange of letters may constitute). When the poems are from a book in print, your publisher will handle reprinting permissions and fees, usually advantageously. Before poems are collected in book form and again after copyright has reverted, the author must handle these permissions and set the fees. Something like two dollars a line is an average rate, but there are variables like the size of the edition, its price, and the likelihood of profitability (which is why your publisher's permissions department knows how to handle these matters advantageously). If anything, err a trifle on what may seem to you the high side in setting fees; the anthologists can always ask you to lower them. You should specify the form the acknowledgment is to take, usually just "Copyright 1978 by Jane Doe," and, if the poem has appeared in a magazine, something like "First printed in *The Other Journal*." It is also important, under the new law, for the author to specify that the permission to reprint is granted only for the present edition, lest the anthology go merrily from revised edition to revised edition, year after year, minting money for everyone but the authors.

Minor revisions may be made in a copyrighted work without any need to record them with the Register of Copyrights. Substantial revision or addition of new material may make it worthwhile to apply for a new copyright.

Copyrights certified prior to 1 January 1978, which are in their first twenty-eight-year term (under the old law), may be renewed in the twenty-eighth year for a renewal term of forty-seven years (Form RE; fee, six dollars). Copyrights certified prior to 1 January 1978, which have already been renewed, are automatically extended to seventy-five years from the date of original publication.

Readings

Oddly enough, poets are likely to earn more from giving readings of their poems in schools or colleges than from actual publication. However small, an audience offers a lively chance to test new poems and provides what publication rarely does—an immediate and personal response. Well-known poets command fees of a thousand dollars or more, but fees of a hundred or so, plus expenses, are common. Beginning poets will do well to accept whatever invitations to read come along, usually for no fee, at their own schools or at public libraries, bookstores, coffeehouses, and sometimes prisons. A poet who has begun to be published should investigate the state's Poets in the Schools program, which funds (generously) visits by local poets to elementary and secondary schools.

Poets develop their own styles in giving readings, and beginning poets will probably have plenty of examples from which to form their own. Listening to poems, especially poems that aren't familiar, takes a lot of concentration; a good reader reads slowly and allows an audience to relax between poems, usually by chatting informally about them. Find out from your host how long you are expected to read and stay within that limit. Ancient mariners quickly wear out their welcome. As a rule, underselling works better than overselling, although a little showmanship may help.

Don't be disappointed when, at your first reading, the audience turns out to be four people (or maybe five, if you count the janitor who stops in the doorway to listen). The fewer they are, the rarer—and so deserving of your best. As Robert Francis says about something else, "Very well. Very well, indeed. But when were rubies and diamonds sold by the peck?"

Book Publication

Even the best magazines are ephemeral, and the poet's goal, as well as the measure of accomplishment, should be publication of a book of poems. Typically, the beginning poet makes a reputation in magazines and, as poems and prestige accumulate, arrives at a book. Faced with rising costs and low sales, trade publishers have cut back severely on poetry in recent years; and the burdens and opportunities have passed to university presses and the small presses that, often subsidized by federal money, flourish throughout the country. The 1977 *Small Press Record of Books in Print* lists nearly 2500 books and chapbooks of poetry! Happy as this proliferation is in many ways, in others it is merely confusion. Neither libraries nor bookstores nor those few periodicals that review poetry, and certainly not readers, can even begin to keep up with the flood. Good books are lost to willing readers who simply never know that they exist. The beginning poet will be wise not to confuse quantity of publication with quality of publication, nor earliness with importance.

A book is an important stage in a poet's growth, a statement of where he or she is, and every poem included should be up to his or her standard. Some of the poems published in magazines may be left out, either because they seem less than best or because, one way or another, they do not fit the tone or shape of the book. Delmore Schwartz moodily made the point: "After much reflection, I've decided that one ought to write as much as possible and publish as little as possible."

The publication of a book may be followed, when the poet is lucky (or unlucky), with reviews. Ideally a review describes fairly and evaluates honestly a book or several books. Alas, many reviewers, out of haste or politics or preening, fall short of being fair or honest. Reviewers who are too friendly, discovering a masterpiece under every stone, praise a mediocre book to the skies; while malicious reviewers find fault with the finest book. Of these two sorts, the too friendly reviewers are the less reprehensible, since it is better to be agreeable than to be churlish, and since poor writing will sink of its own weight. Perhaps the best of reviews are those in E. V. Griffith's tabloid journal, *Poetry Now,* which simply reprints several poems from a book and lets the reader decide for himself.

As for literary politics, the buttering up and the being buttered up, the beginning poet will do well to have as little taste for the one as for the other. Earn what you get by merit, not by sleeping with Caesar's wife (or with Caesar).

Money

One of the freedoms of the poet, since in our society at least poetry doesn't make money, is to do as he or she wishes. Little magazines usually pay in copies—two copies; others may pay a dollar or two per line. A poem that may last as long as the English language, an immortal masterpiece, might bring twenty-five dollars from *Poetry*. The few commercial magazines that still publish poetry do better, but not by much. Given the modest sale of books of poems, the average book earns only several hundred dollars—if that. A lucky poem can earn several hundred dollars from anthologies over the years. And there may be, too, occasional prizes and grants—several hundred dollars here, maybe several thousand dollars there. These days the National Endowment for the Arts is usually the tooth fairy. But, as Ezra Pound's notorious Mr. Nixon (no, not *that* notorious Mr. Nixon) advised the young writer:

". . . give up verse, my boy,
There's nothing in it."

Still, there is the freedom and there is the art of poetry, in which the least of us may be for a time a companion of Geoffrey Chaucer and John Milton and Alexander Pope and William Yeats. Every poet may share the hope of the Roman poet Sextus Propertius (died 15 B.C.), in Ezra Pound's elegant translation "Homage to Sextus Propertius," that he may write a few pages that will not "go to rack ruin beneath the thud of the years."

There is the money, too. If not a living, it is still something. A tidy sum is a tidy sum, and payment at all for doing what one loves is a good wage. As a poet, you need not, at any rate, be modest about expecting or accepting modest payments; nor about claiming, when tax time comes around, the modest privileges of your "small business."

For so, if you have any income to speak of, the Internal Revenue Service must regard you, albeit with suspicion. The proper form is Form C of the 1040: "Profit (or Loss) from Business or Professions (Sole Proprietorships)." Armed with it you may deduct or depreciate your books and your typewriter and your desk. On it you may deduct your expenses, the paper and envelopes and paperclips and manila folders and postage and the like, as well as your mileage and motel bill and tolls when you travel to give readings. You may deduct your copyright fees, anything you pay a typist, long-distance calls about readings or publishing a book, and sometimes even a portion of your rent and utilities. You may even claim, on capital expenses like a typewriter or desk, the 10% Investment Tax Credit (Form 3468). For you are, willy-nilly, a business every bit as much as IBM and General Motors. ("What is good for the poet is good for the country," you may freely declare.)

A good tax accountant (also deductible) can quickly show you the ins and outs, and how to keep the simple records necessary. A little spiral notebook does well, along with the habit of asking for receipts at the post office or stationery store and yet one more manila folder to stuff the receipts into. Profits (or losses) may be carried over to the appropriate line on Form 1040 and added to (or deducted from) the rest of your income. One caveat: even small businesses are expected to operate at a profit more than at a loss, and the IRS is likely to look askance at enormous or continuous losses. A fair general rule is, use writing expenses to offset writing income and don't push. The IRS can also decide that writing is a hobby.

A Last Word

Ben Jonson advised the poet, wisely, "to live merrily, and to trust to good verses."

QUESTIONS AND SUGGESTIONS

1. Here are five very accomplished poems by students. If you were a subeditor for a poetry magazine, would you recommend any for publication? Consider carefully your reaction to each poem. (See Appendix I.)

a) *Miner*

JEANNE FRANK*

Home from the nightshift,
he watches the snow
as it blows and drifts
at the back doorstep,
and curses it to hell.
His workclothes smell

of sweat and the breath
of engines, as he takes
his shovel, shoulders it,
and goes out, tarnishing
the moonlight; miner
in a field of diamonds.

b) *The Invention of the Snowman*

MARK IRWIN*

Somewhere beyond the peripheries of sleep,
my sad bones undressed, rising from their flesh
to become this selfless, falling dust.

It was then that I wanted ears
with which to hear the familiar cries
of those children building me.

And of course, I had no eyes—
only this unfailing bandage of light,
the snow sewing its colorless view.

But worst of all, was this thirst to be living—
to understand those small, clumsy hands
making the same careless mistakes as the gods.

c) *Pandora's Dressing Table*

BONNIE JACOBSON*

The sea was a blue flower
Lolling on a reedy stem
Pandora fingered a moment,
Satisfied her eyes were bluer.

Mark, the moon was a white bee
In the blue flower withering
And the earth was an amber earring
On Pandora's dressing table.

Reason was her bumbling suitor
Stung daft by the waning moon.
Pandora reaching for her rouge
Is wind, whittling dry bee and flower.

d) *The Divers*

JOHN STUPP*

They descend like stones,
leaving air to mark passage.

Once underwater, they
exchange glances, unzip
skin to reveal:
gills, small fins. At night
they sleep with
girls in the village, who will
awake, impaled on
secret hooks. Now, in the morning
they sit grinning
on the docks. This is the photograph
I took of them. Click.

e) *Forgive And Forget*

KATHERINE KINSEY*

Straightening things on my desk,
I find a book of matches,
Matches you pressed on me, though I don't smoke,
Leaving a restaurant after dinner—

After dinner, after our first argument,
Our pairing still unmeasured and unmanaged,
After the first relieved forgiving of wrongs
Still imperfectly imagined.

I put the matches in the top drawer,
A drawer I seldom open, and
Saw unmailed invitations to a party never held
In a time now almost forgotten.

The next time I open the drawer,
Will I know where the matches came from?

2. The **clerihew** is a comic form of four lines of irregular length, of which the
first line is the name of a famous person or historical character. The rhyme
scheme is *a a b b*; and part of the fun is rhyming on the proper name, as well as
making the rest of the poem a pointed comment on the personage. The form's
inventor, Edmund C. (for Clerihew) Bentley (1875—1956), used it to good
purpose:

Sir Christopher Wren
Said, "I am going to dine with some men.
If anybody calls
Say I am designing St. Paul's."

After looking at these other examples, each titled "Clerihew," try a clerihew
of your own:

Zane Grey
Struck pay
Dirt and
Quicksand.

PAUL CURRY STEELE (b. 1928)

Leach, Alexander Archibald
has long been called
more elegant-
ly, Cary Grant.

ANONYMOUS

3. Prepare and send out a group of poems to the first magazine on your list.

POEMS TO CONSIDER

Seven Wealthy Towns

ANONYMOUS

Seven wealthy towns contend for Homer dead
Through which the living Homer begged his bread.

from Homage to Sextus Propertius°   1917

EZRA POUND (1885–1972)

Shades of Callimachus°, Coan ghosts of Philetas°
It is in your grove I would walk,
I who come first from the clear font
Bringing the Grecian orgies into Italy,
                and the dance into Italy.   5
Who hath taught you so subtle a measure,
            in what hall have you heard it;
What foot beat out your time-bar,
      what water has mellowed your whistles?

Out-weariers of Apollo° will, as we know, continue their Martian° gener-
      alities, 10
        We have kept our erasers in order.
A new-fangled chariot follows the flower-hung horses;
A young Muse with young loves clustered about her
        ascends with me into the æther, . . .
And there is no high-road to the Muses. 15

Annalists will continue to record Roman reputations,
Celebrities from the Trans-Caucasus will belaud Roman celebrities
And expound the distentions of Empire,
But for something to read in normal circumstances?
For a few pages brought down from the forked hill° unsullied? 20
I ask a wreath which will not crush my head.
               And there is no hurry about it;
I shall have, doubtless, a boom after my funeral,
Seeing that long standing increases all things
                  regardless of quality. 25
And who would have known the towers
             pulled down by a deal-wood horse°;   *the Trojan horse*
Or of Achilles° withstaying waters by Simois°
Or of Hector° spattering wheel-rims,
Or of Polydmantus°, by Scamander°, and Helenus° and Deiphoibos°? 30
Their door-yards would scarcely know them, or Paris°.
Small talk O Ilion°, and O Troad°
             twice taken by Oetian gods°,   *of Mount Oeta*
If Homer had not stated your case!

And I also among the later nephews of this city 35
             shall have my dog's day,
With no stone upon my contemptible sepulchre;
My vote coming from the temple of Phoebus° in Lycia°, at Patara°,
And in the mean time my songs will travel,
And the devirginated young ladies will enjoy them 40
         when they have got over the strangeness,
For Orpheus° tamed the wild beasts—
           and held up the Threician river;
And Citharaon° shook up the rocks by Thebes
       and danced them into a bulwark at his pleasure, 45
And you, O Polyphemus°? Did harsh Galatea almost
Turn to your dripping horses, because of a tune, under Aetna?
We must look into the matter.
Bacchus and Apollo in favour of it,

There will be a crowd of young women doing homage to my palaver,   50
Though my house is not propped up by Taenarian° columns from Laconia
        (associated with Neptune° and Cerberus°),
Though it is not stretched upon gilded beams;
My orchards do not lie level and wide
                        as the forests of Phaecia,
                        the luxurious and Ionian,   55
Nor are my caverns stuffed stiff with a Marcian° vintage,
My cellar does not date from Numa Pompilius°,
Nor bristle with wine jars,
Nor is it equipped with a frigidaire patent;
Yet the companions of the Muses   60
                will keep their collective nose in my books,
And weary with historical data, they will turn to my dance tune.

Happy who are mentioned in my pamphlets,
        the songs shall be a fine tomb-stone over their beauty.
        But against this?   65
Neither expensive pyramids scraping the stars in their route,
Nor houses modelled upon that of Jove in East Elis°,   *temple of Zeus,*
Nor the monumental effigies of Mausolus°,   *in Greece*
                        are a complete elucidation of death.

Flame burns, rain sinks into the cracks   70
And they all go to rack ruin beneath the thud of the years.
Stands genius a deathless adornment,
                a name not to be worn out with the years.

Sextus Propertius: Roman poet (died 15 B.C.); *Homage to Sextus Propertius:* free
translation (or adaptation) of a number of Propertius's elegies.   1 *Callimachus,*
Philetas: Greek poets of the 3rd and 4th centuries B.C.   10 *Apollo:* Greek sun-god,
patron of all the arts; *Martian:* warlike (of Mars, god of war).   20 *forked hill:*
Parnassus, two-peaked mountain of the Muses.   28–31 *Achilles:* Greek hero of the
Trojan war; *Hector, Polydmantus, Helenus, Deiphoibos, Paris:* Trojans; *Simois,*
Scamander: rivers of Troy.   32 *Ilion:* the citadel; *Troad:* the state.   38 *Phoebus:*
Apollo; *Lycia, Patara:* places in Asia Minor.   42 *Orpheus:* who tamed beasts and
held back rivers by playing his lyre.   44 *Citharaon:* Amphion (of Mount
Citharaon), who raised the walls of the city of Thebes with his music.   46 *Poly-*
phemus: cyclops who loved and was rejected by the sea-nymph Galatea.   51 *Taena-*
rian: marble from quarry at Taenarus, in Greece; *Neptune:* Roman sea-god; *Cerberus:*
three-headed dog guarding the entrance to Hades.   56–57 *Marcian (Ancus*
Marcius), Numa Pompilius: legendary kings of early Rome.   68 *Mausolus:* king
buried in a grand tomb; hence, the word mausoleum.

Selecting a Reader

1974

TED KOOSER   (b. 1939)

First, I would have her be beautiful,
and walking carefully up on my poetry
at the loneliest moment of an afternoon,
her hair still damp at the neck
from washing it. She should be wearing   5
a raincoat, an old one, dirty
from not having money enough for the cleaners.
She will take out her glasses, and there
in the bookstore, she will thumb
over my poems, then put the book back   10
up on its shelf. She will say to herself,
"For that kind of money, I can get
my raincoat cleaned." And she will.

Notes from a Slave Ship

1963

EDWARD FIELD   (b. 1924)

It is necessary to wait until the boss's eyes are on you
Then simply put your work aside,
Slip a fresh piece of paper in the typewriter,
And start to write a poem.

Let their eyes boggle at your impudence;   5
The time for a poem is the moment of assertion,
The moment when you say I exist—
Nobody can buy my time absolutely.

Nobody can buy me even if I say, Yes I sell.
There I am sailing down the river,   10
Quite happy about the view of the passing towns,
When I find that I have jumped overboard.

There is always a long swim to freedom.
The worst of it is the terrible exhaustion
Alone in the water in the darkness, 15
The shore a fading memory and the direction lost.

The Poet Is Audited 1974

ROBERT WALLACE (b. 1932)

The I.R.S. takes a third of what he earns
and to make certain, audits his returns.

Computers punch; pale agents warily
explore the tropes and figures of his Form C:

"Profit (or Loss) from Business or Professions 5
(Sole Proprietorships)" and ask for sessions

critical as his reviews. See him now arrive
at the tall glass-and-aluminum Federal hive,

as he must, sole proprietor of his art,
to lay bare the costs of laying bare his heart; 10

to ride up to the twentieth floor and explain
that to read in Boston he really took a plane

(ticket, cancelled check) or that he tipped a porter
in Chattanooga an unrecorded quarter;

to prove that the books he says he bought, he bought, 15
ink, paper, ribbons, stamps, and as he ought

keeps itemized receipts, and that he spent
the sums he says he did for phoning, rent—

and only used his "office" at home to write,
never letting his dog sleep there at night. 20

Suspiciously they eye the meager income,
the sixty dollar royalty he got from

his latest book, the seven for a sonnet
(he doesn't say he worked a whole month on it,

or hopes that it may last until long after   25
the government's pulled down rafter by rafter).

No fat ten thousands in movie rights for him,
no N.B.A.'s°, nothing from Guggenheim.   *National Book Award*

They're startled how, year by year by year,
he goes along an unprofitable career,   30

mostly showing losses (not counting hair,
or time, or his depreciating flair).

Proved truthful, purified and free, he descends
still faithful to his not-illegal ends

and by the public fountain, in public sun,   35
goes off among the poems still unwritten.

Craft Lost in Texas   1982

PETER KLAPPERT   (b. 1942)

The poet and all
six passengers of
a small poetry reading
were lost late last night
when they went into a dive
outside of Houston.

APPENDIX I

Notes to the Questions
and Suggestions

Chapter 1

1. a) *For a Lady I Know*

COUNTEE CULLEN   (1903–1946)

She even thinks that up in heaven
Her class lies late and snores,
While poor black cherubs rise at seven
To do celestial chores.

b) *Potatoes*

GERALD COSTANZO   (b. 1945)

Grandpa said potatoes
reminded him of school.

Potatoes and school.
He said he'd wake nearly

freezing, kindle a fire
and throw two potatoes

on. Going to school
he carried them to

warm his hands. To
warm his feet he ran.

He said by noontime
those potatoes almost

froze, said he ate a lot
of cold potatoes for lunch.

Chapter 3

1. a) *Epigram: Of Treason*

   Tréasŏn | dŏth névǀĕr prósǀpĕr, whát's | thĕ réasǀŏn?
   Fŏr íf | ĭt prósǀpĕr, nóne | dáre cáll | ĭt tréasǀŏn.

   b) *Death of the Day*

   Mў pícǀtŭres bláckǀĕn ĭn | theĭr frámes
      Ăs níght | cómes ón,
   Ănd yoúthǀfŭl maíds | ănd wrinkǀlĕd dámes
      Ăre nów | áll óne.

   Deáth ŏf | thĕ dáy! | ă stérnǀĕr Deáth
      Dĭd wórse | bĕfóre;
   Thĕ faírǀĕst fórm, | thĕ sweétǀĕst breáth,
      Ăwáy | hĕ bóre.

   c) *Tribute*

   Whát thĕ | beé knóws
   Tástes ĭn | thĕ hónǀĕy
   Sweét | ănd súnǀnў.
   Ŏ wíse | beĕ. Ŏ róse.

   d) *First Sight*

   Lámbs | thăt léarn | tŏ wálk | ĭn snów
   Whén | theĭr bléatǀĭng clóuds | thĕ áir
   Méet | ă vást | ŭnwélǀcŏme, knów

Nóth|ĭng bút | ă sún|lĕss gláre.

Néw|lў stúmb|lĭng tó | ănd fró

Áll | thĕy fínd, | ŏutsíde | thĕ fóld,

Ís | ă wrétch|ĕd wídth | ŏf cóld.

(ˏ)
Ás | thĕy wáit | bĕsíde | thĕ éwe,

Hĕr fléec|ĕs wét|lў cáked, | thĕre líes

Híd|dĕn róund | thĕm, wáit|ĭng tóo,

Éarth's | ĭmméas|ŭrăblĕ⁽ˏ⁾| sŭrpríse.

Thĕy cóuld | nŏt grásp | ĭt íf | thĕy knéw,

Whát | sŏ sóon | wĭll wáke | ănd g[r]ów

Út|tĕrlў⁽ˏ⁾| ŭnlíke | thĕ snów.

e) *The Base Stealer*

Póised bĕ|twĕen gó|ĭng ón | ănd báck, |ˣpúlled,

Bóth wáys | táut lĭke | ă tíght|rópe-wálk|ĕr,

Fíngĕr|típs póint|ĭng thĕ óp|pŏsítes,

Nów bóunc|ĭng típ|tŏe lĭke ă | drópped báll

Ŏr ă kíd skíp|pĭng rópe, | cóme ón, | cóme ón,

Rúnnĭng | ă scát|tĕrĭng⁽ˏ⁾ | ŏf stéps | sídewíse,

Hŏw hĕ téet|ĕrs, skít|tĕrs, tíng|lĕs, téas|ĕs,

(ˏ)
Táunts thĕm, | hóvĕrs | líke ăn | ĕcstát|ĭc bírd,

Hĕ's ón|lў flírt|ĭng, crówd | hĭm, crówd | hĭm,

Délĭcăte, | délĭcăte, | délĭcăte, | délĭcăte|ˣ–nów!

2. Version of the Lewis Thomas passage:

> Afield, a single ant of any kind
> Cannot be said to have much on his mind;
>
> Indeed, it would be hard by rights to call
> His neurons, few, loose-strung, a mind at all,
>
> Or say he had a thought half-way complete.
> He is more like a ganglion with feet.
>
> Circling a moth that's dead, four ants—or ten—
> Will seem more like a real idea then,
>
> Fumbling and shoving, Hill-ward, bit by bit,
> As if by blind chance slowly moving it.

But only when you watch, in crowded dance
Around their Hill, a thousand massing ants

As black and purposeful as scribbling ink,
Do you first see the whole beast, see it think,

Plan, calculate—a live computer's bits
Of dark intelligence, its crawling wits.

Chapter 4

1. Housman tried "sunny," "pleasant," "checkered," "patterned," and "painted" before he hit on the word he finally chose: "colored." Why do you think he preferred "colored" to the other adjectives? Consider the qualities of the scene each suggests.

2. Possible rhymes might include:

circle = *work'll*

stop-sign = *drop mine*

rhinoceros = If ever, outside a zoo,
    You meet a rhinoceros
    And you *cross her, fuss*
    Is exactly what she'll do.
        ANONYMOUS

evergreen = *never seen*

broccoli = Look at the *clock! Oh, me!*

pelican = Ogden Nash used "belly can" and "hell he can."

umbrella = The rain it raineth every day,
    upon the just and unjust *fella,*
    but more upon the just, because
    the unjust hath the just's umbrella.
        ANONYMOUS

4.   *The Fourth of July*

HOWARD NEMEROV (b. 1920)

Because I am drunk, this Independence Night,
I watch the fireworks from far away,
From a high hill, across the moony green
Of lakes and other hills to the town harbor,
Where stately illuminations are flung aloft,   5
One light shattering in a hundred lights
Minute by minute. The reason I am crying,
Aside from only being country drunk,
That is, may be that I have just remembered
The sparklers, rockets, roman candles, and   10

So on, we used to be allowed to buy
When I was a boy, and set off by ourselves
At some peril to life and property.
Our freedom to abuse our freedom thus
Has since, I understand, been remedied   15
By legislation. Now the authorities
Arrange a perfectly safe public display
To be watched at a distance; and now also
The contribution of all the taxpayers
Together makes a more spectacular   20
Result than any could achieve alone
(A few pale pinwheels, or a firecracker
Fused at the dog's tail). It is, indeed, splendid:
Showers of roses in the sky, fountains
Of emeralds, and those profusely scattered zircons   25
Falling and falling, flowering as they fall
And followed distantly by a noise of thunder.
My eyes are half-afloat in happy tears.
God bless our Nation on a night like this,
And bless the careful and secure officials   30
Who celebrate our independence now.

6.   There is a big, old wooden box,
            Without a thing inside.
        It therefore needs, and has, no locks.
            The top is open wide.

        Here is a big, old wooden box
            Which needs, and has, no locks.
        Because it holds nothing inside,
            Its top is opened wide.

        The top is open wide;
            There are no locks.
        For nothing's kept inside
            This wooden box.

Chapter 5

5. "Death of a Soldier" b) is by Wallace Stevens. a) is a homemade imitation.

Chapter 7

3. The speaker in "In 1856 she . . ." is Emily Dickinson.

Chapter 8

2. a) Raspberries *splash*, redly in their leaves
   b) Four cars like *a kite's tail* / behind the hearse
   c) droning, *unzipping* the halves of the air
   d) will shower its peaceful *rockets* / all over the towns
   e) The clarinet, a dark tube / *tallowed* in silver
   f) Big as *wedding cakes*, / two white launches
   g) whirled by a boat's wash / into *Queen Anne's lace*
   h) Dreams are the soul's *home movies*

Chapter 10

4. The original words in "In a Spring Still Not Written Of" are: "burning up" in line 4, "carrying" in line 8, "blossom" in line 12, "astronomies" in line 14, and "untarnished" in line 16.

Chapter 11

2. *Swimmer*

ROBERT FRANCIS (b. 1901)

I

Observe how he negotiates his way
With trust and the least violence, making
The stranger friend, the enemy ally.
The depth that could destroy gently supports him.
With water he defends himself from water.
Danger he leans on, rests in. The drowning sea
Is all he has between himself and drowning.

II

What lover ever lay more mutually
With his beloved, his always-reaching arms
Stroking in smooth and powerful caresses?
Some drown in love as in dark water, and some
By love are strongly held as the green sea
Now holds the swimmer. Indolently he turns
To float.—The swimmer floats, the lover sleeps.

4. a) *The Opening*

DANIEL TOWNER (b. 1952)

Down its length the rifle barrel
is generosity: the smoothness

of steel, the long spiral

down the hole. Try to imagine the gun
without love—impossible.   5
Every report is a sad speech.

I say to you there can be no beauty
greater than that of the cool flower-stem
opening softly, each day, against the forehead.

b) *The Passionate Shepherd to His Love*

CHRISTOPHER MARLOWE (1564–1593)

Come live with me and be my love,
And we will all the pleasures prove
That valleys, groves, hills, and fields,
Woods, or steepy mountain yields.

And we will sit upon the rocks,   5
Seeing the shepherds feed their flocks
By shallow rivers, to whose falls
Melodious birds sing madrigals.

And I will make thee beds of roses
And a thousand fragrant posies,   10
A cap of flowers and a kirtle°   *skirt*
Embroidered all with leaves of myrtle;

A gown made of the finest wool
Which from our pretty lambs we pull;
Fair lined slippers for the cold,   15
With buckles of the purest gold;

A belt of straw and ivy buds,
With coral clasps and amber studs.
And if these pleasures may thee move,
Come live with me and be my love.   20

The shepherd swains° shall dance and sing   *lads*
For thy delight each May morning.
If these delights thy mind may move,
Then live with me and be my love.

c) *The Lark and the Emperor*

W. M. ABERG (b. 1957)

Strangle the Lark.
Place its pink tongue under glass.
Weave the feathers into a coat.
The Hungarians
will build violins from the bones.   5

Pour cinnamon and honey
into the electric fountain.
When you hear the lock turn,
pull the switch.
It will be the Emperor.   10

d) *For One Moment*

DAVID IGNATOW   (b. 1914)

You take the dollar
and hand it to the fellow beside you
who turns and gives it to the next one
down the line. The world being round,
you stand waiting, smoking and lifting   5
a cup of coffee to your lips, talking
of seasonal weather and hinting
at problems. The dollar returns,
the coffee spills to the ground
in your hurry. You have the money   10
in one hand, a cup in the other,
a cigarette in your mouth,
and for one moment have forgotten
what it is you have to do,
your hair grey, your legs weakened   15
from long standing.

e) *Autumn Begins in Martins Ferry, Ohio*

JAMES WRIGHT   (1927–1980)

In the Shreve High football stadium,
I think of Polacks nursing long beers in Tiltonsville,
And gray faces of Negroes in the blast furnace at Benwood,
And the ruptured night watchman of Wheeling Steel,
Dreaming of heroes.   5

All the proud fathers are ashamed to go home.
Their women cluck like starved pullets,
Dying for love.

Therefore,
Their sons grow suicidally beautiful   10
At the beginning of October,
And gallop terribly against each other's bodies.

Chapter 13

2.   *In One Place*

ROBERT WALLACE   (b. 1932)

      —something
holds up two or three leaves
the first year,

           and climbs
and branches, summer
by summer,

      till birds
in it don't remember
it wasn't there.

Chapter 15

1. All five poems have been published.

APPENDIX II

Select Bibliography

A. For Reference.

In addition to a good dictionary:

Norman Lewis, ed., *Roget's New Pocket Thesaurus in Dictionary Form*, rev. ed., Berkley, 1977.

Alex Preminger, ed., *Princeton Encyclopedia of Poetry and Poetics*, Princeton University Press, 1965.

William Strunk, Jr., and E. B. White, *The Elements of Style*, 3rd ed., Macmillan, 1979.

Lewis Turco, *The Book of Forms*, E. P. Dutton, 1968.

Clement Wood, *The Complete Rhyming Dictionary*, rev. ed., Doubleday, 1936.

B. Anthologies.

Donald M. Allen, ed., *The New American Poetry*, Grove Press, 1960.

William S. Baring-Gould, ed., *The Lure of the Limerick*, Crown, 1967.

Willis Barnstone, ed., *Modern European Poets*, Bantam, 1966.

Michael Benedikt, ed., *The Poetry of Surrealism*, Little, Brown, 1974.

Stephen Berg and Robert Mezey, eds., *The New Naked Poetry*, Bobbs-Merrill, 1976.

Hayden Carruth, ed., *The Voice That Is Great Within Us*, Bantam, 1970.

Richard Ellmann and Robert O'Clair, eds., *The Norton Anthology of Modern Poetry*, Norton, 1973.

Paul Engle and Joseph Langland, eds., *Poet's Choice*, Dial, 1962.

Edward Field, ed., *A Geography of Poets*, Bantam, 1979.

Donald Hall, Robert Pack, and Louis Simpson, eds., *New Poets of England and America*, Meridian, 1957.

Donald Hall and Robert Pack, eds., *New Poets of England and America*, Second Selection, 1962.

Daniel Halpern, ed., *The American Poetry Anthology*, Avon, 1975.

William Heyen, ed., *American Poets in 1976*, Bobbs-Merrill, 1976.

Donald Junkins, ed., *The Contemporary World Poets*, Harcourt, Brace Jovanovich, 1976.

Richard Kostelanetz, ed., *Possibilities of Poetry*, Dell, 1970.

Philip Larkin, ed., *The Oxford Book of Twentieth Century English Verse*, Oxford University Press, 1973.

Ron Padgett and David Shapiro, eds., *An Anthology of New York Poets*, Random House, 1970.

Robert Payne, ed., *The White Pony: An Anthology of Chinese Poetry*, John Day, 1947.

A. Poulin, Jr., ed., *Contemporary American Poetry*, 2nd ed., Houghton Mifflin, 1975.

Dudley Randall, ed., *The Black Poets*, Bantam, 1971.

Mark Strand, ed., *The Contemporary American Poets*, World, 1969.

Miller Williams, ed., *Contemporary Poetry in America*, Random House, 1973.

Oscar Williams, ed., *A Little Treasury of Modern Poetry*, 3rd ed., Scribner's, 1970.

Oscar Williams, ed., *The Silver Treasury of Light Verse*, New American Library, 1957.

C. On Poetry, Writing Poetry, and Poets.

Donald M. Allen and Warren Tallman, eds., *The Poetics of the New American Poetry*, Grove Press, 1973.

W. H. Auden, *The Dyer's Hand and Other Essays*, Random House, 1962.

Elaine Berry, *Robert Frost on Writing*, Rutgers University Press, 1973.

Robert Bly, *Talking All Morning*, University of Michigan Press, 1980.

Robert Boyers, ed., *Contemporary Poetry in America*, Schocken Books, 1974.

Paul Carroll, *The Poem in Its Skin*, Big Table, 1968.

Malcolm Cowley, ed., *Writers at Work* (Second Series), Viking, 1963.

Robert Francis, *Pot Shots at Poetry*, University of Michigan Press, 1980.

Robert Francis, *The Satirical Rogue on Poetry*, University of Massachusetts Press, 1968.

Stuart Friebert and David Young, eds., *A Field Guide to Contemporary Poetry and Poetics*, Longman, 1980.

Paul Fussell, *Poetic Meter and Poetic Form*, rev. ed., Random House, 1979.

George Garrett, ed., *The Writer's Voice*, Morrow, 1973.

Walker Gibson, ed., *Poems in the Making*, Houghton Mifflin, 1963.

Harvey Gross, ed., *The Structure of Verse*, new edition, Ecco, 1979.

Donald Hall, *Goatfoot Milktongue Twinbird*, University of Michigan Press, 1978.

John Hollander, *Rhyme's Reason: A Guide to English Verse*, Yale University Press, 1981.

John Hollander, *Vision and Resonance: Two Senses of Poetic Form*, Oxford University Press, 1975.

Humphrey House, ed., *Notebooks and Papers of Gerard Manley Hopkins*, Oxford University Press, 1937.

David Ignatow, *Open Between Us*, University of Michigan Press, 1980.

Randall Jarrell, *Poetry and the Age*, Knopf, 1953.

Randall Jarrell, *The Third Book of Criticism*, Farrar, Straus & Gir   9.

Galway Kinnell, *Walking Down the Stairs*, University of Michigar   978.

Maxine Kumin, *To Make a Prairie*, University of Michigan Press,

Howard Nemerov, *Figures of Thought*, Godine, 1978.

Howard Nemerov, ed., *Poets on Poetry*, Basic Books, 1966.

Charles Norman, ed., *Poets on Poetry*, Free Press, 1962.

Anthony Ostroff, ed., *The Contemporary Poet as Artist and Crit*   Brown, 1964.

George Plimpton, ed., *Writers at Work* (Third Series), Viking,

George Plimpton, ed., *Writers at Work* (Fourth Series), Viking,   .6.

Ezra Pound, *ABC of Reading*, New Directions, 1934.

Rainer Maria Rilke, *Letters to a Young Poet*, trans. M. D. Herter Norton, Norton, 1934.

James Scully, ed., *Modern Poetics*, McGraw-Hill, 1965.

Karl Shapiro, *In Defense of Ignorance*, Random House, 1960.

Louis Simpson, *A Revolution in Taste*, Macmillan, 1978.

W. D. Snodgrass, *In Radical Pursuit*, Harper & Row, 1974.

William Stafford, *Writing the Australian Crawl*, University of Michigan Press, 1978.

Alberta T. Turner, ed., *50 Contemporary Poets: The Creative Process*, Longman, 1977.

Alberta T. Turner, ed., *Poets Teaching*, Longman, 1980.

David Wagoner, ed., *Straw for the Fire: From the Notebooks of Theodore Roethke*, Doubleday, 1972.

Barry Wallenstein, *Visions and Revisions*, Crowell, 1971.

INDEX OF AUTHORS AND TITLES

(continued from page iv)

John Ciardi, "Thematic," © 1977 by John Ciardi, and "Counting on Flowers," © 1962 by John Ciardi. Reprinted by permission.

Gerald Costanzo. Reprinted from In the Aviary by Gerald Costanzo by permission of the University of Missouri Press and the author. Copyright 1974 by Gerald Costanzo.

Robert Creeley. "I Know a Man" from For Love: Poems 1950–1960. Copyright © 1962 by Robert Creeley. (New York: Charles Scribner's Sons, 1962). Reprinted with permission of Charles Scribner's Sons.

Countee Cullen. "For a Lady I Know" from On These I Stand by Countee Cullen. Copyright 1925 by Harper & Row, Publishers, Inc.; renewed 1953 by Ida M. Cullen. Reprinted by permission of Harper & Row, Publishers, Inc.

E. E. Cummings. "Me up at does," © 1963 by Marion Morehouse Cummings, and "l(a," © 1958 by E. E. Cummings. Reprinted from his volume Complete Poems 1913–1962 by permission of Harcourt Brace Jovanovich, Inc. "In Just-" and "O sweet spontaneous" are reprinted from Tulips and Chimneys by E. E. Cummings with the permission of Liveright Publishing Corporation. Copyright 1923, 1925 and renewed 1951, 1953 by E. E. Cummings. Copyright © 1973, 1976 by Nancy T. Andrews. Copyright © 1973, 1976 by George Firmage. "next to of course god america i" reprinted from Is 5 poems by E. E. Cummings with the permission of Liveright Publishing Corporation. Copyright 1926 by Horace Liveright. Copyright renewed 1953 by E. E. Cummings.

J. V. Cunningham. "For My Contemporaries" from The Exclusions of a Rhyme, © 1960 by J. V. Cunningham (The Swallow Press). Reprinted with the permission of The Ohio University Press, Athens.

James Dickey. "Cherrylog Road," copyright © 1963 by James Dickey. Reprinted from Helmets by permission of Wesleyan University Press. First appeared in The New Yorker.

Emily Dickinson. #465 ("I heard a fly buzz when I died"), #747 ("It dropped so low in my regard"), and #1463 ("A route of evanescence") reprinted by permission of the publishers and the Trustees of Amherst College from The Poems of Emily Dickinson, edited by Thomas H. Johnson. Cambridge, Mass.: The Belknap Press of Harvard University Press, Copyright 1951, © 1955, 1979 by the President and Fellows of Harvard College. #747 is the version from The Complete Poems of Emily Dickinson, edited by Thomas H. Johnson. Copyright © 1960 by Mary L. Hampson. Reprinted by permission of Little, Brown and Company.

Reinhard Döhl. Reprinted by permission of the author.

Stephen Dunn. "Outfielder," © 1979 by Stephen Dunn. Reprinted by permission.

Russell Edson. "Oh, My God, I'll Never Get Home," copyright 1961 by Russell Edson. Reprinted from The Clam Theatre by permission of Wesleyan University Press.

T. S. Eliot. Lines from "The Waste Land" from Collected Poems 1909–1962 by T. S. Eliot. Reprinted by permission of Harcourt Brace Jovanovich, Inc., and Faber and Faber Limited.

John Fandel. "Tribute," © 1979 by John Fandel. Reprinted by permission.

David A. Fantauzzi. "Moorings" and draft of same, © 1977 by David A. Fantauzzi. Reprinted by permission.

Edward Field. "Curse of the Cat Woman" and lines from "Graffiti" from Variety Photoplays. Reprinted by permission of the author. Copyright © 1967 by Edward Field. "Notes from a Slave Ship" from Stand Up, Friend, with Me. Reprinted by permission of Grove Press, Inc. Copyright © 1963 by Edward Field.

Michael Finley. "Frankenstein in the Cemetery," © 1977 by Michael Finley. Reprinted by permission.

Robert Francis. "Professional Poet," "The Indecipherable Poem," "Weighed in Balance," and lines from "Defense of Poetry" and "Slender" reprinted by permission from The Satirical Rogue on Poetry by Robert Francis (University of Massachusetts Press, 1965), copyright © 1965 by Robert Francis. "Excellence," copyright 1941, © 1972, "Glass," copyright 1949, and "Aphrodite as History," © 1965, all by Robert Francis, reprinted by permission from Robert Francis: Collected Poems, 1936–1976 (University of Massachusetts Press, 1976), copyright © 1976 by Robert Francis. "Swimmer," copyright 1953 by Robert Francis; "Pitcher," copyright 1953 by Robert Francis; "The Base Stealer," copyright 1948 by Robert Francis; and "Hallelujah: A Sestina," copyright © 1960 by Robert Francis. Reprinted from The Orb Weaver by permission of Wesleyan University Press.

Jeanne Frank. "Miner," © 1977 by Jeanne Frank. Reprinted by permission.

Jill Freshley. "Woman's Work," © 1981 by Jill Freshley. Reprinted by permission.

Robert Frost. "Dust of Snow," "An Old Man's Winter Night," "The Silken Tent," "Provide, Provide," "Stopping by Woods on a Snowy Evening," "Acquainted with the Night," "Home Burial," "The Road Not Taken," and "Design" from The Poetry of Robert Frost edited by Edward Connery Lathem. Copyright 1916, 1923, 1928, 1930, 1939, © 1969 by Holt, Rinehart and Winston. Copyright 1936, 1942, 1944, 1951, © 1956, 1958 by Robert Frost. Copyright © 1964, 1967, 1970 by Lesley Frost Ballantine. Reprinted by permission of Holt, Rinehart and Winston, Publishers. "In White" and text excerpt from The Dimensions of Robert Frost by Reginald L. Cook. Copyright © 1958 by Reginald L. Cook. Reprinted by permission of Holt, Rinehart and Winston, Publishers.

Brendan Galvin. "The Bats" reprinted from No Time for Good Reasons by Brendan Galvin by permission of the University of Pittsburgh Press. © 1974 by Brendan Galvin.

Brad German. "Working Men," © 1982 by Brad German. Used by permission.

Gary Gildner. "The Girl in the Red Convertible" reprinted from Digging for Indians by Gary Gildner by permission of the University of Pittsburgh Press. © 1971 by Gary Gildner.

Allen Ginsberg. "A Supermarket in California" and "America" from Howl & Other Poems by Allen Ginsberg. Copyright © 1956, 1959 by Allen Ginsberg. Reprinted by permission of City Lights Books.

Elton Glaser. "Brief Song," © 1975 by Elton Glaser. Reprinted by permission.

Louise Glück. "The Racer's Widow," © 1968 by Louise Glück. Reprinted by permission.

Albert Goldbarth. "I Learn I'm 96% Water," © 1976 by Albert Goldbarth, and "In 1856 she . . . ," © 1980 by Albert Goldbarth. Reprinted by permission.

John Haines. "The Tree That Became a House," copyright © 1974 by John Haines. Reprinted from Cicada by permission of Wesleyan University Press.

Donald Hall. "The Town of Hill" from The Town of Hill by Donald Hall. Copyright © 1971 by David R. Godine. Reprinted by permission of David R. Godine, Publisher, Inc.

Robert Hayden. "Those Winter Sundays" is reprinted from Angle of Ascent by Robert Hayden with the permission of Liveright Publishing Corporation. Copyright © 1975, 1972, 1970, 1966 by Robert Hayden.

Anthony Hecht. "The Dover Bitch" from Anthony Hecht, The Hard Hours. Copyright © 1967 by Anthony Hecht (New York: Atheneum, 1967). Reprinted with the permission of Atheneum Publishers.

Sheila Heinrich. "disappearances," © 1975 by Sheila Heinrich. Reprinted by permission.

Ernest Hemingway. Vignette from Ernest Hemingway, In Our Time. Copyright 1925, 1930 by Ernest Hemingway; copyright renewed 1953, 1958 by Ernest Hemingway. Reprinted with the permission of Charles Scribner's Sons. October 20, 1922 Toronto Star dispatch from Ernest Hemingway, By-Line: Ernest Hemingway, Selected Articles and Dispatches of Four Decades, edited by William White. Copyright © 1967 by By-Line Ernest Hemingway, Inc. (New York: Charles Scribner's Sons, 1967). Reprinted with the permission of Charles Scribner's Sons.

Conrad Hilberry. "Storm Window," "Fat," © 1980 by Conrad Hilberry. Reprinted by permission.

John Hollander. "Eskimo Pie" from John Hollander, Types of Shape. Copyright © 1969 by John Hollander (New York: Atheneum, 1969). Reprinted with the permission of Atheneum Publishers.

Gerard Manley Hopkins. "Hurrahing in August" and "Pied Beauty" from Poems of Gerard Manley Hopkins (New York: Oxford University Press, 1948).

A. E. Housman. "Bredon Hill," "Loveliest of trees, the cherry now," and "I hoed and trenched and weeded" from "A Shropshire Lad"—Authorised Edition—from The Collected Poems of A. E. Housman. Copyright 1939, 1940, © 1965 by Holt, Rinehart and Winston. Copyright © 1967, 1968 by Robert E. Symons. "In the morning, in the morning" from The Collected Poems of A. E. Housman. Copyright 1922 by Holt, Rinehart and Winston. Copyright 1950 by Barclays Bank Ltd. Reprinted by permission of Holt, Rinehart and Winston, Publishers, and The Society of Authors as the literary representatives of the Estate of A. E. Housman and Jonathan Cape Ltd., publishers of A. E. Housman's Collected Poems.

Ted Hughes. "To Paint a Water Lily" from *Lupercal* by Ted Hughes. Copyright © 1959 by Ted Hughes. Reprinted by permission of Harper & Row, Publishers, Inc., and Faber and Faber Limited.

David Ignatow. "For One Moment," copyright © 1962 by David Ignatow. Reprinted from *Figures of the Human* by permission of Wesleyan University Press.

Mark Irwin. "Icicles," © 1978 by Mark Irwin. Reprinted by permission. "The Invention of the Snowman," *Shenandoah*, Vol. 30, No. 4, 1979. Copyright 1980 by Washington and Lee University; reprinted from *Shenandoah: The Washington and Lee University Review* with the permission of the Editor.

Bonnie Jacobson. "Pandora's Dressing Table," © 1977 by Bonnie Jacobson, and "On Being Served Apples," © 1980 by Bonnie Jacobson. Reprinted by permission.

Robinson Jeffers. "To the Stone-Cutters." Copyright 1924 and renewed 1952 by Robinson Jeffers. Reprinted from *Selected Poems*, by Robinson Jeffers, by permission of Random House, Inc.

Donald Justice. "In Bertram's Garden," copyright 1954 by Donald Justice, and "The Snowfall," copyright © 1959 by Donald Justice. Reprinted from *The Summer Anniversaries* by permission of Wesleyan University Press.

X. J. Kennedy. "First Confession," "In a Prominent Bar in Secaucus One Day," "Little Elegy," and "Ars Poetica" from *Nude Descending a Staircase* by X. J. Kennedy. Reprinted by permission of Curtis Brown, Ltd. Copyright © 1956, 1958, 1959, 1960, 1961 by X. J. Kennedy. "Poets" from *Growing into Love* by X. J. Kennedy. Reprinted by permission of Curtis Brown, Ltd. Copyright © 1964, 1967, 1968, 1969 by X. J. Kennedy.

Katherine Kinsey. "Forgive and Forget," © 1981 by Katherine Kinsey. Reprinted by permission.

Peter Klappert. "Lost Craft in Texas" from *Tuppenny Uprights*, © 1981 by Peter Klappert. Reprinted by permission. "The Trapper" from *Circular Stairs, Distress in the Mirrors* (The Griffin Press), © 1975 by Peter Klappert. Reprinted by permission. "The Invention of the Telephone" from *Lugging Vegetables to Nantucket*, copyright © 1971 by Yale University. Reprinted by permission of Yale University Press.

Kenneth Koch. "You Were Wearing" from *Thank You and Other Poems* (Grove Press, 1962). Reprinted by permission.

Ted Kooser. "Selecting a Reader" and "Abandoned Farmhouse" reprinted from *Sure Signs* by Ted Kooser by permission of the University of Pittsburgh Press. © 1980 by Ted Kooser. "Looking for You, Barbara," © 1976 by Ted Kooser. Reprinted by permission of the author and The Best Cellar Press.

Margaret Lally. "Portrait: Woman in a Grey House," © 1975 by Margaret Lally. Used by permission of the author.

Philip Larkin. "First Sight" and "Talking in Bed" from *The Whitsun Weddings*, © 1964 by Philip Larkin. Reprinted by Faber and Faber Limited.

Richmond Lattimore. "It," "Waiting for the Barbarians," "Apologies to Creston," "A Siding Near Chillicothe," "Catania to Rome," and "Hiroshima" reprinted from *Poems from Three Decades* by Richmond Lattimore by permission of The University of Chicago Press. Copyright © 1972 by Richmond Lattimore.

D. H. Lawrence. "Piano," "The Piano," and lines from "The Bat" from *The Complete Poems of D. H. Lawrence*. Copyright © 1964 by Angelo Ravagli and C. M. Weekley, Executors of the Estate of Frieda Lawrence Ravagli.

Philip Levine. "Animals are Passing from Our Lives," copyright © 1968 by Philip Levine. Reprinted from *Not This Pig* by permission of Wesleyan University Press.

Ronald R. Louie. "A man I met in Cincinnati . . ." Copyright © 1975 by Ronald R. Louie. Reprinted by permission.

Timothy Lucas. "Belfast Ballad," © 1981 by Timothy Lucas. Reprinted by permission.

Curt Manley. "The Butterfly Collective," © 1981 by Curtis R. Manley. Reprinted by permission.

Peter Meinke. "Teaching Poetry at a Country School in Florida." Originally appeared in *The New Republic*, May 10, 1975. Reprinted by permission of the author.

W. S. Merwin. "Elegy," "Shoe Repairs," and "Memory of Spring" from W. S. Merwin, *The Carrier of Ladders*. Copyright © 1970 by W. S. Merwin (New York: Atheneum, 1970). "For the Anniversary of My Death" from W. S. Merwin, *The Lice*. Copyright © 1967 by W. S. Merwin (New York: Atheneum, 1967.) Reprinted with the permission of Atheneum Publishers.

Marianne Moore. "To a Steam Roller," "The Fish," "Critics and Connoisseurs," and "Poetry" reprinted with permission of Macmillan Publishing Co., Inc. from *Collected Poems* by Marianne Moore. Copyright 1953 by Marianne Moore, renewed 1963 by Marianne Moore and T. S. Eliot. "Nevertheless" reprinted with permission of Macmillan Publishing Co., Inc. from *Collected Poems* by Marianne Moore. Copyright 1944 by Marianne Moore, renewed 1972 by Marianne Moore. "Poetry" (1967 version) from *The Complete Poems of Marianne Moore*. Copyright © 1967 by Marianne Moore. Reprinted by permission of Viking Penguin Inc. "Poetry" (1924 version) reprinted by permission from *Observations* (Dial Press), p. 31, as quoted in George W. Nitchie, *Marianne Moore* (Columbia University Press, 1969), pp. 36–37.

Joseph S. Napora. "Sore Eros," © 1979 by Joseph S. Napora. Reprinted by permission.

Ogden Nash. "The Cobra" from *Verses from 1929 On* by Ogden Nash. Copyright 1931 by Ogden Nash. By permission of Little, Brown and Company.

Warren Nelson. "Loan," © 1978 by Warren Nelson. Reprinted by permission.

Howard Nemerov. "Power to the People," "Learning by Doing," "Make Big Money at Home! Write Poems in Spare Time!" "The Fourth of July," and "Lion & Honeycomb." © 1958, 1962, 1967, 1973 by Howard Nemerov. Reprinted by permission.

Frank O'Hara. "Why I Am Not a Painter." Copyright © 1960 by Maureen Granville-Smith, Administratrix of the Estate of Frank O'Hara. Reprinted from *The Collected Poems of Frank O'Hara*, by Frank O'Hara, edited by Donald Allen, by permission of Alfred A. Knopf, Inc. "Poem" ("The eager note on my door . . .") from *Meditations in an Emergency*. Reprinted by permission of Grove Press, Inc. Copyright © 1957 by Frank O'Hara.

Mary Oliver. "Strawberry Moon" and "The Black Snake" from *Twelve Moons: Poems by Mary Oliver*. Copyright © 1979 by Mary Oliver. By permission of Little, Brown and Company in association with the Atlantic Monthly Press. "Music at Night" from *The Night Traveler* (Bits Press, 1978); Copyright © 1978 by Mary Oliver. Reprinted by permission.

Wilfred Owen. "Arms and the Boy" from *Collected Poems* of Wilfred Owen. Copyright © Chatto & Windus Ltd., 1946, 1963. Reprinted by permission of New Directions.

Kenneth Patchen. "The Murder of Two Young Men by a Kid Wearing Lemon-colored Gloves" from *Collected Poems* of Kenneth Patchen. Copyright 1945 by Kenneth Patchen. Reprinted by permission of New Directions.

Roger Pfingston. "The Perfect Suicide," © 1977 by Roger Pfingston. Reprinted by permission.

Marge Piercy. "Sentimental Poem," © 1978 by Marge Piercy. Reprinted by permission.

Ezra Pound. "In a Station of the Metro," "The Garden," "Homage to Sextus Propertius" (Section I), "The Three Poets," "The Bath Tub," and lines from "The Return" from Ezra Pound, *Personae*. Copyright 1926 by Ezra Pound. Lines from Canto II from *The Cantos* of Ezra Pound. Copyright 1934 by Ezra Pound. Reprinted by permission of New Directions.

Suzanne Raschke. "Move into the Wheat," © 1981 by Suzanne Raschke. Reprinted by permission.

J. D. Reed. "The Weather Is Brought to You" from J. D. Reed, *Expressways*. Copyright © 1969 by J. D. Reed. Reprinted by permission of Simon & Schuster, a Division of Gulf & Western Corporation.

Edwin Arlington Robinson. "Richard Cory" from Edwin Arlington Robinson, *The Children of the Night*. Copyright under the Berne Convention. (New York: Charles Scribner's Sons, 1897). Reprinted with the permission of Charles Scribner's Sons.

Theodore Roethke. "My Papa's Waltz" (Copyright 1942 by Hearst Magazine, Inc.) and "I Knew a Woman" (Copyright 1954 by Theodore Roethke) from *The Collected Poems of Theodore Roethke*. Reprinted by permission of Doubleday & Company, Inc.

Jan M. W. Rose. "Spider," © 1977 by Jan M. W. Rose. Reprinted by permission.

Vern Rutsala. "The Mill Back Home," © 1978 by Vern Rutsala. Reprinted from *Walking Home from the Icehouse*, Carnegie-Mellon University Press, 1981, by permission of the author.

David St. John. "Iris" from *Hush* by David St. John. Copyright © 1976 by David St. John. Reprinted by permission of Houghton Mifflin Company.

Rucky Seligman. "Planting," © 1975 by Ruth Seligman. Reprinted by permission.

Karl Shapiro. "Auto Wreck." Copyright 1942 and renewed 1970 by Karl Shapiro. Reprinted from *Collected Poems 1940–1978*, by Karl Shapiro, by permission of Random House, Inc.

Richard Shelton. "Encounter" reprinted from *The Bus to Veracruz* by Richard Shelton by permission of the University of Pittsburgh Press. © 1978 by Richard Shelton.

Charles Simic. "The Prisoner," reprinted from *Charon's Cosmology* by Charles Simic by permission of the publisher, George Braziller, Inc. Copyright, Charles Simic, 1977. "Stone," reprinted from *Dismantling the Silence* by Charles Simic by permission of the publisher, George Braziller, Inc. Copyright, Charles Simic, 1971. "Watermelons," reprinted from *Return to a Place Lit by a Glass of Milk* by Charles Simic by permission of the publisher, George Braziller, Inc. Copyright, Charles Simic, 1974.

Louis Simpson. "On the Lawn at the Villa," "American Poetry," and "My Father in the Night Commanding No." Copyright © 1963 by Louis Simpson. Reprinted from *At the End of the Open Road* by permission of Wesleyan University Press. "My Father in the Night Commanding No" first appeared in *The New Yorker.*

Frances T. Slack. "I think the needle is stuck," © 1982 by Frances T. Slack. Used by permission.

Barry Spacks. "In the Fields," © 1978 by Barry Spacks. Reprinted by permission.

Elizabeth Spires. "At the Bambi Motel," © 1979 by Elizabeth Spires. First appeared in *Poetry.*

William Stafford. "Traveling Through the Dark" from *Stories That Could Be True* by William Stafford. Copyright © 1960 by William Stafford. Reprinted by permission of Harper & Row, Publishers, Inc. "Ask Me" by William Stafford from *50 Contemporary Poets,* edited by Alberta T. Turner. Copyright © 1977 by Longman Inc. Reprinted by permission of Longman Inc., New York.

George Starbuck. "Lamb" from "Translations from the English" from *White Paper: Poems* by George Starbuck. Copyright © 1965 by George Starbuck. First appeared in the *Atlantic.* By permission of Little, Brown and Company in association with the Atlantic Monthly Press.

Paul Curry Steele. "Clerihew," © 1976 by Paul Curry Steele. Reprinted from *Anse on Island Creek and Other Poems* by permission of Mountain State Press and of the author.

Wallace Stevens. "The Idea of Order at Key West" (Copyright 1936 by Wallace Stevens and renewed 1964 by Holly Stevens), "A Rabbit as King of the Ghosts" (Copyright 1942 by Wallace Stevens and renewed 1970 by Holly Stevens), "The Poem That Took the Place of a Mountain" and "The Plain Sense of Things" (Copyright 1952 by Wallace Stevens), and "Death of a Soldier" (Copyright 1923 and renewed 1951 by Wallace Stevens). Reprinted from *The Collected Poems of Wallace Stevens,* by Wallace Stevens, by permission of Alfred A. Knopf, Inc. Excerpt from "Two or Three Ideas" from *Opus Posthumous* by Wallace Stevens, edited by Samuel French Morse. Copyright © 1957 by Elsie Stevens and Holly Stevens. Reprinted by permission of Alfred A. Knopf, Inc.

Mark Strand. "Eating Poetry" and "Keeping Things Whole" from Mark Strand, *Reasons for Moving.* Copyright © 1968 by Mark Strand (New York: Atheneum, 1968). Reprinted with the permission of Atheneum Publishers.

John Stupp. "The Divers," © 1975 by John C. Stupp. Reprinted by permission.

May Swenson. "The Universe" from *New & Selected Things Taking Place* by May Swenson. Copyright © 1963 by May Swenson. First appeared in the *Hudson Review.* By permission of Little, Brown and Company in association with the Atlantic Monthly Press.

Dylan Thomas. "Do not go gentle into that good night," "Fern Hill," and "Twenty-four Years" from *The Poems* of Dylan Thomas. Copyright 1939, 1946 by New Directions; Copyright 1945 by the Trustees for the Copyrights of Dylan Thomas; Copyright 1952 by Dylan Thomas. Reprinted by permission of New Directions, J. M. Dent & Sons Ltd., and the Trustees for the Copyrights of the late Dylan Thomas.

Lewis Thomas. An excerpt from "On Societies as Organisms" in *The Lives of a Cell* by Lewis Thomas. Copyright © 1971 by Massachusetts Medical Society. Originally appeared in *The New England Journal of Medicine.* Reprinted by permission of Viking Penguin Inc.

Eric Torgersen. "Wearing Mittens," © 1976 by Eric Torgersen. Reprinted by permission.

Daniel Towner. "The Opening," © 1980 by Daniel Towner. Reprinted by permission.

John Updike. "Dog's Death," from *Midpoint and Other Poems,* by John Updike. Copyright © 1969 by John Updike. Reprinted by permission of Alfred A. Knopf, Inc. "Player Piano," © 1958 by John Updike. Reprinted by permission.

Joseph T. Urban, Jr. "Cherries Jubilee," © 1982 by Joseph T. Urban, Jr. Used by permission.

David Wagoner. "Walking in Snow" from *Collected Poems 1956–1976* by David Wagoner. Copyright 1976 by Indiana University Press. Reprinted by permission.

Robert Wallace. "The Double Play," "A Problem in History," and "In a Spring Still Not Written Of" from *Views from a Ferris Wheel.* Copyright 1965 by Robert Wallace. "Ungainly Things," "In the Field Forever," and "Ballad of the Mouse" from *Ungainly Things.* Copyright 1968 by Robert Wallace. "In One Place," "Swimmer in the Rain," "Myth, Commerce, and Coffee on United Flight #622 from Cleveland to Norfolk," "The Girl Writing Her English Paper," and "The Poet is Audited" from *Swimmer in the Rain.* Copyright 1979 by Robert Wallace. Used by permission of Carnegie-Mellon University Press.

Richard Wilbur. "Junk," © 1961 by Richard Wilbur. Reprinted from his volume *Advice to a Prophet and Other Poems* by permission of Harcourt Brace Jovanovich, Inc. "Juggler" and "Year's End," copyright 1949, 1977 by Richard Wilbur. Reprinted from his volume *Ceremony and Other Poems* by Harcourt Brace Jovanovich, Inc. First published in *The New Yorker.* "Praise in Summer," from *The Beautiful Changes,* copyright 1947, 1975 by Richard Wilbur. Reprinted by permission of Harcourt Brace Jovanovich, Inc. "Love Calls Us to the Things of This World" from *Things of This World,* © 1956 by Richard Wilbur. Reprinted by permission of Harcourt Brace Jovanovich, Inc. Six drafts of the opening lines of "Love Calls Us to the Things of This World," © 1964 by Richard Wilbur. Reprinted by permission.

Peter Wild. "Natural Gas," © 1978 by Peter Wild. Reprinted from *The Lost Tribe,* Wolfsong Press, 1979, by permission of the author.

William Carlos Williams. "The Nightingales," "To Waken an Old Lady," "Poem" (cat), "The Red Wheelbarrow," and "Great Mullen" from *Collected Earlier Poems of William Carlos Williams.* Copyright 1938 by New Directions Publishing Corporation. Reprinted by permission of New Directions. "Poem" ("The rose fades") and lines from "Asphodel, That Greeny Flower" from William Carlos Williams, *Pictures from Breughel and Other Poems,* Copyright 1954, © 1955, 1962 by William Carlos Williams. Reprinted by permission of New Directions. Excerpt from *Kora in Hell: Improvisations,* pp. 50–51, by William Carlos Williams. Copyright © 1957 by William Carlos Williams. Reprinted by permission of City Lights Books. Excerpt from an unpublished letter to Robert Wallace. Copyright © 1960 by William E. and Paul H. Williams. Used by permission of New Directions, Agents.

Charles Wright. "Spider Crystal Ascension." Copyright © 1977 by Charles Wright. Reprinted from *China Trace* by permission of Wesleyan University Press.

James Wright. "Before a Cashier's Window in a Department Store," © 1965 by James Wright. "Autumn Begins in Martins Ferry, Ohio," © 1962 by James Wright. "I Try to Waken and Greet the World Once Again" and "A Blessing," © 1961 by James Wright. "In Memory of the Horse, David, Who Ate One of My Poems," © 1971 by James Wright. Reprinted from *Collected Poems* by permission of Wesleyan University Press. "Before a Cashier's Window in a Department Store" appeared first in *The New Yorker.* "A Blessing" first appeared in *Poetry.*

William Butler Yeats. "After Long Silence" (Copyright 1933 by Macmillan Publishing Co., Inc., renewed 1961 by Bertha Georgie Yeats), "Lapis Lazuli" (Copyright 1940 by Georgie Yeats, renewed 1968 by Bertha Georgie Yeats, Michael Butler Yeats and Anne Yeats), "Adam's Curse," and "The Sorrow of Love" (1906 version) reprinted with permission of Macmillan Publishing Co., Inc., M. B. Yeats, Anne Yeats, and Macmillan London Limited from *Collected Poems* by William Butler Yeats. "The Sorrow of Love" (1893 version) and untitled poem "The friends that have it I do wrong . . ." reprinted with permission of Macmillan Publishing Co., Inc., M. B. Yeats, Anne Yeats, and Macmillan London Limited from *The Variorum Edition of the Poems of W. B. Yeats,* edited by Peter Akkt and Russell K. Alspach. Copyright 1957 by Macmillan Publishing Co., Inc. Epigraph to *Collected Works,* Vol. II, and drafts of "After Long Silence" reprinted with permission of M. B. Yeats, Anne Yeats, and Macmillan London Limited.